Introduction to Experimental Mathematics

Mathematics is not, and never will be, an empirical science, but mathematicians are finding that the use of computers and specialized software allows the generation of mathematical insight in the form of conjectures and examples, which pave the way for theorems and their proofs. In this way, the experimental approach to pure mathematics is revolutionizing the way research mathematicians work.

As the first of its kind, this book provides material for a one-semester course in experimental mathematics that will give students the tools and training needed to systematically investigate and develop mathematical theory using computer programs written in Maple. Accessible to readers without prior programming experience, and using examples of concrete mathematical problems to illustrate a wide range of techniques, the book gives a thorough introduction to the field of experimental mathematics, which will prepare students for the challenge posed by open mathematical problems.

Søren Eilers is a professor of mathematics at the University of Copenhagen, who heads the VILLUM Foundation Network for Experimental Mathematics in Number Theory, Operator Algebras, and Topology. He has received numerous teaching prizes as well as an outreach prize for developing the mathematics of LEGO, and is an expert of the classification of C*-algebras.

Rune Johansen was the first postdoc in experimental mathematics in Denmark, specializing in symbolic dynamics.

Introduction
to
Experimental
Mathematics

Søren Eilers
University of Copenhagen, Denmark

Rune Johansen
University of Copenhagen, Denmark

CAMBRIDGE
UNIVERSITY PRESS

University Printing House, Cambridge CB2 8BS, United Kingdom

One Liberty Plaza, 20th Floor, New York, NY 10006, USA

477 Williamstown Road, Port Melbourne, VIC 3207, Australia

314-321, 3rd Floor, Plot 3, Splendor Forum, Jasola District Centre, New Delhi - 110025, India

79 Anson Road, #06-04/06, Singapore 079906

Cambridge University Press is part of the University of Cambridge.

It furthers the University's mission by disseminating knowledge in the pursuit of education, learning and research at the highest international levels of excellence.

www.cambridge.org
Information on this title: www.cambridge.org/9781107156135

First published 2017

A catalogue record for this publication is available from the British Library

Library of Congress Cataloging in Publication data
Names: Eilers, Søren. | Johansen, Rune (Mathematician)
Title: Introduction to experimental mathematics / Søren Eilers, University of Copenhagen, Denmark, Rune Johansen, University of Copenhagen, Denmark.
Description: Cambridge : Cambridge University Press, [2017] | Includes bibliographical references and index.
Identifiers: LCCN 2016044166 | ISBN 9781107156135 (alk. paper)
Subjects: LCSH: Experimental mathematics – Textbooks. | Mathematics – Textbooks.
Classification: LCC QA9 .E45 2017 | DDC 510.72/4 – dc23
LC record available at https://lccn.loc.gov/2016044166

ISBN 978-1-107-15613-5 Hardback

Contents

Preface

Mathematics is not, and never will be, an empirical science, but mathematicians are finding that the use of computers and specialized software allows the generation of mathematical insight in the form of conjectures and examples that pave the way for theorems and their proofs. In this way, the experimental approach to pure mathematics is revolutionizing the way research mathematicians work.

However, research mathematicians who take to experimentation are largely self-taught, both in the use of various software packages and when it comes to designing useful experiments, and the rapid growth of the use of experimentation in the formulation and development of mathematical theory has not been accompanied by a corresponding development of courses and textbooks. It is our immodest ambition to change that situation with this textbook.

About This Book

Being largely self-taught experimental mathematicians ourselves, we originally adopted an experimental approach to the teaching of experimental mathematics, and the book has evolved by trial and error for more than a decade in the form of lecture notes for various courses taught at the University of Copenhagen.

Like our courses, the book is aimed at beginning graduate students and advanced undergraduate students in mathematics. We assume that the reader has a corresponding general level of mathematical maturity, including knowledge of calculus, analysis, and linear algebra corresponding to the curriculum covered by standard introductory courses. A few isolated examples and exercises in the book require command of more advanced mathematical topics, but these instances are clearly marked and can be skipped with no hidden consequences.

Whereas we know of no textbook with similar ambitions to this one, there is a rich and beautiful literature aimed at the more accomplished mathematician, discussing the philosophy of experimentation in mathematics and establishing by generous collections of examples how and why experimental mathematics should be done. Standing very much on the shoulders of the giants who pioneered the field of experimental mathematics, we have incorporated the work of many of these in the book as worked examples or exercises. As will be obvious from the remarks closing each chapter, we are particularly indebted to the works of David Bailey, Jonathan Borwein, Peter Borwein, and Doron Zeilberger.

For the Student

Experimental mathematics is not a spectator sport, even less so than traditional pure mathematics. As a consequence, this book contains fewer theorems and more examples than a traditional mathematics textbook. It is of paramount importance that you immerse yourself in these and try your hand at conducting small- to medium-scale experiments as you read through the book, especially if you are using this book for self-study. In a traditional mathematical textbook, examples and exercises are crucial for grasping difficult theoretical content, but to some extent, they can be seen as the means to an end: the goal is to understand the theory. In this book, on the other hand, examples and exercises constitute the backbone of the learning process, whereas the general explanations and expositions of theory should provide for rather light reading.

We invite you to consider using experimental methods while studying for other courses alongside your studies of experimental mathematics. Be warned, however, that such approaches may yield shortcuts that disturb the original purpose of a traditional exercise. While such examples provide excellent motivation for the study of experimental mathematics, by showcasing the way experiments can be used to gain insight, they may not give you the training in traditional mathematical methods that you would have gotten by solving such exercises by traditional means. Sometimes, experimental mathematics by computer-based computation is just *too* efficient.

For the Teacher

Like the authors, you are very likely a largely self-taught experimental mathematician yourself, and probably embark on teaching a course on experimental mathematics with some hesitation. Teaching a course in experimental mathematics is obviously very different from teaching a standard upper-level theoretical course, and you may find yourself wondering how to fill the lectures and exercise sessions when there are (almost) no theorems to prove.

In spite of the nonstandard subject matter in this book, we have found that traditional lectures over the general descriptions of the experimental modus operandi combined with selected aspects of relevant mathematical theory and discussions of some of the worked examples contained in the book combine well to keep the students interested and their learning process organized. In our experience, the essential key to a successful course in experimental mathematics is to get the students involved in the design, execution, and evaluation of small experiments as early and as often as possible. In each chapter, we include exercises of varying length and difficulty that can be used for this purpose.

Depending on the students' technical background, they may need assistance to digest the more technical chapters in the book. We have found that this need is hard to address through lectures, but is effectively handled by providing easy access to technical consultations (say, using a teaching assistant with the appropriate technical qualifications).

In the courses we have taught, students have always reacted very positively when presented with examples and exercises based on our own research. In this book, we have tried to provide a diverse collection of examples and exercises, many of which are rooted in the experimental mathematics literature rather than our experiments. We warmly recommend that you involve examples and exercises inspired by your own research in addition to the ones presented here.

In our experience, students that have completed a course in experimental mathematics based on this book are fully capable of tackling open research problems experimentally. Indeed, a major motivation for many of our students has been the promise that they would be allowed to try their hands at open problems as a part of the course.

About Maple

Throughout the book, Waterloo Maple® is used to write the computer programs needed in experimental mathematics. The book is targeted at mathematicians with no prior programming experience, and to make it accessible to this audience, we have included an introduction to basic programming in Maple. However, this is not intended to be a book on computer programming.

To make the book useful to students without much programming experience, we have found it necessary to focus on a single programming language. We chose Maple because it contains all the tools we need and because it is already in use as a computer algebra system in many universities.

Code examples are given using a notation matching the classic Maple input in Worksheet Mode rather than the 2d-mathematics notation of Document

Mode. This choice was made to make sure that it is always clear to the reader what to type into Maple to reproduce the given results. While pretty, the formatting of Document Mode will sometimes obscure the text that actually has to be input in order to reproduce the 2d-mathematics notation. This is most clearly seen when working with indices of sequences and related data structures. Document Mode's 2d input, on the other hand, has the benefit of providing useful syntax highlighting for control structures and other commands, and we leave it to the readers to decide their personal preferences. The examples given should work equally well copied into either type of Maple input. The Maple code is also available on the website of this book.

The output shown in the book has been produced with Maple 2015 (beautified for legibility in a few cases), but any recent version of Maple, say Maple 15 onwards, will support the examples and serve as a vessel for the experiments suggested throughout.

The Contents of This Book

An introduction of the basic methodology of experimental mathematics is given in Chapter 1. Focus is on the use of experimental mathematics in the development of mathematical conjectures and on the special role that counterexamples play in the experimental investigation of hypotheses. The chapter concludes with a collection of case studies, showcasing the application of experimental mathematics to a variety of mathematical problems. Some of these examples are of a historical nature, while others have been developed specifically for this book. Most of them will be revisited in later chapters and examined more carefully with the tools introduced there.

Chapter 2 contains an introduction to basic programming in Maple, laying the foundation needed for the programs discussed in the rest of the book. The topics covered include variables, procedures, control structures, and debugging. Particular focus is given to the development and use of procedures for the automated testing of hypotheses. The goal of the chapter is to develop the necessary programming skills, and the examples are mainly technical in nature. The exercises, however, give students ample opportunity to apply the programming skills they have acquired to genuine mathematical experiments. Readers already familiar with programming in Maple can skip this chapter, but not its exercises.

One of the great benefits of using computers in experimental mathematics is their ability to generate and investigate extremely large collections of data. To do this efficiently requires programming techniques involving iteration and recursion. Such techniques are presented in Chapter 3 and applied to a collection of mathematical experiments. In the case of recursion, it is shown how Maple's built-in tools can be used to drastically speed up computations.

Finally, the chapter contains a discussion of how much experimental evidence you need before believing sufficiently in a hypothesis to invest your time in the search for a proof, and we present a number of examples to show how far one may need to look to find counterexamples to a hypothesis.

As mentioned above, computers allow experimenting mathematicians to generate vast quantities of data, and in order to investigate such data systematically it must be presented in a form that is understandable and manageable to the human investigator. The visualization of mathematical structures and results plays a crucial role in this process, and Chapter 4 is devoted to the discussion of such tools. This includes an introduction to many of Maple's different plotting commands and a discussion of the construction of automated figures. Novel visualization techniques that are, for example, useful for the investigation of matrices, are investigated and applied to experimental problems. Additionally, the chapter contains a discussion of data transformations and the use of both linear and nonlinear fitting in the extraction of information from data.

Generating and visualizing data is one thing, but the real power of experimental mathematics comes from the tools that allow mathematicians to detect patterns in the investigated data, for example by recognizing the first terms of a sequence or the digits of a well-known mathematical constant like π. We call this process *symbolic inversion*, and Chapter 5 presents a collection of tools that help the experimenting mathematician detect such connections. The chapter is split into two main parts dealing with sequences and floating point numbers, respectively. Sequences are investigated using transformations, generating functions, and the *Online encyclopedia of integer sequences*. For floating point numbers, it is shown how to search for patterns using, for example, continued fractions and the powerful PSLQ algorithm. The chapter also contains a discussion of some of the fascinating *mathematical* results behind these wide-ranging tools.

In some experiments, randomness (or rather pseudorandomness) can play a crucial part in avoiding biases in the construction and investigation of experimental data, and such tools are discussed in Chapter 6. To give the reader a clear understanding of the purpose and applicability of pseudorandomness, the chapter contains a discussion of the construction of pseudorandom number generators as well as an introduction to the randomization tools that are provided in Maple. The use of pseudorandomness in experiments is highlighted by a number of examples, and the application of pseudorandomness in nondeterministic algorithms is presented via an application to primality testing.

Chapter 7 concerns the challenge of balancing the desired precision with the available time and computational resources. To facilitate this, the chapter starts out with a discussion of computational complexity and O-notation before giving a series of general purpose performance tips. In many applications, there is a trade-off between time and memory consumption, and it is shown what one can do to tip this scale in order to achieve better performance. In many cases, there is also a trade-off between precision and computational resources, and in such cases it is important to know how precisely a given quantity has been calculated. To this end, it is shown how one may gauge errors using heuristic estimates or achieve stringent bounds through the use of interval arithmetic.

Finally, Chapter 8 discusses the use of linear algebra and graph theory in efficient experimental investigations. This is meant to showcase how experimental investigations into largely unknown territory may benefit from importing ideas and results from more mature mathematical subjects. Linear algebra and graph theory are by no means the only fields that can play this role, but they do show up sufficiently often to warrant special attention. In particular, it is shown how Maple can be used for linear algebra over non standard fields and rings that may play a role in experimental mathematics. Additionally, the chapter uses graphs as the foundation for a discussion of the important mathematical concepts of *isomorphism* and *equivalence* which can sometimes be used to drastically reduce the number of cases an experimental mathematician needs to consider.

EX. 1.5.1 →   Throughout the book, the exposition is supported and driven by a large collection of concrete examples. Some of these case studies are revisited several times in the book, and notes in the margin are used to track such transversal connections through the text. This makes it clear whether a given example has been examined previously in the text and whether it will be discussed again later. Specifically, the margin notes shown here would signify that the current text is a continuation of something considered in Example 1.5.1 and
EX. 3.4.1 ← that this subject will be discussed again in Example 3.4.1.

Scattered throughout the text, there are boxes with short descriptions of notable events in the history of experimental mathematics. These boxes are intended to provide context and interesting anecdotes relevant to the main material, but they are largely independent of the rest of the text and are generally very light reading. Every chapter concludes with a collection of miscellaneous notes relevant to the covered material and suggestions for further reading. Most citations are deferred to these sections to increase the readability of the main text.

Exercises and Projects

Each chapter contains a collection of exercises subdivided into three categories: *warmup*, *homework*, and *projects and group work*. Warmup exercises are meant to be fast and straightforward training exercises testing the concepts and basic tools introduced in the chapter. Most are suitable for self-testing as well as unprepared classroom discussions. *Homework* exercises are generally more difficult and time-consuming than *warmup* exercises and are meant to train the use of experimental methods introduced in the chapter. Particularly long and/or hard exercises are <u>underlined</u>.

The final category contains advanced experimental projects that require the use of a wide range of the ideas and tools introduced in the preceding chapters. Each project description introduces a concrete mathematical problem that can be investigated experimentally. The questions posed in each case are meant to guide the initial investigation, but as always, the experimenter should keep an open mind and pursue all interesting results. In addition to the experimental projects, this section also contains exercises that are not particularly long or hard, but require students to work in groups.

Projects generally require a lot more work than homework exercises, and some are harder than others: <u>Underlined</u> exercises in this category are genuine open problems where the authors do not know the answers to all questions posed, so it may well be hard or impossible to formulate satisfactory hypotheses. After all, even an exemplary experimental investigation will not reveal interesting results if there is no structure to find. This is a fundamental condition of the experimental process that students of experimental mathematics will have to face sooner or later. We hope that these open-ended projects will give the reader a chance to experience the thrill of possible discovery that comes with developing new mathematical theory.

Acknowledgements

We are grateful to our colleagues at the Department of Mathematics at University of Copenhagen for sharing their insight and for providing us with ideas for examples and exercises. In particular, we would like to thank Morten Risager and Jesper Lützen for enlightening discussions about, respectively, number theory and the history of mathematics. We would also like to thank the participants in the 2013 and 2014 versions of the course Experimental Mathematics taught at the University of Copenhagen for acting as test subjects for the first versions our lecture notes. In particular, we are grateful to Dimitrios Askitis, Nicolas Bru Frantzen, Jeanette Kjølbæk, and Mikkel Bøhlers Nielsen for finding a number of typos and errors. We are also grateful to librarian Mikael Rågstedt at Institut Mittag-Leffler for invaluable help with illustrative materials.

Finally, we wish to express our gratitude to VILLUM FONDEN for funding the Network in Experimental Mathematics which has allowed the experimental mathematics community at the University of Copenhagen to blossom and given us the opportunity to pursue goals of experimental mathematics in our own research.

Copenhagen, July 21, 2016

1 *Experimental Method*

Mathematical textbooks and research papers normally present mathematical objects and results in a concise manner, where the most efficient techniques and proofs are used. This has several obvious advantages, but such a condensed presentation may leave the reader wondering how the ideas for the definitions and theorems came to be, and one of the things that are almost always omitted from such a presentation are the many concrete examples that the author may have had to investigate before finding the optimal formulation of the theorem and getting the ideas needed for the proof. In contrast, the focus of this book is the work that comes before the neatly formulated theorems and clever proofs, and in this chapter, we will lay the foundation for this presentation. We will introduce and define mathematical experimentation as a tool in the formulation of conjectures and proofs, and present basic methodology common to most mathematical experiments.

1.1 Experimenting with Mathematics

We will define experimental mathematics very broadly to be: *The systematic investigation of concrete examples of a mathematical structure in the search for conjectures about its properties (using computers).* This definition mirrors the way experiments are used in the (other) natural sciences, but there is a very important difference in the way experiments can be used to gain knowledge in mathematics and other sciences. In the natural sciences, knowledge and established facts are ultimately rooted in experiments, and experimental evidence is sufficient to draw conclusions about the true nature of the world. Indeed, the results of experiments are the cornerstones of our understanding of the physical world and once a sufficient number of rocks have been dropped from the leaning tower of Pisa, we can (and should) conclude that heavier objects do not fall faster than lighter objects. This is obviously not the case in mathematics where results and truths are established deductively. No amount of fruitless searches for solutions to $x^n + y^n = z^n$ could ever be used to justify Fermat's Last Theorem as a mathematical result. Hence, the fundamental difference between experimentation in mathematics and experimentation in the natural sciences is that most mathematical experiments will not produce mathematical knowledge directly. Instead, the result of such an experiment will often be a conjecture which must then be treated with traditional mathematical tools to produce a theorem with a formal proof.

What, then, is the use of experimentation in mathematics? Primarily, experimentation has an important place in mathematics as a tool to come up with the ideas needed to formulate conjectures and proofs. Mathematicians have always had this need to investigate simple concrete cases before being able to formulate conjectures and proofs, but the advent of modern computers has made it possible to do so much more quickly and efficiently than previously. This has led to a blossoming of the use of experimentation in mathematics and to an increased recognition of the place that experimentation has in the development of mathematical theory. In particular, there is now a research journal (aptly named *Experimental Mathematics*) dedicated to the publication of formal results inspired by experimentation, conjectures suggested by experiments, and data supporting significant hypotheses. Unlike traditional journals, *Experimental Mathematics* publishes significant conjectures or explorations in the hope of inspiring other, perhaps better-equipped researchers to carry on the investigation.

There is another application of computers to the development of mathematical theory which does not fall within the scope of this book: Automated proofs are computer programs used to prove theorems—typically by testing a large number of cases such as in the original proof of the four-color theorem (see box on p. 267). Such automated proofs will not generally fall under the definition of experimentation given above even though there may be some overlap in the applied techniques.

Example 1.1.1: Towers of Hanoi. *The Towers of Hanoi* (also known as *Towers of Brahma* or *Lucas's Tower*) is a classic puzzle with the following setup: There are three identical pegs, and $n \in \mathbb{N}$ discs with holes matching the size of the pegs. No two discs have the same size, and the discs start out stacked in descending order of size on one of the pegs. The setup is sketched in Figure 1.1. The objective of the puzzle is to move all the discs to one of the other pegs while obeying the following rules:

- Only the topmost disc may be removed from a stack.
- Only one disc may be moved at a time.
- No disc may be placed on a smaller disc.

The associated mathematical problem is to find the smallest number of moves required to finish the puzzle. There are several different ways to find this bound, but the obvious approach, if one has never encountered the problem before, is to first look at a number of examples in order to become familiar

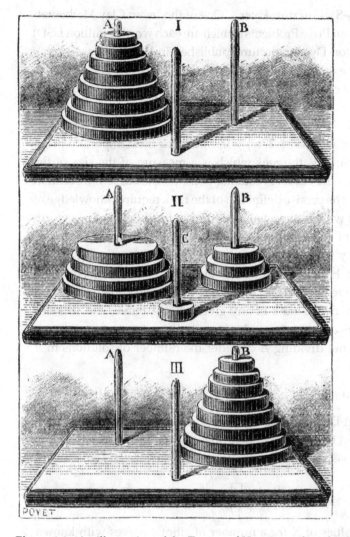

Figure 1.1 An illustration of the Towers of Hanoi puzzle published in [Luc85].

with the mechanics of the problem. This leads to a hypothesis which can easily be proved to be correct (see Exercise 1.1).

This makes the Towers of Hanoi a problem where experimentation is a natural part of the solution and an example of why an experimental investigation does not necessarily have to involve computer programs. In this case, there is no need to turn to computers to complete the experiment since sufficient information can be gained from investigating the problem by hand for small values of n. ◁

While the previous example showed how experimentation can be a natural tool in the solution of a simple mathematical exercise, the next example shows the scope of experimental mathematics as a tool in the formulation of fundamental conjectures.

Example 1.1.2: Birch–Swinnerton-Dyer.   One of the seven Clay Mathematics Institute Millennium Prize Problems (which are each worth 1 million USD) is the Birch–Swinnerton-Dyer conjecture, published in 1965 and based on an analysis of computer experiments [BSD65].

Consider an elliptic curve

$$E : y^2 = x^3 + ax + b, \quad a, b \in \mathbb{Z}$$

with discriminant $\Delta = -16(4a^3 + 27b^2) \neq 0$. One of the most important properties of an elliptic curve is the *rank* which is a measure of the size of the set of *rational points* on the curve. A rational point on the curve is a solution (x, y) where $x, y \in \mathbb{Q}$. The precise definition of the rank requires knowledge of group theory beyond what is expected of readers of this book, but it is worth noting that the rank of an elliptic curve, like the determinant of a matrix, is an important property which contains a lot of useful information about the behavior of the object. However, unlike the determinant of a matrix, the rank is generally very hard to compute. In particular, there is no known algorithm guaranteed to determine the rank of any given elliptic curve, and it is unknown which integers occur as the rank of an elliptic curve.

For every prime p not dividing Δ consider the number of solutions to E modulo p and define

$$N_p = 1 + \left| \{ 0 \leq x, y \leq p - 1 \mid y^2 \equiv x^3 + ax + b \pmod{p} \} \right|.$$

Birch and Swinnerton-Dyer had the idea that this number of solutions modulo p should be related to the number of rational points as given by the rank. Over a period of five years in the late 1950s and early 1960s they computed

$$\pi_E(X) = \prod_{p \leq X, p \nmid \Delta} \frac{N_p}{p}$$

for many different values of X for a number of elliptic curves with known ranks. Plotting these data gave graphs like the ones shown in Figure 1.2. This led Birch and Swinnerton-Dyer to conjecture that

$$\pi_E(X) \to C \ln(X)^{\mathrm{rank}(E)} \text{ for } X \to \infty$$

for some C that depends only on E. The story of this discovery is partially told in the introduction to Birch and Swinnerton-Dyer's original paper. The conjecture also contains a more advanced part which requires detailed knowledge of elliptic curves to formulate, and it will not be given here.

As a Clay problem, the Birch–Swinnerton-Dyer conjecture is recognized as one of the most important open questions in mathematics, so a significant amount of work—both theoretical and experimental—has been dedicated to investigating it. This work has resulted in a great number of interesting mathematical results, even though the conjecture itself remains an open problem. In this way, the experimentally founded conjecture has had an enormous
EX. 1.2.1 ← influence on the development of this branch of mathematics.   ◁

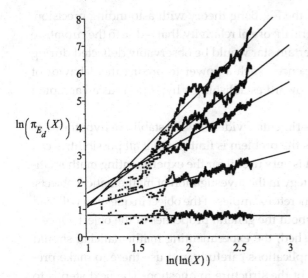

Figure 1.2 Data for the elliptic curves $y^2 = x^3 - d^2x$ at $d = 1, 5, 34, 1254, 29274$.

1.2 Basic Methodology

The experimenting mathematician can learn a lot from the basic philosophy and methodology of fields with a stronger experimental tradition even though there is a fundamental difference between how the results of an experiment can be used in mathematics and in other natural sciences.

1.2.1 Initial Investigation

When faced with a new problem or mathematical structure that is going to be investigated experimentally, the experimenting mathematician should first make sure that the definitions and basic premises of the mathematical objects involved are well understood. Next, the investigator should use computer programs to generate a number of examples that should be collected and studied to make it possible to find common features among them. Later chapters will give several different techniques (such as visualization and symbolic inversion) that will be useful in this initial investigation of examples. A successful investigation should result in one or more clearly defined hypotheses, which can then be made the subject of further experimentation, or theoretical analyses.

1.2.2 Hypotheses and Counterexamples

In the natural sciences, a hypothesis is judged by its suitability to make predictions about the behavior of the investigated object, and the history of science is full of theories with bold predictions backed by later experiments. This was the case for the results of the investigations carried out with the COBE satellite which gave a map of the cosmic background radiation matching the predictions of the Big Bang theory with astounding precision. Or the prediction of the general theory of relativity, that—due to the curvature of space—the light from a certain star would be observably deflected during an eclipse. In the natural sciences, such a power to predict the behavior of our world goes a long way toward establishing a hypothesis as an accepted fact.

Clearly, no amount of experimental evidence will establish a hypothesis as a mathematical truth (unless the problem is finite so that all possibilities can be checked). Nevertheless, it is very useful for the experimenting mathematician to employ a similar strategy in the investigation of mathematical objects. An initial investigation of concrete examples of the object in question will lead to one or more hypotheses about the general properties of the object. Once a hypothesis has been established, the experimenting mathematician should investigate its theoretical implications carefully and use these to make predictions about the behavior of the structure in question. The next step is to design experiments to check whether the structure has these predicted properties or not. If not, then the hypothesis has been proved false by the counterexample. A series of confirmations of the predictions of the hypothesis is naturally not sufficient to establish the hypothesis as a mathematical result, but it is often possible to extract useful knowledge from the process which may in turn support the formulation of a proof. At the very least, having a clearly defined conjecture that the investigator has reason to believe in makes it much easier to work towards a proof, and sometimes—as in the case of the Birch–Swinnerton-Dyer conjecture—the conjecture itself may turn out to be an important goal for the development of mathematical theory even though it cannot be proved immediately.

Even if a hypothesis is disproved by a counterexample, it may not be necessary to abandon it completely. The common features of a collection of counterexamples will often supply the input needed to refine the hypothesis into a new form which should then be tested in the same manner. Thus, the experimental process can be seen as a stepwise refinement of the initial hypothesis through a systematic search for counterexamples as illustrated in Figure 1.3. Once a final hypothesis has been established, to which no counterexamples can be found, it is time to start looking for a proof.

In order to be able to use computer programs to search for counterexamples to hypotheses, it is very important that the hypotheses are clearly defined so they can be used to make definite predictions about the behavior of the structure in question.

EX. 1.1.2 → **Example 1.2.1: Predictions.** In the original paper, Birch and Swinnerton-Dyer emphasized their conjecture's ability to predict the behavior of elliptic curves:

We were in fact able to predict the number of generators of A for specific curves Γ, with fairly consistent success, by examining the values of f(P).

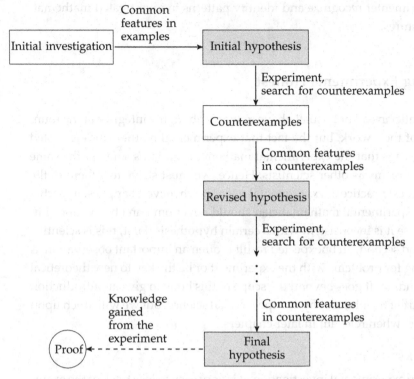

Figure 1.3 Stepwise refinement of hypotheses through a systematic search for counterexamples.

This is an example of how a mathematical experiment has resulted in a hypothesis that is judged on its ability to make predictions.   ◁

1.3 From Hypothesis to Proof

When the iterative process described above has resulted in a hypothesis that careful experimental investigation cannot disprove, it is time to start searching for a proof. It is difficult—if not impossible—to give general guidelines about how to use the knowledge gained through an experimental process to formulate a proof of the final conjecture, but in the examples, exercises, and projects given later, it will be shown how this can be done in concrete cases.

Naturally, a counterexample may be a result in its own right, and in such a case, little or no work is needed to turn the experimental work into a mathematical result (see Figure 3.6 for a spectacular example of this phenomenon). After all, a single counterexample is sufficient to disprove a hypothesis, and this is exactly why several of the highest profiled unproved mathematical conjectures, such as the Birch–Swinnerton-Dyer conjecture or Fermat's Last Theorem, are supported by so much experimental evidence: Mathematicians have been trying (and failing) to disprove them by searching for counterexamples for a long time. In Chapter 5, we will discuss useful tools that can help the experimenter recognize and identify patterns in investigated mathematical structures.

1.4 Keeping Experiments Honest

Mathematicians do not usually have to worry about the integrity of the foundations of their work, but the fact that experimental mathematics is rooted in data means that the experimental mathematician faces some of the same ethical problems as other scientists. Hence, we must strive to adhere to the accepted best practice in experimental sciences whenever it applies. In particular, an experimental mathematician should never omit an observation simply because it is inconsistent with a certain hypothesis. First, this is scientific fraud. And second, an unexpected result is often an important observation as it may flag for problems with the experiment or be the key to new theoretical understanding. It goes beyond the scope of this book to give an introduction to this part of the philosophy of experimental science, but we will touch upon the subject when relevant in later chapters.

1.4.1 Logbooks

During an experimental investigation, it is very easy to lose track of the examples and hypotheses that have been investigated. For this reason, investigators in the traditional experimental sciences will normally use a logbook (lab book) to record the details of their experiments while working. This could be an electronic record such as a simple text file, but in a laboratory it may be more desirable to use a physical book, partly to keep the computer away from the lab equipment, and partly to make sure that records are not deleted or altered either on purpose or by accident. Many laboratories are now using tablets with dedicated software for this purpose.

In experimental mathematics, the logbook plays an equally vital role. In a nutshell, it should be used to record all the information needed to recreate the experiment, so that counterexamples and other interesting features can be investigated in greater detail later and so that errors can be found and fixed. Generally, it is a good idea to write the logbook as if it was going to be read by somebody else rather than yourself. Things that seem obvious while doing the experiment can easily be forgotten before it is time to analyze the results.

Since experimental mathematics does not involve fluids that might be hazardous to the computer, or samples that must be kept clean, the experimenting mathematician will normally choose to use a text file rather than a physical book for these records. This has the advantage that one can easily copy counterexamples and other output from computer programs to the logbook. However, it is still worth thinking of the logbook as something written on paper in permanent ink: Nothing should ever be deleted or altered once it has been entered in the log.

1.5 Dangers

Experimentation should be a complement to—and never a substitute for—careful theoretical considerations. In particular, the experimenting mathematician should be careful to make sure that the definitions and basic properties of the objects at hand are well understood before elaborate computer programs are written. It is very easy to waste time on poorly planned computer code if the fundamental premises of the problem are not properly taken into account.

The great benefit of using computers to investigate mathematical objects is that they allow the consideration of far more examples than it is possible to handle by hand. However, such an investigation threatens to produce enormous amounts of output that the human investigator cannot digest. For this reason, it is important for the experimenting mathematician to have access to computer tools that can facilitate the organization and visualization of data. This will be treated in detail in Chapter 4.

The human mind is very good at recognizing patterns, and this is naturally an essential part of the process of digesting experimental evidence and forming hypotheses. However, the experimenting mathematician is faced with a fundamental challenge that also arises in the traditional experimental sciences: We *want* to see patterns, and this may lead to erroneous conclusions when accidental patterns are encountered. Hence, the experimenter should always remain skeptical and remember that the fundamental goal of an experimental investigation of a hypothesis is always to disprove it by finding a counterexample.

Example 1.5.1: Mersenne and Fermat primes. In 1644, the French mathematician and music theorist Marin Mersenne conjectured that for $n \leq 257$, the *Mersenne number* $M_n = 2^n - 1$ is a prime if and only if

$$n \in \{2, 3, 5, 7, 13, 17, 19, 31, 67, 127, 257\}.$$

However, the numbers involved are so large that neither Mersenne nor his peers could prove that all of these are primes. Indeed, it took approximately a century before Leonhard Euler was able to verify that M_{31} is a prime. However, the conjecture is false: In 1883 the first omission was found when Ivan Mikheevich Pervushin proved that M_{61} is also a prime, and in 1903 Frank Nelson Cole demonstrated that M_{67} is composite. In fact, these are not the only errors in the list (see Exercise 2.33).

To illustrate that even great mathematicians may be led astray by an apparent pattern, consider the following cautionary tale: Pierre de Fermat conjectured that for each n, the *Fermat number* $F_n = 2^{2^n} + 1$ is prime. This conjecture was refuted by Euler, who showed that it fails for $n = 5$. Indeed,

$$F_5 = 2^{2^5} + 1 = 2^{32} + 1 = 4294967297 = 641 \cdot 6700417.$$

Gauss

Unter	gibt es Primzahlen	Integral $\int \frac{dn}{\log n}$	Differ	Ihre Formel	Abweich.
500 000	41 556	41 606,4	+50,4	41 596,9	+40,9
1 000 000	78 501	78 627,5	+126,5	78 672,7	+171,7
1 500 000	114 112	114 263,1	+151,1	114 374,0	+264,0
2 000 000	148 883	149 054,8	+171,8	149 233,0	+350,0
2 500 000	183 016	183 245,0	+229,0	183 495,1	+479,1
3 000 000	216 745	216 970,6	+225,6	217 308,5	+563,6

Dass Legendre sich auch mit diesem Gegenstande beschäftigt hat, war mir nicht bekannt; auf Veranlassung Ihres Briefes habe ich in seiner Theorie des Nombres nachgesehen, und in der zweiten Ausgabe einige darauf bezügliche Seiten gefunden, die ich früher übersehen (oder seitdem vergessen) haben muss. Legendre gebrauchte die Formel

$$\frac{n}{\log n - A}$$

According to his own recollection, the great German mathematician Carl Friedrich Gauss (1777–1855) considered the distribution of primes at age 15 or 16 after receiving a book containing logarithms of numbers with up to 7 digits and a table of primes less 10,009. In a letter from 1849, he claimed that this study led him to observe that the density of prime numbers over an interval $[x - \delta, x + \delta]$ seemed to average $2\delta / \ln(x)$. An excerpt from this letter is shown above. Clearly, such an investigation must have involved very time-consuming hand calculations, and this illustrates how the experimental approach was central to the development of mathematics long before the advent of modern computers.

Assuming that the probability that a small interval around x contains a prime is proportional to $1/\ln(x)$ leads to the conjecture that the number of primes less than $X \in \mathbb{R}$ should be approximated by the function

$$\text{Li}(X) = \int_{x=2}^{X} \frac{dx}{\ln(x)}.$$

If Gauss's observation was correct, there should be approximately $x/\ln(x)$ primes smaller than x for each $x > 2$. In particular, this led to the conjecture that

$$\lim_{x \to \infty} \frac{\pi(x)}{x/\ln(x)} = 1,$$

where $\pi(x)$ is the number of primes less than x. This result is known as the *prime number theorem*, and it was proved independently by Jacques Hadamard (1865–1963) and Charles Jean de la Vallée-Poussin (1866–1962) in 1896.

Even without guessing a divisor or employing modern computational tools, it is not hard to prove that 641 is a factor of F_5. Note that $641 = 2^7 \cdot 5 + 1$, so $2^7 \cdot 5 \equiv -1 \pmod{641}$, and hence, $2^{28} \cdot 5^4 \equiv 1 \pmod{641}$. On the other hand, the equality $641 = 2^4 + 5^4$ implies that $5^4 \equiv -2^4 \pmod{641}$, and together, these congruences imply that $-2^{32} \equiv 1 \pmod{641}$, proving that $641|F_5$.

It is believed that Fermat knew of the congruences Euler used to disprove the conjecture, and if that is true, one might wonder why he failed to find the counterexample. An explanation could be that he made a computational error and that his belief in the correctness of the conjecture meant that he failed to check the results thoroughly.

Interestingly, F_n is composite for $n \geq 5$ in all known cases. Hence, a modern experimenting mathematician will be led to the reverse of the original EX. 3.4.1 ← conjecture: F_n is only prime in the four cases known to Fermat.   ◁

It is worth noting that certain areas of mathematics lend themselves better to an experimental investigation than others. In particular, problems involving objects that cannot easily be represented in a finite manner are inherently unsuited for experimentation. In Chapter 7, it will be discussed how the restraints of time and computing resources limit the problems that can be attacked, and how such limitations force the experimenter to make choices in the experimental design.

Finally, if the subject of the investigation is a publicly known problem, it is very important to find out whether it has already been investigated with computer experiments by other mathematicians. Often, other investigators with access to better resources will already have investigated such problems in great detail, and there is little hope that further computer experiments will reveal new knowledge in such cases. Unfortunately, the results of such investigations are often left unpublished, so to find out whether the problem has already been subjected to an experimental investigation, it may be necessary to contact experts in the field.

Example 1.5.2: Collatz conjecture.   Define a function $f : \mathbb{N} \to \mathbb{N}$ by

$$f(n) = \begin{cases} n/2 & n \text{ even} \\ 3n+1 & n \text{ odd.} \end{cases}$$

The *Collatz conjecture* states that given $m \in \mathbb{N}$, there exists $j \in \mathbb{N}$ such that $f^{\circ j}(m) = 1$, that is, a sufficiently long iteration will end at the number 1. This problem seems well suited for experimental investigation since it is clearly not hard to write a computer program to test the conjecture with various starting values. One could hope that such an investigation would solve the problem, either by resulting in a counterexample (by finding a starting value terminating in a cycle not containing the number 1) or by supplying enough insight into the behavior of the iterations to prove the conjecture. However, the conjecture has already been tested for all starting values up to 2^{60}, well

La Métode des Exclusiones

4	1	5
9	1	10
9	4	13
16	1	17
16	4	20
16	9	$25 = 5^2$
25	1	26
25	4	29
25	9	34
25	16	41

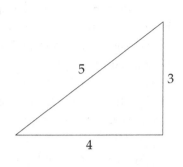

In *La Métode des Exclusiones*, Bernard Frénicle de Bessy (c. 1605–1675) proposed to base the (experimental) investigation of mathematical problems on 10 concrete rules.

Rules 2, 3, and 7 emphasize the importance of carrying out systematic investigations and using a simple order of progression to avoid omissions. Rules 4–6 state that you should limit the search space if it is possible to do so, a strategy which will be applied several times in the following. Rules 9 and 10 concern the formulation of ideas based on observations and stress the importance of investigating counterexamples. In this way, Frénicle's rules give an early introduction to experimental mathematics with many fundamental similarities with the methods discussed in this book, in spite of the vast difference between the available tools. Another difference between our approach and the methods presented in *La Métode des Exclusiones* is that Frénicle did not worry about finding formal proofs of the observed patterns. Instead, he was satisfied with an experimental verification of the results.

To illustrate how these rules could be applied, Frénicle used them to investigate 10 concrete problems, one of which was the question of which integers occur as the length of the hypotenuse of a right-angled triangle. This is the proposed experimental strategy: First, compile a table of the squares of the numbers $1, \ldots, N$ for some suitably large N. For each square m^2 in this table, construct a table of the form shown above, computing $m^2 + n^2$ for each $n < m$. To determine whether the result is the hypotenuse of a right-angled triangle, it is sufficient to check whether the resulting number is listed in the original table of squares. Note how this systematic investigation ensures that all relevant numbers are considered.

beyond the levels that can be reached without clever algorithms and very
EX. 3.3.2 ← powerful computers.   ◁

Example 1.5.3: The ABC conjecture.   Another example of a conjecture that
has been the subject of an intensive experimental investigation is the *ABC
conjecture*. Let *a*, *b* and *c* be positive integers such that $a + b = c$, $a < b < c$,
and a, b, c have no common divisors. The *radical*, $\text{rad}(abc)$, is the product of
the distinct prime factors of *a*, *b*, and *c*. It seems that for most such triples,
$c < \text{rad}(abc)$.

The ABC conjecture states that for each $\epsilon > 0$ there are only finitely many
triples such that $c > \text{rad}(abc)^{1+\epsilon}$. The *quality* of a triple is

$$q(a, b, c) = \frac{\log c}{\log \text{rad}(abc)},$$

and the conjecture is clearly equivalent to the statement that for each $h > 1$
there are only finitely many triples a, b, c such that $q(a, b, c) > h$. The largest
known value of this quality is 1.6299 which is achieved by $a = 2, b = 3^{10} \cdot 109$,
and $c = 23^5$.

A lot of work has gone into identifying triples with $q(a, b, c) > 1$, and there
is no real hope that an experimental investigation carried out on a single
computer will be able find a substantial number of new triples. However,
the *abc@home* project has made a very large number (23827716 at the time of
writing) of these triples publicly available, and conceivably one could hope
to discover interesting structure in this dataset.   ◁

1.6 Case Studies

The following case studies give examples of mathematical problems that can
be investigated with experimental tools. They will all be revisited in later
examples and exercises.

Example 1.6.1: Derivatives.   Consider the function $f : \mathbb{R}_+ \to \mathbb{R}$ defined by

$$f(x) = \frac{\ln x}{x}.$$

The first eight derivatives are

$$f'(x) = \frac{1}{x^2} - \frac{\ln x}{x^2} \qquad f''(x) = -\frac{3}{x^3} + \frac{2\ln x}{x^3}$$

$$f'''(x) = \frac{11}{x^4} - \frac{6\ln x}{x^4} \qquad f^{(4)}(x) = -\frac{50}{x^5} + \frac{24\ln x}{x^5}$$

$$f^{(5)}(x) = \frac{274}{x^6} - \frac{120\ln x}{x^6} \qquad f^{(6)}(x) = -\frac{1764}{x^7} + \frac{720\ln x}{x^7}$$

$$f^{(7)}(x) = \frac{13068}{x^8} - \frac{5040\ln x}{x^8} \qquad f^{(8)}(x) = -\frac{109584}{x^9} + \frac{40320\ln x}{x^9}.$$

Is there a pattern to the higher order derivatives of f, and is it possible to predict them without doing all the intermediate calculations?

It would not be difficult to solve this problem without using computers, but pretend for a moment that we have no theoretical tools with which to handle the problem. Exercise 1.4 illustrates how an experimental investigation can
EX. 3.2.1 ← reveal the general structure and help in the formulation of a proof.　　　　◁

BOX P. 12 → **Example 1.6.2: Pythagorean triples.**　The problem of determining which integers that occur as the hypotenuses of right-angled integer triangles is well suited for simple experimentation by hand. Even a moderately sized table of the kind considered in the box on p. 12 allows the formulation of an interesting hypothesis about the form of these numbers. Furthermore, the challenge of writing down tables for larger integers necessitates an instructive reduction of the search space. To avoid spoiling the experiment, no more details will be given here, but the problem will be examined in detail in Exercises 1.2–1.6.　　　　◁

Example 1.6.3: Coefficient patterns.　The formulas

$$\sum_{k=1}^{n} k = \frac{n^2 + n}{2} \quad \text{and} \quad \sum_{k=1}^{n} k^2 = \frac{2n^3 + 3n^2 + n}{6}$$

may be known to the reader, and it is not hard to see that for any $m \in \mathbb{N}$,

$$q_m(n) = \sum_{k=1}^{n} k^m$$

is a polynomial of degree $m + 1$. In fact,

$$q_0(n) = n$$
$$q_1(n) = \tfrac{1}{2}n^2 + \tfrac{1}{2}n$$
$$q_2(n) = \tfrac{1}{3}n^3 + \tfrac{1}{2}n^2 + \tfrac{1}{6}n$$
$$q_3(n) = \tfrac{1}{4}n^4 + \tfrac{1}{2}n^3 + \tfrac{1}{4}n^2$$
$$q_4(n) = \tfrac{1}{5}n^5 + \tfrac{1}{2}n^4 + \tfrac{1}{3}n^3 - \tfrac{1}{30}n$$
$$q_5(n) = \tfrac{1}{6}n^6 + \tfrac{1}{2}n^5 + \tfrac{5}{12}n^4 - \tfrac{1}{12}n^2$$
$$q_6(n) = \tfrac{1}{7}n^7 + \tfrac{1}{2}n^6 + \tfrac{1}{2}n^5 - \tfrac{1}{6}n^3 + \tfrac{1}{42}n$$
$$q_7(n) = \tfrac{1}{8}n^8 + \tfrac{1}{2}n^7 + \tfrac{7}{12}n^6 - \tfrac{7}{24}n^4 + \tfrac{1}{12}n^2$$
$$q_8(n) = \tfrac{1}{9}n^9 + \tfrac{1}{2}n^8 + \tfrac{2}{3}n^7 - \tfrac{7}{15}n^5 + \tfrac{2}{9}n^3 - \tfrac{1}{30}n$$
$$q_9(n) = \tfrac{1}{10}n^{10} + \tfrac{1}{2}n^9 + \tfrac{3}{4}n^8 - \tfrac{7}{10}n^6 + \tfrac{1}{2}n^4 - \tfrac{3}{20}n^2$$
$$q_{10}(n) = \tfrac{1}{11}n^{11} + \tfrac{1}{2}n^{10} + \tfrac{5}{6}n^9 - n^7 + n^5 - \tfrac{1}{2}n^3 + \tfrac{5}{66}n$$
$$q_{11}(n) = \tfrac{1}{12}n^{12} + \tfrac{1}{2}n^{11} + \tfrac{11}{12}n^{10} - \tfrac{11}{8}n^8 + \tfrac{11}{6}n^6 - \tfrac{11}{8}n^4 + \tfrac{5}{12}n^2$$
$$q_{12}(n) = \tfrac{1}{13}n^{13} + \tfrac{1}{2}n^{12} + n^{11} - \tfrac{11}{6}n^9 + \tfrac{22}{7}n^7 - \tfrac{33}{10}n^5 + \tfrac{5}{3}n^3 - \tfrac{691}{2730}n.$$

Considering these equations reveals certain patterns in the coefficients. Some are easy to formulate while others are fairly complex. These patterns will be
EX. 3.2.3 ← examined in the exercises.　　　　◁

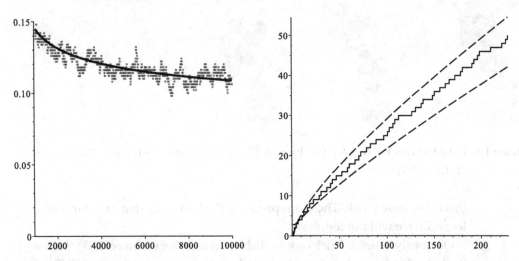

Figure 1.4 Left: The density of primes in the interval $[n - 250, n + 250]$ plotted as a function of $n \in \{1000, \dots, 10000\}$ and compared to the graph of the function $1/\ln$. Right: Plot of the functions $\pi(x)$ (solid line), $x/\ln(x)$ (bottom dashed line), and $\mathrm{Li}(x)$ (top dashed line).

BOX P. 10 → **Example 1.6.4: Primes.** As discussed in the historical intermezzo on p. 10, Gauss considered the distribution of primes and conjectured that the number of primes in a small interval $[x - \delta, x + \delta]$ is approximately $2\delta/\ln(x)$. Using computer programs, it is straightforward to replicate Gauss's experiment, and Figure 1.4 shows the result of such an investigation. Note that the data in this figure were in principle available to Gauss, though one must assume that he used significantly fewer data points to formulate the hypothesis. Considering this figure, there certainly seems to be merit to Gauss's hypothesis, though there are clearly large local deviations from the pattern.

The prime counting function $\pi : \mathbb{R}^+ \to \mathbb{N}$ is defined by

$$\pi(x) = |\{p \leq x \mid p \text{ is a prime}\}|.$$

If Gauss's observation is correct, then $\mathrm{Li}(x)$ and $x/\ln(x)$ should both be good approximations of $\pi(x)$. For now, we disregard the question of what is meant by a good approximation and simply appeal to Figure 1.4 where the functions are plotted together. Note that it looks like $\mathrm{Li}(x)$ and $x/\ln(x)$ provide upper and lower bounds for $\pi(x)$. The relationship between these functions will be investigated in greater detail in the exercises in Chapter 2. ◁

Example 1.6.5: LEGO towers. We will call any LEGO building that can be made by stacking 2×2 bricks on top of each other, in the same plane, a *LEGO tower*. We wish to study the number, β_N, of LEGO towers made with N bricks, having the property of being *stable* in the sense that the center of gravity falls

Figure 1.5 LEGO towers for $N = 6$ given by $x_1 = (-1, 0, 1, 1, 0)$, $x_2 = (-1, 1, 0, 1, 1)$, and $x_3 = (1, 1, 0, 1, -1)$.

inside the base block. These are precisely the buildings that can stand on a level surface without toppling.

Obviously, when N bricks are available, the number of towers is 3^{N-1} since the lower brick may be considered fixed, and any other brick may be affixed to the one just below it in three different ways, so an efficient model for such buildings is given by the elements in $\{-1, 0, 1\}^{N-1}$. Indeed, for each $(N-1)$-tuple $(x_i)_{i=1}^{N-1}$ one may construct a LEGO tower by placing each block on the next according to the entries. An entry 0 signifies putting the next block directly on top of its predecessor, -1 placing it once to the left, and 1 placing it once to the right. It is easy to see that the relevant coordinate of the center of gravity is then given by

$$\tau(\mathbf{x}) = \frac{1}{N} \sum_{i=1}^{N-1} (N-i) x_i, \tag{1.1}$$

and hence we have

$$\beta_n = |\{\mathbf{x} \in \{-1, 0, 1\}^{N-1} \mid -1 < \tau(\mathbf{x}) < 1\}|.$$

(Having $|\tau(\mathbf{x})| = 1$ will result in structures that very easily tip, as one may see by real-life experiments.) In Figure 1.5, we have

$$\tau(\mathbf{x}_1) = 0, \quad \tau(\mathbf{x}_2) = 1/3, \quad \tau(\mathbf{x}_3) = 5/3,$$

so that the towers associated to $\mathbf{x}_1$ and $\mathbf{x}_2$ are stable, while the one associated

EX. 3.3.4 ← to $\mathbf{x}_3$ is not.   ◁

Example 1.6.6: LEGO pyramids. We wish to study the number of pyramids which can be made with LEGO bricks of width 2 (equivalent with what is usually called *dimers*). As in Example 1.6.5, we require all bricks to be placed in the same vertical plane, and to rest on a base block, but in this case two bricks will be allowed to be attached to the same lower brick. This entails that each level of the pyramid can contain several bricks, as opposed to the case for the towers studied there. See Figure 1.6 for a number of

EX. 5.1.10 ← examples.   ◁

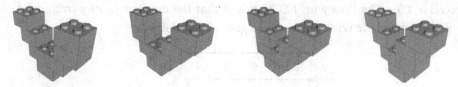

Figure 1.6 Four pyramids with $n = 7$.

1.7 Exercises

Warmup

EX. 1.1.1 → **Exercise 1.1** Given $n \in \mathbb{N}$, find the number of moves required to complete the n-disc Towers of Hanoi game.

EX. 1.6.2 → **Exercise 1.2** Construct tables of sums of squares by hand as outlined in Example 1.6.2. Use them to find small integers that are the lengths of hypotenuses of right-angled integer triangles.

BOX P. 10 → **Exercise 1.3** Compare the entries in Gauss's table to the values obtained by numtheory[pi].

Homework

EX. 1.6.1 → **Exercise 1.4** Let f be the function defined in Example 1.6.1.

  (a) Study the calculated derivatives, and formulate a hypothesis about the form of $f^{(n)}$ for all $n \in \mathbb{N}$.

  (b) Test your hypothesis by comparing the predicted answer for $f^{(i)}$ with the actual answer for a number of values of $i \in \mathbb{N}$.

EX. 3.2.1 ← (c) Prove the hypothesis using induction.

EX. 1.6.2 → **Exercise 1.5** Some of Frénicle's rules deal with the exclusion of numbers that a priori can be seen to be irrelevant to the investigation. Find a way to rule out as many pairs a, b as possible. How much does this speed up the computations?

EX. 1.6.2 → **Exercise 1.6** Consider the hypotenuses found in Exercises 1.2 and/or 1.5. What do these numbers have in common? Formulate a hypothesis based on the observation. In the spirit of Frénicle, test the hypothesis by considering larger values of a, b, and c. Can you predict the next hypotenuse?

EX. 1.6.3 → **Exercise 1.7** Spot as many patterns as possible in the coefficients of the polynomials considered in Example 1.6.3.

EX. 1.6.5 → **Exercise 1.8** Experiment with actual LEGO bricks to determine β_N for as many N as possible.

EX. 1.6.6 → **Exercise 1.9**   Confirm with LEGO bricks that the number p_n of pyramids that can be made with n bricks is as given in the table:

n	1	2	3	4
p_n	1	3	10	35

Can you determine p_5 without actually building all the pyramids?

1.8 Notes and Further Reading

See [RS02] for an introduction to problems involving ranks of elliptic curves and the Birch–Swinnerton-Dyer conjecture. For information about this and the other Clay Millennium Problems, see the web page of the Clay Mathematics Institute http://www.claymath.org/millennium/.

Fermat numbers and Euler's counterexample to Fermat's original conjecture are discussed in [KLS01], and a good introduction to the Mersenne primes discussed in Example 1.5.1 can be found in [Rob54]. For more information about the state of the Collatz problem discussed in Example 1.5.2, see [Lag10] which covers both experimental and theoretical aspects of the investigation in depth. If you want to devote idle computing resources to experimental mathematics, consider the abc@home project (www.abcathome.com).

The letter from Gauss shown in the box on p. 10 is discussed in detail in [Tsc06], and the presentation of *La Métode des Exclusiones* given in the box on p. 12 is based on the discussion in [Gol08].

2 *Basic Programming in Maple*

In the following, it will be assumed that the reader has a basic knowledge of how to use Maple as a computer algebra system for solving problems in calculus and basic algebra. No prior knowledge of programming in Maple or otherwise is expected.

2.1 Statements, Execution and Groups

An *execution group* is a container for a block of Maple code that can be executed by pressing Enter once. In Worksheet mode, each execution group is enclosed to the left by a single (stretched) [with a > on the first line. In Document mode, each execution group is enclosed in a dashed box. An execution group may contain more than one line of code. Extra lines can be added by pressing Shift+Enter.

A *statement* is a block of code starting at the beginning of an execution group—or at the end of the previous statement—and ending at the first encountered semicolon or colon. In Document mode, the end of an execution group can also be used to terminate a statement, but in some versions of Maple, this will produce an error message in Worksheet mode. A statement may contain more than one line of code and an execution group may contain more than one statement.

When you press Enter while the cursor is inside an execution group, the statements contained in the execution group will be executed one at a time starting from the top. Control structures are special pieces of code that can be used to break away from this basic pattern to introduce repetition or conditionality into the flow, and these will be discussed later in this chapter.

2.1.1 Comments

The character # is used for *comments*. In each line, all code that is preceded by the character # will be ignored by Maple in all computations. This is useful for adding comments about the code to improve readability. Note that colons and semicolons are also ignored when occurring inside a comment.

```
[> # A simple calculation                                        1
    2+2;                                                         2
```

Comments are used to document code to make it more accessible both for the programmer and for others who might need to understand it later. While writing a program, it will normally be obvious to the programmer what each piece of code is supposed to accomplish, but this information can be forgotten surprisingly quickly, so one should always write comments while coding. In fact, it may be a good idea to pretend that the code will be have to be read by someone who has no idea about what it is supposed to accomplish.

2.1.2 *Command Line*

It is most common to use the standard graphical interface of Maple discussed above, but Maple can also be launched in a *command line version* that has a very simple graphical user interface but precisely the same computational capabilities as the regular version. In fact, one could think of the regular version as a pretty facade on top of this basic layer where the actual computations are performed. To carry out computations, simply type the relevant commands. As in worksheet mode, statements should be followed by semicolons. The command line version of Maple is particularly useful for running large experiments on servers for hours or even days at a time. See the Maple help system for more information about how to launch the command line version under various operating systems.

2.2 Variables, Functions and Expressions

Functions in Maple are defined using the operator `->`. For example, the function f given by $f(x) = x^2$ is defined in Maple by the command:

```
[> f := x -> x^2;
```

As in the mathematical assignment $f(x) = x^2$, the x is simply a placeholder. The function can be evaluated using commands such as f(2) and f(y). In Maple, f is now defined as a mathematical object that can be acted on by various operators:

```
[> 2*f, D(f);
```

A function with several input and/or output variables can also be defined in this way:

```
[> f := (x,y,z) -> (x+y,x+z);
```

Evaluating f(1,2,3) yields 3,4.

In Maple, an *expression* is a mathematical expression involving one or more specific variables. Unlike a function, an expression depends on the specific variable used in the definition, and changing the underlying variable will also change the value of the expression, as illustrated here:

```
[> a := 2*x;                                              1
   a;                                                     2
   x := 3;                                                3
   a;                                                     4
```

$$a := 2x$$

$$2x$$

$$x := 3$$

$$6$$

Expressions and functions can often be used for the same purposes, but one should notice that Maple has two sets of commands for performing similar tasks involving respectively functions and expressions. Generally, commands involving expressions will need to be called with the underlying variable given explicitly as input, while this is not necessary for functions, where the variable used in the definition is simply a placeholder. Interchanging such commands may cause an error.

Example 2.2.1: Functions vs. expressions. To illustrate how to perform a few basic tasks with either functions or expressions, consider the function $f: \mathbb{R} \to \mathbb{R}$ given by $f(x) = x^2$ which can be defined, plotted, and differentiated in Maple using the following commands:

```
[> f := x -> x^2;                                         1
   plot(f,0..10);                                         2
   D(f);                                                  3
```

The following commands will do the same to the corresponding expression:

```
[> a := x^2;                                              1
   plot(a,x=0..10);                                       2
   diff(a,x);                                             3
```
◁

Note that if f is a function defined in Maple, then f(x) is an expression. The reverse operation—constructing a function from an expression—is done using the command unapply:

```
[> a := x^2*y;                                            1
   f := unapply(a,x);                                     2
   f(2);                                                  3
```

$$f := x \to x^2 y$$

$$4y$$

This is the only way to turn an expression into a function. As shown in Exercise 2.1, the naive assignment f := x -> a will not produce the desired result.

2.3 Sets, Lists, Sequences, Matrices and Strings

Maple can work with *sets* as mathematical objects and manipulate them using unions, intersections and differences as illustrated by the following commands

```
[> A := {1,2,3,3};                                    1
   B := {1,4};                                        2
   A union B;                                         3
   A intersect B;                                     4
   A minus B;                                         5
   is(2 in A);                                        6
```

$$A := \{1, 2, 3\}$$
$$B := \{1, 4\}$$
$$\{1, 2, 3, 4\}$$
$$\{1\}$$
$$\{2, 3\}$$
$$true$$

As expected of the mathematical object, sets in Maple do not count elements with multiplicity.

A *list* is used to store a collection of data where the order of data points matters. The following commands show how to define and access a list

```
[> L := [11,12,13,14];                               1
   L[3];                                              2
   nops(L);                                           3
```

$$L := [11, 12, 13, 14]$$
$$13$$
$$4$$

The command nops (short for *number of operands*) counts the number of elements of a list. It is worth noting that the input L[i] needed to access the ith element of L will be typeset as L_i when using 2d-mathematics notation.

The following commands show how lists can be nested, and how such nested lists are accessed

```
[> L := [1,[2,3],[4,[5,6],7],8,9]:                                1
  L[3,2];                                                          2
  L[3][2];                                                         3
```

$$[5, 6]$$
$$[5, 6]$$

Maple comes with a number of *packages* that can be loaded individually. Each of these contains a collection of commands relevant to a particular class of problems. For instance, the package `ListTools` contains a number of very useful tools for manipulating lists and it can be loaded using the command `with(ListTools)`. See the Maple help system for a description of the concrete functions available in this and other packages.

In Maple, a *sequence* is the underlying data structure used in the definition of both sets and lists. It is simply a comma-separated list of values. The command `op` (short for *operands*) can be used to convert a set or list to the corresponding sequence:

```
[> L := [2,3,5,7]:                                                1
  op(L);                                                          2
```

$$2, 3, 5, 7$$

The following command is used to generate sequences with a predefined internal structure given by an expression

```
[> seq(n^2,n=1..5);
```

$$1, 4, 9, 16, 25$$

It is worth noting that both input and output of most of Maple's commands take the form of sequences, and that they can be accessed as such:

```
[> solution := solve(x^3-2*x^2+x-2=0,x);                          1
  solution[1];                                                    2
```

$$solution := I, 2, -I$$
$$I$$

A *string* is a special kind of sequence designed to store text. A string is defined by enclosing a series of characters in quotation marks. As the following commands illustrate, the resulting variable behaves like a sequence in many ways

```
[> s := "this is a string";                                      1
  s[2];                                                           2
```

$$s := \text{"this is a string"}$$
$$\text{"h"}$$

This data type is often used for text, and the package `StringTools` contains a number of useful commands for the analysis of such text, for example

```
[> with(StringTools):                                             1
   FirstFromLeft("c","abcabcabc");                                2
```

3

Many of the commands from `StringTools` are also useful in the investigation of the structure of sequences that are not actual text.

The command `Matrix` can be used to define matrices from a wide range of input. The most basic approach is to give the entries explicitly. For instance, the 2×2 identity matrix can be defined using `Matrix([[1,0],[0,1]])`. However, for larger matrices in particular, it is more useful to specify the entries using a function of two variables that maps each pair consisting of a row and a column number to the corresponding entry, as in:

```
[> f := (r,c) -> r-c:                                             1
   Matrix(2,3,f);                                                 2
```

$$\begin{bmatrix} 0 & -1 & -2 \\ 1 & 0 & 1 \end{bmatrix}$$

2.4 Control Structures

Control structures are special commands used to make Maple deviate from the basic pattern of executing statements one at a time in the order they are encountered. The control structures `for` and `while` are used for repetitions, and the control structure `if` is used to introduce conditionality such that a part of the code is only executed under certain conditions.

2.4.1 *for*

A `for`-loop is used to execute a piece of code repeatedly with sequential input variables. A `for`-loop is initiated by code of the form `for i from s to e do`. It works by executing all the statements enclosed between the keyword `do` and first subsequent matching occurrence of the keyword `end` once for every value of the index variable `i` from the start value `s` to the end value `e`. The index variable `i` is incremented by one each time the loop has been completed.

Example 2.4.1: A `for`-loop. The following example shows how a basic `for`-loop can be used to print the numbers from 1 to 10.

```
[> for i from 1 to 10 do                                         1
     print(i);                                                   2
   end do;                                                       3
```

Here, i is the index variable of the loop. The start and end values are, respectively, 1 and 10.   ◁

Two (or more) for-loops can be nested so that the inner loop is executed, and hence repeated a number of times, each time the outer loop is completed once. This can, for instance, be used to vary the start and/or end values of the inner loop as shown in the following example.

Example 2.4.2: Nested for-loops. The following code uses an inner loop where the end value is dependent on the index variable of the outer loop.

```
[> for i from 0 to 10 do                                    1
      for j from 0 to i do                                  2
          print(j);                                         3
      end do;                                               4
   end do;                                                  5
```

This will print the sequence $0, 0, 1, 0, 1, 2, \ldots$ to the screen.   ◁

It is worth noting that for-loops can be replaced by more efficient tools in many applications. For instance, the tasks performed by the commands seq, map, add, and mul can also be handled using for-loops, but the built-in commands usually require less time and computer resources.

Example 2.4.3: for-loop variations. There are a few variations of the basic structure of the for-loop that can be used when one is interested in a repetition that does not involve a sequence of consecutive values of the index variable. The following form can be used if one is only interested in an evenly spaced subset of the values between the starting value and end value. For instance, the following command will print out a sequence of odd numbers:

```
[> for i from 1 to 100 by 2 do                              1
      print(i);                                             2
   end do;                                                  3
```

Another option is to put the desired values of the index variable in a list. The following command will print the elements of the list L:

```
[> L := [2,3,7,19];                                         1
   for i in L do                                            2
       print(i);                                            3
   end do;                                                  4
```

This approach is often useful for processing data that have been returned from another part of the program.   ◁

It is possible to change the behavior of the for-loop if the index variable is modified in the code enclosed between do and end. For instance, a manual incrementation of the index variable inside the loop can be used as an alternative to the first variation of the `for`-loop used to print out odd numbers in Example 2.4.3:

```
[> for i from 1 to 100 do                                           1
       print(i);                                                     2
       i := i+1:                                                     3
   end do:                                                           4
```

This means that it is possible to make a `for`-loop that never terminates, that is, an *infinite loop*. When executing such a loop, Maple will be caught in an infinite repetition until the process is aborted by the user. It is often impossible to exit Maple cleanly in such cases, so there is a risk of loosing unsaved work. Hence, one should always be careful when testing loops. Here is a simple example of an infinite loop:

```
[> for i from 1 to 2 do                                             1
       # An infinite loop. Save before executing!                   2
       print("Infinite loop!");                                     3
       i := i-1;                                                     4
   end do;                                                          5
```

2.4.2 *while*

Like the `for`-loop, a `while`-loop is used to repeat a block of code, but where the `for`-loop uses a counter to control how many times the block is executed, the `while`-loop will repeat as long as a specified condition is met.

A `while`-loop is initiated using the syntax `while C do`, where `C` is a condition that is either true or false. If the condition `C` is satisfied, then all the statements enclosed between the keyword `do` and the first matching occurrence of the keyword `end` will be executed. Then the condition `C` will be tested again. If it is still satisfied, then the statements in the loop will be executed again, if not, then Maple will move on to the first statement after the loop. The statements in the loop will continue to be executed in this manner as long as the condition `C` is true. If the condition is false from the beginning, the code contained in the loop is not going to be executed at all.

Example 2.4.4: Continuity. Given a continuous f, $\epsilon > 0$, and a suitable value x_0 in the domain of f, the following piece of code will find a $\delta > 0$ such that $|f(x_0 - \delta) - f(x_0 + \delta)| \leq \epsilon$ (but there is naturally no guarantee that this inequality holds for all x between $x_0 - \delta$ and $x_0 + \delta$)

```
[> f := x -> exp(x):                                                1
   x0 := 0.5:                                                        2
   epsilon := 0.1:                                                   3
   delta := 1:                                                       4
```

```
    while abs(f(x0-delta)-f(x0+delta)) > epsilon do        5
        delta := delta/2:                                  6
    end do:                                                7
    delta;                                                 8
```

$$\frac{1}{64}$$ ◁

Unlike a `for`-loop, a `while`-loop has no automatic incrementation. This increases the risk of accidentally constructing an infinite loop if the code contained in the loop does not eventually change the value of the condition C. One should be extra careful when testing new `while`-loops.

The condition C appearing in the statement of the loop can be any *boolean expression*, that is, an expression that Maple can evaluate as true or false. This is, for instance, the case for equations and inequalities. For the formulation of composite boolean expressions, use the logical operations `and`, `or`, and `not`. For more details, search for *boolean expressions* in the Maple help system.

Note that using clever assignments to the index variables, `for`-loops and `while`-loops can in principle be used to solve precisely the same programming task. However, each is designed to minimize the amount of bookkeeping needed in specific types of situations, and the programmer should use them accordingly. Both `for`- and `while`-loops can be nested in any desired order.

2.4.3 `if`

The `if`-statement is used to construct a piece of code that is only executed under certain conditions. Let C be a boolean expression and let S1 and S2 be collections of one or more statements, then an `if`-statement can be constructed by using the following syntax:

```
[> if C then                                               1
       S1                                                  2
   else                                                    3
       S2                                                  4
   end if;                                                 5
```

Executing code with this syntax will cause the statements S1 to be executed if and only if the boolean expression C is true. Reversely, the statements in S2 will be executed if and only if C is false. Note that the keyword `else` and the second collection of statements can be omitted.

Example 2.4.5: `break`. The keyword `break` is used to make Maple stop the execution of a loop prematurely. Whenever Maple encounters the keyword `break` inside a `for` or `while` loop, it will continue with the first statement after the loop instead of executing the remaining statements and looping as normal. In case of nested loops, only the innermost loop will be exited. The following code illustrates how break can be used to exit the inner loop in a pair of nested for-loops:

```
[> for i from 1 to 100 do                                      1
      for j from 2 to i do                                     2
         if i mod j = 0 then                                   3
            print(i,j);                                        4
            break;                                             5
         end if;                                               6
      end do;                                                  7
   end do;                                                     8
```

Note that this command will print a sequence of pairs (n, d) where $1 \leq n \leq 100$ and d is the smallest nontrivial divisor of n.   ◁

Often, it is useful to be able to test more than one condition at the same time and to act based on the outcomes of these tests. Naturally, this can be done using a series of nested if-statements, but Maple also has a variation of the basic if-statement designed specifically to handle such cases.

Example 2.4.6: Multiple cases.   In the following code, one of three strings will be printed depending on the value of the input variable x:

```
[> if x > 0 then                                               1
      print("Positive");                                       2
   elif x < 0 then                                             3
      print("Negative");                                       4
   else                                                        5
      print("Zero");                                           6
   end if;                                                     7
```

Note that the code enclosed between else and end if will be executed in every case that is not covered by one of the preceding tests.   ◁

2.5 Procedures

A procedure is a generalized function that can take zero or more variables as input and execute a block of code before returning results. Procedures can be used to perform any number of different tasks, and they are very useful for dividing a program into natural pieces with clearly defined purposes. This makes it much easier to develop and maintain the code by facilitating the construction of well-structured programs.

Example 2.5.1: Hello world. A simple procedure without input can be defined by:

```
[> hello := proc()                                    1
       print("Hello world!");                         2
   end proc;                                           3
```

To run this procedure, use the command:

```
[> hello();                                           1
```

"Hello world!"

The empty parenthesis signifies that the procedure does not take any input variables.   ◁

Example 2.5.2: Average. The following procedure takes two variables as input, and returns the average.

```
[> average := proc(a,b)                               1
       return (a+b)/2:                                 2
   end proc:                                           3
```
◁

If Maple does not encounter the keyword `return` when a procedure is executed, it will simply return the last computed result. However, to keep the intent of the code clear, it is a good idea to always include return-statements explicitly.

As discussed in Sections 2.1, Maple will execute statements in the order they are written in the code, and as seen in Section 2.4, this basic pattern can be altered by using control structures. Procedures give another very powerful way of modifying this flow of control, since calling a procedure will execute a piece of code that is defined in completely different part of the program. This feature is very important in the design of simple well-structured programs, because it allows the program to be broken down into a number of natural pieces, each handled by a procedure with a clearly defined purpose.

A great benefit of using procedures is that the same code lines can be reused over and over again. For that reason, one should aim to make procedures that will solve the given problem in a generalized form if that is possible. For example, a procedure that takes a list as input and performs some task on it (printing, sorting, etc.) should not be limited to lists of a specific length, so it can more easily be reused in later applications.

Example 2.5.3: Chebyshev's bias. Consider the list C_n consisting of the modulo 4 remainders of the first n primes. For instance, it is easily verified that

$$C_{10} = [2, 3, 1, 3, 3, 1, 1, 3, 3, 1].$$

In 1853, the Russian mathematician Pafnuty Lvovich Chebyshev observed that the number 3 seems to occur more often than the number 1 in these lists and this phenomenon is known as *Chebyshev's bias* or the *prime race*. In order to investigate it experimentally, define the following two procedures in Maple. The first one generates the list of remainders:

```
[> RemainderList := proc(N)                                          1
      local n, Cn;                                                   2
      Cn := [];                                                      3
      for n from 1 to N do                                           4
         Cn := [op(Cn), ithprime(n) mod 4];                          5
      end do;                                                        6
      return Cn;                                                     7
   end proc:                                                         8
```

The other one uses the result of this procedure and calculates the *bias*, that is, the difference between the number of occurrences of the number 3 and the number of occurrences of the number 1.

```
[> ChebyshevBias := proc(N)                                          1
      local Cn, bias, i;                                             2
      bias := 0;                                                     3
      Cn := remainderList(N);                                        4
      for i in Cn do                                                 5
         if i = 3 then                                               6
            bias := bias +1;                                         7
         elif i = 1 then                                             8
            bias := bias -1;                                         9
         end if;                                                    10
      end do;                                                       11
      return bias;                                                  12
   end proc:                                                        13
```

A plot of the bias as a function of N is shown in Figure 2.1.

Note that there is a lot of redundancy in this approach to the computation of the bias since the remainders are recomputed each time `chebyshevBias` is called. A more efficient program will be constructed in Exercise 2.14.   ◁

2.5.1 Data Types

Unlike most programming languages, Maple does not generally require the user to specify what kind of data that is going to be stored in a variable. For instance, the following series of assignments is perfectly valid:

```
[> a := 2;                                                           1
   a := ([[0,1],[1,0]]);                                             2
   a := "Test";                                                      3
```

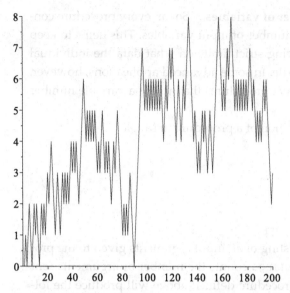

Figure 2.1 A plot of Chebyshev's bias. The number of occurrences of the number 3 in C_N minus the number of occurrences of 1 is plotted as a function of N.

This has an obvious advantage in flexibility, and even without experience of other programming languages, one can imagine that a certain amount of bookkeeping is avoided by not having to specify the type of data that a variable is going to store. However, this freedom comes at a price. Efficient memory allocation is precluded by the fact that the amount of memory needed to store a given variable cannot be known in advance, and the fluidity of the data types in use makes it hard to detect errors caused by sending unexpected input to homemade procedures. For instance, a procedure designed to take a matrix as input will return unexpected results if called with a string or a plot-structure as input. To avoid such errors, one should specify the data types of the input variables in the definition of a procedure. To see a complete list of the available data types, search for *type* in the Maple help system.

Example 2.5.4: Declaring variables.   The following procedure restricts the allowed input. Calling it with input that is not of the specified data type will result in an error.

```
[> CheckLength := proc(n::integer,s::string)          1
       if Length(s) >= n then                          2
          return true;                                 3
       else                                            4
          return false;                                5
       end if;                                         6
    end proc:                                          7
                                                       ◁
```

Example 2.5.5: Variable number of variables. So far, every procedure considered has had a predefined number of input variables. This helps to keep programs structured by enforcing strict limits on what data the individual procedures can be used to handle. In some advanced applications, however, it becomes necessary to construct procedures that accept a variable number of input variables.

Consider the following definition of a procedure in Maple:

```
[> printInput := proc()                                    1
      print(nargs);                                        2
      print(args);                                         3
   end proc:                                               4
```

Here, args is a sequence consisting of all input arguments given to the procedure at execution. Similarly, nargs counts the number or arguments sent to the procedure. Hence, the procedure defined above will produce the following output:

```
[> printInput(1,2,3,a,b,c);
```

$$6$$
$$1, 2, 3, a, b, c$$

Note how this makes it possible to define a procedure accepting a variable number of input variables. However, this option should not be used if there is another way to solve the task at hand, since it can make programs less structured and harder to read. In particular, it can be seen as step in the opposite direction compared to the specification of data types for input variables discussed above.   ◁

2.5.2 *Local and Global Variables*

As seen in the examples given earlier in this chapter, the definition of a procedure will often require a number of variables in addition to the ones given as input. These are, for instance, used for computations and indexation in the body of a procedure. When introducing such variables, the programmer has a choice: Should the variable be available outside the body of the procedure, or should it only be possible to access it from within the procedure itself. Such variables are, respectively, called *global* and *local*. The following example shows how global and local variables are defined and used.

Example 2.5.6: Local vs. global. The following code defines a procedure, localExample, and executes it. The keyword local preceding the variable s in the definition of the procedure means that inside the procedure, s behaves like a new variable completely unrelated to the definition of s outside the body of the procedure.

```
[> s := 0:                                                   1
  localExample := proc()                                     2
    local s;                                                 3
    s := 7                                                   4
    print("Inside the procedure", s);                        5
  end proc:                                                  6
  print("Before executing the procedure", s);               7
  localExample();                                            8
  print("After executing the procedure", s);                9
```

"Before executing the procedure", 0

"Inside the procedure", 7

"After executing the procedure", 0

Note that the changes made to the local s during an execution of the procedure are forgotten as soon as the procedure has terminated. This is seen in the output which prints values of s before, during, and after execution.

The following code defines a similar procedure, globalExample. Here, the definition of s is preceded by the keyword global which means that the variable s is the same both inside and outside the procedure's body.

```
[> s := 0:                                                   1
  globalExample := proc()                                    2
    global s;                                                3
    s := 7;                                                  4
    print("Inside the procedure", s)                         5
  end proc:                                                  6
  print("Before executing the procedure", s);               7
  globalExample();                                           8
  print("After executing the procedure", s);                9
```

"Before executing the procedure", 0

"Inside the procedure", 7

"After executing the procedure", 7

Now, the changes made to s during the execution of the procedure will remain after the procedure has terminated. Note how this is reflected in the output. ◁

It is worth noting that variables passed to a procedure as input cannot be modified directly by the procedure. This feature helps protect programs from unwanted and accidental changes to variables. Hence, the only way to modify a variable appearing outside the definition of procedure from within the procedure is to declare the variable as a global variable in the procedure definition.

Programs should generally be defined so information is made available to procedures on a *need to know basis* in the sense that a procedure should only have access to a variable if it actually needs to use it to retrieve or store data. This helps keeping programs organized and limits the errors the procedure can cause. In Maple, this means that one should aim to use local variables as much as possible, and most tasks can actually be solved without using global variables.

However, using local rather than global variables does come at a cost. Passing a variable to a procedure as input will cause an extra copy of the contained data to be stored in the computer's memory. If the same data were stored in a global variable then they could be accessed without the need to copy. This saves time and memory, and if big amounts of data are involved, this could be necessary in order to make a program that will finish in a reasonable amount of time. However, an untrained programmer should aim to make clear and well-structured—rather than fast—programs. Even in cases where the extra speed-up is really needed, one should first construct a basic implementation using the guidelines given above before starting to worry about optimization of the code.

Local and global variables are special cases of what is known as the *scope* of a variable. Loosely, the scope of a variable is the part of the code where the variable if available to be used in computations. This is a complex concept in Maple because the user has the freedom to execute statements in arbitrary order, and it will not be treated in further detail here.

2.5.3 *Procedures in Structured Programming*

Procedures are invaluable tools in the construction of structured programs. Fundamentally, the program should be split into a number of procedures that each solves a single clearly defined problem, delegating sub-tasks to other procedures to make the code clear and manageable. Each procedure should, however, solve its task in the most general manner possible, so it has a better chance of being reused in other contexts. In this way, complex tasks can be solved by calling a series of simpler procedures.

Maple itself relies on procedures for the majority of its functionality: Each command is a procedure with a specific purpose, and many commands solve their tasks by calling other, more general commands. For instance, the command `Determinant` from the package `LinearAlgebra` solves the problem of finding the determinant of a given matrix. However, it does so in a very general manner: It is not limited to matrices with certain dimensions or certain kinds of entries. Indeed, it is not even limited to matrices over the fields $\mathbb{R}$ and $\mathbb{C}$.

A *magic number* is any number appearing in the code that might as well have been replaced by another number. Such magic numbers should generally be avoided, because they severely limit the possibilities to reuse and generalize the code. Instead, such numbers should in most cases be replaced by parameters passed to the procedure in question or by a command that computes the desired quantity directly. For instance, a procedure should not use an explicitly given ending value in a `for`-loop when investigating a sequence, but rather use a command like `nops` to get access to the number of elements in the actual sequence under investigation.

There are more advanced approaches to the construction of well-structured computer programs. In particular, certain programming languages (like C++, C♯, Java, and Python) give a whole new level of tools that allows the programmer to define and work with homemade objects consisting of both data and procedures. In many cases, this *object oriented programming* allows a more natural manipulation of (mathematical) structures and a code that is easier to read. For instance, in many ways, it is more natural to think of the determinant of a matrix as an intrinsic property of the matrix rather than the value of a function applied to the matrix. Maple does contain tools for this approach, but they are not easy to use for an inexperienced programmer, and object oriented programming will not be discussed in detail here.

Example 2.5.7: $\{0, 1\}$-sequences. This case study concerns the properties of a specific kind of sequences of zeroes and ones and the goal will be to arrive at hypotheses about their properties. Given an irrational $\alpha \in (0, 1) \setminus \mathbb{Q}$, define the sequence $\mathbf{s}[\alpha] = (s_n)_{n \in \mathbb{N}_0}$ by $s_n = \lfloor (n + 1)\alpha \rfloor - \lfloor n\alpha \rfloor$. To start the investigation, consider the following two examples:

$$
\begin{aligned}
\mathbf{s}\left[\tfrac{\sqrt{5}-1}{\sqrt{5}+1}\right] = (&0, 0, 1, 0, 0, 1, 0, 1, 0, 0, 1, 0, 0, 1, 0, 1, 0, 0, 1, 0, 1, 0, 0, 1, 0, 0, 1, \\
&0, 1, 0, 0, 1, 0, 0, 1, 0, 1, 0, 0, 1, 0, 1, 0, 0, 1, 0, 0, 1, 0, 1, 0, 0, 1, 0, \\
&1, 0, 0, 1, 0, 0, 1, 0, 1, 0, 0, 1, 0, 0, 1, 0, 1, 0, 0, 1, 0, 1, 0, 0, 1, 0, 0, \\
&1, 0, 1, 0, 0, 1, 0, 0, 1, 0, 1, 0, 0, 1, 0, 1, 0, 0, 1, 0, 0, 1, 0, 1, 0, 0, 1, \\
&0, 1, 0, 0, 1, 0, 0, 1, 0, 1, 0, 0, 1, 0, 0, 1, 0, 1, 0, 0, 1, 0, 1, 0, 0, 1, 0, \\
&0, 1, 0, 1, 0, 0, 1, 0, 1, 0, 0, 1, 0, 0, 1, 0, 1, 0, 0, 1, 0, 0, 1, \ldots)
\end{aligned}
$$

$$
\begin{aligned}
\mathbf{s}[\pi/4] = (&0, 1, 1, 1, 0, 1, 1, 1, 1, 0, 1, 1, 1, 0, 1, 1, 1, 1, 0, 1, 1, 1, 1, 0, 1, 1, 1, \\
&0, 1, 1, 1, 1, 0, 1, 1, 1, 1, 0, 1, 1, 1, 0, 1, 1, 1, 1, 0, 1, 1, 1, 1, 0, 1, 1, \\
&1, 0, 1, 1, 1, 1, 0, 1, 1, 1, 1, 0, 1, 1, 1, 0, 1, 1, 1, 1, 0, 1, 1, 1, 1, 0, 1, \\
&1, 1, 0, 1, 1, 1, 1, 0, 1, 1, 1, 1, 0, 1, 1, 1, 0, 1, 1, 1, 1, 0, 1, 1, 1, 1, 0, \\
&1, 1, 1, 0, 1, 1, 1, 1, 0, 1, 1, 1, 1, 0, 1, 1, 1, 0, 1, 1, 1, 1, 0, 1, 1, 1, 1, \\
&0, 1, 1, 1, 0, 1, 1, 1, 1, 0, 1, 1, 1, 1, 0, 1, 1, 1, 0, 1, 1, \ldots).
\end{aligned}
$$

Studying these two sequences should give a hint that such sequences have a strict internal structure which further experiments can illuminate. In the following, these sequences will simply be referred to as $\{0, 1\}$-sequences. Their structure is well understood, but for now, the discussion of the theory will be limited to a minimum, to show how much information it is possible to extract from a purely experimental investigation.

The following two functions generate the initial terms of such sequences:

```
[> s := (alpha,n) -> floor((n+1)*alpha)-floor(n*alpha);          1
   generateSequence := (alpha, N) ->                              2
                        seq( s(alpha,n) , n = 0..N-1);            3
```

Using this generator on a collection of concrete cases and investigating their properties can quickly lead to a wide range of hypotheses (*cf.* Exercises 2.19 and 2.41). One of the simplest of these is that the average over the first N
EX. 2.8.1 ← elements of $s[\alpha]$ converges to α.   ◁

2.6 Pseudocode and Stepwise Refinement

When writing computer programs, it is very important to prepare properly. In order to make effective and well structured programs, the programmer should know in detail what the program is meant to do before starting to write the code. Hence, the design of a computer program should normally start on a piece of paper, not at the keyboard.

Pseudocode is a broad term covering descriptions of computer programs using the structural conventions of a programming language but giving information in a human readable format. It is used to write detailed descriptions of computer programs (on paper) before the actual programming starts. The great benefit of this is that one can focus on the ideas and structures of the program instead of the details of the technical implementation. The pseudocode description can omit the details that—while necessary to make the code perform in the computer—are distracting to a human reader. Using pseudocode, the programmer can plan the program carefully without being distracted by the errors that inevitably occur while writing and testing actual computer code. Having said that, it is important to note that it is almost impossible to get everything right the first time around when writing computer programs. Often, the process and the challenges encountered shape the program, so the development becomes an iterative procedure.

Another benefit of pseudocode notation is that it is to a great extent independent of the programming language used. Many programming languages solve similar tasks in similar manners, and even though the notation and conventions of two languages may differ wildly, the same pseudocode can be used as the foundation of a program written in either language. This means that pseudocode written with a specific programming language in mind is often just as suitable for the development of a program solving the same problem in another language, and often such a piece of pseudocode will be much more accessible than the finished program. This is worth keeping in mind if one is searching for help in the construction of an algorithm solving a specific task.

When one is documenting experimental work in a paper or similar written report, it is customary to include pseudocode for the important parts of the experimental design. The actual code is often relegated to an appendix or simply made available online. This has the advantage of giving readers an understandable description of the programs without slowing down the presentation with all the details of the implementation.

Pseudocode should be written using indentations to highlight the structure of the program in the same manner as in the examples of code given in this chapter. Keywords like `for`, `while`, and `if` should be used whenever it makes sense in the design of the program. Over time, most programmers develop their own conventions and shorthand notations for writing pseudocode. The following example shows what a piece of pseudocode can look like, and in the rest of the notes, a similar notation will be used to describe various algorithms.

Example 2.6.1: Sieve of Eratosthenes. *The Sieve of Eratosthenes* is a simple algorithm for exhaustively finding the primes less than or equal to a given upper bound N. Pseudocode for the sieve is given in Algorithm 2.1. ◁

Algorithm 2.1 Sieve of Eratosthenes

1: **procedure** SIEVE(N)
2:     Construct a list $L = [2, \ldots, N]$
3:     Let $p = 2$
4:     **while** $p < N$ **do**
5:         Remove ip from L for each integer $i \geq 2$
6:         Let p be the smallest element in L greater than p
7:     **end while**
8: **return** L ▷ L contains all primes smaller than N
9: **end procedure**

Stepwise refinement is the process of turning a loosely formulated idea for a computer program into a detailed piece of pseudocode through steps consisting of progressively more detailed pseudocode. When the pseudocode is sufficiently refined, the programmer can start implementing it by writing the actual program. Using the conventions of pseudocode described above, this process can be described by Algorithm 2.2.

Algorithm 2.2 Stepwise refinement

1: identify the problem that you want to solve

2: write initial pseudocode for the program

3: **while** the pseudocode is not detailed enough to write the program **do**

4:       modify and refine the pseudocode

5: **end while**

6: write the program

Example 2.6.2: Winning strategy. Two players, A and B, agree on an $n \in \mathbb{N}$ and proceed to play the following game: Starting with A, they take turns to write either 0 or 1 as the next entry in a sequence. The loser is the player who first writes a digit so that the last n digits form a sub-sequence that has already occurred once. For $n = 2$, the game could proceed in the following manner:

$$00101.$$

Here, player B wins when 01 is written for the second time by player A.

In this case, player B even has a *winning strategy*, that is, a strategy that leads to victory no matter what player A chooses to play: After player B had written his first 0, player A was forced to write 1 to avoid a repetition of 00. In the third move, Player A has to repeat either 01 or 00. If player A had started with a 1, then player B could have won in a similar manner by answering with a 1. We say that this strategy has *depth* 2 because player B only needs to look at the last two elements of the sequence to determine what to play. Letting $*$ indicate the position before the start of the game, this strategy can be described as follows:

$$*0 \to 0, \quad *1 \to 1, \quad 01 \to 0, \quad 10 \to 1.$$

There is no need to list 00 and 11 as they cannot appear just before player B's turn.

This is a finite two-player game that cannot result in a draw, and each player has complete information about the preceding moves. In such a game, one player will always have a winning strategy. Note that the number of

---

Algorithm 2.3 Finding the winner of the game considered in Example 2.6.2

1: **procedure** WINNER(Integer n and strategies for A and B)

2:       create an empty string w

3:       **while** the game has not yet been won **do**

4:            Add a digit to w according to the strategy of the current player

5:       **end while**

6: **return** identity of winning player

7: **end procedure**

---

possible ways the game can end grows exponentially with n, making it highly nontrivial to investigate the game exhaustively for large n.

In order to be able to investigate the game further and find winning strategies for $n > 2$, we will define a procedure play which can play the game given *strategies* for the two players, that is, given two procedures A and B determining how the players make their moves, the procedure play should finish the game and determine a winner. Pseudocode for this procedure is given in Algorithm 2.3.

In order to define play, it is first necessary to define a procedure capable of determining when the game has been won. The following procedure solves this problem. It takes an integer n and a string w as input. If w is sufficiently long, the procedure determines whether w contains a repetition of the final n digits:

```
[> gameHasBeenWon := proc(n, w) local ending;        1
    if(length(w)<=n) then                            2
      return false;                                  3
    else                                             4
      ending := substring(w,-n..-1);                 5
      if Search(ending, w) <= length(w)-n then       6
        return true;                                 7
      else                                           8
        return false;                                9
      end if;                                       10
    end if;                                         11
  end proc:                                         12
```

The following procedure is more complicated than the ones considered so far in that it takes *procedures* as input. The idea is to pass the strategies of the two players to the procedure which then places digits according to these rules until the game is decided when one of the players creates a repetition:

```
[> play := proc(n::integer,A::procedure,B::procedure)   1
    local w;                                             2
    w := "";                                             3
    while(gameHasBeenWon(n,w) = false) do                4
      if type(length(w),even) then                       5
        w := cat(w,A(w));                                6
      else                                               7
        w := cat(w,B(w));                                8
      end if;                                            9
    end do;                                             10
    return length(w) mod 2, w;                          11
  end proc:                                             12
```

The procedure returns a bit (0 or 1) to specify the winning player followed by the sequence of digits that the game has produced.

As an example of a function which could be used as input to play, consider the function which simply returns a random binary digit without regard for the input:

```
[> randomMove := w -> rand(0..1)():
```

To generate a random example of a game for $n = 3$, use:

```
[> play(3,randomMove,randomMove);
```

Using this and other concrete strategies, it is straightforward to generate examples.

The goal of Exercise 2.43 is to use the tools constructed here to find a winning strategy for as many values of n as possible. This is easy for some values of n and very difficult for other values.   ◁

EX. 6.5.5 ←

2.7 Errors

When writing computer code, there are several different types of errors that can occur. In Maple, one will normally encounter errors in the following two broad categories:

Maple user errors: Maple gives an error message when a piece of code is executed. This happens whenever Maple is unable to make sense of a statement.

Logical errors: The program runs without error messages, but the output is corrupted. These errors are often the hardest to find and correct because it may not be obvious that there is an error at all.

2.7.1 *Avoiding Errors*

Every nontrivial computer program is going to have errors while it is being developed. However, there are a number of simple things that can be done to reduce the number of errors and make it easier to correct the errors that do show up:

- Know what you want any given piece of code to accomplish before you start writing it. Use pseudocode and stepwise refinement in this process.
- Divide the program into natural pieces and let each piece be handled by a single procedure (that may need to call other procedures).
- Every procedure should have a name that reflects its purpose. If it is difficult to find a good name, then it is likely that the purpose of the procedure is too unspecific. In that case, it is a good idea to split it into several procedures with clearly defined purposes.
- Use meaningful names for variables.

- Do not reinvent the wheel. If you are attempting to solve a basic task then Maple probably already contains a procedure that can handle the problem.
- Comment your code.
- Use line breaks and spaces to structure the code for readability.

2.7.2 Debugging

Errors in computer code are known as *bugs*, and the process of finding and fixing such errors is known as *debugging*. Maple contains a dedicated tool for debugging known as the *Maple debugger*. However, an untrained programmer working on smaller projects such as the ones presented in this book is normally better served by a simpler approach, and the Maple debugger is not going to described in detail here.

The main problem when attempting to fix a Maple error is to pinpoint the exact piece of code where things went wrong. Maple will try to help by displaying an error message and placing the cursor where the error was detected. However, this only shows where Maple noticed the error, and the actual error may stem from a neighboring part of the code. To locate the actual error, one can insert the command `print` at strategic places in the code. Only the `print`-commands occurring before the error will be executed, so the approach can be used to find the exact line where things went wrong. In the most simple form, the command `print` is simply used to print a string of text to identify the position of the error. In more complex cases, it is often useful to print the values of key variables instead, since this makes it easier to gather information about the program that will help identify the error.

2.7.3 A Short Catalog of Common Maple Error Messages

Here is a short description of some of the more common Maple error messages:

Error, attempting to assign to ... which is protected is displayed if the user attempts to save data to one of the variables that Maple has reserved for specific commands or constants (notably I and D).

Error, invalid subscript selector occurs when attempting to access the nth element of a sequence (or similar data structure) that has fewer than n elements. It also occurs if the argument n is not an integer and hence does not give a valid specification of a position.

Warning, premature end of input occurs when the user attempts to execute an unfinished statement (i.e. a `for`-loop without the keyword `end`). This often happens when pressing Enter rather than Shift+Enter while writing a statement.

Error, ... expects its ... argument, ..., to be of type ... occurs if a procedure receives an argument of a different type than expected, see

Section 2.5.1. The problem may be that the arguments are given in the wrong order. Note that the error mentions both the expected and the received type of data; this can often help identify the error.

See also the *Error Message Guide Overview* in the Maple help system for detailed descriptions of these and many other error messages.

2.8 Automated Testing of Hypotheses

As discussed in Chapter 1, the fundamental process in an experimental investigation of a mathematical problem is the testing of hypotheses. We loosely define an *automated test* of a hypothesis H, to be the systematic investigation of the validity of H for all cases in some subset of the possible cases. Often, the fundamental challenge for the experimenting mathematician will be to extend the subset of cases considered sufficiently to get interesting results.

It is important to keep in mind that the aim of an automated test should always be to falsify the hypothesis under investigation by finding a counterexample. Naturally, any computer-assisted test of the validity of a hypothesis requires that the hypothesis is formulated clearly, so a procedure can be designed to check whether it is satisfied in any given case.

Automated tests are most efficiently carried out by programs that investigate large numbers of examples automatically and output any counterexamples found. Depending on the problem at hand, the examples may be generated systematically or randomly.

This approach is described unspecifically in Algorithm 2.4, but there are many ways to vary this basic pattern of an automated test. For instance, it might be beneficial to keep track of the investigated systems to avoid repetition. In some cases, one can systematically investigate all cases up to some degree of complexity while it might be more practical to investigate a random selection in other cases. This will be discussed in greater detail in Chapters 6 and 7.

Algorithm 2.4 Automated testing of a hypothesis

 1: **procedure** AUTOMATICTEST(A hypothesis H concerning a structure S)
 2:     **while** not enough examples have been investigated **do**
 3:         construct an example of S
 4:         **if** the example does not satisfy H **then**
 5:             save and/or print the counterexample
 6:         **end if**
 7:     **end while**
 8: **return** all counterexamples
 9: **end procedure**

In some cases, it may not be possible to know for certain whether a given example is in fact a counterexample to the hypothesis. Consider, for instance, the Collatz conjecture given in Example 1.5.2. For any given starting value, it may take a very long time for the iterated values to reach 1, and for large starting values, there is a very real danger of running out of time or computer resources before doing so. In such cases, the automated test will need to operate with *possible* counterexamples which should be stored so they can be investigated in greater detail later.

Note that it is very important to keep track of the counterexamples that show up in an automated investigation because such examples should always be investigated carefully. After all, it is not particularly useful if the result of a long computation is that there exists a counterexample, while the actual counterexample remains unknown. Common features in counterexamples often give the necessary input to reformulate and refine hypotheses. In other cases, the counterexamples are actually a product of logical errors in the program code, and in such cases, the collection of counterexamples will help the programmer find and fix the errors.

In the construction of automated tests, one should always aim to output all relevant information about a counterexample as soon as it becomes available. Otherwise, a later error may cause the program to crash or otherwise corrupt the data, so the information about the counterexample becomes unavailable.

EX. 2.5.7 → **Example 2.8.1: Automated test.** As mentioned in Example 2.5.7, it seems that the average of the first N elements of the sequence $s[\alpha]$ converges to α as N tends to infinity. The next goal is to develop a program that can carry out an automated test of this hypothesis.

In this example, there is clearly no way to examine all possible irrational values of α, so to avoid bias in the tested cases, it would be nice to be able

---

Algorithm 2.5 Automated test of the hypothesis discussed in Example 2.8.1

```
 1: procedure AUTOMATICTEST(N, k ε)
 2:     for n from 1 to N do
 3:         construct an α
 4:         construct the k first elements of s[α]
 5:         compute the average
 6:         find the difference between the average and α
 7:         if the difference > ε then
 8:             print α
 9:             store α in collection of counterexamples
10:         end if
11:     end for
12: return all counterexamples
13: end procedure
```

to test a random selection of values of α. The feasibility of that option will be discussed in greater detail in Chapter 6. For now, we will settle for constructing new irrational numbers from a single base number $\alpha_0 \in (0, 1) \setminus \mathbb{Q}$ by setting $\alpha_i = |\alpha_0 - 1/2(1 + \cos(n))|$. This is not optimal, as there is a serious risk of introducing bias into the results if the constructed numbers share some property that is not universal to all irrational numbers.

The goal is to construct a procedure that can test the hypothesis given a base number α_0, a number N of terms in the constructed sequences, and a tolerance ϵ specifying how far the average should be from the examined α before α is filed as a possible counterexample. Pseudocode for such a procedure is given in Algorithm 2.5. This pseudocode is easy to translate into functioning Maple code relying on the procedure constructed in Example 2.5.7 which generates the first N terms of $\mathbf{s}[\alpha]$ (cf. Exercises 2.20 and 2.21).   ◁

The final example of this chapter concerns a kind of sequence that can be analyzed in much the same way as the ones considered in Examples 2.5.7 and 2.8.1, but in this case, the entire experimental investigation is deferred to the exercises.

Example 2.8.2: Beta-sequences.   Define, for any pair of numbers $\beta \in (1, \infty)$ and $x \in [0, 1]$, a sequence $(x_n)_{n \in \mathbb{N}_0}$ by

$$x_0 = x$$
$$x_n = \beta^{-n}\langle \beta^n x_{n-1}\rangle, \qquad n \in \mathbb{N}.$$

Using these sequences, define $\mathbf{b}[\beta, x] = (b_n)_{n \in \mathbb{N}}$ by

$$b_n = \lfloor \beta^n x_{n-1} \rfloor, \qquad n \in \mathbb{N}.$$

The notation $\langle y \rangle$ is used for the *fractional part* $y - \lfloor y \rfloor$, when $y \in (0, \infty)$. For instance, $\langle 2.7 \rangle = \langle 1.7 \rangle = 0.7$. Letting $\beta = \frac{5}{2}$ and $x = 1$ yields the sequence

$$
\begin{aligned}
\mathbf{b}[5/2, 1] = [&2, 1, 0, 1, 1, 1, 0, 0, 0, 0, 1, 1, 0, 1, 2, 1, 0, 0, 0, 1, 1, \\
&1, 1, 1, 2, 1, 0, 0, 0, 1, 0, 0, 2, 0, 0, 0, 1, 0, 0, 1, 2, 0, \\
&1, 0, 0, 1, 1, 1, 1, 1, 0, 0, 0, 1, 1, 0, 0, 1, 2, 0, 0, 0, 1, \\
&2, 0, 0, 1, 2, 0, 1, 1, 1, 1, 0, 0, 0, 2, 0, 1, 0, 0, 2, 0, 0, \\
&1, 0, 1, 0, 1, 1, 0, 1, 1, 0, 1, 1, 0, 1, 2, 0, 0, 1, 1, 1, 1, \\
&2, 0, 1, 1, 0, 0, 0, 1, 1, 2, 0, 0, 0, 0, 2, 0, 2, 0, 0, 0, 1, \dots].
\end{aligned}
$$

It is straightforward to write a procedure which, given β, x, and N, computes the first N terms of $\mathbf{b}[\beta, x]$. The structure of these sequences are investigated EX. 7.4.3 ← in Exercises 2.22, 2.23, 2.24 and 2.44.   ◁

2.9 Exercises

Warmup

Exercise 2.1 As mentioned above, the following assignment will not define a function in Maple:

```
[> a := x^2+1;                                                    1
   f := x -> a;                                                   2
```

What properties does the object f have?

Exercise 2.2 Use Maple's internal help-function to identify the commands from the StringTools package that can solve the following problems given strings s_1 and s_2:

- Determine whether s_1 is a sub-string of s_2.
- Determine whether s_1 is a prefix of s_2.
- Find the first occurrence (if any) of s_1 as a sub-string of s_2.
- Given n_1, n_2, extract the sub-string of s_1 consisting of characters number n_1 through n_2.
- Given $n \in \mathbb{N}$, find all sub-strings of s_1 of length n.

Use each command in an example.

Exercise 2.3 Identify a closed form expression for $\sum_{k=1}^{N} k^5$.

Exercise 2.4 Use a for-loop to output the first 100 prime numbers.

Exercise 2.5 Use command line Maple to solve $8x^3 - 14x^2 + 7x - 1 = 0$.

Exercise 2.6 Use the usual plotting command to make a plot of the parabola given by the equation $y = x^2 + 2x - 3$ in command line Maple.

Homework

Exercise 2.7 Write Maple code that produces all polynomials in one variable with degree at most 3 and coefficients in $\{0, \ldots, 3\}$.

Exercise 2.8 Construct a procedure based on the answer to Exercise 2.7 that given $d, k \in \mathbb{N}$ returns all polynomials in one variable with degree at most d and coefficients in $\{0, \ldots, k\}$. Modify this procedure to make it able to produce polynomials in more than one variable.

EX. 1.5.2 → **Exercise 2.9** Use a while-loop to test the Collatz Conjecture for starting values 8, 17, 100, 219. For each value, find the number of iterations needed to reach 1.

Exercise 2.10 Use nested while-loops to recreate the output shown in Example 2.4.2.

Exercise 2.11 Define procedures capable of solving the following problems and test each procedure on at least three suitable examples.

- Given numbers a and b, return the function defined by $f(x) = \cos(ax + b)$.
- Given a list L of numbers, return the sum and the average.
- Given a matrix, return the largest entry.

Exercise 2.12 Write a procedure which uses `args` and `nargs` to compute the average of an a priori unspecified number of input variables. Solve the same problem using a list instead.

Exercise 2.13 Look through the examples given in this chapter and identify the magic numbers in each case. Pick one of these examples and rewrite it as a procedure where the magic numbers are replaced by input variables to a procedure.

EX. 2.5.3 → **Exercise 2.14** Use the procedures constructed in Example 2.5.3 to look for a counterexample to Chebyshev's conjecture. Rewrite the procedures to avoid computing the remainders multiple times. Compare the results and speed of the two procedures.

EX. 2.6.1 → **Exercise 2.15** Prove that the sieve of Eratosthenes produces all primes less than or equal to N.

Exercise 2.16 Write pseudocode for the Euclidean algorithm and implement it.

Algorithm 2.6 A simple sorting algorithm

```
procedure SORT(L)
    for i from 1 to the size of L do
        index of smallest value := i
        for j from i + 1 to the size of L do
            if L[j] < L[index of smallest value] then
                index of smallest value := j
            end if
        end for
        interchange L[i] and L[index of smallest value]
    end for
return L
end procedure
```

Exercise 2.17 Explain how Algorithm 2.6 works. Use it to write a procedure that can sort a list. Identify a built-in command in Maple that solves the same problem.

EX. 1.5.1 → **Exercise 2.18** Write a procedure which given n tests whether M_n is a prime. Use this procedure to find as many errors in Mersenne's original conjecture as possible. Note that M_n is composite if n is composite, so it is sufficient to consider primes.

EX. 2.5.7 → **Exercise 2.19** Generate the first 100 elements of $s[\alpha]$ for at least 10 different values of α. Record any interesting patterns.

EX. 2.8.1 → **Exercise 2.20** Implement the pseudocode given in Algorithm 2.5.

EX. 2.8.1 → **Exercise 2.21** Use the procedure constructed in Exercise 2.20 to conduct an automatic test. How many terms of the sequences must be included to make sure that there are no counterexamples for $\epsilon = 0.1$ and $\epsilon = 0.01$, respectively? Formulate a hypothesis about the precision of the approximation based on the number of terms N and test it. How well does this compare to the optimal approximation of α as the frequency of ones in a sequence of N zeroes and ones?

EX. 2.8.2 → **Exercise 2.22** Construct a procedure which, given β, x and $N \in \mathbb{N}$, will return the first N elements of $b[\beta, x]$ (e.g. in a list).

EX. 2.8.2 → **Exercise 2.23** Consider $\beta = 5/2$. Which words of length 1, 2, and 3 occur in $b[5/2, x]$ for $x \in (0, 1]$? Choose another $\beta \in (1, 3)$ and answer the same question. Do you see a pattern?

EX. 2.8.2 → **Exercise 2.24** Formulate and test a hypothesis about the relation between $b[\beta, x]$ and $s(\beta, x) = \sum_{n=1}^{\infty} b_n / \beta^n$.

EX. 1.6.2 → **Exercise 2.25** Write a procedure to carry out the construction of integers that are hypotenuses of right-angled integer triangles as considered in Exercise 1.6. Formulate a precise hypothesis about the form of the numbers that can occur and test this hypothesis using a procedure.

Exercise 2.26 Consider an integer sequence $(x_n)_{n \in \mathbb{N}}$. Let $(d_n)_{n \in \mathbb{N}}$ be defined by $d_n = |x_{n+1} - x_n|$. Investigate what happens when one iterates this process on the sequence of primes. Explain the observation and formulate a conjecture.

In each of the following exercises, write a program to investigate the hypothesis and output any counterexamples. Do you believe the hypothesis is true?

Exercise 2.27 Hypothesis: Every even integer greater than 2 can be expressed as the sum of two primes.

Exercise 2.28 Hypothesis: Every odd integer greater than 5 can be expressed as the sum of three primes.

Exercise 2.29 Hypothesis: Every odd number is either a prime or a sum of a prime and two times a square, that is, for each $n \in \mathbb{N}_0$ there exist a prime p and $m \in \mathbb{N}_0$ such that $2n + 1 = p + 2m^2$.

Exercise 2.30 Hypothesis: For each $n \in \mathbb{N}$,

$$\left\lceil \frac{2}{\sqrt[n]{2} - 1} \right\rceil = \left\lfloor \frac{2n}{\ln 2} \right\rfloor$$

EX. 2.5.3 → **Exercise 2.31** For each $n \in \mathbb{N}$, let P_n be the list of the modulo 3 remainders of the first n primes except 2 and 3. Hypothesis: For each n, the number 2 occurs more often in P_n than the number 1. Note the similarity with the problem considered in Example 2.5.3 and Exercise 2.14.

EX. 1.5.1 → **Exercise 2.32** Hypothesis: For each $n \geq 5$, the Fermat number $F_n = 2^{2^n} + 1$ is composite.

EX. 1.5.1 → **Exercise 2.33** Hypothesis: For each prime p, the Mersenne number M_p is square-free.

EX. 1.6.4 → **Exercise 2.34** Hypothesis: The inequalities $\text{Li}(x) > \pi(x) > x/\ln(x)$ hold for all $x > 1$.

Exercise 2.35 Given $n \in \mathbb{N}$, let $\#(n)$ denote the number of prime factors of n counted with multiplicity. Hypothesis: For each $N > 1$,

$$|\{n \leq N \mid \#(n) \text{ odd}\}| \geq |\{n \leq N \mid \#(n) \text{ even}\}|.$$

Exercise 2.36 For each $n \in \mathbb{N}$, let p_n denote the nth prime number. Hypothesis: For each $n \in \mathbb{N}$, $\sqrt{p_{n+1}} - \sqrt{p_n} < 1$.

Exercise 2.37 Hypothesis: Given $\alpha, \beta \in \mathbb{R}$,

$$\liminf_{n \to \infty} n \, ||n\alpha|| \, ||n\beta|| = 0,$$

where $||x|| = \min(x - \lfloor x \rfloor, \lceil x \rceil - x)$ is the distance from x to the nearest integer.

Exercise 2.38 Hypothesis: $p \in \mathbb{N}$ is a prime number if and only if

$$\sum_{i=1}^{p-1} i^{p-1} \equiv -1 \pmod{p}.$$

Exercise 2.39 Hypothesis: Consider positive integers A, B, C, x, y, z with $x, y, x > 2$ and $A^x + B^y = C^z$, then A, B, and C have a common prime factor.

Exercise 2.40 Hypothesis: For every integer $n \geq 2$, there exist positive integers x, y, and z such that

$$\frac{4}{n} = \frac{1}{x} + \frac{1}{y} + \frac{1}{z}.$$

Projects and Group Work

EX. 2.5.7 → **Exercise 2.41** Formulate at least three clearly defined hypotheses about the general behavior of $s[\alpha]$. Investigate the hypotheses using automated tests.

EX. 1.5.2 → **Exercise 2.42** Construct a program capable of carrying out an automatic test of the Collatz conjecture introduced in Example 1.5.2. Design this program using pseudocode and stepwise refinement. The procedure should test all starting values between two numbers that are sent to the procedure as input. The procedure should also take a variable as input that controls how many iterations the test will go through before giving up on reaching 1 and reporting the current value as a possible counterexample. It may be useful to modify the program constructed in Exercise 2.9.

EX. 2.6.2 → **Exercise 2.43** The aim of this exercise is to formulate and test winning strategies for the game considered in Example 2.6.2. For some values of n, it is still an open problem to formulate the winning strategy, but here the focus will be on the cases where it is possible to identify and verify simple winning strategies.

- Define a procedure implementing the winning strategy considered in the example and use the procedure `play` to test it against a player who places binary digits at random. Find a winning strategy for Player B when $n = 3$.
- Formulate a hypothesis about the $n \in \mathbb{N}$ that allow a simple winning strategy for player B, and express these winning strategies as concisely as possible
- Implement the strategies and construct an automatic test to check that they are winning strategies.
- Prove that the strategies are indeed winning strategies.

EX. 2.8.2 → **Exercise 2.44** Continue the investigation started in Exercises 2.22 and 2.23: Formulate and test as many hypotheses as possible about the sequences.

2.10 Notes and Further Reading

For a thorough general introduction to Maple, see the *Maple User Manual* [map16]. Maplesoft also publishes a comprehensive guide to programming in Maple [BCD+16], as well as a more accessible introduction [BCD+05]. For a good introduction to mathematical computing with Maple, see for example [BS11] or [Gar16].

The discussion of the game considered in Example 2.6.2 is based on the presentation in [MN98a]. The sequences considered in Example 2.5.7 are known as *Sturmian sequences* [Fog02]. The ones discussed in Example 2.8.2 are known as *beta-sequences* or *β-expansions* [Bla89].

Table 2.1 *Overview of famous problems considered in the exercises*

Ex.	Name(s)	Status	Ref.
2.26	Gilbreath	Unresolved	[Guy04, A10]
2.27	Goldbach	Unresolved, holds up to 10^{18}	→ Example 3.4.4
2.28	Goldbach	Confirmed 2013	→ Example 3.4.4
2.29	Goldbach	Fails at 5777	→ Example 3.4.5
2.30	–	Fails at 777451915729368	→ Example 5.1.11
2.31	Chebyshev	Fails at 23338590792	[BH78]
2.32	Fermat	Unresolved	[Guy04, A3]
2.33	Mersenne	Unresolved	[Guy04, A3]
2.34	Skewes	False, no known counterexample	[Ske33], [Ske55]
2.35	Pólya	Fails at 906150257	→ Example 3.4.6
2.36	Andrica	Unresolved	[Guy04, A8]
2.37	Littlewood	Unresolved	[HW79]
2.38	Agoh–Giuah	Unresolved	[BBBG96]
2.39	Beal	Unresolved	[Mau97]
2.40	Erdős–Straus	Unresolved, holds up to 10^{14}	[Guy04, D11]

Exercises 2.26–2.40 are based on well-known mathematical conjectures and problems. These are listed in Table 2.1 which gives information about the current status of the problem and references to both the literature and later chapters in this book, where the problems are investigated further. Naturally, information about the status of these problems is likely to be invalidated in the future as more information is uncovered through experimental and theoretical work.

3 *Iteration and Recursion*

One of the most fundamental features of using computers for mathematical experiments is the ability to repeat or iterate computations, thus allowing the production of a large body of data which can then be used for further study, or to search through such data for counterexamples or specific features. In the present chapter, we will look at the basic techniques for doing so with a special emphasis on contrasting the programming methods associated to *iteration* and to *recursion*. At the end of the chapter, we look at some famous examples where a brute-force search by iteration has produced useful mathematical insight in the form of counterexamples, and other examples where more sophisticated approaches proved necessary.

3.1 Iteration versus Recursion

The distinction between iteration and recursion will be well known to mathematicians, for instance in the context of sequences. An iteratively defined sequence $(a_n)_{n=1}^{\infty}$ is given by a direct—closed form—expression for each term a_n, such as

$$a_n = 3n^2 - 7,$$

whereas a recursive definition of a sequence $(b_n)_{n=1}^{\infty}$ is given by defining most of the terms by way of earlier terms in the sequence, such as

$$b_1 = 2$$
$$b_2 = -5$$
$$b_n = b_{n-1} - b_{n-2}^2, \qquad n \geq 3.$$

Note that when such a definition is attempted, one or more initial terms must be given explicitly to get the recursion started.

Of course, the nature of the sequences or other mathematical objects one wishes to study will often dictate whether iteration or recursion is appropriate—it is not very natural to define $(\cos(n))_{n=1}^{\infty}$ recursively, or $(n!)_{n=1}^{\infty}$ iteratively. But indeed many sequences are easy to formulate both ways.

Choosing between these basic approaches to iteration, or combining them, is the first order of business for the experimental mathematician desiring to perform a repeated computation. In the next subsections we will discuss the advantages of each method separately, but first let us use them in different constellations to perform the same task.

Example 3.1.1: Power sets.   When a finite set M is given, the *power set*, sometimes denoted $\mathcal{P}(M)$, is the set of subsets of M. Producing such a power set is a built-in feature in Maple which can be accessed using

```
[> with(combinat):                                                    1
   powerset({a,b,c,d});                                               2
```

$$\{\{\}, \{a\}, \{b\}, \{c\}, \{d\}, \{a, b\}, \{a, c\}, \{a, d\}, \{b, c\}, \{b, d\}, \{c, d\},$$
$$\{a, b, c\}, \{a, b, d\}, \{a, c, d\}, \{b, c, d\}, \{a, b, c, d\}\}$$

We now implement the procedure ourselves in three different ways, drawing on iteration and recursion in varying ways. One possibility is to follow the pseudocode in Algorithm 3.1, leading to an implementation such as

```
[> powerset1:=proc(M)                                                 1
   local e, S, G, tempG;                                              2
      G:={{}};                                                        3
      for e in M do                                                   4
         tempG:={};                                                   5
         for S in G do                                                6
            tempG:={op(tempG),S union {e}};                           7
         end do;                                                      8
         G:= G union tempG;                                           9
      end do;                                                         10
      return G;                                                       11
   end proc;                                                          12
```

Algorithm 3.1 Powerset, version 1

1: **procedure** POWERSET1(M)

2:     $\mathcal{G} := \{\emptyset\}$

3:     **for** every e in M **do**

4:         **for** every S in $\mathcal{G}$ **do**

5:             Collect both S and $S \cup \{e\}$ in $\mathcal{G}$

6:         **end for**

7:     **end for**

8:     **return** $\mathcal{G}$

9: **end procedure**

This is an example of a *nested* for loop in which the outer iteration works its way through the elements of M one at a time, and the inner iteration duplicates the sets already found into one containing the element from the outer loop, and one not containing it.

A few comments on the implementation of powerset1 are in order. Note how we were forced to collect the results of the inner loop in a temporary copy of the variable G to ensure that the newly added sets were not involved in the outer loop to avoid unnecessary repetition of subsets. Note also how line 7 has the effect of adding $S \cup \{e\}$ to the set being created in tempG. We will explain this further in Section 3.2.3.

Dealing with the dichotomy of keeping or discarding each element in a very different way, we could also try the approach associated to the observation that

$$\mathcal{P}(M) = p(M, \{\emptyset\})$$

when one defines p recursively as

$$p(\emptyset, \mathcal{G}) = \mathcal{G}$$

$$p(\{a_1, a_2, \ldots, a_n\}, \mathcal{G}) = p\left(\{a_2, \ldots, a_n\}, \mathcal{G} \cup \bigcup_{G \in \mathcal{G}} (G \cup \{a_1\})\right)$$

for any $\mathcal{G} \subseteq \mathcal{P}(M)$. Understanding how this works is perhaps easiest by contemplating that the definition gives

$$
\begin{aligned}
p(\{a, b, c\}, \{\emptyset\}) &= p(\{b, c\}, \{\emptyset, \{a\}\}) \\
&= p(\{c\}, \{\emptyset, \{a\}, \{b\}, \{a, b\}\}) \\
&= p(\emptyset, \{\emptyset, \{a\}, \{b\}, \{a, b\}, \{c\}, \{a, c\}, \{b, c\}, \{a, b, c\}\}) \\
&= \{\emptyset, \{a\}, \{b\}, \{a, b\}, \{c\}, \{a, c\}, \{b, c\}, \{a, b, c\}\}.
\end{aligned}
$$

We may implement it as

```
[> pset2:=proc(M, G) local e;                              1
       if(nops(M)=0) then                                  2
           return G;                                       3
       end if;                                             4
       e:=op(1,M);                                         5
       return pset2(M minus {e},                           6
           G union map(x->x union {e},G));                 7
   end proc;                                               8
```

where the use of map in line 7 has the effect of adding, to each element in a given set of sets, the element e, as we will explain in Section 3.2.1. The fact that pset2 calls itself is what makes the programming recursive, and we may now compute power sets by running this algorithm recursively with an initial value of $\{\emptyset\}$, as in

```
[> powerset2:=M->pset2(M,{{}});
```

An entirely different approach to the problem is to find an *enumeration* of the elements in the power set, so that they can be generated in some predefined order using `for`. When M has n elements, there are 2^n elements in the power set, and we may produce a bijection from $\{0, \ldots, 2^n - 1\}$ to $\mathcal{P}(M)$ by writing out each number in the range as a binary number, letting the ith digit indicate whether or not element number i should be in the set. One way of obtaining such a map is

```
[> with(Bits):                                                      1
    extractElements3:=proc(n,E) local i,M,L;                        2
       L:=Split(n);                                                 3
       M:={};                                                       4
       for i from 1 to nops(L) do                                   5
          if L[i]=1 then                                            6
             M:={op(M),E[i]};                                       7
          end if;                                                   8
       end do;                                                      9
       return M;                                                    10
    end proc;                                                       11
```

which works since we have, for example,

```
[> Split(11);
```

$$[1, 0, 1, 1]$$

corresponding to the set $\{a, c, d\}$. We now get the desired power set algorithm using

```
[> powerset3:=proc(M)                                              1
       return {seq(extractElements3(i,M),                          2
                        i=0..(2^nops(M)-1))};                       3
    end proc;                                                      4
```

Each of these methods has independent merits. The first implementation is very simple and would be easy to augment with further code dealing with the details of the individual power sets, if desired. The second is perhaps less transparent, but very short and mathematically elegant. And the third method allows each element in the power set to get an index which can then be used to keep track of some elements of particular interest. In particular, it is much more space efficient to talk about element 11 rather than

EX. 7.1.6 ← $\{a, c, d\}$.   ◁

3.2 Iteration

As noted in Section 2.4, iteration in Maple is handled via either `for` or `while`. We may also implement it using `seq` as seen in Section 2.3. Thus we could have the first integer squares computed by either

```
[> seq(n^2,n=1..10);
```

$$1, 4, 9, 16, 25, 36, 47, 64, 81, 100 \tag{3.1}$$

or by

```
[> for i from 1 to 10 do i^2; end do;
```

or even

```
[> i:=1;                    1
   do                       2
       print(i^2);          3
       i:=i+1;              4
   end do:                  5
```

The latter code is set aside from the two first by running indefinitely, until the computation is halted by the user. Note also that the first piece of code is computed by Maple in one go, with no partial results being presented during the computation. This is fine for a short computation like the one given here, but often one desires to have some results presented or collected along the way in a long computation, to give the user an indication that the computation is proceeding as planned and to allow the user to elect to stop the computation at a given time, when enough information has been extracted. This point of view is of course necessary when the computation runs indefinitely in an infinite loop. Using `for` or `while` will yield continual output to serve such needs.

3.2.1 `seq`

The most immediate method for iteration in Maple is the `seq` command, which produces an ordered tuple of observations as seen in (3.1). The indices may range over any finite segment of the integers. The advantage of the `seq` command is that it delivers all output in one shipment, which can then be stored and manipulated later. Most often, it is convenient to convert the `seq` output to a list by enclosing it in brackets, using a command like

```
[> L:=[seq(f(n),n=1..100)]:
```

The data produced can then be visualized or manipulated further; we will show in the following a few useful methods for doing so. Note also that it is often convenient to suppress the printing of long lists as the one computed above by the use of colon instead of semicolon, since long lists will clutter the display and tends to slow down Maple. If one wishes to inspect the end of the list, one can use commands like L[-20..-1] which displays the last 20 entries.

The Maple command map is a very flexible tool for manipulating lists. It works by applying a designated mapping to each entry in the list, as in

```
[> M:=map(g,L);                                                          1
    map(x->x^2,M);                                                       2
```

The mapping used can be predefined or defined using the arrow notation, as shown.

3.2.2 Output Compression

It is often essential to perform *output compression* on the results of a computation in order to make it possible for the humans processing the data to extract the key features. We give a few examples of how this is easily obtained using map and conversion between lists and sets.

EX. 1.6.1 → **Example 3.2.1: Extracting coefficients.**   In Example 1.6.1, we studied the derivatives of the function $f(x) = \ln(x)/x$, trying to extract information about the coefficients by inspection of the functions found. Let us use map to extract the first 30 coefficients more systematically, taking for granted that the nth derivative is of the form

$$\frac{a_n}{x^{n+1}} + \frac{b_n \ln(x)}{x^{n+1}}.$$

To extract the numbers a_n and b_n, we ask Maple to compute the terms $x^{n+1} f^{(n)}$ using

```
[> f := x -> ln(x)/x;                                                    1
    S := [seq(x^(n+1)*(D@@n)(f)(x),n=1..30)]:                            2
```

but as we can see by inspecting a single entry

```
[> S[4];
```

$$x^5 \left(-\frac{50}{x^5} + \frac{24 \ln(x)}{x^5} \right)$$

this does not quite give the results on a useful form; what we were aiming for was

```
[> simplify(S[4]);
```

$$-50 + 24 \ln(x)$$

It is, however, not necessary to recompute the list S, instead we can simplify each term using

```
[> S:=map(simplify,S):
```

Note that we assign the simplified list to S again, letting the original data go in the process. This may of course not always be desirable, in which case a different name should be used for the manipulated sequence instead, but here there is no reason to hang on to the original list. Now we use the command op to extract the coefficients, noting that at every term of the data one can extract a_n by a command of the form

```
[> op(1,S[4]);
```

$$-50$$

and b_n by

```
[> op(2,S[4]),op(1,op(2,S[4])));
```

$$24 \ln(x), 24$$

Putting this together we may set

```
[> S:=map(x->[op(1,x),op(1,op(2,x))],S):      1
   S[1..9];                                    2
```

$$[[1, -1], [-3, 2], [11, -6], [-50, 24], [274, -120], [-1764, 720], \qquad (3.2)$$
$$[13068, -5040], [-109584, 40320], [1026576, -362880]$$

This gives the desired list of coefficients as a list of pairs $[a_n, b_n]$. If necessary, we could separate them in two lists as

```
[> SA:=map(x->x[1],S);
   SB:=map(x->x[2],S);
```

Note now that it would be very easy to generate the numbers a_n and b_n in much longer intervals by simply replacing 30 with a larger number and run-

EX. 5.2.6 ← ning the code again. ◁

Example 3.2.2: Cyclotomic polynomials. Running

```
[> seq(factor(x^n-1),n=1..9);
```

produces

$$x - 1, (x - 1)(x + 1), (x - 1)(x^2 + x + 1), (x - 1)(x + 1)(x^2 + 1),$$
$$(x - 1)(x^4 + x^3 + x^2 + x + 1), (x - 1)(x + 1)(x^2 + x + 1)(x^2 - x + 1),$$
$$(x - 1)(x^6 + x^5 + x^4 + x^3 + x^2 + x + 1),$$
$$(x - 1)(x + 1)(x^2 + 1)(x^4 + 1), (x - 1)(x^2 + x + 1)(x^6 + x^3 + 1)$$

which seems to suggest that every coefficient of the complete factorization, over $\mathbb{Z}$, of the cyclotomic polynomial $x^n - 1$ is either -1 or 1. It is trivial to get many more terms of the sequence, but the expressions become very long and hence it is not easy to visually process all coefficients to ensure that this remains the case for larger n.

Thus we seek a more condensed output from such an experiment. The command `coeffs` extracts all coefficients from a polynomial, so we can get a list of coefficients without repetitions by converting to a set with brackets { . . . } as in

```
[> coeffs(x^4-x^3+x^2-x+1,x);                                          1
   {coeffs(x^4-x^3+x^2-x+1,x)};                                        2
```

$$1, -1, 1, -1, 1$$
$$\{-1, 1\}$$

However, `coeffs` cannot be applied to a factorized polynomial, so we have to be more careful before trying to apply it. The help page for `factor` leads to the variant `factors` which returns a list of factors on a specified form, from which we extract a list of factors in a useful form by

```
[> factors(x^10-1);                                                   1
   map(x->x[1],factors(x^10-1)[2]);                                   2
```

$$[1, [[x^4 - x^3 + x^2 - x + 1, 1], [x^4 + x^3 + x^2 + x + 1, 1], [x - 1, 1], [x + 1, 1]]]$$
$$[x^4 - x^3 + x^2 - x + 1, x^4 + x^3 + x^2 + x + 1, x - 1, x + 1]$$

Thus with

```
[> convert(map(x->coeffs(x[1]),factors(x^10-1)[2]),set);
```

$$\{-1, 1\}$$

we can check our hypothesis in such a way that a screen easily fits all relevant data for n up to 200. A counterexample is found at $n = 105$:

```
[> factor(x^105-1);
```

$$(x - 1)(x^6 + x^5 + x^4 + x^3 + x^2 + x + 1)(x^4 + x^3 + x^2 + x + 1)$$
$$(x^{24} - x^{23} + x^{19} - x^{18} + x^{17} - x^{16} + x^{14} -$$
$$x^{13} + x^{12} - x^{11} + x^{10} - x^8 + x^7 - x^6 + x^5 - x + 1)$$
$$(x^2 + x + 1)(x^{12} - x^{11} + x^9 - x^8 + x^6 - x^4 + x^3 - x + 1)$$
$$(x^8 - x^7 + x^5 - x^4 + x^3 - x + 1)$$
$$(x^{48} + x^{47} + x^{46} - x^{43} - x^{42} - 2x^{41} - x^{40} - x^{39} + x^{36} + x^{35} + x^{34} +$$
$$x^{33} + x^{32} + x^{31} - x^{28} - x^{26} - x^{24} - x^{22} - x^{20} + x^{17} + x^{16} +$$
$$x^{15} + x^{14} + x^{13} + x^{12} - x^9 - x^8 - 2x^7 - x^6 - x^5 + x^2 + x + 1)$$

Note how difficult it is to spot the two exceptional coefficients even when one has been told that they are there!   ◁

EX. 1.6.3 → **Example 3.2.3: Coefficient patterns.**   We saw in Example 1.6.3 that the polynomials $q_m(n)$ defined there were best understood by writing

$$q_m(n) = c_m^{(0)} n^{m+1} + c_m^{(1)} n^m + c_m^{(2)} n^{m-1} + \cdots + c_m^{(m)} n$$

and analyzing each series of coefficients $\{c_m^{(i)}\}$ separately, with i fixed and m varying. For instance, it was easy to see that $c_m^{(0)} = \frac{1}{m+1}$ for every $m \geq 0$ and that $c_m^{(1)} = \frac{1}{2}$ for $m \geq 1$. To study the more complex sequence $c_m^{(4)}$ we can compute terms in a list by

```
[> N:=25:                                                                 1
   L:=[seq(coeff((expand(sum(r^m,r=1..n))),n,m-3),              2
        m=1..N)];                                                          3
```

$$\left[0, 0, 0, -\frac{1}{30}, -\frac{1}{12}, \frac{1}{6}, -\frac{7}{24}, -\frac{7}{15}, \frac{7}{10}, -1, -\frac{11}{8}, \frac{11}{6}, -\frac{143}{60}, \frac{91}{30}, -\frac{91}{24}, \right.$$

$$\left. -\frac{14}{3}, -\frac{17}{3}, -\frac{34}{5}, -\frac{323}{40}, -\frac{19}{2}, \frac{133}{12}, -\frac{77}{6}, \frac{1771}{120}, -\frac{253}{15}, -\frac{115}{6} \right]$$

Even with more terms, it is far from obvious how to understand this sequence, but we do notice that many of the denominators are repeated. Indeed, we may extract the denominators and delete repetitions by

```
[> convert(map(denom,L),set);
```

$$\{1, 2, 3, 5, 6, 8, 10, 12, 15, 24, 30, 40, 60, 120\}$$

Rewriting the code to allow more systematic experimentation, we may compute similar lists for other i by

```
[> CList:=(i,N)-> [seq(coeff((expand(sum(r^m,r=1..n))),        1
                    n,m+1-i),m=1..N)];                                      2
   for i from 4 to 10 by 2 do                                              3
      convert(map(denom,CList(i,200)),set);                                4
   end;                                                                    5
```

we get

$$\{1, 2, 3, 4, 5, 6, 8, 10, 12, 15, 20, 24, 30, 40, 60, 120\}$$
$$\{1, 2, 3, 4, 6, 7, 9, 12, 14, 18, 21, 28, 36, 42, 63, 84, 126, 252\}$$
$$\{1, 2, 3, 4, 5, 6, 8, 10, 12, 15, 16, 20, 30, 40, 48, 60, 80, 120, 240\}$$
$$\{1, 2, 3, 4, 6, 11, 12, 22, 33, 44, 66, 132\}$$

Note that as we increased N from 25 to 200, two new denominators 4 and 20 appeared at $i = 4$. This is a symptom that the computations carried out above EX. 5.1.8 ← are insufficient, as further discussed in Exercise 3.7.   ◁

3.2.3 *for and while*

When it is not a priori known how long an iterated process must run, the seq command is not available and must be replaced by a programming construct such as for or while. Also, the use of for and while allows us to have partial computations output to a screen or a file, hence enabling the experimenter to monitor the progress of a long computation.

As opposed to what was the case with seq, we now need to concern ourselves with collecting the computed values for future use. An efficient way
of doing so is to define an empty list before the loop is executed, and then
appending each computed value to the end of the list inside the loop, as in

```
[> L:=[];                                                              1
   for i from 1 to 10 do                                              2
       L:=[op(L), i^2];                                               3
   end do;                                                            4
```

The syntax L:=[op(L),i^2] reads as follows: We assign to L the list composed of the old entries in L succeeded by the value i^2. We will use this
frequently.

When one is attempting a long computation via for or while one must
prepare for the eventuality that the process will take too long to process to
the end, or that Maple needs to force quit for some reason. One may even
wish to design the program to run in an infinite loop, as a *kamikaze process*,
until either the experimenter's patience runs out, or Maple breaks down. But
then one must also take steps to salvage the computed data for later use.

It is usually a good idea to collect large amounts of data computed this
way in a global variable, even though that violates our general *need to know*
principle explained in Section 2.5.2, for if a process does not make it to the
final return statement, all local variables will be lost. Even safer (but more
time-consuming) is to make Maple output such data to a text file on the experimenter's general file system, so that the data will preserved even if Maple
crashes completely.

Were we attempting to generate a lot of squares, we could do it using a
procedure like

```
[> manySquares:=proc(filename, N)                                     1
       local outfile, i;                                             2
       outfile:=fopen(filename,WRITE);                               3
       for i from 1 to N do                                          4
         fprintf(outfile,"[%d,%d]\n",i,i^2);                         5
         flush(outfile);                                             6
       end do;                                                       7
       close(outfile):                                              8
   end proc;                                                         9
```

Here, the command fopen will open a file and produce a *file handle* for it,
which may then be stored (here in outfile) used to output data. We format
the data for the file in the fprintf command using the formatting string
[%d,%d] to tell Maple that the data supplied are integers and should be
printed enclosed in brackets. See the help pages for fprintf for details of
how this is done.

The file should be closed using close, but because of the command flush,
every line of output will be added to the file as soon as it has been computed.

Hence, if the program was to be terminated before reaching the end in a call such as

```
[> manySquares("severalsquares.txt",100000);
```

we would still have a copy of all computed data in the format required.

3.2.4 Case Studies

In this section, we give examples of iteration.

Example 3.2.4: Ruin probability. A gambler walks into a casino with N dollars in her pocket, intending to play M fair games where she may lose or win one dollar each time. Since the casino will only let her play when she has at least one dollar to put at stake, there is a certain probability that she will go bankrupt before the intended M games have been played. We wish to investigate this probability experimentally using a simulation.

The core of a simulation of this nature is a pseudorandom variable which simulates the effect of flipping a fair coin. We will discuss such tools in detail in Chapter 6, so let us here just note that the desired effect is attainable using a command rand(0..1)(). Indeed, we get by

```
[> seq(rand(0..1)(),n=1..30);
```

$$0, 1, 1, 0, 0, 1, 1, 1, 1, 0, 0, 0, 1, 0, 1, 0, 1, 0, 1, 0, 0, 1, 0, 0, 0, 0, 0, 1, 0, 0$$

a sequence of zeroes and ones which is very hard to distinguish from something truly random. We now program a simulation of the situation described above using the code

```
[> ruin:=proc(capital, games)              1
    local cap,i;                           2
    cap:=capital;                          3
    for i from 1 to games do               4
      if cap=0 then                        5
        return true;                       6
      end if;                              7
      if rand(0..1)()=0 then               8
        cap:=cap+1;                        9
      else                                 10
        cap:=cap-1;                        11
      end if;                              12
    end do;                                13
    return false;                          14
  end proc;                                15
```

which will return true when the gambler goes bankrupt before the desired number of games is played, having an initial capital as indicated. Note that it is necessary (in line 3) to copy the given value in the variable capital to a local variable cap in order for Maple to change it, cf. Section 2.5.2. Note also that the program is written so that the maximal number of games is only carried out when the player does not go bankrupt, as the command in the line 6 will exit the procedure and the `for` loop when the gambler reaches a capital of 0.

Using further iteration, we define a procedure

```
[> ruinFrequency:=                                          1
   proc(capital, games, experiments)                        2
       local ruins,i;                                       3
       ruins:=0;                                            4
       for i from 1 to experiments do                       5
           if(ruin(capital,games)) then                     6
               ruins:=ruins+1;                              7
           end if;                                          8
       end do;                                              9
       return ruins/experiments;                           10
   end proc;                                                11
```

which performs this experiment a number of times, keeping track of the proportion of events resulting in ruin for the gambler. To get an idea of how the ruin probability varies with the initial capital we will try to simulate it over a lot of experiments and with all initial values ranging from 1 to 40. Since we are going to use the data generated in a plot, it would be easiest to do this in a `seq` command, but anticipating long computation times we elect to do it in a `for` loop, collecting data as outlined above:

```
[> ruinSimulation:=                                         1
   proc(capitalStart, capitalEnd,                           2
       games, experiments)                                  3
       local i; global L;                                   4
       L:=[];                                               5
       for i from capitalStart to capitalEnd do             6
           L:=[op(L),[i,evalf(ruinFrequency                 7
               (i, games, experiments))]];                  8
           print(L[i]);                                     9
       end do;                                              10
   end proc;                                                11
```

Note that we have elected to design the procedure with the list `L` a global variable, deviating from our general principle to use only local variables. Our motivation for doing so stems from the fact, discussed above, that we intend to run the simulation a large number of times, so that there is a risk that we will be forced to terminate the computation before it is completed. If `L` had been a local variable, all data collected would have been lost in such a situation.

After running `ruinSimulation`, we can visualize the results of the simulation using `pointplot(L)` as in Figure 3.1.

We might like to perform a very long simulation, in which case it is convenient to put data in a text file which can then be pasted into Maple later. For

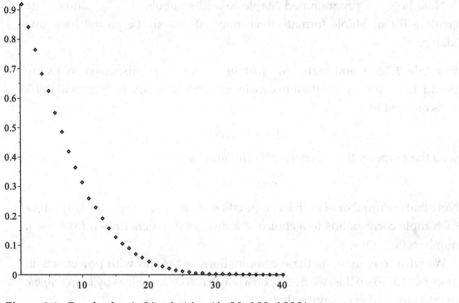

Figure 3.1 Result of `ruinSimulation(1,50,100,1000)`.

instance, we could implement `longruinsimulation` as in Figure 3.2 which with a call of, say,

```
[> longRuinSimulation(10,15,100,100000,                    1
        "tmp/longruinouti.txt");                           2
```

could produce a text file containing

```
[[10, .3162300000],[11, .2729700000],[12, .2275900000],
[13, .1943500000],[14, .1575400000],[15, .1339900000]]
```

```
[> longRuinSimulation:=proc(capitalStart, capitalEnd,       1
                    games, experiments, filename)           2
    local i, outfile;                                       3
    outfile:=fopen(filename,WRITE);                         4
    fprintf(outfile,"[");                                   5
    for i from capitalStart to capitalEnd do                6
        fprintf(outfile,"[%d,%g]",i,                        7
            evalf(ruinFrequency(i, games,                   8
                experiments)));                             9
        if(i<capitalEnd) then                               10
            fprintf(outfile,",");                           11
        end if;                                             12
        flush(outfile);                                     13
    end do;                                                 14
    fprintf(outfile,"];");                                  15
    close(outfile);                                         16
end proc;                                                   17
```

Figure 3.2 `longruinsimulation`.

Note how we programmed Maple to add symbols "[", "," and "]" to create a list in Maple format which may effortlessly be pasted back into

EX. 3.3.3 ← Maple.   ◁

Example 3.2.5: Combinations. Just like power sets discussed in Example 3.1.1, it is often important to consider *k-combinations*, which we will think of as ordered lists

$$[c_1, c_2, \ldots, c_k]$$

with the property that every $c_i \in \mathbb{N} \cup \{0\}$ and that

$$c_1 < c_2 < \cdots < c_k.$$

Note that the number of such k-combinations with $c_k < n$ is precisely $\binom{n}{k}$ since each tuple corresponds to a choice of k distinct numbers drawn from the n numbers $0, \ldots, n - 1$.

We wish to enumerate these combinations as we did with power sets in powerset3. To do this, we decide on a way to order these lists by *lexicographic (right-to-left) ordering*, saying that

$$[c_1, c_2, \ldots, c_k] < [c_1', c_2', \ldots, c_k']$$

if for some i we have

$$c_i < c_i' \quad \text{and} \quad c_{i+1} = c_{i+1}', \ldots, c_k = c_k'.$$

This means for instance that we have

$$[0, 2, 3, 7] < [0, 2, 4, 7] < [0, 3, 7, 8].$$

Fixing $k = 4$, we list the first 10 combinations:

$$[0, 1, 2, \underline{3}], [0, 1, \underline{2}, 4], [0, \underline{1}, 3, 4], [\underline{0}, 2, 3, 4], [1, 2, 3, \underline{4}],$$
$$[0, 1, \underline{2}, 5], [0, \underline{1}, 3, 5], [\underline{0}, 2, 3, 5], [1, 2, \underline{3}, 5], [0, \underline{1}, 4, 5] \tag{3.3}$$

and note how one goes from one combination to the one immediately succeeding it by first locating the lowest index i with the property that $c_i + 1 < c_{i+1}$, or setting $i = k$ if no such i exists, as indicated in the example by underlining the relevant entry. Then one gets the successor by adding 1 to c_i, preceding that entry with the minimal choice possible, namely $[0, \ldots, i - 2]$, and letting what is read to the right of c_i stay fixed.

One can implement this procedure in Maple as

```
[> getNext:=proc(L) local i;                              1
        for i from 1 to nops(L)-1 do                       2
            if L[i+1]-L[i]>=2 then                          3
                break;                                      4
            end if;                                         5
        end do;                                             6
        return [seq(j,j=0..i-2),L[i]+1,                     7
                    seq(L[j],j=i+1..nops(L))];              8
    end proc;                                               9
```

and produce lists of k-combinations as

```
[> generateCombinations:=proc(M, N) local L,CL,i;       1
      L:=[seq(i,i=0..M-1)];                             2
      CL:=[L];                                          3
      for i from 2 to N do                              4
         L:=getNext(L);                                 5
            CL:=[op(CL),L];                             6
      end do;                                           7
      return CL;                                        8
   end proc;                                            9
```

With these definitions, we can produce lists of combinations for use in a variety of situations.   ◁

3.3 Recursion

Implementing recursive mathematical definitions in Maple is usually completely straightforward in the sense that all one needs to do is to have a procedure or a function call itself. Maple provides the syntax f@@n to return the result of composing a function f with itself n times (often denoted f^{on} in the mathematical literature, but $f^{(n)}$ in Maple), so that for instance

```
[> (f@@10)(x), (sqrt@@10)(x);
```

$$f^{(10)}(x), x^{1/1024}$$

Parallel to the distinction we saw in the previous section between seq on the one hand and for/while on the other, the @@ command only applies when it is known a priori how many levels of recursion are required. It also only works when the recursion takes the straightforward form of a single map composed with itself. In most cases, we thus need to implement recursion by providing nested calls in procedures, like in

```
[> fibonacci1:=proc(n) option remember;               1
      if(n<=1) then                                    2
         return n;                                     3
      else                                             4
         return fibonacci1(n-1)+fibonacci1(n-2);       5
      end if;                                          6
   end proc;                                           7
```

computing the Fibonacci numbers defined by the recursive definition

$$f_0 = 0$$
$$f_1 = 1$$
$$f_n = f_{n-1} + f_{n-2}, \qquad n \geq 2.$$

n	6	5	4	3	2	1	0
# calls	1	1	2	3	5	8	5

Figure 3.3 Number of calls needed for `fibonacci(6)`.

One notes that the Maple procedure is defined in direct correspondence with the mathematical definition, dealing first with the initial cases for $n = 0$ and $n = 1$, and then with the general case.

3.3.1 *Option* remember

As we shall see, there are several potential pitfalls to be aware of when a recursive program is designed and implemented. Most substantially, if we had left out the option `remember` in the program defining `fibonacci1` above, it would not have been able to compute much farther than a_{10}.

The `remember` option feature in Maple works by maintaining a list—the *remember table*—of all the calls to any procedure defined with the `remember` option, noting the input and the output for each such call. If at any point the procedure is called with an input value that has already occurred, Maple returns the stored value rather than recomputing it.

Using remember tables can be relevant in many contexts when duplication of calls occurs frequently, and in contexts with recursion this can lead to dramatic reductions of run time at a modest expense of memory, since one saves not only the time expended for the concrete call replaced by the remembered value, but also the time for the recursive calls.

Example 3.3.1: Computing Fibonacci numbers. If we were to implement `fibonacci` above without a remember table, a call `fibonacci(6)` would result in a total of 41 calls of the form `fibonacci(n)` as described in Figure 3.3, since the number of calls follow the Fibonacci numbers until we reach the base values $n = 1$ and $n = 0$. By contrast, a total of 7 calls would suffice with `option remember`, and even less if some of the values had been previously computed. The efficient computation of Fibonacci numbers will be discussed
EX. 5.1.5 ← further below.   ◁

It is sometimes useful to inspect the remember table, and this is done by an apocryphal command such as

```
[> L:=op(op(4,eval(fibonacci1)));
```

to the effect

$$L := [0 = 0, 1 = 1, 2 = 1, 3 = 2, 4 = 3, 5 = 5, 6 = 8]$$

The rather un-mathematical form of the table matches Maple's `rtable` syntax. We will often find it convenient to extract either the input or the output values with Maple's `lhs` and `rhs` commands, as in

```
[> [map(lhs,L)], [map(rhs,L)];
```

to the effect

$$[0, 1, 2, 3, 4, 5, 6], [1, 1, 2, 3, 5, 8, 13]$$

A remember table may be reset using

```
[> forget(fibonacci1);
```

EX. 1.5.2 → **Example 3.3.2.** To initially investigate the Collatz conjecture (Example 1.5.2, Exercise 2.9), we may use recursion to compute the *Collatz depth d* of numbers n defined mathematically as

$$d(n) = \begin{cases} 0 & n = 1 \\ d(f(n)) + 1 & n > 0 \end{cases}$$

and in Maple as

```
[> CollatzDepth:=proc(n) option remember;          1
       if n=1 then                                  2
          return 0;                                 3
       else                                         4
          return CollatzDepth(f(n))+1;              5
       end if;                                      6
    end proc;                                       7
```

where as in Example 1.5.2, f is defined by

```
[> f:=n->if(n mod 2=0) then                         1
       n/2;                                          2
    else                                             3
       3*n+1;                                        4
    end if;                                          5
```

The depth can easily be computed up to $n = 100$ and visualized as in Figure 3.4 by

```
[> plot([seq([n,CollatzDepth(n)],n=1..100)]);
```

The remember table can be investigated post festum to see which values had to be computed to determine $\{d(1), d(2), \ldots, d(100)\}$. For instance, we can run

```
[> nops(op(op(4,eval(CollatzDepth))));             1
    max(map(lhs,op(op(4,eval(CollatzDepth)))));    2
```

to find that 251 values of $d(n)$ had to be computed, the largest occurring at $n = 9232$.   ◁

3.3.2 Case Studies

EX. 3.2.4 → **Example 3.3.3: Ruin probabilities computed exactly.** In Example 3.2.4 above, we used a nested iterative program to estimate the probability that a gambler with C dollars in her pocket would fail to be able to play g fair games for a possible loss or gain of 1 dollar without losing all her money in

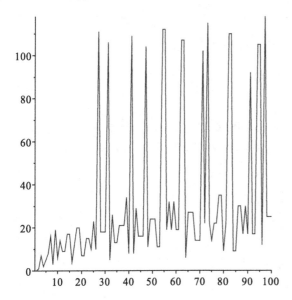

Figure 3.4 Collatz depths.

the process. Let us try to compute these probabilities exactly using a recursive procedure. Indeed, if we denote the probability that the gambler must leave the casino without completing the g games by $r_{C,g}$ we have

$$r_{C,g} = \frac{r_{C-1,g-1} + r_{C+1,g-1}}{2}, C \geq 1, g \geq 1.$$

Indeed, when the gambler is willing and able to play a game, she will get either one dollar more or one dollar less to stake depending on the outcome of that game, and one less game to play in either case. Combining this observation with straightforward claims such as

$$r_{C,g} = 0, C \geq g$$
$$r_{0,g} = 1, g \geq 1$$

(which include the convention that $r_{0,0} = 0$), we have a recursive definition which, at least in principle, allows the computation of $r_{C,g}$ for any pair of nonnegative C, g. We can implement it by

```
[> ruinP:=proc(capital, games)                          1
      if(capital>=games) then                           2
        return 0;                                        3
      elif(capital=0) then                               4
        return 1;                                        5
      else                                               6
        return((ruinP(capital-1,games-1)+               7
              ruinP(capital+1,games-1))/2);              8
      end if;                                            9
    end proc;                                            10
```

but will probably not be too surprised that the program will not terminate in any reasonable amount of time if run `ruinP(10,100)`. Indeed, since most calls of `ruinP(C,g)` will lead to the call of both `ruinP(C-1,g-1)` and `ruinP(C+1,g-1)`, we are a priori looking at something like 2^{100} calls of this procedure.

Note, however, that many of these calls will be repeated. To compute $r_{10,100}$, we need $r_{9,99}$ and $r_{11,99}$, and in both these numbers there is a factor $r_{10,98}$, etc. Using `remember`, we ask Maple to keep an index of which calls of `ruinP` have already been made, and reuse the results whenever possible. The augmented program computes $r_{10,100}$ almost instantaneously; indeed it is

$$\frac{31184193974503243566665087963}{99035203142830421991929933792}.$$

To understand how this is possible, we can inspect the content of the remember table and see precisely which instances of `ruinP` were computed. We call

```
[> L:=op(op(4,eval(ruinP)));
```

which assigns to the variable L a list of entries such as

$$(4, 10) = \frac{23}{128}, \tag{3.7}$$

indicating that at some point in the computation, $R_{4,10}$ was found to be the fraction given. With `nops(L)` we see that precisely 1539 probabilities were computed, explaining the speed with which the result was found.

To better understand the computation made, we apply some of the methods from Section 3.2.1. Indeed, forgetting the actual probability in an entry such as (3.7) is easy using `lhs` as explained above. To be able to plot this structure with `pointplot` we need to place brackets around each pair, replacing an entry of the form `(4,10)` by one of the form `[4,10]`, so we do

```
[> plots[pointplot](map(x->[lhs(x)],L));
```

to arrive at the left part of Figure 3.5. We see that the computation is limited not only by the reuse of values already computed, but also by the procedure employing the facts that when $g > C = 0$ or $C \geq g$, no further computations EX. 6.1.2 ← are required to arrive at the probabilities 1 or 0, respectively. ◁

EX. 1.6.5 → **Example 3.3.4: Counting towers.** We have already seen how to represent LEGO towers with N bricks by tuples $\mathbf{x} \in \{-1, 0, 1\}^{N-1}$, and how to compute the x-coordinate of their center of gravity $\tau(\mathbf{x})$. In the paper [Wat80] P.J.S. Watson proposed the study of the number β_N of stable LEGO towers as defined in Section 1.6.5, as well as the number of *maximally stable* buildings: The number

$$B_N = |\{\mathbf{x} \in \{-1, 0, 1\}^{N-1} \mid \tau(\mathbf{x}) = 0\}|$$

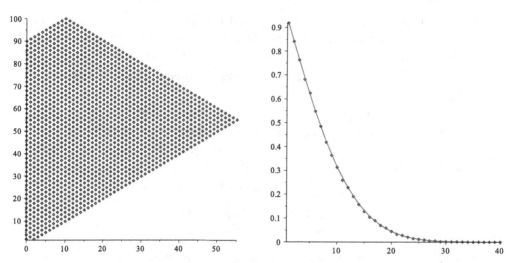

Figure 3.5 Left: Computed values for `ruinP(10,100)`. Right: Exact results plotted with simulation results from Figure 3.1.

of buildings with the center of gravity just on top of the center of the base block. In Figure 1.5, we have that the tower associated to x_1 is maximally stable, the one associated to x_2 is stable but not maximally so, and the one associated to x_3 is not stable at all.

Watson himself managed to compute the 12 terms

$$1, 3, 7, 19, 53, 149, 419, 1191, 3403, 9755, 28077, 81097$$

of the infinite sequence (β_n) and the terms

$$1, 1, 1, 3, 7, 15, 35, 87, 217, 547, 1417, 3735 \qquad (3.8)$$

of the infinite sequence (B_n). Let us attempt to compute further.

A strategy for computing these numbers is to let $t_{N,w}$ designate the number of towers with N bricks having the center of gravity over the x-coordinate w/N, and noting that $B_N = t_{N,0}$ while

$$\beta_N = \sum_{i=-(N-1)}^{N-1} t_{N,i}, \qquad (3.9)$$

so that all we need is a way to compute $t_{N,w}$. We can come up with a simple recursive formula for these numbers; indeed

$$t_{N,w} = t_{N-1,w+N-1} + t_{N-1,w} + t_{N-1,w-N+1}$$

for $N > 1$, and we have

$$t_{1,w} = \begin{cases} 1 & w = 0 \\ 0 & w \neq 0 \end{cases}.$$

We easily put this in the Maple form:

```
[> towers:=proc(n, weight) option remember;        1
        if n=1 then                                 2
            if weight=0 then                        3
                return 1;                           4
            else                                    5
                return 0;                           6
            end if;                                 7
        else                                        8
            return towers(n-1,weight+n-1)+          9
                   towers(n-1,weight)+              10
                   towers(n-1,weight-n+1);          11
        end if;                                     12
    end proc;                                       13
```

where the option `remember` is extremely important for the execution times just as in Section 3.3.3. Indeed, without it, we can only count a few terms longer than Watson, whereas with it, we may reach several hundred observations. A program such as

```
[> # WARNING runs indefinitely - save your work!   1
    L:=[];                                          2
    n:=1;                                           3
    do                                              4
        c:=towers(n,0);                             5
        L:=[op(L),c];                               6
        n:=n+1;                                     7
    end do;                                         8
```

will grind to a halt at $n = 18$ when there is no `remember` option. Including the option allows the program to run rather effortlessly until $n = 457$ before running out of memory with an error message. Inspecting the remember table, we learn that the number of values computed is counted in millions before the program must give up.

Supposing that 457 terms of the sequence is not enough for our purposes, which—as we shall see—is quite realistic, we hence need to concern ourselves with saving space in the remember table for the procedure `towers`. To do so we may exploit the obvious symmetry relation

$$t_{N,w} = t_{N,-w}$$

to halve the number of values computed, and use that for any building x with N bricks we will have

$$\tau(\mathbf{x}) \le \frac{1}{N}\sum_{i=1}^{N-1}(N-i) \le \frac{1}{N} \cdot \frac{N(N-1)}{2} = \frac{N-1}{2}$$

so that we may see that $t_{N,w} = 0$ when

$$2w > N(N-1).$$

To employ these two observations, we divide the recursive procedure in two; one named rTower which will use a remember table, and one named dTower which will not. These two procedures will call each other alternately, with dTower employing the reductions without storing anything, and rTower working as before, except that it calls dTower instead of itself. We can code dTower as follows

```
[> dTower := proc(N,w)                                    1
     if(w<0) then                                         2
        return rTower(N,-w);                              3
     end if;                                              4
     if(2*w>N*(N-1)) then                                 5
        return 0;                                         6
     end if;                                              7
     return rTower(N,w);                                  8
  end proc;                                               9
```

◁

EX. 4.2.4 ←   We end this section with an advanced example showing how to use @@.

Example 3.3.5: The Stern–Brocot tree.   The *Stern–Brocot* tree provides an efficient way of generating fractions in lowest terms for testing hypotheses over the rationals. Indeed, one may prove that by employing "freshman addition" of fractions, adding numerators and denominators independently, one will traverse all elements of $\mathbb{Q}^+$ by starting with the list

$$\frac{0}{1}, \frac{1}{0}$$

(where $\frac{1}{0}$ is to be interpreted as an auxiliary formal symbol) and then interspersing successive fractions this way to obtain

$$\frac{0}{1}, \frac{1}{1}, \frac{1}{0}$$
$$\frac{0}{1}, \frac{1}{2}, \frac{1}{1}, \frac{2}{1}, \frac{1}{0}$$
$$\frac{0}{1}, \frac{1}{3}, \frac{1}{2}, \frac{2}{3}, \frac{1}{1}, \frac{3}{2}, \frac{2}{1}, \frac{3}{1}, \frac{1}{0}$$

This can be implemented as

```
[> sb:=proc(L) local i,M;                                 1
     M:=[];                                                2
     for i from 1 to nops(L)-2 do                          3
        M:=[op(M),[L[i],                                    4
          (numer(L[i])+numer(L[i+1]))/                      5
          (denom(L[i])+denom(L[i+1]))]];                    6
     end do;                                                7
     M:=[op(M),[L[i],                                       8
```

Table 3.1 *Suggested run times (CPU hours)*

Before...	$N \geq$
telling a friend	5
telling a teacher/colleague	50
reporting in a paper or talk	500

```
        (numer(L[i])+1)/denom(L[i])],L[i+1]];                    9
      return(ListTools[Flatten](M));                            10
  end proc;                                                     11
```

where we represent 1/0 by a placeholder value (below we choose ∞) and produce a list of pairs of fractions which is then transformed to a list of fractions using the command `Flatten` from the package `ListTools`. Thus, with

```
  [> (sb@@5)([0,infinity]);                                      1
```

we get

$$\left[0, \frac{1}{5}, \frac{1}{4}, \frac{2}{7}, \frac{1}{3}, \frac{3}{8}, \frac{2}{5}, \frac{3}{7}, \frac{1}{2}, \frac{4}{7}, \frac{3}{5}, \frac{5}{8}, \frac{2}{3}, \frac{5}{7}, \frac{3}{4}, \frac{4}{5}, 1, \right.$$
$$\left. \frac{5}{4}, \frac{4}{3}, \frac{7}{5}, \frac{3}{2}, \frac{8}{5}, \frac{5}{3}, \frac{7}{4}, 2, \frac{7}{3}, \frac{5}{2}, \frac{8}{3}, 3, \frac{7}{2}, 4, 5, \infty\right]$$

◁

3.4 Knowing When to Stop

Suppose a systematic search for a counterexample to a conjecture remains fruitless for some time. How many hours N of computer time should the experimental mathematician expend before it is reasonable to say that computer experiments support the conjecture? And on the other hand, when is it time to realize that further experimentation will be fruitless to avoid falling prey to the phenomenon that pioneering experimental mathematician D. H. Lehmer described as "happiness is always just around the corner"?

As we will discuss below, there are at least two good reasons to refuse to answer such a question, but even though it may be ill-advised, let us try to do so in the form of Table 3.1. The main point of the table is that the amount of computing power spent should reflect the forum in which the "computer experiments support the conjecture" statement is uttered; a few hours would be sufficient for informal claims to a close associate, whereas the scientific community at large would expect a much more thorough investigation before such claims were made in the formal guise of a talk or a paper.

The first reason that the question is mathematically ill-posed is, of course, that the history of mathematics is full of examples where an exhaustive search of all immediately tractable examples seemed to support a conjecture which subsequently turned out to fail. It is an interesting observation that the advent of computers has not changed this basic characteristic of mathematical research, even though the considered collections of "immediately tractable" examples are now much larger. The second reason is that the number of examples that can be covered by N hours of computing time can vary dramatically with the efficiency of the methods used and with the capacity of the computer used. We have already seen this in Example 1.6.5 and will provide a more systematic discussion of such matters in Chapter 7.

We will end this section by examples from the early history of experimental mathematics to illustrate the two points made above, and show that making conjectures based solely on the lack of counterexamples is a very risky business.

EX. 1.5.1 → **Example 3.4.1: Fermat numbers.**   One of the first instances of a conjecture being disproved due to a computerized experiment was due to John Selfridge in 1953, as recorded in [Sel53]. Using the SWAC machine (see box on p. 75), he addressed a special case (see [Rob58]) of the Fermat conjecture: Must numbers of the form

$$2^{2^{2^{\cdot^{\cdot^{\cdot}}}}} + 1$$

always be prime? The first open case (*cf.* Example 1.5.1) was the enormous number

$$F_{16} = 2^{2^{16}} + 1 = 2^{65536} + 1 \simeq 2.003529930 \cdot 10^{19728},$$

which to this day remains unfactored, but Selfridge on August 14, 1953 managed to disprove the conjecture by a search for factors of the form $d = (2k+1)2^r + 1$, using that Euler had proved that when such a d divides F_m, $r \geq m + 2$. Thus such factors of F_{16} must have $r \geq 18$, and looking at all possible $d \leq 2^{36}$, Selfridge found the factor

$$825753601 = 1575 \cdot 2^{19} + 1.$$

It is straightforward to repeat Selfridge's experiment by something like

```
[> f:=2^(2^16)+1;                                    1
    for r from 18 to 36 do                           2
        for k from 1 to 2^min((35-r),15) do          3
            if f mod ((2*k+1)*2^r+1) = 0 then        4
                print((2*k+1)*2^r+1);                5
            end if;                                  6
        end do;                                      7
    end do;                                          8
```

$$825753601$$

This takes less than two seconds, but since Maple without hesitation reserves almost 18 MB of memory to do the computation one may wonder how Selfridge managed to complete the task on a machine with just more than 1 KB. We will return to such issues in Chapter 7.   ◁

SWAC: The Standard Western Automatic Computer

The SWAC was custom built in 1950 for the United States National Bureau of Standards to be used as an interim computer designed to be built quickly and put into operation while the bureau waited for more powerful computers to come on the market, and when it went into operation, it was the fastest computer in the world. And although the SWAC's primary purpose was quite different, access was granted to California-based mathematicians making the SWAC one of the most important early vessels for experimental mathematics.

The machine used 2300 vacuum tubes. It had 256 words of memory, using Williams tubes, with each word being 37 bits. Thus, measured in standard bytes of 8 bit each, the memory capacity of the SWAC was 1.2 KB. The machine operated with the seven basic operations: add, subtract, and multiply (single precision and double precision versions); comparison, data extraction, input and output.

After being replaced at the National Bureau of Standards, the SWAC remained in operation at the University of California until the late 1950s.

Example 3.4.2: Sums of like powers. Euler conjectured in 1769 that the equation

$$x_1^n + x_2^n + \cdots + x_m^n = y^n$$

could only have solutions $x_1, x_2, \ldots, x_n, y \in \mathbb{N}$ when $n > m > 2$; that is, that for a sum of nth powers to itself be an nth power it must have either only one or at least n summands.

COUNTEREXAMPLE TO EULER'S CONJECTURE ON SUMS OF LIKE POWERS

BY L. J. LANDER AND T. R. PARKIN

Communicated by J. D. Swift, June 27, 1966

A direct search on the CDC 6600 yielded

$$27^5 + 84^5 + 110^5 + 133^5 = 144^5$$

as the smallest instance in which four fifth powers sum to a fifth power. This is a counterexample to a conjecture by Euler [1] that at least n nth powers are required to sum to an nth power, $n > 2$.

REFERENCE

1. L. E. Dickson, *History of the theory of numbers*, Vol. 2, Chelsea, New York, 1952, p. 648.

Figure 3.6 The first counterexample to Euler's conjecture.

The conjecture remained open until 1966 when it was disproved in the short paper ([LP66]) by Leon J. Lander and Thomas R. Parkin illustrated in Figure 3.6. Let us re-enact the experiment and satisfy ourselves that the example provided in [LP66] is minimal in an appropriate sense.

We adopt the strategy of going through all 4-tuples (x_1, x_2, x_3, x_4) with

$$x_1 \leq x_2 \leq x_3 \leq x_4$$

by implementing a procedure to return the successor in the lexicographic order (left-to-right) of any such tuple by

```
[> nextList:=proc(L) local i;                              1
      for i from nops(L) to 2 by -1 do                     2
        if L[i-1]>L[i] then                                3
          return [seq(L[j],j=1..i-1),L[i]+1,               4
                        seq(1,j=i+1..nops(L))];            5
        end if;                                            6
      end do;                                              7
      return [L[1]+1,seq(1,j=2..nops(L))];                 8
    end proc;                                              9
```

so that, for instance

```
[> seq((nextList@@i)([1,1,1,1]),i=1..10);
```

$$[2, 1, 1, 1], [2, 2, 1, 1], [2, 2, 2, 1], [2, 2, 2, 2], [3, 1, 1, 1],$$
$$[3, 2, 1, 1], [3, 2, 2, 1], [3, 2, 2, 2], [3, 3, 1, 1], [3, 3, 2, 1]$$

To test whether or not a sum x of Nth powers is itself an Nth power of integers, we can compute

$$x - \lfloor \sqrt[N]{x} \rfloor^N,$$

which will be zero precisely when this is the case. Thus, by defining

```
[> isPower:=proc(L, n) local x;                          1
     x:=sum(L[i]^n, i=1..nops(L));                        2
     return is(x-floor(x^(1/n))^n=0);                     3
   end proc;                                              4
```

we can search for a counterexample by a kamikaze process. After a couple of hours we reach the desired output

$$[133, 110, 80, 22]$$

Looking further gives no immediate hits. We return to a discussion of how to speed up the search significantly in exercises.   ◁

Example 3.4.3: Sum of biquadrates. The example described in Example 3.4.2 motivated a lot of interest in the question of whether

$$a^4 + b^4 + c^4 = d^4 \tag{3.10}$$

could have integer solutions (Euler himself had essentially proved his conjecture in the case for $n = 3$, a special case of Fermat's last theorem). This question did not immediately give way to brute-force searches such as the one applied in Example 3.4.2, but instead, Noam Elkies in [Elk88] resolved the question in 1987 by a combination of stringent reductions and qualified guesswork. Indeed, he established that when (u, v) is a solution to

$$u^2 = 22030 + 28849v - 56158v^2 + 36941v^3 - 31790v^4 \tag{3.11}$$

then

$$(85v^2 + 484v - 313)^4 + (68v^2 - 586v + 10)^4 + (2u)^4 \tag{3.12}$$
$$= (357v^2 - 204v + 363)^4.$$

Thus, since Elkies could find a solution to (3.11) with u and v rational (see Exercise 3.16), he could feed them into (3.12), cancel all denominators, and arrive at the solution

$$2682440^4 + 15365639^4 + 18796760^4 = 20615673^4.$$

Shortly after, Roger Frye in [Fry88] carried out an exhaustive search and found the smallest possible counterexample:

$$95800^4 + 217519^4 + 414560^4 = 422481^4. \tag{3.13}$$

This again was done on one of the fastest computers in the world: The Connection Machine developed by Thinking Machines primarily for uses in artificial intelligence, which quickly became popular for computational problems due to its massively parallel architecture. Nevertheless, the analysis of the problem done by Frye (who was an employee of Thinking Machines at the time) shows that in spite of the impressive specifications of the Connection

Machine, a naive brute-force approach is not possible, and the search to the range needed is only made possible by a combination of reductions of the search space suggested by Elkies. These reductions are very instructive, so we will discuss them in detail.

The starting point of [Fry88] is the observation that

$$0^4 \equiv 0 \qquad 1^4 \equiv 2^4 \equiv 3^4 \equiv 4^4 \equiv 1 \qquad (\mathrm{mod}\, 5)$$

so that any solution to (3.10) must be of one of the forms

$$0 + 0 + 0 = 0 \quad 1 + 0 + 0 = 1$$
$$0 + 1 + 0 = 1 \quad 0 + 0 + 1 = 1$$

modulo five. A solution of the first such form would only be possible in the case when 5 was a divisor of all of a, b, c, d, so since we are looking for the minimal such solution, this case may be ignored and we may without loss of generality assume that

$$a \equiv b \equiv 0 \qquad c \not\equiv 0 \qquad d \not\equiv 0 \qquad (\mathrm{mod}\, 5).$$

The fundamental idea is then to divide the search process in two, first locating all pairs (c, d) that could possibly lead to a solution to (3.10), being very careful to reduce the number of (c, d) candidates as much as possible, and then look for matching (a, b) by a brute force search.

Our observations this far show that we may discard any pair (c, d) so that $5^4 = 625$ does not divide $d^4 - c^4$, and a similar analysis based on

$$0^4 \equiv 2^4 \equiv 0 \qquad 1^4 \equiv 3^4 \equiv 1 \qquad (\mathrm{mod}\, 4)$$

shows that we may assume that d is odd.

We next turn to a result by Gauss concerning biquadratic residues to conclude that if p is an odd prime with $p \not\equiv 1 (\mathrm{mod}\, 8)$, then (as we shall discuss in Exercise 4.25)

$$p \mid (a^4 + b^4) \Longrightarrow p \mid a, p \mid b. \tag{3.14}$$

This has two consequences for our computation. First, with such a p, if $p \mid c$ and $p \mid d$ then we could conclude that $p \mid a$ and $p \mid b$, and hence the entire tuple could be replaced by a smaller tuple by dividing every entry by p. Thus we may discard any such pair (c, d). Further, we see that if such a p divides $d^4 - c^4$, it must divide both a and b, and hence also

$$p^4 \mid a^4 + b^4 = d^4 - c^4.$$

We can then also discard any pair (c, d) which has such a p as a prime divisor a number of times which is not a multiple of 4. Thus if the prime factorization

$$d^4 - c^4 = 2^{n_1} 3^{n_2} 5^{n_3} \cdots p_i^{n_i} \cdots$$

does not satisfy

$$p_i \not\equiv 1 (\mathrm{mod}\, 8) \Longrightarrow 4 \mid n_i \tag{3.15}$$

for some $i > 1$ then the pair (c, d) may be discarded.

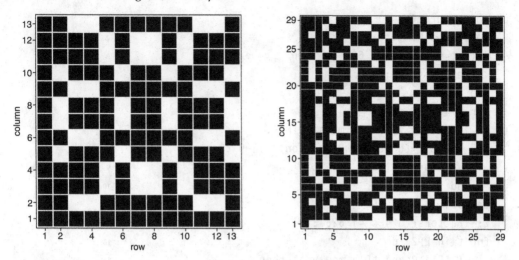

Figure 3.7 Possible residues for (c, d) at $r = 13$ (left) and $r = 29$ (right).

Finally, Frye implemented specialized testing modulus $r = 9, 13$ and 29, but as the preparatory computations become more complicated, let us use Maple to do them. Focusing on $r = 13$, the idea is simply to consider all solutions to (3.10) modulo r and extract what they say about the pair (c, d). Using msolve we find all 1297 solutions

```
[> sols:=[msolve(a^4+b^4+c^4=d^4,13)]:
```

and extract the possible residues for (c, d) as

```
[> cdsols:=map(x->subs(x,[c,d]),sols):          1
   cdsols[1..5];                                2
   nops(cdsols);                                3
```

$$[[0, 0], [1, 1], [1, 5], [1, 8], [1, 12]]$$
$$121$$

We can organize that information obtained into a matrix with entries in $\{0, 1\}$ using

```
[> Matrix(13,13,map(x->(x[1]+1,x[2]+1)=1,{op(cdsols)}));
```

which works by the map command producing a set of all the nonzero entries on the form

$$\{(1, 1) = 1, (2, 2) = 1, (2, 6) = 1, (2, 9) = 1, (2, 13) = 1, \ldots\}$$

which is then passed to Matrix and visualized as in Figure 3.7 using the matrixplot command we will discuss in Section 4.1.5.

Combining these observations, we design a procedure precheck as noted in Figure 3.8, where MML is a list of the three matrices obtained at $r = 9, 13, 29$ as described above. Then with

```
[> precheck:=proc(c, d)                                                  1
    local L,t,M; global MML;                                             2
    if(not d^4-c^4 mod 625=0) then                                       3
       return false;                                                     4
    end if;                                                              5
    for M in MML do                                                      6
       if M[1+(c mod RowDimension(M)),                                   7
             1+(d mod RowDimension(M))]=0 then                           8
          return false;                                                  9
       end if;                                                          10
    end do;                                                             11
    L:=ifactors((d^4-c^4)/625);                                         12
    for t in L[2] do                                                    13
       if t[1]>2 and t[1] mod 8<>1 then                                 14
          if d mod t[1]=0 and c mod t[1] =0 then                        15
             return false;                                              16
          end if;                                                       17
          if t[2] mod 4<>0 then                                         18
             return false;                                              19
          end if;                                                       20
       end if;                                                          21
    end do;                                                             22
    return true;                                                        23
end proc;                                                               24
```

Figure 3.8 precheck.

```
[> for d from 1 to N do                                                  1
      if((not d mod 5=0) and d mod 2=1) then                            2
         for c from 1 to d-1 do                                         3
            if(not c mod 5=0) then                                      4
               if(precheck(c,d)) then                                   5
                  fprintf(output,"%d %d %d\n",                          6
                     d,c,(d^4-c^4)/625);                                7
               end if;                                                  8
            end if;                                                     9
         end do;                                                       10
      end if;                                                          11
   end do;                                                             12
```

we can search through all pairs (c, d) with $c < d < N$ and save all candidates in a file for the second part of the experiment.

For the second part, we of course use that we know that 5 must divide a and b to search instead for a solution to

$$x^4 + y^4 = \frac{d^4 - c^4}{625} = z.$$

We may assume that $z \geq y^4 \geq x^4$, so we conclude that $y^4 \geq z/2$ or $y \geq 2^{-1/4}z^{1/4}$ which reduces the search space further, to the simple test

```
[> postcheck:=proc(z) local y;                                          1
        for y from ceil((z/2)^(1/4)) to floor(z^(1/4)) do               2
        if floor((z-y^4)^(1/4))^4=(z-y^4) then                          3
            return true;                                                 4
        end if;                                                         5
    end do;                                                            6
    return false;                                                       7
end proc;                                                              8
```

But in spite of our careful following of Frye's recipe, and the fact that the CPUs of our personal computers easily outperform the individual CPUs of the Connection Machine, we see that the first part of the experiment does not terminate in any reasonable amount of time, so although we can certainly use it to rediscover Frye's solution by looking in a narrow interval around it, we are far from being able to complete the search which guarantees that the solution is minimal. Somewhat humbled by 1980s technology, we postpone further discussion to after we have discussed efficiency issues in

EX. 7.1.7 ← Chapter 7. ◁

Example 3.4.4: Goldbach's conjecture. In 1742, Christian Goldbach formulated the conjecture that any even number $2n > 2$ is the sum of two primes. The conjecture remains open in spite of very serious attempts to falsify it by experimental methods. In fact, it is known ([OeS]) that the conjecture holds for any even number up to 10^{18}.

Such a wide range has been examined using a very simple search based on a small elaboration of Eratosthenes' sieve (Algorithm 2.1). We proceed according to Algorithm 3.2 as described in the following.

First, the array is initialized with false except at $i = 4$, which is special by being the sum of two even primes:

3	4	5	6	7	8	9	10	11	12	13	14	15	16	17

After having processed $i = 3$, the array reads

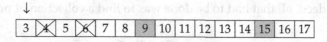

where we have established that 6 is not a counterexample and that 9, 15 are not primes. The next step is $i = 5$ which gives

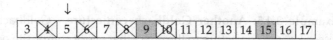

Although the extensive search discussed above has not lead to any conclusion regarding Goldbach's primary question, it plays as key role in the recent

---

Algorithm 3.2

1: **procedure** GOLDBACH(N)
2:      **for** i from 3 to N **do**
3:          $L[i]$:=false
4:      **end for**
5:      $L[4]$:=true
6:      **for** i from 3 to N **do**
7:          **if** $\neg L[i]$ **then**
8:              **if** i is even **then**
9:                  i is a counterexample to Goldbach's conjecture
10:             **end if**
11:             **if** i is odd **then**
12:                 Set $L[ki]$:=true for all odd $k, 3 \leq k \leq N/i$
13:                 **for** odd j from 3 to i **do**
14:                     **if** $\neg L[j]$ **then**
15:                         $L[i+j]$:=true
16:                     **end if**
17:                 **end for**
18:             **end if**
19:         **end if**
20:     **end for**
21: **end procedure**

---

resolution of Goldbach's *weak* (also known as odd, or ternary) conjecture: Is every odd number larger than 7 the sum of three primes? The weak Goldbach conjecture was proved ([Vin37]) in 1937 to hold for all "sufficiently large" odd numbers, and shortly after the conjecture was proved to hold for odd numbers larger than $C = 3^{3^{15}} \simeq 3.2 \cdot 10^{6846168}$. Improved estimates were obtained over the years, and in 2002 it was established that $C = e^{3100} \simeq 2.1 \cdot 10^{1346}$ was enough, but of course it was still not feasible to check the remaining finite segment of odd numbers.

Introducing completely new methods, Helfgott ([Hel13]) managed to lower C to 10^{30}, and this allowed a proof of the weak Goldbach conjecture by appealing to the partial verification of the original conjecture up to 10^{18}. Indeed, all that had to be done was to find a collection of primes

$$p_1 < p_2 < \cdots < p_n$$

with $p_k - p_{k-1} < 10^{18}$ and $p_n > C$. This was obtained in [HP13], see also
EX. 6.6.8 ← Exercise 3.20.   ◁

Example 3.4.5: Another Goldbach conjecture. Goldbach made a much lesser-known conjecture to the effect that every composite odd number is the sum of a prime and twice a square. We can reformulate the conjecture by requiring that

$$2n + 1 = p + 2m^2$$

has a solution with p a prime and $m \in \mathbb{N}_0$ for any $n > 1$. This was suggested by Goldbach to Euler in 1752, and Euler in 1753 reported back that he had confirmed the conjecture for $2n + 1 \leq 2500$.

We can easily test the conjecture by the procedure

```
[> otherGoldbach:=proc(x) local m;              1
     for m from 0 to floor(sqrt(x/2)) do        2
       if isprime(x-2*m^2) then                 3
         return true;                           4
       end if;                                  5
     end do;                                    6
     return false;                              7
   end proc;                                    8
```

But we do not have to look very far to locate the two counterexamples 5777 and 5993. These were found by Moritz Stern (the same Stern as in Example 3.3.5) long before the advent of computers in 1856. Interestingly, these are the only counterexamples known, but the conjecture is not as thoroughly studied as *the* Goldbach conjecture, so we will return to the problem in
EX. 7.3.3 ← Chapter 7.   ◁

Example 3.4.6: Pólya's conjecture.   Joseph Liouville studied

$$\lambda(n) = \begin{cases} -1 & n \text{ has an odd number of prime factors} \\ 1 & n \text{ has an even number of prime factors} \end{cases}$$

and George Pólya conjectured that most numbers have an odd number of prime factors, in the sense that the accumulated Liouville function

$$L(n) = \sum_{i=1}^{n} \lambda(i)$$

would remain nonpositive for all $n > 1$.

It is easy to use Maple to test this conjecture for small n (cf. Exercise 2.35); furthermore we see that $L(n) = 0$ for n among

$$2, 4, 6, 10, 16, 26, 40, 96, 586$$

but for no other n in the immediate range of such an experiment. All of this was of course known to Pólya.

Since Pólya had established that his conjecture would imply the Riemann hypothesis, it attracted quite a lot of attention, and it was checked before the advent of computers all the way to $n = 20000$ ([Gup40]). It was initially widely believed, but when Ingham [Ing42] proved that it would imply that

```
14.134725142
21.022039639
25.010857580
30.424876126
32.935061588
37.586178159
```

Figure 3.9   Zeroes of $\zeta(\frac{1}{2} + \alpha i)$

there was an infinite number of linear integral relations among the imaginary parts of the zeroes of ζ, the general sentiment shifted toward the conjecture being false. When it was finally disproved by Brian Haselgrove in 1958 ([Has58]) the result failed to generate the sensation that would probably have accompanied it earlier.

Haselgrove chose an approach which was computational in nature, but did not lead directly to a concrete counterexample. Indeed, extending L to all of $\mathbb{R}_+$ by

$$L(x) = L(\lfloor x \rfloor),$$

Ingham had established

$$\limsup_{x \to \infty} e^{-x/2} L(e^x) \geq \limsup_{x \to \infty} A_M(x)$$

where

$$A_M(x) = \frac{1}{\zeta(1/2)} + 2\Re\left(\sum_{\rho_n < M} \frac{(1 - \frac{\rho_n}{M})\zeta(1 + 2i\rho_n)e^{i\rho_n x}}{(\frac{1}{2} + i\rho_n)\zeta'(\frac{1}{2} + i\rho_n)}\right)$$

with $0 < \rho_1 < \rho_2 < \cdots < \rho_N$ the imaginary parts of the first N zeroes of the Riemann zeta-function $\zeta(z)$ (see box on p. 109). Haselgrove could establish that $A_{1000}(831.847) \simeq 0.00495 > 0$, proving that indeed $L(n)$ must be positive at infinitely many n since A_M is almost periodic.

Not much later, R. Sherman Lehman—who had also worked on the SWAC—in [Leh60] provided a concrete counterexample to Pólya's conjecture by an experimental approach which deserves close study. To do so, we must implement $A_M(x)$ in Maple for relatively large M, but while certainly $\zeta(z)$ is implemented in Maple, its zeroes must be found elsewhere. A dependable internet source is ([Odl]), providing a text file on the form indicated in Figure 3.9 so we can prepare an array ZL with zeroes using

```
[> N:=1000;                                                    1
   input:=fopen("zeroes1.txt",READ);                          2
   ZL:=fscanf(input,"%{1000,1}ac")[1];                        3
   close(input);                                              4
```

where we import 1000 values in one call of fscanf using a format string as described in the documentation of this command. We confirm by

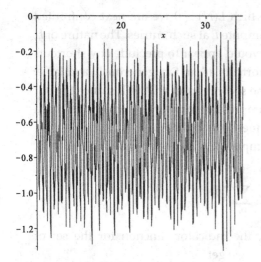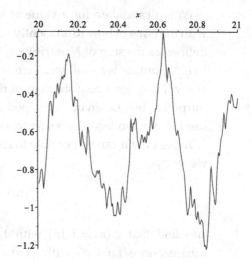

Figure 3.10 Plots of $A_{1000}(x)$.

```
[> ZL[649], ZL[650];
```

$$999.791571557, 1001.349482638$$

that the largest $\rho_N < 1000$ occurs at $N = 649$, and then define AA by

```
[> AA:=x->1/Zeta(1/2)+                                    1
      2*Re(add((1-ZL[i]/1000)*Zeta(1+2*I*ZL[i])/         2
      ((1/2+I*ZL[i])*D(Zeta)(1/2+I*ZL[i]))*              3
      exp(I*ZL[i]*x),i=1..649));                          4
```

We check our program against Haselgrove's computation to find

```
[> evalf(AA(831.847));
```

$$0.0049451718$$

which is consistent with what Haselgrove had computed.

The starting point of Lehman's work is the heuristic observation that in fact $e^{-x/2}L(e^x) \approx A_M(x)$ for large M, something that we may easily convince ourselves of for small x (Exercise 3.2). Haselgrove's computation would then indicate that L was positive around

$$e^{831.847} \simeq 1.847404035 \cdot 10^{361}$$

but confirming this for numbers in this range was (and remains to this day) impossible. Instead, Lehman searched for smaller x where $A_M(x)$ was large and was led to consider the local maxima we can see in Figure 3.10. The most promising such local maximum, at $x \simeq 33.5$, would lead to 15-digit n-values, so we choose the more modest local maximum at 20.6 at which we have 9-digit integers. We may zoom in to read off the value $x \simeq 20.6245$ and see that this corresponds to $N = 905704815$.

With a candidate for a value at which $L(N) > 0$ we are next confronted with the issue of how to efficiently compute L at such entries. The nature of L, defined as the sum of N entries ± 1, would appear to preclude any shortcuts to $L(N)$, but, as we shall see, such shortcuts are in fact generously available. We will just describe a shortcut of the second order that will suffice for our purposes, but Lehman developed impressive machinery which has been used also in modern attacks on this question ([BFM08]).

To see how it can be possible to compute $L(N)$ without knowing $L(N-1)$, we study

$$\Lambda(n) = \sum_{k|n} \lambda(k)$$

and find that $\Lambda(n) = 1_S(n)$ with 1_S the indicator function for the set of squares, since if $n = p^r a$ with $(p, a) = 1$ we get

$$\Lambda(n) = \sum_{i=0}^{r} \sum_{k|a} \lambda(p^i k) = \sum_{i=0}^{r} \sum_{k|a} (-1)^i \lambda(k) = \sum_{i=0}^{r} (-1)^i \Lambda(a)$$

so that Λ vanishes when p divides n an odd number of times and can be reduced to $\Lambda(1) = 1$ when all primes occur with even multiplicity. Thus we have

$$\lfloor \sqrt{x} \rfloor = \sum_{1 \le n \le x} 1_S(n) = \sum_{1 \le n \le x} \sum_{k|n} \lambda(k)$$
$$= \sum_{1 \le k \le x} \lambda(k) \left\lfloor \frac{x}{k} \right\rfloor = \sum_{1 \le n \le x} L(x/n), \qquad (3.16)$$

showing that we may compute $L(N)$ if we know $L(N/2), L(N/3), \ldots, L(1)$, without worrying about $L(N-1)$. In our setting, however, this reduction is insufficient, so we use it instead to establish

$$\sum_{1 \le m \le \frac{x}{w}} \mu(m) \left\lfloor \sqrt{\frac{x}{m}} \right\rfloor = \sum_{1 \le m \le \frac{x}{w}} \mu(m) \sum_{n \le x} L(x/n),$$

where μ is the Möbius function:

$$\mu(n) = \begin{cases} \lambda(n) & n \text{ is square-free} \\ 0 & \text{otherwise.} \end{cases} \qquad (3.17)$$

This gives that

$$\sum_{1 \le m \le \frac{x}{w}} \mu(m) \sum_{n \le \frac{x}{mw}} L(x/mn) = \sum_{1 \le \ell \le \frac{x}{w}} L(x/\ell) \sum_{m|\ell} \mu(m) = L(x)$$

so that we may compute L by

$$L(x) = \sum_{1 \le m \le x/w} \mu(m) \left(\left\lfloor \sqrt{\frac{x}{m}} \right\rfloor - \sum_{1 \le k < w} \lambda(k) \left(\left\lfloor \frac{x}{km} \right\rfloor - \left\lfloor \frac{x}{mv} \right\rfloor \right) \right).$$

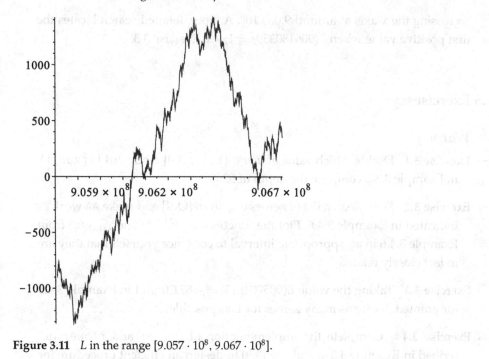

Figure 3.11 L in the range $[9.057 \cdot 10^8, 9.067 \cdot 10^8]$.

We implement this, taking $w = \lfloor \sqrt{x} \rfloor$, by

```
[> lambdar:=proc(k) option remember;                          1
       return (-1)^bigomega(k);                                2
   end proc;                                                   3
   LL:=proc(x) local w;                                        4
     w:=floor(x^(1/2));                                        5
     return(add(mobius(m)*(floor(evalf(sqrt(x/m)))-            6
       add(lambdar(k)*(floor(evalf(x/(k*m)))-                  7
       floor(evalf(w/m))),k=1..ceil(x/w-1))),m=1..w));         8
   end proc;                                                   9
```

electing to use a remember table for values of λ since they will be used
repeatedly in the inner sum. Testing LL against the naive implementation L
up to 10000 we satisfy ourselves that it works, but although it is much faster
than L, we must still allow Maple more than 4 hours computation time to
reach

```
[> LL(905704815);
```

$$-871$$

This is a bit of an anticlimax; indeed the value is negative. But having a single
value of L in this range makes it easy to compute L in an interval around it,
and it takes only 10 minutes to produce the graph in Figure 3.11 which shows

L crossing the x-axis at around $9.06 \cdot 10^8$. A more detailed search locates the

EX. 7.1.5 ← first positive value when $L(906180359) = 1$, see Exercise 3.3.   ◁

3.5 Exercises

Warmup

EX. 3.3.2 → **Exercise 3.1**   Decide which value of n, $n \in \{1, \ldots, 100\}$ made `collatzDepth` in Example 3.3.2 compute the depth of 9232.

EX. 3.4.6 → **Exercise 3.2**   Download a list of zeroes of ζ from [Odl] and make AA work as indicated in Example 3.4.6. Plot the functions $e^{-x/2}L(e^x)$ and $A_{1000}(x)$ from Example 3.4.6 in an appropriate interval to convince yourself that they are in fact closely related.

EX. 3.4.6 → **Exercise 3.3**   Taking the value $L(905704815) = -871$ found in Example 3.4.6 for granted, locate as many zeroes for L as possible.

EX. 3.3.4 → **Exercise 3.4**   Complete the implementation of `dTower` and `rTower` described in Example 3.3.4, and use (3.9) to design an efficient procedure for computing β_n. How far can you compute $\beta_1, \ldots, \beta_n$ in 10 minutes?

EX. 3.4.3 → **Exercise 3.5**   Perform the computations leading to the 9×9, 13×13 and 29×29-matrices described in Example 3.4.3 and place them in a Maple list `MML`. Then run the procedure given to find all pairs (c, d) up to $N = 5000$.

EX. 3.4.1 → **Exercise 3.6**   What happens if we try to factorize the Fermat number F_{16} directly by

    [> ifactor(2^(2^16)+1);

Compare with

    [> ifactor(2^(2^16)+1,easy);

and explain using Maple's help system.

Homework

EX. 3.2.3 → **Exercise 3.7**   Design a strategy to ensure that the N discussed in Example 3.2.3 is sufficiently large for the list produced to contain all denominators. Formulate a conjecture on the nature of the sets found. Test it for values $i > 10$.

Exercise 3.8   Make a procedure `countup(N)` which returns exacly N digits of the number

$$0.123456789101112131415161718192021 \cdots$$

[Hint: Look in the documentation of the `StringTools` *package.]*

Exercise 3.9 In combinatorial game theory, one often works with a function mex which to some finite subset G of $\mathbb{N} \cup \{0\}$ associates the smallest element in $\mathbb{N} \cup \{0\}$ which is *not* in G. Hence we have

$$\mathrm{mex}(\{0, 1, 4\}) = 2$$
$$\mathrm{mex}(\{1, 5, 7\}) = 0$$
$$\mathrm{mex}(\{0, 1, 2, 3, 4, 5, 6\}) = 7.$$

Implement this in a Maple procedure mex.

Exercise 3.10 In combinatorial game theory, for any $N \in \mathbb{N} \cup \{0\}$, one defines a recursive sequence of numbers by

$$s_n = \mathrm{mex}\left(\{\mathrm{xor}(s_k, s_\ell) \mid k \geq 0,\, \ell \geq 0,\, k + \ell = n - N\}\right), \qquad n \geq N$$
$$s_n = 0, \qquad n < N$$

with mex as defined in Exercise 3.9.

Here, we define $\mathrm{xor}(a, b)$ to be the result of writing each number a and b in binary notation, and using the exclusive-or rule

$$0\,\mathrm{xor}\,0 = 0 \qquad 1\,\mathrm{xor}\,0 = 1 \qquad 0\,\mathrm{xor}\,1 = 1 \qquad 1\,\mathrm{xor}\,1 = 0$$

at every individual digit. Hence we have, for instance, $\mathrm{xor}(12, 9) = 5$.

Implement this as a Maple procedure s and compute $s_1, \ldots s_{100}$ for $N = 2$. Is it important to use remember here?

EX. 3.2.5 → **Exercise 3.11** Apply max to each entry of generateCombinations(5,30) or other lists generated as described in Example 3.2.5. Explain the pattern. One may prove that when a k-combination $[c_1, \ldots c_k]$ is given, then the index of the combination within the enumeration described above (starting at 0) is given by

$$\binom{c_1}{1} + \binom{c_2}{2} + \cdots + \binom{c_k}{k}$$

where we have $c_i \geq i - 1$ and let $\binom{i-1}{i} = 0$. Note, for example, that

$$\binom{0}{1} + \binom{1}{2} + \binom{4}{3} + \binom{5}{4} = 0 + 0 + 4 + 5 = 9,$$

consistent with the fact that we find the combination at the tenth entry, (3.3). Implement this formula as a Maple procedure getIndex. Find a way to test it using map.

Exercise 3.12 For any $N \in \mathbb{N}_0$, consider the sequence of integers $(t_{m,N})_{m=0}^{\infty}$ defined recursively as

$$t_{m,N} = (N - 1)t_{m-1,N} + (N + 1)^{m-1}, \qquad m > 0$$
$$t_{0,N} = 1.$$

Implement it as a recursive procedure t in Maple so that

```
[> for N from 0 to 9 do                                                    1
    seq(t(m,N),m=0..9);                                                    2
   end do;                                                                 3
```

generates a hundred values organized in ten rows of ten entries each. Try to guess a closed form for $t_{m,N}$ and implement it as tt. Explain why is it desirable if a run of

```
[> Q:=100;                                                                 1
   max([seq(seq(abs(t(m,N)-tt(m,N)),m=0..Q),N=0..Q)]);                     2
```

has the output 0.

EX. 3.4.2 → **Exercise 3.13** In Example 3.4.2, we searched for solutions to

$$x_1^5 + x_2^5 + x_3^5 + x_4^5 = y^5 \tag{3.18}$$

$$x_1 \leq x_2 \leq x_3 \leq x_4$$

going through all tuples (x_1, x_2, x_3, x_4) and then testing for the existence of a y. This was easy to program, but is not computationally efficient. In this exercise we design a more efficient procedure to systematically check for solutions to (3.18) for a given y using a recursive procedure.

(*a*) Prove that when

$$\sum_{i=1}^{k} x_i^n = y \tag{3.19}$$

with $1 \leq x_1 \leq x_2 \leq \cdots \leq x_k$ then $x_1 \geq (y/k)^{1/n}$.

(*b*) Program a recursive procedure isPower(y,n,k,z) which returns true precisely when (3.19) has a solution with $1 \leq x_1 \leq x_2 \leq \cdots \leq x_k \leq z^n$.

(*c*) Search after the smallest y admitting a solution to (3.19) using isPower.

(*d*) Adjust isPower to store the solution $x_1, \ldots, x_k$ in a global variable.

EX. 3.3.3 → **Exercise 3.14** Using the left-hand side of Figure 3.5, produce an estimate of how many values need to be computed to determine ruinP(C,g) when the remember table is empty. Compare the estimate to the size of the remember table with a selection of values of C and g, using forget to empty the remember table between the experiments.

EX. 2.6.2 → **Exercise 3.15** Write a recursive procedure win(s,n) which returns true when the next player can win the game in Example 2.6.2 after the moves contained in the string s have been played. Use the fact that the player who is next to move can win precisely if one of the moves s0 or s1 has the property that the next player to move can *not* win. Run win("",n) for as many n as possible and conclude which player has a winning strategy.

EX. 3.4.3 → **Exercise 3.16** In this exercise we follow Elkies's original approach to an integer solution of (3.10). Let

$$f(v) = 22030 + 28849v - 56158v^2 + 36941v^3 - 31790v^4.$$

(a) Find an interval I so that $f(v) < 0$ for $v \in \mathbb{R} \backslash I$.

(b) Write a procedure to search for rational solutions to $f(v) = u^2$.

(c) Use any solutions found to produce a counterexample for Euler's conjecture at $n = 4$.

EX. 3.2.2 → **Exercise 3.17** Find $n > 105$ so that the factorization of $x^n - 1$ over $\mathbb{Z}$ (*cf.* Example 3.2.2) has a coefficient which is not ± 1. Do the n found have properties in common?

EX. 3.4.6 → **Exercise 3.18** Lehman in fact established that for $1 \le v \le w \le x$, $L(x)$ could be expressed as

$$\sum_{\substack{1 \le m \le x/w \\ m \text{ odd}}} \mu(m) \left(\left\lfloor \sqrt{\frac{x}{m}} \right\rfloor - \left\lfloor \sqrt{\frac{x}{2m}} \right\rfloor + \left\lfloor \frac{x + mv}{2mv} \right\rfloor \sum_{k < v} \lambda(k) - \left\lfloor \frac{x + km}{2km} \right\rfloor \sum_{k < v} \lambda(k) \right)$$

$$- \sum_{\substack{x/w < \ell \le x/v \\ \ell \text{ odd}}} L\left(\frac{x}{\ell}\right) \sum_{\substack{1 \le m \le x/w \\ m|\ell}} \mu(m).$$

Use this to implement a more efficient version of L.

Projects and Group Work

EX. 3.4.2 → **Exercise 3.19** Adjust the program used in Example 3.4.2, or the improved program of Exercise 3.13, to search for solutions to

$$x_1^n + x_2^n + \cdots + x_n^n = y^n$$

with $x_1, x_2 \ldots, x_n, y \in \mathbb{N}$, for $n = 2, 3, 4, 5, 6$. Note the relation to Exercise 1.5 at $n = 2$.

EX. 3.4.4 → **Exercise 3.20** Use Maple's isPrime command to find primes

$$p_1 < p_2 < \cdots < p_n$$

with $p_k - p_{k-1} < 10^{18}$ and $p_n > C$ for C as large as possible. Can you verify Goldbach's weak conjecture (*cf.* Example 3.4.4) up to Helfgott's bound this way?

Exercise 3.21 Is it possible to start a Fibonacci-type recursive sequence

$$u_n = u_{n-1} + u_{n-2}, \qquad n \ge 2$$

by $u_0 = A, u_1 = B$ so that the sequence u_n contains only composite numbers even though $\gcd(A, B) = 1$?

EX. 3.3.5 → **Exercise 3.22**   The output given in Example 3.3.5 shows that sb@@5 returns
all of the fractions i/n with $0 \leq i \leq n$ when $n \leq 5$, but that the fractions $\frac{1}{6}, \frac{5}{6}$
are not present at this stage. We note also that there are two fractions in
lowest terms of the form $i/8$, but no larger denominators occur.

   (*a*) Formulate a hypothesis about how many times, as a function of n, sb
       should be run before *all* fractions $0/n, 1/n, \ldots, n/n$ occur.

   (*b*) Formulate a hypothesis about the largest denominator in a fraction
       found by applying sb m times.

Test your hypotheses with Maple.

3.6 Notes and Further Reading

Many of the examples given in Section 3.4 were contributed by several mathematicians to a discussion on stackexchange.org starting with a user request for "Conjectures that have been disproved with extremely large counterexamples?" and a similar discussion on mathoverflow.net on "Examples of eventual counterexamples." Both fora are excellent sources for further
such examples.

   Exercise 3.21 was inspired by [Guy04]; this book is a rich source of
interesting problems that may be attacked experimentally. The website
projecteuler.net has a similarly rich supply of interesting problems in
experimental and computational mathematics.

   Another useful source for early examples of experimental mathematics is
the column "Computers and mathematics" which ran in the Notices of the
American Mathematical Society from 1989 to 1996. An index is provided in
the 1995 volume 42 issue, pp. 248–259.

   The particular variation of a ruin problem given in Example 3.2.4 was suggested to the authors by Ernst Hansen.

   The enumeration scheme for combinations, and many other relevant ideas,
are discussed in [Knu]. The Stern–Brocot tree is beautifully explained in
[GKP94].

4 *Visualization*

The great benefit of using computers to generate and investigate examples of mathematical structures as described in the previous chapters is the ability to handle much larger amounts of complicated data than possible when using less sophisticated tools like pen and paper. However, such investigations will often result in large quantities of output, which are only useful if they can be represented in a way that gives the investigator the opportunity to notice interesting features and trends. To make sense of such output, it is essential to be able to use computer programs to represent data in a human readable manner.

4.1 Plotting Data

The basic Maple command for visualizing functions and expressions is `plot`. For instance, `plot(x^2)` produces a plot of a parabola. Note that Maple creates such plots by computing a number of reference points and interpolating between them. A *plot structure* is a Maple data type designed to contain the information needed to make a visual display of a graphic such as the plot of a function. This is the data type returned by Maple's various plotting commands such as `plot` and `plot3d`. A plot structure can be saved to a variable and reused later using a simple assignment such as

```
[> p := plot(x^2);
```

4.1.1 *Specialized Plotting Commands*

As seen in Exercise 4.2, the basic command `plot` is very versatile, but various specialized figures still require specifically tailored commands. Many of these commands are contained in the package `plots`.

As an example, consider the command `pointplot` which is used to plot a family of data points. It is of particular interest to experimental mathematicians because it allows easy overview of a data set. Input can be given as a

The Mandelbrot set

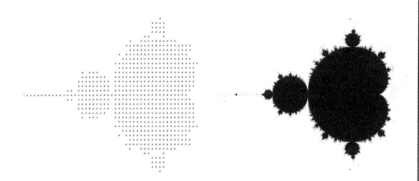

"When seeking new insights, I look, look, look and play with many pictures (One picture is never enough)."

– Benoit Mandelbrot

For each $c \in \mathbb{C}$, define $P_c \colon \mathbb{C} \to \mathbb{C}$ by $P_c(z) = z^2 + c$ and consider the sequence of iterated function values $(P_c^{\circ n}(0))_{n \in \mathbb{N}}$. The *Mandelbrot set* is defined to be the set of points c for which this sequence is bounded, that is,

$$M = \{c \in \mathbb{C} \mid \exists s \in \mathbb{R}, \forall n \in \mathbb{N} \ |P_c^{\circ n}(0)| \leq s\}.$$

In 1980, a visualization of M similar to the figure shown above (left) came to the attention of Benoit Mandelbrot (1924–2010), who embarked on a detailed investigation of M based on computer generated visualizations. Concretely, Mandelbrot would print out images of (parts of) the set and study these. In an early set of print-outs, Mandelbrot observed what appeared to be specks of dirt surrounding the main image. Due to the quality of the printer, this was a very reasonable explanation, but a symmetry in the specks led Mandelbrot to investigate them more closely. Writing a new program to zoom in on the mysterious points revealed that the specks were not the result of a mechanical error but simply very small parts (or *islands*, as Mandelbrot called them) of M. More importantly, each of these islands resembled a miniature copy of the whole set and the magnification revealed that they were connected to the rest of the set. This led Mandelbrot to conjecture that M is connected, a fact that was subsequently proved by Douady and Hubbard in 1982.

The visualization of the Mandelbrot set was featured on the cover of the August 1985 issue of *Scientific American* and in a touring art exhibition of the German Goethe Institute. Later, the Mandelbrot set got even more exposure when the visualizations became popular as screen savers. Indeed, the stunning images of the Mandelbrot set have become the archetypical example of visualization in mathematics.

list of vectors/lists or as a matrix. For instance, the following two commands produce the same plot.

```
[> with(plots):                                          1
   pointplot([[seq(i,i=1..10)],                          2
              [seq(ithprime(i),i=1..10)]]);              3
   pointplot([<seq(i,i=1..10)>,                          4
              <seq(ithprime(i),i=1..10)>]);              5
```

Maple also has extensive tools for constructing three-dimensional plots and inspecting their properties. The command `plot3d` is used to plot surfaces in three dimension, and as such, it serves a purpose analogous to `plot`. To investigate the structure of such a plot, commands such as `contourplot` can be very useful.

4.1.2 *Plot Options*

A number of optional arguments can be used to customize most of the plotting commands in Maple. Many of these options can also be applied after making an initial plot by right-clicking on the resulting figure and choosing from the menu. However, in order to be able to automate the process of constructing figures from data, it is necessary to be able to make such alterations by giving options directly to the plotting command as in:

```
[> plot([2*x,exp(x)],x=-1..1, color=[blue,red]);
```

Information about the various optional arguments can be found by searching for `plot, options` in the Maple help system. The ones most likely to be useful in a mathematical experiment are:

`a..b`: Explicitly determines the part of the vertical axis displayed.

`discont=true`: Removes vertical lines at the points of discontinuity from discontinuous functions.

`scaling=constrained`: Gives the axes the same scale.

`numpoints=N`: Can be used to increase the minimum number of reference points used when drawing graphs. This can be useful for increasing the resolution, but Maple employs an adaptive algorithm to determine the number of points required and will often use more than the minimum number of points anyway.

Maple's built-in plotting tools generally do a good job at choosing the points where the function should be sampled, but one should always be aware that plots are prone to give inaccurate information when the function values vary violently. This is particularly true for commands like `plot3d` and `complexplot3d` that operate with fairly small sample sizes by default.

Plaster models

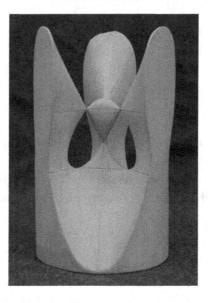

These geometric investigations were pursued almost like botanical studies in which the geometer went about collecting various specimens associated with certain classes of equations. These then had to be classified according to some larger scheme, certainly less ambitious than the Linnaean framework, but nevertheless with a similar purpose in mind.

David E. Rowe

A major theme in 19th-century geometry was the search for surfaces, for example algebraic, with extreme behavior such as a having a maximal number of nodes or containing a maximal number of lines.

Substantial work was invested in the production of models in wood or metal allowing researchers to visually communicate their findings. In the late 19th century, a production of mathematical models, mainly in plaster, was initiated by Alexander Wilhelm von Brill (1842–1935) in Munich. Perhaps surprisingly, these models became a commercial success, and many of them can still be found in mathematics departments around the world. The model depicted above is a surface with four real conic points.

Most of the models were produced using a method not unlike that employed by Maple's visualization procedures: Shapes of two-dimensional cuts through such a surface were computed, and drawn on carton. These two-dimensional shapes were cut out and assembled into spatial figures that were then used to cast the models.

There is still a market for physical models of mathematical surfaces, but the advent of 3d printers has made plaster and carton obsolete.

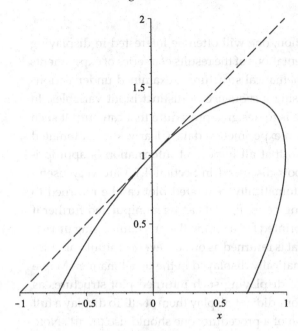

Figure 4.1 The plot constructed in Example 4.1.1 using `display`.

4.1.3 Combining Plots

Often, one is interested in making a plot combining features of some of the basic plot commands or emphasizing certain features of a plot. For such applications, the command `display` from the package `plots` is a powerful tool for the creation of useful graphical representations. The command `display` takes a list of plot structures as input and returns the plot obtained by displaying them on top of one another. It cannot be used to combine 2d and 3d plots without first transforming the 2d plot, but the output of almost all other standard plotting commands can be combined in this way. It is worth noting that most of the options mentioned in Section 4.1.2 can also be used as options for `display`. For instance, general formatting commands such as titles and legends should rather be given to `display` than to the individual plots.

Example 4.1.1: Display. The following commands combine a plot of a straight line with a plot of a parametric curve. The resulting plot is shown in Figure 4.1.

```
[> p1 := plot(x+1,x=-1..1, linestyle = dash):                    1
   p2 := plot([cos(t), sin(t)+cos(t), t=0..2*Pi],                2
                -1..1,-0..2):                                    3
   display([p1,p2], scaling = constrained);                      4
```

◁

4.1.4 Automated Figures

In an experimental investigation, one will often be interested in displaying complicated graphical representations of the results of a series of experiments where the behavior of a mathematical structure is examined under various conditions, for instance by using a sequence of distinct input variables. In such cases, the obvious choice is to design a procedure that can output such graphical representations given experimental data. Clearly, such automated figures should be designed so that all important information is appropriately emphasized, and the tools discussed in Section 4.1.3 are very useful for that purpose. Such an automatically generated plot can be returned to the surrounding program using `return`, so it can be manipulated further if necessary, or it can simply be printed from within the procedure using `print`.

Note that a plot structure that is returned as one of several output variables from a procedure is not automatically displayed in the usual manner. Maple 2015 introduced the feature of displaying such returned plot structures as miniatures, while earlier versions did not display them at all. To display a full sized plot during the execution of a procedure, one should use `print`. Note that plot structures potentially contain a lot of data, so it can be problematic to maintain a large collection of plots in the program.

Example 4.1.2: Automated plot. The following procedure takes a function f and an interval $[a, b]$ as input. It will plot the graph of f on the interval $[a, b]$, color the area between the graph and the horizontal axis, print the value of the integral $\int_a^b f(x)dx$, and return the value of the integral.

```
[> with(plots):                                                          1
   intPlot := proc(f, a, b)                                              2
       local p, textCoordinate, text, x;                                3
       p := plot(f,a..b,                                                 4
               filled = [color="grey", transparency=0.9]);              5
       x := a + (b-a)/2;                                                 6
       text := textplot([x,f(x)/2,'typeset'(int(f,a..b))],              7
                                   color = black);                       8
       print(display([p,text]));                                        9
       return int(f,a..b);                                              10
   end proc:                                                            11
```

Executing this procedure with the following input produces the plot shown in Figure 4.2.

```
[> f := x -> -x^2+2*x+1;                                                 1
   intPlot(f,-1,3);                                                      2
                                                                        ◁
```

Example 4.1.3: The Koch curve. Define a map on the set of line segments in the real plane by

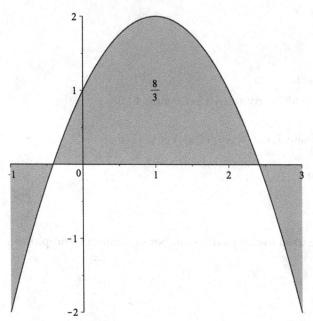

Figure 4.2 The automated plot constructed in Example 4.1.2.

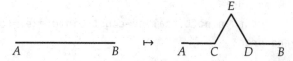

where $|AC| = |CD| = |DB| = \frac{1}{3}|AB|$ and CDE is an equilateral triangle. Loosely, the *Koch curve* is a fractal defined to be the limit of this iteration.

The following procedure implements the basic iterative step. It takes two points as input and returns the points obtained by applying the map described above to the corresponding line segment.

```
[> KochMove := proc( A, B )                                    1
    local v;                                                   2
    v := B-A;                                                  3
    return  A,                                                 4
            A+1/3*v,                                           5
            A+1/2*v+1/2*[-v[2]/sqrt(3),v[1]/sqrt(3)],          6
            A+2/3*v;                                           7
  end proc:                                                    8
```

The next procedure takes a list of points as input and applies `KochMove` to all pairs of adjacent points in the list:

```
[> KochIteration := proc( L )                                 1
    local n, newL;                                            2
    newL := [];                                               3
    for n from 1 to nops(L)-1 do                              4
```

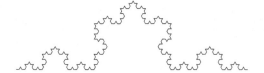

Figure 4.3   Fourth iteration of the map KochPlot considered in Example 4.1.3.

```
        newL := [op(newL),KochMove(L[n],L[n+1])];          5
    end do;                                                6
    newL := [op(newL),L[-1]];                              7
    return newL;                                           8
end proc:                                                  9
```

The final procedure can be used to carry out a number of iterations and plot the resulting curve:

```
[> KochPlot := proc(n)                                     1
    local L,i;                                             2
    L := [[0,0],[1,0]];                                    3
    for i from 1 to n do                                   4
        L := KochIteration(L);                             5
    end do;                                                6
    return plot(L,scaling=constrained,axes=none);          7
end proc:                                                  8
```

Figure 4.3 shows an example of the output from KochPlot. In the exercises, it will be examined how the same general program structure can be used for the visualization of other fractals as well.   ◁

4.1.5 *Visualization by Matrices*

As discussed in Section 2.3, the command Matrix can produce a matrix from a list defining the entries. However, Matrix can also be used to define matrices based on the evaluation of a function. More specifically, consider the problem of constructing an N by M matrix A where $A_{ij} = f(i, j)$ for some known function f. Assuming that f has been defined in Maple as a function (or procedure) f taking two integers as input, A can be defined with the command

```
[> A := Matrix(N,M,f);
```

Among other things, this gives an easy way to tabulate results.

When using this approach to produce tables of results, one is often hampered by the fact that Maple does not display large (dimensions bigger than 10) matrices on the screen. To override this behavior, one can use the command interface(rtablesize=n) to set the maximal dimension to n.

Sometimes, the structure of a sequence of numbers becomes much more apparent if the sequence is displayed in a rectangular array rather than as

---

The Costa–Hoffman–Meeks surface

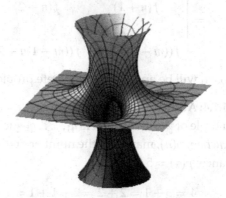

For approximately 200 years, the known *complete*, *embedded minimal* surfaces of finite topology were just the *plane*, the *catenoid* and the *helicoid*, and it was widely believed that there were no others.

In 1984, Celso Costa (1949–) constructed a new complete minimal surface, and the defining equations suggested that the surface somehow contained a plane and two catenoids. However, it was not initially possible to determine whether the surface intersected itself. If not, then it would be an new example of a complete, embedded minimal surface and a revolution in the field of differential geometry.

Suspecting that Costa's surface could be embedded, David Hoffman (1944–) and William Meeks III (1947–) used computer graphics to create a visualization. These plots showed no self-intersections and revealed previously unnoticed symmetries that eventually allowed Hoffman and Meeks to prove that this was indeed a new example of an embedded surface. It is worth noting that the visualization was crucial in the construction of the proof: The surface could not be understood before it could be seen.

This result inspired a great deal of work in the field of differential geometry and paved the way for the construction of many new complete, embedded minimal surfaces.

---

a list. For this purpose, it can be useful to have an easy way to assign the elements in a sequence to the entries of a matrix. To look for structure in the values of $f(n)$ for $n \in \mathbb{N}$, we may define:

```
[> entryNumber := (r,c,n) -> c + (r-1)*n:          1
    m:= 5: n := 15:                                 2
    fill := (r,c) -> f(entryNumber(r,c,n)):         3
    A := Matrix(m,n,fill);                          4
```

The result will be the matrix

$$A = \begin{bmatrix} f(1) & f(2) & \cdots & f(n) \\ f(n+1) & f(n+2) & & f(2n) \\ \vdots & & \ddots & \vdots \\ f((m-1)n+1) & f((m-1)n+2) & \cdots & f(mn) \end{bmatrix}$$

This approach will be applied to a concrete problem in the next example.

Example 4.1.4: Additive partitions. An *additive partition* of a number n is an unordered tuple of positive integers $q_1, \ldots, q_k$ such that $n = q_1 + \cdots + q_k$. The *partition function*, $p(n)$, maps n to the number of distinct additive partitions of n. For instance, $p(4) = 5$ since

$$4 = 3 + 1 = 2 + 2 = 2 + 1 + 1 = 1 + 1 + 1 + 1.$$

In Maple, $p(n)$ is computed by the procedure numbpart from the package combinat. Using this, the first 20 values of $p(n)$ are:

$$1, 2, 3, 5, 7, 11, 15, 22, 30, 42, 56, 77, 101, 135, 176, 231, 297, 385, 490, 627.$$

Reducing this modulo 5 yields

$$1, 2, 3, 0, 2, 1, 0, 2, 0, 2, 1, 2, 1, 0, 1, 1, 2, 0, 0, 2.$$

There is no readily apparent structure, but representing the sequence by matrices with various numbers of columns as described above will quickly reveal a pattern. Specifically, applying the function fill defined above to

```
[> f := k -> numbpart(k) mod 5;
```
1

results in the matrix

$$\begin{bmatrix} 1 & 2 & 3 & 0 & 2 & 1 & 0 & 2 & 0 & 2 & 1 & 2 & 1 & 0 & 1 \\ 1 & 2 & 0 & 0 & 2 & 2 & 2 & 0 & 0 & 3 & 1 & 0 & 3 & 0 & 4 \\ 2 & 4 & 3 & 0 & 3 & 2 & 2 & 0 & 0 & 3 & 3 & 4 & 1 & 0 & 4 \\ 3 & 4 & 3 & 0 & 1 & 3 & 4 & 1 & 0 & 1 & 3 & 4 & 0 & 0 & 2 \\ 0 & 1 & 4 & 0 & 3 & 0 & 4 & 0 & 0 & 3 & 0 & 3 & 4 & 0 & 4 \end{bmatrix}$$

This representation makes it easy to see that $p(n) \equiv 0 \pmod 5$ when $n \equiv 4 \pmod 5$. This and other patterns were first noted by Ramanujan who had access to the values of $p(n)$ for $n \in \{1, \ldots, 200\}$. ◁

In the preceding example, the zeroes line up in columns, making it easy to identify the pattern. However, this particular visual clue clearly depends on the number of columns in the matrix under consideration. Changing the number of columns will give a different, and probably less recognizable, pattern of zeroes. Hence, one may need to resize such a matrix repeatedly in order to find an illustrative representation. If all entries in a sequence have the same number of digits, then there is an easy way to handle this: simply

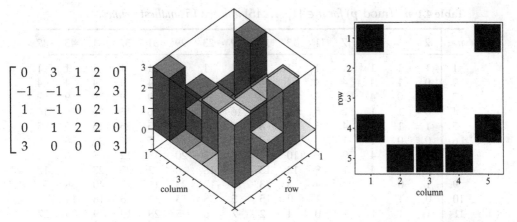

Figure 4.4 Output of `matrixplot(A,heights=histogram)` (center) and `sparsematrix-plot(A,matrixview,zeroes)` (right) for the given matrix A.

list the elements of the sequence on the screen, and resize the entire *window* of the Maple worksheet until the desired number of columns is achieved.

Maple has two commands that facilitate the study of patterns in the entries of a matrix using graphical representations; both are part of the `plots` package.

The command `matrixplot` can be used to construct a 3d-plot of the points $(n, m, A_{n,m})$ when A is a matrix with entries that can be evaluated to floating point values using `evalf`. By default, the result is displayed as a continuous surface and in some cases, this may obscure the structure of the matrix. A more faithful rendition can be achieve by adding the option `heights=histogram` to obtain a plot where the value of each entry defines the height of the bar in a two-dimensional histogram. An example of the output from `matrixplot` is given in Figure 4.4.

The command `sparsematrixplot` is very useful if one is only interested in *sparsity patterns*. Given a $m \times n$ matrix A, `sparsematrixplot` will display an m by n array of squares colored based on the value of the corresponding entry: a white square if $A_{m,n} = 0$ and a black square if $A_{m,n} \neq 0$. This is very useful for identifying structure in the entries of a matrix. By default, the columns of A are used as rows in the plotted array and *vice versa* . To reverse this, use the option `matrixview`. To emphasize entries equal to zero rather than nonzero, use the option `zeroes`. An example of the output from `sparsematrixplot` is given in Figure 4.4. Note how knowing the sparsity pattern may make it easier to recognize structure.

Example 4.1.5: Quadratic residues. Let p be a prime. An integer a is said to be a *quadratic residue modulo p* if $a \equiv b^2 \pmod{p}$ for some $0 < b < p$. If no such b exists, a is said to be a *quadratic nonresidue modulo p*. A good way to start the investigation of quadratic residues is to tabulate $n^2 \pmod{p}$ for small

Table 4.1 n^2 (mod p) *for* $n \in \{1, \ldots, 15\}$ *and the 15 smallest primes.*

n	2	3	5	7	11	13	17	19	23	29	31	37	41	43	47
1	1	1	1	1	1	1	1	1	1	1	1	1	1	1	1
2	0	1	4	4	4	4	4	4	4	4	4	4	4	4	4
3	1	0	4	2	9	9	9	9	9	9	9	9	9	9	9
4	0	1	1	2	5	3	16	16	16	16	16	16	16	16	16
5	1	1	0	4	3	12	8	6	2	25	25	25	25	25	25
6	0	0	1	1	3	10	2	17	13	7	5	36	36	36	36
7	1	1	4	0	5	10	15	11	3	20	18	12	8	6	2
8	0	1	4	1	9	12	13	7	18	6	2	27	23	21	17
9	1	0	1	4	4	3	13	5	12	23	19	7	40	38	34
10	0	1	0	2	1	9	15	5	8	13	7	26	18	14	6
11	1	1	1	2	0	4	2	7	6	5	28	10	39	35	27
12	0	0	4	4	1	1	8	11	6	28	20	33	21	15	3
13	1	1	4	1	4	0	16	17	8	24	14	21	5	40	28
14	0	1	1	0	9	1	9	6	12	22	22	10	11	32	24	8
15	1	0	0	1	5	4	4	16	18	22	8	3	20	10	37

values of n and p. As described above, this can be done in Maple using the commands:

```
[> squareModPrime := (n,m) -> n^2 mod ithprime(m);          1
   squaresModPrimes := Matrix(15,15,squareModPrime);        2
```

The result of this computation is shown in Table 4.1. A number a appears in the (infinite) column corresponding to a prime p if and only if there exists a solution to $a \equiv x^2$ (mod p). Since $(n + p)^2 = n^2 + p^2 + 2np \equiv n^2$ (mod p), it is in fact sufficient to consider the first $p - 1$ entries in each column. In particular, the table gives complete information about the solvability of $a \equiv x^2$ (mod p) for $p \in \{2, 3, 5, 7, 11, 13\}$. The following investigation will attempt to find patterns in the numbers that appear in the individual columns.

The case $a = 1$ is trivial for all p, so consider the case $a = -1$ instead. The idea is to use the columns of the table to identify the primes where there exists a solution to $-1 \equiv x^2$ (mod p). For instance, $4 \equiv -1$ (mod 5) and 4 occurs in the column corresponding to $p = 5$, so there exists a solution to $-1 \equiv x^2$ (mod 5). Specifically, 2 and 3 are solutions. Carrying out analogous investigations for the remaining primes yields:

> -1 is a quadratic residue modulo p for $p \in \{2, 5, 17, 29, 37, 41\}$
> -1 is a quadratic nonresidue modulo p for $p \in \{3, 7, 11\}$.

Note that the table has insufficient information to make conclusions about the remaining primes. However, disregarding 2, it is striking that 5, 17, 29, 37, 41 are all congruent 1 modulo 4 while the remaining primes considered are congruent 3 modulo 4. This pattern is easy to formulate as a hypothesis: For an odd prime p, there exists a solution to $-1 \equiv x^2$ (mod p) if and only if

$p \equiv 3 \pmod 4$. In the following, the investigation will be restricted to quadratic residues modulo odd primes.

Investigating the case $a = 2$ in the same manner as above yields

> 2 is a quadratic residue modulo p for $p \in \{7, 17, 23, 31, 47\}$
> 2 is a quadratic nonresidue modulo p for $p \in \{3, 5, 11, 13\}$.

Analyzing these data as above easily leads to the hypothesis: For an odd prime p, there exists a solution to $2 \equiv x^2 \pmod p$ if and only if $p \equiv \pm 1 \pmod 8$. Analogously, the table can be used to formulate a conjecture for $a = -2$, this will be examined in Exercise 4.21.

Next, consider the case $a = -3$. An analysis similar to the one carried out above reveals that

> -3 is a quadratic residue modulo p for $p \in \{7, 13, 19, 31, 43\}$
> -3 is a quadratic nonresidue modulo p for $p \in \{5, 11\}$.

As in the previous cases, it is possible to establish a common property of the listed primes: -3 is a quadratic residue modulo p when $p \equiv 1 \pmod 3$. Conversely, 5 and 11 are both congruent 2 modulo 3. There are two apparent problems with the hypothesis at this point. First, the table only gives information about two quadratic nonresidues. Second, $37 \equiv 1 \pmod 3$, so if the observed pattern holds in general, 37 should be a quadratic residue modulo 3, but the table holds insufficient information to determine whether this is the case. Fortunately, both problems can be remedied by considering more data, and at this point, it would be natural to extend the table to see if the suggested pattern holds for more quadratic nonresidues and for the problematic prime 37. In fact, it is only necessary to extend it by one row: $-3 \equiv 16^2 \pmod{37}$. Noting that 1 is the only quadratic residue modulo 3, the hypothesis can be reformulated to:

$$-3 \text{ is a quad. res. mod } p \text{ if and only if } p \text{ is a quad. res. mod. 3.} \qquad (4.1)$$

Next, consider the case $a = 5$. Analyzing as above reveals that:

> 5 is a quadratic residue modulo p for $p \in \{11, 19, 29, 31, 41\}$
> 5 is a quadratic nonresidue modulo p for $p \in \{3, 7, 13\}$.

In this case, the pattern is a little harder to determine, but the data supports the following hypothesis: 5 is a quadratic residue modulo p if and only if $p \equiv \pm 1 \pmod 5$. In other words, the hypothesis is:

$$5 \text{ is a quad. res. mod } p \text{ if and only if } p \text{ is a quad. res. mod 5.} \qquad (4.2)$$

The intriguing relations discovered in (4.1) and (4.2) warrant closer investigation, and a continuation of the investigation will reveal similar relations for other small primes. Such an investigation is carried out in Exercise 4.23 in the cases $a = \pm 7$ and $a = \pm 11$. Based on this, it is natural to suspect a

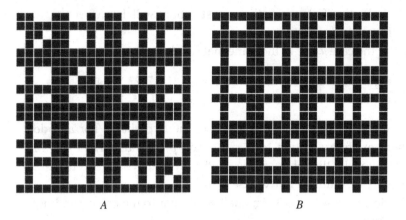

A   B

Figure 4.5   Visualization of sparsity patterns in the matrices A (left) and B (right) considered in
Example 4.1.5.

relation between the solvability of $p \equiv x^2$ (mod q) and the solvability of
$q \equiv x^2$ (mod p) (up to a sign change).

In Maple, this pattern can be investigated further using the built-in function quadres from the package numtheory. The command quadres(a,b)
computes a *generalized Legendre symbol*:

$$\left(\frac{a}{b}\right) = \begin{cases} 1 & a \text{ is quadratic residue modulo } b \\ -1 & a \text{ is quadratic nonresidue mod } b \end{cases}.$$

Let p, q be odd primes. Then $\left(\frac{p}{q}\right)\left(\frac{q}{p}\right) = 1$ if and only if

- p is a quad. res. mod q and q is a quad. res. mod p, or
- p is a quad. nonres. mod q and q is a quad. nonres. mod p.

In other words, computing $\left(\frac{p}{q}\right)\left(\frac{q}{p}\right)$ will determine whether the pattern
seen above for $a = 5$ holds in the case of p and q. Similarly, computing
$\left(\frac{-p}{q}\right)\left(\frac{q}{p}\right)$ will determine whether p and q follow the pattern observed in the
case $a = -3$.

In order to investigate the observed patterns systematically, we will
construct matrices

$$A = \left[\left(\frac{p_i}{p_j}\right)\left(\frac{p_j}{p_i}\right) + 1\right]_{i,j} \quad \text{and} \quad B = \left[\left(\frac{-p_i}{p_j}\right)\left(\frac{p_j}{p_i}\right) + 1\right]_{i,j},$$

where p_k is the kth odd prime number. The offset achieved by adding 1 to each
entry in the definitions above is added to ensure that the structures under
investigation are described by the sparsity patterns, so they can be visualized
using sparsematrixplot. The result of such a visualization is shown in
Figure 4.5.

Considering the rows of these two matrices (and disregarding the diagonal) reveals that for some p, $\left(\frac{p}{q}\right)\left(\frac{q}{p}\right) = 1$ for all q. Analogously, some p give $\left(\frac{-p}{q}\right)\left(\frac{q}{p}\right) = 1$ for all q. This observation is tabulated here:

p	3	5	7	11	13	17	19	23	29	31	37	41	43
$\left(\frac{p}{q}\right)\left(\frac{q}{p}\right)$		1			1	1			1		1	1	
$\left(\frac{-p}{q}\right)\left(\frac{q}{p}\right)$	1		1	1			1	1		1			1

Considering the table above, it is easy to summarize the observed patterns: Let p, q be odd primes, then

- If $p \equiv 1$ (mod 4), then $p \equiv x^2$ (mod q) is solvable if and only if $q \equiv x^2$ (mod p) is solvable.
- If $p \equiv 3$ (mod 4), then $-p \equiv x^2$ (mod q) is solvable if and only if $q \equiv x^2$ (mod p) is solvable.

In fact, this result holds in general and is known as the *Quadratic reciprocity theorem*. It was first proved by Gauss who proceeded to published a total of six different proofs. Privately, he dubbed it *Aurema Theorema* (the golden theorem). ◁

4.1.6 Scatter Plots

Formally, a *scatter plot* is simply a plot of a set of points in $\mathbb{R}^2$. A well-known example is the graph consisting of the points $(x, f(x))$ for some function f. In experimental mathematics, it is often useful to consider scatter plots of sets of the form:

$$S_P = \{(x, y) \mid x \in A, y \in B, P(x, y) = \text{true}\}$$

where A and B are finite subsets of $\mathbb{R}$, and P is a predicate in two variables related to the mathematical structure under consideration. Examples of such predicates could be: $f(x, y) = 0$, f is continuous in (x, y), or the series $\sum_{n=1}^{\infty} f_n(x, y)$ is convergent. In Maple, such plots can be generated by constructing a list of points satisfying the relevant predicate and using `pointplot`. This approach is applied to the famous Mandelbrot set in the following example.

BOX P. 94 → **Example 4.1.6: Plotting the Mandelbrot set.** It can be proved that the iterated sequence $P_c^{\circ n}(z)$ diverges if $|z| > 2$. This gives a criterion that can be used to exclude points from the Mandelbrot set, M. However, there is no certain way of distinguishing points inside the set from points where the sequence simply diverges very slowly. Hence, it is necessary to use a finite threshold T

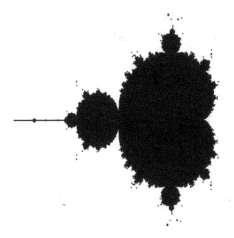

Figure 4.6 Visualization of the Mandelbrot set discussed in Example 4.1.6. Note the outlying points discussed in the box on p. 94.

as an indication of divergence: If $P_c^{\circ n}(0) < 2$ for all $n \leq T$, c will be assumed to be an element of M. This leads to the following test:

```
[> ElementOfM := proc(T, c)                                    1
       local i,z;                                              2
       z := evalf(c);                                          3
       for i from 1 to T do                                    4
           if abs(z) > 2 then return false end if;             5
           z := P(c,z);                                        6
       end do;                                                 7
       return true;                                            8
   end proc:                                                   9
```

To use this to create a list of points in the Mandelbrot set, simply check the predicate defined above for a suitable grid of points in the plane. The result obtained by doing this for a grid consisting of a million points is shown in Figure 4.6.   ◁

4.1.7 Approximations and Plots

In experimental mathematics, it is often interesting to plot functions that are not completely understood. In particular, the function under consideration may not have a known explicit closed definition. Even if such a definition exists, it may be too unwieldy to use in practical computations. However, an approximated plot will often reveal the information needed in experiments.

BOX P. 109 → **Example 4.1.7: Plotting the Riemann ζ function.**   Here, the goal is to produce and examine a plot of the Riemann zeta function, ζ. Naturally, the zeta function is known to Maple, and in applications, one should normally rely on the built-in function `Zeta` for computations involving the zeta function.

The Riemann hypothesis

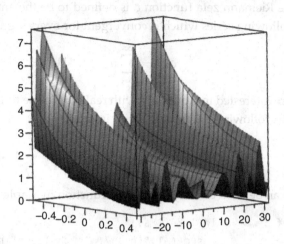

In 1859, Bernhard Riemann (1826–1866) introduced the *zeta function* as the analytic continuation of

$$\zeta(s) = \sum_{n=1}^{\infty} n^{-s}, \qquad \Re(s) > 1.$$

It is not hard to show that $\zeta(s) = 0$ when $s = -2k$ for $k \in \mathbb{N}$, and these are called the trivial zeroes of ζ. In his 1859 memoir, Riemann conjectured that every nontrivial zero of ζ has $\Re(s) = 1/2$. This is the *Riemann hypothesis*, unquestionably one of the greatest open problem in mathematics (and a Clay problem like the Birch–Swinnerton-Dyer conjecture). One of the many fascinating consequences of the Riemann hypothesis is that it would give precise information about the distribution of primes: the error term in the prime number theorem (see the box on p. 10) is closely related to the position of the zeroes.

As with many other great mathematical results and conjectures, the experimental work that went into formulating the Riemann hypothesis was not originally made available to the public. But when Riemann's notes were examined in 1929, it was found that he had computed some of the lowest-order zeroes of the zeta function with several decimals' precision. As can be expected for such a prominent problem, the zeroes of the zeta function have since been investigated very carefully using computer experiments, and by 2004, it had been proved that the 10^{13} nontrivial zeroes closest to the origin all lie on the critical line with $\Re(s) = 1/2$.

However, in order to illustrate the challenges involved in constructing a plot of such a function, we will define it from scratch instead.

The Riemann zeta function ζ is defined to be the analytic continuation of the following series which is convergent for every $s \in \mathbb{C}$ with $\Re(s) > 1$:

$$\zeta(s) = \sum_{n=1}^{\infty} n^{-s}, \qquad \Re(s) > 1.$$

We are interested in values of s with real parts close to $1/2$, so we will have to use the following alternating series instead:

$$\zeta(s) = \frac{1}{1 - 2^{1-s}} \sum_{n=1}^{\infty} (-1)^{n-1} n^{-s}, \qquad \Re(s) > 0. \tag{4.3}$$

This can be used directly to define a function in Maple:

```
[> f := s -> 1/(1-2^(1-s))*                                          1
           sum((-1)^(n-1)/(n^s),n=1..infinity);                      2
```

However, computing f(3) gives the unhelpful answer $\zeta(3)$. Unsurprisingly, Maple knows this series and immediately connects it to ζ. For the purpose of this discussion, we prefer to force Maple to do a numerical computation based on Equation (4.3). For that purpose, define

```
[> zeta := (s,N) -> evalf(1/(1-2^(1-s))*                             1
           add((-1)^(n-1)/(n^s),n=1..N));                            2
```

Here, the variable N determines the number of terms in the series to use for the approximation. The challenge of choosing N large enough to give a good approximation, but small enough to allow practical computation, will be discussed in Chapter 7. For now, we will simply use $N = 200$, hoping that this will provide a suitable compromise.

The figure in the box on p. 109 shows a plot of the absolute value of zeta(s,200). Inspecting this figure reveals deep valleys in the absolute value of the function (this is much easier to see on the screen where the plot can be rotated). Considering the warning about the resolution of 3d plots given earlier, one might suspect that these valleys could actually be zeroes of the function. Specifically, it seems interesting to investigate certain points around the line $1/2 + it$ further:

```
[> fsolve(zeta(s,300) = 0,s=1/2+14*I,complex);                       1
   fsolve(zeta(s,300) = 0,s=1/2+22*I,complex);                       2
   fsolve(zeta(s,300) = 0,s=1/2+25*I,complex);                       3
   fsolve(zeta(s,300) = 0,s=1/2+30*I,complex);                       4
```

According to these calculations, there are zeroes of ζ near $0.508 + 14.147i$, $0.507 + 21.012i$, $0.490 + 25.019i$, and $0.493 + 30.432i$. From this, it looks like our guess based on the visual inspection was correct, and we have found approximations of 4 zeroes of the zeta function. Indeed, the numbers match the ones presented in Figure 3.9. This is clearly a very limited investigation, but note that the data supports the Riemann hypothesis. As could be expected, the approximation used results in zeroes that lie close to, but not precisely on, the critical line $1/2 + it$.

◁

4.1.8 Transforming Data

The great benefit of plotting data is that it allows the experimenter to search for interesting structures visually. This will often make it possible to notice trends and dependencies that are hidden when considering the raw data.

Given a set of data consisting of points in $\mathbb{R}^2$, it is generally fairly easy for the human eye and mind to tell whether there might be a linear dependency between the first and the second coordinates. However, it is much harder to recognize dependencies given by more complicated functions, and hence, several tools have traditionally been used to transform data into a form where a complicated dependency will be translated into a linear relation, for example single and double logarithmic paper and various types of probability distribution paper.

The fundamental idea when transforming a data set consisting of points $(x_1, y_1), \ldots, (x_n, y_n) \in \mathbb{R}^2$ is to a apply a pair of functions f_x, f_y (one of which could be the identity) to each element to produce the transformed values $\{(f_x(x_i), f_y(y_i))\}$. Usually, both f_x and f_y are going to be injections to create a direct correspondence between the original and the transformed data points. If it is possible to find a (hypothesis about) a simple dependency between the first and the second coordinate of the transformed data points, then this can be translated into a similar statement about the original data points.

Logarithms are the most commonly used transformations, and in Maple, it is easy to see how a data set behaves under a logarithmic transformation by plotting it (using `pointplot`) and changing the way the axes are represented (by right-clicking on the resulting figure and choosing from the menu). However, it is also straightforward to make much more complicated transformations: given functions f_x, f_y, the corresponding transformation of data can be carried out in Maple using `map` to construct new lists or vectors of data from the originals. Obviously, it can be highly nontrivial to find the transformations that make the underlying structure of the dataset apparent.

Example 4.1.8: Transforming data. Figure 4.7 shows a plot of the following data set before and after transforming with $f_x(t) = t^3$ and $f_y(t) = \ln t$.

x	0.2	0.4	0.6	0.8	1.0	1.2	1.4	1.6	1.8
y	2.0	2.0	2.2	2.6	3.2	4.6	8.2	15	36

The transformation reveals that the data seem to follow a relation of the form $y = b \exp(ax^{1/3})$ for some undetermined values of a and b. The next section is dedicated to the search for the best possible educated guess of the values of parameters like a and b in situations like this.

◁

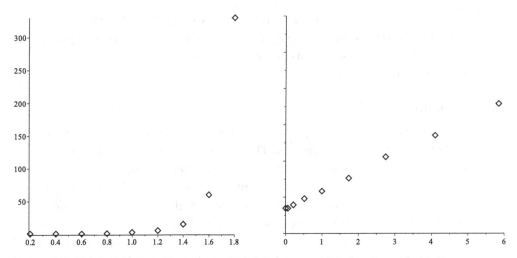

Figure 4.7 Original (left) and transformed (right) data considered in Example 4.1.8.

So far, only transformations of two-dimensional data have been discussed.
A similar approach could clearly be applied to higher-dimensional data sets,
but then the visual inspection is more difficult and will require 3d-plots and
other related plotting commands.

4.2 Fitting

Given a set of data points $(x_1, y_1), \ldots, (x_n, y_n) \in \mathbb{R}^2$ and a *model* $f_{\bar{p}} \colon \mathbb{R} \to \mathbb{R}$ depending on the *parameters* $\bar{p} \in \mathbb{R}^m$, *fitting* is the process of finding the value of
$\bar{p}$ that gives the best possible global match between $f_{\bar{p}}(x_i)$ and y_i. The precise
definition of what is meant by *best possible* will be given in Section 4.2.2.

4.2.1 *Choosing a Model*

The first and most important step when attempting to fit a function to data
is naturally to choose the right model based on the behavior of the data. If
it is possible to transform the data into an approximately linear data set, as
discussed in the previous section, then this immediately gives input that can
be used to determine a suitable model. For instance, considering the data and
transformation from Example 4.1.8, one might choose a model of the form
$y = b \exp(ax^{1/3})$. In this way, transformation of data becomes an important
tool when selecting a model to use in a fit.

Clearly, any kind of function could potentially serve as the model for a
set of data, but certain models are used much more extensively than others
because they can be applied in many different applications and/or are easy
to work with. Commonly used models include: linear functions ($y = ax + b$),
exponential functions ($y = ba^x$) power functions ($y = bx^a$) and polynomials.

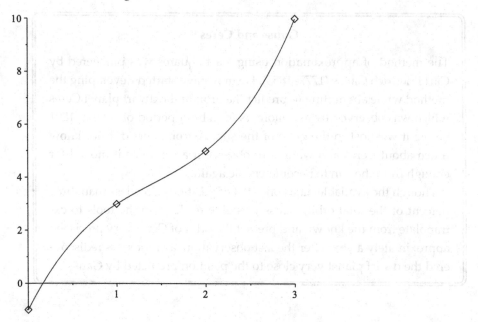

Figure 4.8 Fitting a third order polynomial to four data points.

Unless there is a theoretical reason to expect polynomial behavior, one should generally think of polynomial models as power series approximations to a true underlying, but undetermined, model. If one is considering a part of the domain where a specific term of the polynomial dominates the others, it will be hard to distinguish polynomial data from the corresponding power data, and if two or more terms are significant in the considered range, it can be difficult to determine their relationship.

Generally, one will be able to get smaller errors in a fit by introducing more parameters to the model. Given a collection of n points in the plane, there is, for instance, precisely one polynomial of degree $n - 1$ that intersects all the points. In this sense, the polynomial gives a very good fit to the data. However, that does not mean that such a polynomial model gives a good description of underlying behavior of the data. This is illustrated in Figure 4.8 where a third order polynomial has been designed to pass through each of the four data points. Clearly, this does not imply that the polynomial gives a good description of the underlying structure of the data. Indeed, the points seem to lie approximately on a straight line.

4.2.2 Least Squares

Let $(x_1, y_1), \ldots, (x_n, y_n) \in \mathbb{R}^2$ be a set of data points, and let $f_{\bar{p}} \colon \mathbb{R} \to \mathbb{R}$ be a model depending on the parameters $\bar{p} \in \mathbb{R}^m$. The aim of this section is to formalize the notion of a fit. To do this, we need to establish a suitable measure of the quality of the match between the values $f_{\bar{p}}(x_i)$ and y_i in order to be able to find the best possible match.

Gauss and Ceres

The method of approximation using least squares was pioneered by Carl Friedrich Gauss (1777–1855). He may have started developing the method while attempting to predict the orbit of the dwarf planet Ceres which was observed by astronomers for a brief period of time in 1801 before it was lost in the glare of the sun. Astronomers did not know much about Ceres and wanted to observe it again once it moved far enough from the sun to become visible again.

Though the available data consisted of positions from less than three percent of the total orbit, Gauss was able to develop the tools to extrapolate from the known and predict the orbit of Ceres very precisely: approximately a year after the last observation, astronomers rediscovered the dwarf planet very close to the position predicted by Gauss.

Let $\bar{x} = (x_1, \ldots, x_n), \bar{y} = (y_1, \ldots, y_n) \in \mathbb{R}^n$, and define $f_{\bar{p}}(\bar{x})$ to be the vector $(f_{\bar{p}}(x_1), \ldots, f_{\bar{p}}(x_n)) \in \mathbb{R}^n$. Now, the obvious choice for a measure of the distance between $f_{\bar{p}}(\bar{x})$ and $\bar{y}$ is the standard 2-norm on $\mathbb{R}^n$:

$$||f_{\bar{p}}(\bar{x}) - \bar{y}|| = \left(\sum_{i=1}^{n} (f_{\bar{p}}(x_i) - y_i)^2 \right)^{1/2}.$$

Normalizing by the number of observations to get a quantity that does not increase simply by adding more observations yields the *mean squared error*:

$$\frac{1}{n} ||f_{\bar{p}}(\bar{x}) - \bar{y}||^2 = \frac{1}{n} \sum_{i=1}^{n} (f_{\bar{p}}(x_i) - y_i)^2.$$

The process of fitting is then a search for the choice of $\bar{p}$ that gives the smallest possible value of the norm $||f_{\bar{p}}(\bar{x}) - \bar{y}||$—or equivalently—of the mean squared error. In some cases, it can be natural and beneficial to use other measures of the quality of a fitted function than the mean square error, but it goes beyond the scope of this book to discuss them.

While searching for a fit, the observations $\bar{x}, \bar{y} \in \mathbb{R}^n$ are considered to be constant, while the parameters $\bar{p} \in \mathbb{R}^m$ are variable. Hence, it is natural to consider the model as a function—not of the observations—but of the parameters. Define $F \colon \mathbb{R}^m \to \mathbb{R}^n$ by $F(\bar{p}) = f_{\bar{p}}(\bar{x})$. The goal in finding a fit then becomes to find the point in the image $\operatorname{im} F \subseteq \mathbb{R}^n$ closest to $\bar{y} \in \mathbb{R}^n$. In general, the subset $F(\mathbb{R}^m)$ may be very complicated and that makes the problem of finding the point closest to $\bar{y}$ highly nontrivial. However, as discussed in the next section, it is possible to give a closed form solution when F is a linear function.

4.2.3 Linear Fitting

Let $\bar{x}, \bar{y} \in \mathbb{R}^n$, let $f_{\bar{p}} \colon \mathbb{R} \to \mathbb{R}$ be a model depending on parameters $\bar{p}$, and let $F \colon \mathbb{R}^m \to \mathbb{R}^n$ be defined as in the previous section. Assume that F is linear, and let A be the matrix such that $F(\bar{p}) = A\bar{p}$ for all $\bar{p} \in \mathbb{R}^m$. A will be denoted the *parameter matrix*. Then $\operatorname{im} F = F(\mathbb{R}^m)$ is a subspace of $\mathbb{R}^n$ which will be denoted the *model space*. This makes it possible to use the powerful tools of linear algebra to examine the problem.

Example 4.2.1: Linearity. Note that the assumption is that the model function is linear in the parameters. This does not imply that it is also linear in the variables of the data. Consider, for instance, the model $f_{(a,b,c)}(x) = ax^2 + bx + c$ which is linear in the parameters (a, b, c), but not in x.   ◁

Let $\bar{y}'$ be the orthogonal projection of $\bar{y}$ on $\operatorname{im} F$. Then $\bar{y}'$ is closer to $\bar{y}$ in norm than any other element of $\operatorname{im} F$, so in order to solve the least squares problem, it is sufficient to find $\bar{p} \in \mathbb{R}^m$ such that $F(\bar{p}) = A\bar{p} = \bar{y}'$.

Hence, $\bar{p}$ is a solution to the least squares problem if and only if $A\bar{p} - \bar{y} \in (\operatorname{im} F)^{\perp}$. This is the case if and only if $A\bar{p} - \bar{y} \in \ker F^*$. Hence, the goal is to solve the equation $0 = A^{\mathsf{T}}(A\bar{p} - \bar{y}) = A^{\mathsf{T}}A\bar{p} - A^{\mathsf{T}}\bar{y}$ which is equivalent to

$$A^{\mathsf{T}}A\bar{p} = A^{\mathsf{T}}\bar{y}. \tag{4.4}$$

This system of n equations in n unknowns is called the *normal equations* of the least squares problem. In general, the matrix $A^{\mathsf{T}}A$ will not be invertible, so this equation does not necessarily have a unique solution. However, note that there always exists a solution and that the orthogonal projection $\bar{y}'$ is unique, so if $\bar{p}_1, \bar{p}_2$ are both solutions to (4.4) then $A\bar{p}_1 = \bar{y}' = A\bar{p}_2$. In other words, the models given by parameters $\bar{p}_1$ and $\bar{p}_2$ have precisely the same values at all the data points given by $\bar{x}$.

If $A^{\mathsf{T}}A$ is invertible, then the unique solution to the least squares problem is $\bar{p}' = (A^{\mathsf{T}}A)^{-1}A^{\mathsf{T}}\bar{y}$, and the element of the model space $\operatorname{im} F$ closest to $\bar{y}$ in norm is $A(A^{\mathsf{T}}A)^{-1}A^{\mathsf{T}}y$. The matrix $A(A^{\mathsf{T}}A)^{-1}A^{\mathsf{T}}$ is known as the *projection matrix*.

If $(A^{\mathsf{T}}A)$ is not invertible, then the solution to the normal equation is not unique, and it is necessary to employ powerful specialized algorithms to find a solution. These algorithms will often employ numerical solutions rather than exact solutions to speed up the process. Such fitting algorithms are implemented in Maple, but it goes beyond the scope of this book to discuss them in detail.

Example 4.2.2: Fitting by hand. As an example of a linear fit, consider the data set given by

$$\bar{x} = \begin{bmatrix} 0 \\ 1 \\ 2 \\ 3 \end{bmatrix} \quad \text{and} \quad \bar{y} = \begin{bmatrix} -1 \\ 3 \\ 5 \\ 10 \end{bmatrix}$$

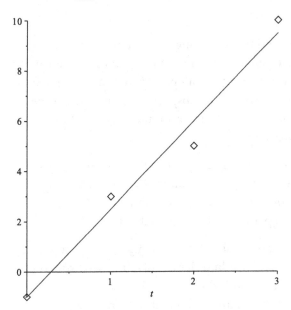

Figure 4.9 The linear fit constructed in Example 4.2.2.

with the model $f_{(a,b)}(x) = ax + b$. The model function $F \colon \mathbb{R}^2 \to \mathbb{R}^4$ is given by the matrix

$$A = \begin{bmatrix} 0 & 1 \\ 1 & 1 \\ 2 & 1 \\ 3 & 1 \end{bmatrix}$$

which should be interpreted as $f_{(a,b)}(x_4) = a \cdot 3 + b$, and so forth. Now,

$$A^{\mathrm{T}}A = \begin{bmatrix} 14 & 6 \\ 6 & 4 \end{bmatrix} \quad \text{and} \quad (A^{\mathrm{T}}A)^{-1} = \frac{1}{10} \begin{bmatrix} 2 & -3 \\ -3 & 7 \end{bmatrix}$$

so the optimal choice of parameters is

$$\begin{bmatrix} a' \\ b' \end{bmatrix} = (A^{\mathrm{T}}A)^{-1}A^{\mathrm{T}}y = \begin{bmatrix} 7/2 \\ -1 \end{bmatrix}.$$

The resulting line is plotted together with the data in Figure 4.9.   ◁

4.2.4 Nonlinear Fitting

Generally, it is much harder to fit a nonlinear model to data than it is to fit a linear model, and several specialized tools have been developed to handle such problems. Consider a set of data points $(x_1, y_1), \ldots, (x_n, y_n) \in \mathbb{R}^2$ and a model $f_{\bar{p}} \colon \mathbb{R} \to \mathbb{R}$ depending on the parameters $\bar{p} \in \mathbb{R}^m$. Unlike in the linear case, there is generally not a unique element $\bar{y}' \in \operatorname{im} F$ closest to $\bar{y}$, and this makes it much harder to find a good fit.

A nonlinear fit is often obtained through a series of successive approximations, and this leaves the process vulnerable to being caught in a local minimum of the quantity being minimized, for example the distance. The successive approximations are normally initiated from given starting values of the variables in question, and the approximation process may very well depend greatly on these chosen starting values. Hence, it is important to try several different relevant starting values, so the resulting fits can be compared. In very nonlinear problems, it can be difficult to find a good fit, even for data without much noise. This is examined in Exercise 4.31.

4.2.5 Fitting in Maple

Maple has a single command, called `Fit`, that can handle both linear and nonlinear models. It will call an underlying procedure to carry out either a linear or a nonlinear fit depending on the model given. The basic syntax is

```
[> with(Statistics):                                              1
   X := <1,2,3,4,5,6,7,8,9,10>:                                   2
   Y := <1.2,1.8,2.9,4.5,5.1,6.1,7.0,7.5,8.9,10.2>:              3
   Fit(a*x+b,X,Y,x);                                              4
```

$$.983030303030303x + .113333333333334$$

Note that the data set is given in the form of two *vectors* and that the independent variable(s) must be given explicitly to distinguish them from the parameters. The command `convert(L, vector)` is useful for converting a list of data to the format required by `Fit`. Note also that Maple will use the full precision specified by the current value of the variable `Digits` when returning the result. This is not to be taken as an indication that the data allows the coefficients to be determined with that kind of precision.

4.2.6 Quality of Fit

Assume that a model has been fitted to a data set so that the least squares error has been minimized as described in the previous sections. How good is this fit actually? After all, if the model is wrong, even the best possible fit may not match the data very well.

The first and most important test of the quality of a fit should always be a visual inspection of a plot of the data together with the fitted function. This will often give a very good idea about whether the function gives a good approximation or not.

For a rigorous analysis of the goodness of a fit, one could use the huge body of statistical tools developed for the investigation of experimental data in all branches of science. This could potentially be very useful for the experimenting mathematician, but unlike the other sciences, experimental mathematics does not rely on statistical inference to draw final conclusions from data. No

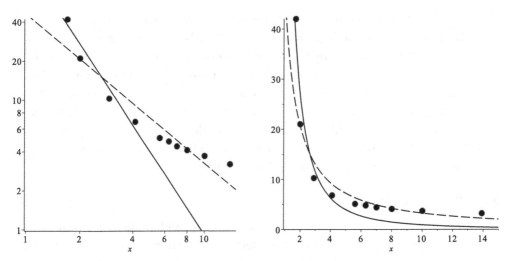

Figure 4.10 Data and functions considered in Example 4.2.3. The solid curve is the graph of the
function obtained trough a nonlinear fit to the original data while the dotted curve is
the graph of the function obtained by fitting a linear model to the transformed data.
The axes in the left figure are logarithmic while the axes on the right are not.

matter how well a hypothesized model corresponds to a set of data, the experimenting mathematician is not going to conclude that this model captures
the true behavior of the system. A good correspondence will be the basis of
a reasonable hypothesis, but the hypothesis does not become a mathematical result before there is a proof. Hence, the experimenting mathematician
may well be less dependent on rigorous statistical analysis than colleagues in
other natural sciences, and statistical tools are not going to be a major topic
in this book.

Example 4.2.3: Fitting to transformed data.   The following table shows a
sequence of observations.

x	1.7	2.0	2.9	4.1	5.6	6.3	7.0	8.0	10.0	13.9
y	42.0	21.0	10.3	6.8	5.1	4.8	4.4	4.1	3.7	3.2

Assume that we are asked to find the best possible fit of a decaying power
function to these data:

```
[> X := <1.7,2.0,2.9,4.1,5.6,6.3,7.0,8.0,10.0,13.9>:          1
   Y := <42.0,21.0,10.3,6.8,5.1,4.8,4.4,4.1,3.7,3.2>:          2
   f := unapply(Fit(b*x^a,X,Y,x),x);                           3
```

$$f := x \to \frac{115.71107860347986}{x^{2.1019491692315294}}$$

To check the validity of the fit, consider the first graph in Figure 4.10, where
the function f (the solid line) has been plotted together with the data in a logarithmic coordinate system. This figure makes it clear that the points do not

approximate a straight line very well. In fact, there seems to be a completely
different trend that makes the points lie on a convex curve. Clearly, the model
is not very good, and this illustrates the paramount importance of inspecting
fits visually.

In an experimental investigation, this plot would be sufficient evidence to
drop the proposed model. However, here we will use the bad model to expose
another problem: If you attempt to make the same fit on a calculator or in a
spreadsheet, it may well result in a completely different function. Such tools
may not be able to make an exponential fit by minimizing the least squares
error as described above. Instead, they will carry out a logarithmic transformation of the data, construct a straightforward linear fit to the transformed
values, and retransform the resulting answer. Generally, this will result in a
drastically different fit, because the method lends much more weight to small
errors on small values than a fit to the untransformed data does.

To illustrate this difference between fitting before and after transforming
the data, the following commands serve to transform the data and fit a linear
model to the transformed data set.

```
[> X_transformed := map(x -> ln(x),X):                    1
   Y_transformed := map(y -> ln(y),Y):                    2
   Fit(a*x+b,X_transformed,Y_transformed,x);              3
```

$$-1.15357277252544x + 3.83071571265096$$

Based on this, the fitted function should be $g(x) = \exp(3.83)x^{-1.2}$.

To compare the two fits visually, use the following commands to define g
and plot the functions together with the data.

```
[> g := x -> exp(3.8)*x^(-1.2);                           1
   display([pointplot([X,Y],symbolsize=20,                2
           symbol=solidcircle),                           3
           plot([f(x),g(x)], x=1..15,                     4
           linestyle=[solid,dash])]);                     5
```

The result is shown in Figure 4.10, f is the solid curve and g is the dotted
curve. In the left-hand figure, it looks like g gives the best approximation,
but in the right-hand figure it becomes apparent that g is only better for large
values of x, and that there is a significant deviation from the data for small
values of x.   ◁

The previous example may serve as a warning about the dangers associated
with fitting to transformed data rather than carrying out a nonlinear fit to the
original data. However, nonlinear fitting is a nontrivial operation, and Maple
may not always be able to produce a reasonable fit using the normal method.
In such cases, it is certainly worthwhile to attempt a fit to transformed
data.

4.2.7 Discarding Data

When considering (a graphical representation of) a data set, it will sometimes happen that a number of data points deviate significantly from the apparent trend of the rest of the data. In such cases, one might be tempted to disregard the troublesome points in order to get a better fit from the rest of the data. In general, this can be a very dangerous undertaking because the experimenter runs the risk of discarding interesting examples or (subconsciously) modifying the data to match a hypothesis.

Nevertheless, it might be worth investigating what happens when discarding such data points, particularly considering that the experimental process is a tool for the formulation of conjectures, and not a direct source for mathematical results. In such cases, one should keep careful track of the points being left out and make sure that they are not actually caused by an undiscovered counterexample to the hypothesis under consideration. This is one part of the experimental process that should not normally be automated.

In particular, when considering a hypothesis concerning the eventual behavior of a sequence of numbers (e.g. that the numbers converge to a specific number or increase with a certain rate of growth) it is perfectly reasonable to discard some of the first observations. After all, the eventual behavior is independent of any finite subsequence. This approach is employed in the following example.

EX. 3.3.4 → **Example 4.2.4: A nonlinear fit.** Consider again the problem concerning balanced LEGO towers from Example 3.3.4. Based on the observation of $(B_n)_{n=1}^{12}$ and $(\beta_n)_{n=1}^{12}$, Watson conjectured that the two sequences (B_n) and (β_n) grow, respectively, as

$$\frac{3^{n-1}}{n \log_3(n)} \quad \text{and} \quad \frac{3^{n-1}}{\log_3(n)}.$$

As we shall see, this was certainly a very reasonable conjecture based on the data available to Watson. Using the fact that $B_N = t_{N,0}$ and $\beta_N = \sum_{i=-(N-1)}^{N-1} t_{N,i}$, the efficient computation of $t_{N,i}$ developed in Example 3.3.4 can be used to generate far more terms of the sequences than the 12 available to Watson, and we can use this extra data to challenge the conjecture.

It appears evident that the sequences (B_n) and (β_n) grow exponentially, so the first goal is to test whether Watson's conjecture about the growth rates is correct. To do this, we will fit a suitable model to the data. However, due to the large variation in the data values, Maple has problems finding a good nonlinear fit. Hence, we will settle for a linear fit to the transformed data sets $(n, \ln(\beta_n))$ and $(n, \ln(B_n))$. Considering the first 300 terms, this yields

$$\ln(B_n) \approx 1.08n - 5.51 \text{ and } \ln(\beta_n) \approx 1.09n - 2.24.$$

These functions are plotted together with the first 50 terms of the sequences in Figure 4.11.

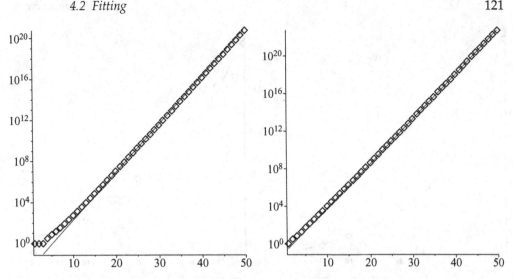

Figure 4.11 Plots of $(B_n)_{n=1}^{50}$ (left) and $(\beta_n)_{n=1}^{50}$ (right) together with the functions fitted in Section 4.2.4. Note the mismatch due to the nonlinear behavior for small values of n.

Looking at Figure 4.11, the sequences seem to have a nonlinear behavior for small values of n while they are progressively better approximated by the lines as n grows. Since we are interested in the (eventual) rate of growth, it makes sense to consider only, say, the last 50 observations. This yields the fits

$$\ln(B_n) \approx 1.093n - 8.182 \quad \text{and} \quad \ln(\beta_n) \approx 1.097n - 2.885.$$

Plotting these function with the data points reveals an extremely good correspondence, in fact, the points appear to lie exactly on the lines.

This experiment appears sufficient to determine the slopes with approximately two decimals of precision. Considering that $\ln 3 = 1.0986\ldots$, it is natural to assume that both sequences grow like 3^n. This conjecture is supported by the fact that the sequences are derived from $\{-1, 0, 1\}^{(N-1)}$, so we will assume that this is true and focus on the less significant components of the rate of growth by studying the sequences $(\widehat{B}_n)$ and $(\widehat{\beta}_n)$ given by

$$\widehat{B}_n = B_n/3^{-n+1} \quad \text{and} \quad \widehat{\beta}_n = \beta_n/3^{-n+1}.$$

These numbers give the fractions of all buildings that are, respectively, stable and maximally stable.

According to Watson's conjecture, these numbers should decrease as, respectively,

$$\frac{1}{n\log_3(n)} \quad \text{and} \quad \frac{1}{\log_3(n)}.$$

Figure 4.12 shows such functions fitted to the data consisting of the first 12 terms of $(\widehat{B}_n)$ and $(\widehat{\beta}_n)$ which were available to Watson. For $(\widehat{B}_n)$, the fit matches the data remarkably well, but for $(\widehat{\beta}_n)$, there could be a systematic deviation.

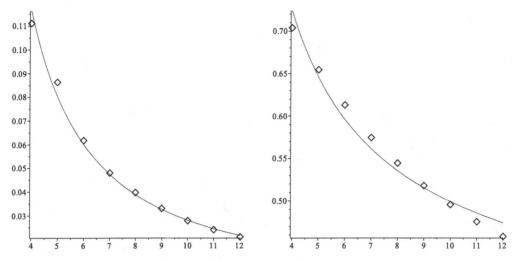

Figure 4.12   Watson's fits to $(\widehat{\beta}_n)$ and $(\widehat{B}_n)$. Left: Plot of $(\widehat{B}_n)_{n=4}^{12}$ and the function $\frac{0.58}{x\log_3 x}$ fitted to the data. Right: Plot of $(\widehat{\beta}_n)_{n=4}^{12}$ and the function $\frac{0.71}{\log_3 x} + 0.16$ fitted to the data.

However, plotting far more observations of $(\widehat{B}_n)$ and $(\widehat{\beta}_n)$ in a double logarithmic coordinate systems as in Figure 4.13 reveals that both Watson's conjectures fail: the sequences tend toward a power function dependency on n, and the two conjectures are not supported much beyond the observations available to Watson himself. Indeed, the curves shown in Figure 4.13 are the same functions as seen in Figure 4.12, and apparently these models do not give very good descriptions of the data for large values of n.

Hence, we must abandon Watson's conjecture; searching instead for a power function decay of the form bn^{-a}. To do this, we fit linear models to the transformed data $(\ln(n), \ln(\widehat{\beta}_n))$ and $(\ln n, \ln(\widehat{B}_n))$. Considering the first

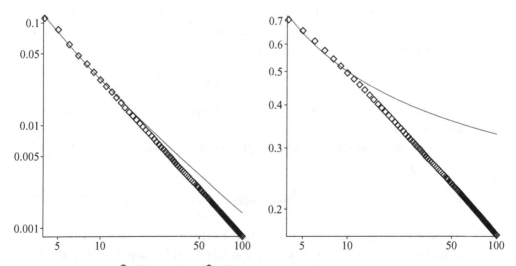

Figure 4.13   Plots of $(\widehat{B}_n)_{n=1}^{100}$ (left) and $(\widehat{\beta}_n)_{n=1}^{100}$ (right) in double logarithmic coordinate systems. The curves are the same as in Figure 4.12.

300 terms, this yields

$$\ln(\widehat{B}_n) \approx -1.507n - 0.126 \text{ and } \ln(\widehat{\beta}_n) \approx -0.470n + 0.372.$$

Considering only the terms from $n = 250$ to $n = 300$, gives

$$\ln(\widehat{B}_n) \approx -1.501n - 0.157 \text{ and } \ln(\widehat{\beta}_n) \approx -0.497n + 0.506.$$

Plotting these final fits with the relevant data points reveals an extremely good correspondence. Noting that the coefficient of the first order terms are close to $-3/2$ and $-1/2$, respectively, we formulate the hypothesis that there exist b_1, b_2 such that $\widehat{\beta}_n = b_1 n^{-1/2}$ and $\widehat{B}_n = b_2 n^{-3/2}$. Clearly, the fits are not precise enough to confidently claim that this is the true behavior, but it is certainly a very reasonable conjecture that would warrant closer theoretical

EX. 4.3.1 ← investigation. ◁

As seen above, the ability to recognize constants from floating point approximations greatly facilitates the formulation of concise, testable hypotheses. For numbers like $1/2$ or $2/3$, this is straightforward, but many interesting mathematical constants are not so easy to recognize, and the next chapter will introduce a collection of tools that can help in such an identification.

4.3 Probability Distributions

In the other natural sciences, data from an experiment will often take the form of a series of observations—called a *sample*—of an underlying stochastic variable. This is less common in mathematical experiments where the uncertainty in measurements plays a much smaller role, but the finite precision of the calculations done by a computer may mean that aggregated computational errors result in noise comparable to the uncertainties of measurement encountered in other fields. Hence, experimental mathematics can also benefit from the tools that facilitate the identification of the statistical distribution of a stochastic variable based on a sample. Additionally, statistical distributions show up in various counting problems. We will touch on this subject again, when we discuss confidence intervals in Section 6.5.

In Maple, one can use the function `ProbabilityPlot` to investigate whether a model distribution matches a given sample. To determine whether two samples were drawn from the same underlying distribution, one can use a `QuantilePlot` which works by comparing the *quantiles* of the samples.

EX. 4.2.4 → **Example 4.3.1: Distribution.** Consider again the problem of counting (maximally) balanced LEGO towers that was introduced in Example 1.6.5. As seen previously, for each N, the sequence $t_{N,w}$ can be used to compute the number of balanced and maximally balanced LEGO towers efficiently. Since this sequence is so central to the problem, it might be possible to get more insight by investigating the sequences $t_{N,w}$ directly.

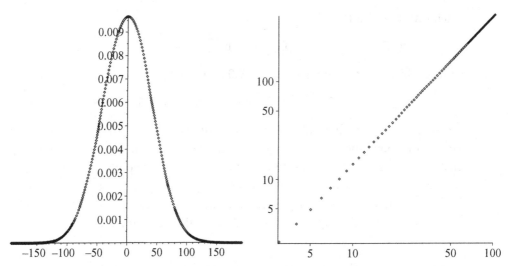

Figure 4.14 Left: A plot of $(w, t_{20,w})$. Right: A plot of the variance of $t_{N,w}$ as a function of N in a double logarithmic coordinate system.

Figure 4.14 shows the points $(w, t_{20,w})$. Note that the graph seems to look like the graph of the probability function of a *normal distribution* with mean 0. Such a probability function is given by

$$p(x) = \frac{1}{\sqrt{2\pi}\sigma} e^{-\frac{x^2}{2\sigma^2}},$$

where σ^2 is the *variance* of the distribution. Considering this as a model with a single parameter σ, it is straightforward to obtain a fit using Maple. This gives the value $\sigma = 41.18$, and a graph that matches the points extremely well (examined in Exercise 4.33).

Clearly, such a variance σ_N^2 can be computed for every value of N. Figure 4.14 shows a plot of σ_N as a function of N. The axes are logarithmic, so this indicates that the variance grows as a power function. Fitting a power EX. 5.2.7 ← function to these data yields $0.45x^{1.50}$.   ◁

4.4 Exercises

Warmup

Exercise 4.1 Execute the following command:

```
[> plot([seq(x^2+n*x,n=0..10)], x =-1..1,               1
        color = [seq(HUE(1/10*n),n=0..10)]);            2
```

Explain how HUE may be useful in an automated construction of figures.

Exercise 4.2 How does plot handle each of the following kinds of input?

- A list of points (each point given as a list of two elements)
- A list or set containing several functions.
- A list or set containing both functions and expressions.

Exercise 4.3 Search for *plotting guide* in the Maple help system to get an overview of the various plotting commands. Identify the commands suitable for solving the following tasks and use each of them in an example.

- Plotting a parametric curve.
- Plotting an implicitly given curve.

Exercise 4.4 Make a plot of the functions $f, g \colon \mathbb{R} \to \mathbb{R}$ defined by $f(x) = x^3$ and $g(x) = \cos(\pi x)$ on the interval $[-1, 1]$. Use optional arguments to

- add a caption and labels for the axes,
- move or remove the axes,
- change the colors of the graphs and change the solid lines to dotted and dashed lines, respectively.

Exercise 4.5 Make a nice-looking plot of $f(x) = x$ and $g(x) = 1/(x-1)$ on the interval $[-5, 5]$ in the same coordinate system.

Exercise 4.6 Which line does $y = ba^x$ correspond to when y is transformed by a logarithm? Which line does $y = bx^a$ correspond to when both coordinates are transformed by logarithms?

Exercise 4.7 Define a procedure that takes a model and a data set as input, and returns a fit of the model to the data after plotting the data points and the resulting function in the same coordinate system.

EX. 4.2.2 → **Exercise 4.8** Consider the data and model from Example 4.2.2. Make a fit in Maple and plot the resulting function together with the data. Compare with the result given in the example.

Homework

Exercise 4.9 Use `display` to combine plots of the circle with center $(0, 0)$ and radius 1, the line $y = \frac{1}{3}(1 + x)$, and your own choice of symbols for the points of intersection (use `implicitplot` for the circle).

Exercise 4.10 Design a procedure that given a function $f \colon \mathbb{R} \to \mathbb{R}$ and a value $x_0 \in \mathbb{R}$ displays and returns a plot of f on an interval around x_0 together with lines connecting $(x_0, f(x_0))$ with respectively $(x_0, 0)$ and $(0, f(x_0))$. Add information about the coordinates of the point $(x_0, f(x_0))$ at an appropriate place in the plot.

Exercise 4.11 Consider the model $y = ax^2 + bx + c$ and the data given in the following table.

x	1	2	3	4	5
y	1.3	1.9	3.5	5.9	9.5

Construct the parameter matrix A. Use Maple to compute A^TA, and use this to compute the least squares solution. Plot the result together with the data.

Exercise 4.12 Consider the data and model from Exercise 4.11. Make a fit in Maple and plot the resulting function together with the data. Compare with the result obtained in Exercise 4.11.

Exercise 4.13 For each $N \in \mathbb{N}$, a sequence (s_n) is defined in Exercise 3.10. In combinatorial game theory, it is desirable to find out whether such sequences are *periodic*. For each $N \in \{1, \ldots, 5\}$, plot the points (n, s_n) for n from 1 to 100. Does this representation make it easier to look for repeating patterns?

EX. 1.6.4 → **Exercise 4.14** Write a procedure that given $X > 0$ plots $\pi(x)$, $\mathrm{Li}(x)$ and $x/\ln(x)$ on the interval $[0, X]$. Use it to recreate Figure 1.4.

EX. 1.6.2 → **Exercise 4.15** Write a procedure that given three integers (a, b, c) will draw a triangle with these side lengths (if possible), placing tick marks at every integer value to make it easy to see by inspection that the sides indeed are integral.

EX. 1.6.2 → **Exercise 4.16** Write a procedure which, given $N \in \mathbb{N}$, produces a plot of all points (a, b) with $a, b < N$ and $a^2 + b^2 = c^2$ for some $c \in \mathbb{N}$. For sufficiently large N, (at least) two patterns can be observed in the distribution of these points. Describe and explain these patterns.

EX. 4.1.4 → **Exercise 4.17** Identify as many patterns as possible in the sequence of partition function values $(p(n))_{n \in \mathbb{N}}$.

Exercise 4.18 Quantify the difference in the least squares error between an exponential fit and the linear fit to the corresponding transformed data. How does this influence the resulting fits?

EX. 3.3.3 → **Exercise 4.19** Consider again the procedure `ruinProbability`. The command `[seq([i,ruinProbability(i,100)],i=1..90)]` will generate a list of points (n, P_n), where P_n is the probability of ruin after playing 100 games with a starting capital of n. Identify the transformation that must be applied to a data set (x_i, y_i) to put it on a straight line if $y = e^{-\beta x^\alpha}$ and apply it to the given data set. Does this model give a good description of the data? Can you find a better model for the data?

EX. 4.1.3 → **Exercise 4.20** Many other fractals can be defined using iterations of maps like the one considered in Example 4.1.3, one of them is the *Minkowski sausage* which is generated by iterations of the following substitution:

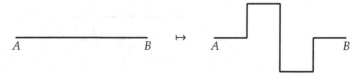

Write a procedure that produces a plot of the iterations of this map. Can you create similar iterated plots based on other substitutions?

EX. 4.1.5 → **Exercise 4.21** Use Table 4.1 to formulate a conjecture about the solvability of $-2 \equiv x^2 \pmod{p}$. Test the hypothesis by considering larger primes.

EX. 4.1.5 → **Exercise 4.22** Write a procedure for testing whether a is a quadratic residue modulo p, its output should be equal to that of the built-in procedure quadres. (Hint: use the same test as in Example 4.1.5). Test the procedure against quadres by visualizing a matrix where each entry is the difference between the values of the two procedures.

EX. 4.1.5 → **Exercise 4.23** Identify patterns in the primes modulo which a is a quadratic residue for $a \in \{\pm 7, \pm 11\}$. Check that the result is in accordance with the quadratic reciprocity theorem.

EX. 4.1.5 → **Exercise 4.24** Construct a procedure that given a positive integer N plots two $N \times N$ matrices analogous to the ones considered in Figure 4.5.

EX. 4.1.5 → **Exercise 4.25** Let p be a prime. An integer a is said to be a *biquadratic residue modulo p* if $a \equiv b^4 \pmod{p}$ for some $0 < b < p$.

(a) Make experiments to formulate a hypothesis on which p allow -1 to be a biquadratic residue.

(b) Assuming that the hypothesis is true, prove (3.14).

Exercise 4.26 To return a single random sample from the normal distribution with mean mu and variance sigma, one can use the command

```
[> Statistics[Sample](Normal(mu,sigma),1);                                    1
```

Write a procedure that given a real function $f, \sigma \in \mathbb{R}$, and x in the domain of f, returns a sample y from the normal distribution with mean $f(x)$ and variance σ.

Exercise 4.27 Write a procedure which takes a predicate P in two variables and a specification of a grid of points in $\mathbb{R}^2$ as input and returns a plot visualizing the points (x, y) on the grid satisfying $P(x, y)$.

EX. 4.1.6 → **Exercise 4.28** Reproduce the plot of the Mandelbrot set shown in Figure 4.6.

EX. 4.1.7 → **Exercise 4.29** Plot the real and imaginary parts of the Riemann zeta function.

EX. 4.2.3 → **Exercise 4.30** Compute the least squares error of the two investigated model functions f and g with respect to the original data. Do the same for the corresponding linear functions and the logarithmically transformed data.

Exercise 4.31 Use the procedure constructed in Exercise 4.26 on the function given by $f(x) = 3\cos(2x + 1)$ on the interval $[0, 4\pi]$ for variance 0.2, 0.1, and 0.01. Use Fit and the model $A\cos(Bx + C)$ on each data set and comment on the results. Is it possible to get a better fit by giving starting values for the parameters? Does it help to specify A, B, or C in the model, so it only has one or two parameters? What happens if the domain of the function is reduced, so it only contains a single period of the function or even less?

EX. 4.2.4 → **Exercise 4.32** Carry out the nonlinear fits mentioned in Example 4.2.4. Compare with results obtained in the example using linear fits to transformed data.

EX. 4.3.1 → **Exercise 4.33** Construct the fit to the data $(w, t_{20,w})$ considered in Example 4.3.1. Check with the value of σ given in the example and plot the function together with the data.

EX. 4.3.1 → **Exercise 4.34** Compute the variance of the $t_{20,w}$ data set and plot the probability function of the corresponding normal distribution together with the data. Do the same for other values of N and translate the findings to a hypothesis regarding B_N.

Exercise 4.35 Write a procedure that given a list of integers $(x_1, y_1), \ldots,$ (x_n, y_n) draws n boxes of width N and height M with the lower left-hand corner of the ith box at (x_i, y_i).

EX. 3.2.3 → **Exercise 4.36** Reproduce the graph to the left in Figure 4.15 by invoking

```
[> pointplot3d([seq(seq(                                                    1
    [i,m,coeff(expand(sum(r^m,r=1..n)),n,m+1-i)],                           2
    i=0..m+1), m=1..50)],                                                   3
    color=black,view=[0..50,0..50,-500..500]);                             4
```

Find a way to extract the most interesting features of the observations as a 2d plot with colors.

EX. 3.2.3 → **Exercise 4.37** The sparsematrixplot to the right in Figure 4.15 indicates which of the small primes $2, 3, \ldots, 71$ divide $120c_m^{(4)}$. Reproduce the figure and experiment with $252c_m^{(6)}$ and $240c_m^{(8)}$ the same way.

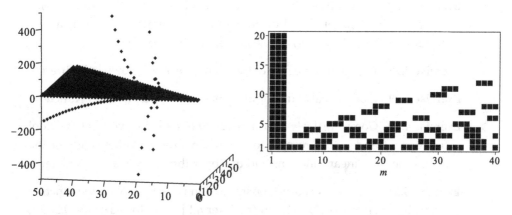

Figure 4.15 Left: 3d plot of values $c_n^{(m)}$. Right: Divisibility concerning $c_n^{(4)}$.

EX. 3.2.3 → **Exercise 4.38** Use the information experimentally obtained in Exercises 4.36 and 4.37 to formulate a hypothesis about how the values $c_m^{(i)}$ vary with m for fixed i.

EX. 2.8.2 → **Exercise 4.39** Continue the investigation carried out in Exercises 2.22 and 2.44 by plotting the frequencies of the numbers 0, 1 and 2 as a functions of $\beta \in [1, 3)$. Can you identify any simple dependencies in the three plots?

Exercise 4.40 In most cases, the number of subwords of length k of an infinite sequence will grow exponentially with k, and the growth rate is known as the *entropy* of the sequence. Write a procedure that returns an approximation of the entropy of a sequence when passed the first N elements. Beware of the problems that occur when N is not much larger than k.

Projects and Group Work

Exercise 4.41 This exercise involves at least two teams consisting of one or more people. Each team should choose five specific functions from among the models considered in Section 4.2.1. The parameters should be integers. For each function, use the procedure constructed in Exercise 4.26 to construct a randomized data set. Exchange data with another team, guess their models, and use Fit to estimate the parameters. Check your results with the other team and discuss.

BOX P. 101 → **Exercise 4.42** Look up a parametrization of the Costa–Hoffman–Meeks surface and use it to construct a plot. In order to avoid singularities, it may be necessary to construct the plot by piecing together several parts. Investigate the plot.

EX. 4.1.6 → **Exercise 4.43** Modify the plot of the Mandelbrot set constructed in Example 4.1.6 and Exercise 4.28 in the following ways:

- Add an optional parameter to the function that makes it possible specify the rectangular subset of the plane where the set should be plotted.
- Add a color gradient based on the number of iterations required to escape.
- Use display to turn an appropriate sequence of plots into an animation illustrating the self-similarity of the set by zooming in on a subset which looks identical to the whole set.

EX. 2.5.7 → **Exercise 4.44** Consider the sequences introduced in Example 2.5.7. Define a procedure that takes α and $N \in \mathbb{N}$ as input, computes the first N terms of $s(\alpha)$, and constructs a new sequence by deleting one 0 from every block of two or more 0's and one 1 from every block of two or more 1's. Let α' be the average of the terms in the modified sequence. Plot α' as a function of α. Is there a systematic dependency? If so, construct a model and make a fit.

Exercise 4.45 The logarithm function can be approximated with

$$\frac{x}{1+x} \le \ln(1+x) \le x \text{ for } x > -1,$$

and this is of great importance in, for example information theory, but it is of interest to look for better approximations with rational functions, say of the form

$$\Phi_n(x) = \frac{xP_{n-1}(x)}{Q_n(x)} \text{ and } \Psi_n(x) = \frac{xR_{n-1}(x)}{S_{n-1}(x)}.$$

The given indices indicate the degree of the polynomial, and we may assume, by normalizing, that the leading coefficients in Q_n and R_n are both 1. We require

$$\Phi_n(x) \le \ln(1+x) \le \Psi_n(x)x \qquad x \ge 0,$$

since the interval $(-1, 0)$ is not relevant in the context. Are there good (or even: best) approximations of this type for small n? Can you, based on such, devise an entire sequence of optimal approximands?

Exercise 4.46 The *moment sequence* of a probability measure v on $[0, 1]$ is the sequence (m_n) given by

$$m_n = \int_0^1 t^n dv.$$

It is interesting to study the measure μ with moment sequence given recursively by

$$m_0 = 1, \qquad m_{n+1}^2 + \frac{m_{n+1}}{m_n} = 1, \qquad m_n \ge 0,$$

and this can be done by investigating

$$f(z) = \int_0^1 \frac{1-t^z}{1-t} d\mu(t)$$

which is defined when $\Re(z) > 0$, and it can be extended to other values of z as well. It can be proved that

$$f(z) = \lim_{n \longrightarrow \infty} \psi^{\circ n} \left(\frac{1}{m_{n-1}} \left(\frac{m_{n-1}}{m_n} \right)^z \right) \tag{4.5}$$

when $z \in [0, 1]$, with $\psi(z) = z - 1/z$. Can equation (4.5) be used to visualize f on the interval $[0, 1]$? Does the right hand side of (4.5) converge for other values of z?

Exercise 4.47 Let $f_c \colon \mathbb{C} \to \mathbb{C}$ be defined by $f_c(z) = z^2 + c$ and let $s \in \mathbb{C}$. The *Julia set* $J(f_c, s)$ is defined to be the set of limit points of the set of $f_c^{-n}(z)$. Write a procedure that plots an approximation of the Julia set. Check visually wether this procedure produces a reasonable approximation. How does the plot depend on s and c?

4.5 Notes and Further Reading

For an excellent introduction to the art of designing graphical representations of numerical data, see [Tuf01].

The problem discussed in Example 4.2.3 was part of the May 2011 exam in A-level math in Danish high-schools. The bad model did not become apparent to the students solving the problem, because they were not asked to judge the quality of the fit either visually or quantitatively. The students were expected to solve the problem using a tool, for example a spread sheet, that handles exponential fits by transforming the data logarithmically and making a linear fit to the transformed data. In this particular case, the answer to the questions posed became nonsenscal if one used a true nonlinear fit instead.

As mentioned in the text, it goes beyond the scope of this book to give an introduction to all the statistical tools that may prove useful in an experimental investigation. Instead, we refer the reader to standard texts on the statistical analysis of experimental data. The choice [Was04] comes recommended.

The paragraph quoted in the box on p. 96 is from [Row13], and the plaster models constructed under the supervision of Brill, Klein and others are catalogued in [Mül04]. Modern versions created with 3d printers can for instance be bought at `http://blog.mo-labs.com`.

The original paper on the Costa–Hoffman–Meeks surface considered in the box on p. 101 is [HM90], and additional information can be found in [FGM96].

Example 4.1.4 was adapted from [Bor15, Ex. 4.7], and Exercise 4.46 was inspired by [BD08]. Exercise 4.45 was devised by Flemming Topsøe.

5 *Symbolic Inversion*

As discussed earlier, mathematical experiments only rarely lead directly to mathematical insights in any conclusive form. When a mathematical experiment has produced results, the task for the experimenter is thus to extract as much insight as possible from the results to the end of producing mathematical theory in the form of useful definitions or theorems. Sometimes, it will be obvious to the experimenter that results obtained hint at certain results being true or certain methods being useful, but most often, a systematic analysis of the results is required. Envisioning a direct forward map from an unknown mathematical theory to the results found as indicated on Figure 5.1, we call this systematic analysis *experimental inversion*.

Experimental inversion often falls in one of two categories: visualization or symbolic inversion. Both have the purpose of providing the experimenter with an improved understanding of the mathematical consequences that could be inferred from the experiment. Having dealt with visualization already, we will discuss symbolic inversion in the chapter at hand, focusing on integer sequences and floating point arithmetic. As we shall see, experimental inversion is not a strictly mathematical discipline, being based on vague notions such as plausibility, but it can be aided by mathematical methods and algorithms which are completely mathematically well founded. We will present some of these key tools here.

5.1 Overview

In this section, we introduce all the key tools for symbolic inversion in the dual contexts of integer sequences and floating point constants. In the subsequent sections, we then discuss the two problems in detail separately.

Sequences of integers are common output from mathematical experiments, and hence, the process of establishing a theory of how they may have arisen by way of symbolic inversion is central to experimental mathematics. The process resembles one which may be familiar to the reader, for example from

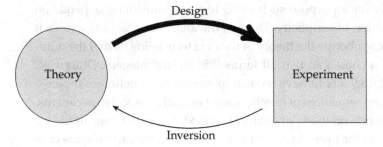

Figure 5.1 Experimental inversion.

IQ tests in the form: What is the next term of the sequence

$$2, 5, 10, 17, ?$$

Most mathematicians would probably analyze such a sequence by computing the relative differences 3,5,7, and then propose to continue with the number 26 given by continuing the sequence of relative differences by 9, assuming that it was just the sequence of odd numbers. But certainly the sequence of relative differences could also have been a segment of the sequence of odd primes, and the next term hence 28. As a more complicated example, consider what would be a reasonable next term in sequence

$$120, 60, 80, 90, ? \tag{5.1}$$

which has been used to IQ test Danish men (including the authors) for the draft for decades. The correct answer, according to the designer of this problem, is 96, since he would like us to consider 120 as an initially given term, and the ensuing terms as $n/(n+1)$ times that term. However, from a mathematical point of view, this is not a very satisfactory explanation since after $n = 5$ we leave the integers by such an explanation. Also, a formula of the form

$$\frac{120n}{n+1}$$

can not be arranged to match the first term. Indeed, perhaps a better mathematical explanation would be that the next term is 120 because we are looking at the sequence whose nth term is ten times the number of ones in the binary expansions of the prime factors of $n + 23$, cf. Exercise 5.19.

These examples demonstrate, first and foremost, that the art of symbolic inversion is not a purely mathematical discipline since the underlying questions are not mathematically well posed; there is obviously no unique answer to a question of how to expand an initially given segment to an infinite sequence, and no unique way of explaining how an infinite sequence has been generated. Nevertheless, being able to answer such questions is fundamental to experimental mathematics and very often this will be possible using notions of heuristic plausibility. When it comes to analyzing sequences which have been made for a purpose such as IQ testing, plausibility depends on some human notion of simplicity. Thus, in the analysis of sequence (5.1), it would seem to corroborate the theory of the next term being 96 that the number 120 has been chosen so that all terms this far are integers. Otherwise, the sequence 12,6,8,9 would have seemed to provide for a better—simpler— exercise. But when sequences of numbers arise in mathematical experiments, plausibility depends on the mathematical context. Counting ones in the binary expansions of the prime factors of $n + 23$ could be relevant in some contexts, but not in most.

Perhaps surprisingly, the notions of plausibility in man-made sequences and those arising from experiments often seem to coincide. Explanations arising from fundamental mathematical concepts, in particular basic arithmetic and combinatorics, are certainly always plausible. And the opposite is surprisingly often true as well: An explanation which is simple enough to be plausible often hints at underlying mathematical truth.

In the discussion above, we divided the task of analyzing a sequence

$$a_1, \ldots, a_N$$

arising from a mathematical experiment into two moments; expanding it to the infinite sequence $(a_n)_{n=1}^{\infty}$ and providing a formula (or similar) to compute a_n for all $n \in \mathbb{N}$. (Of course it is conceivable that a mathematical experiment only makes sense for some finite number of n, but usually such examples are difficult to analyze). Computations will be limited by time and memory consumption of the mathematical experiment, so N will usually not be easily negotiable, but of course as many terms as possible are useful.

Another frequent problem of inversion occurs when some experiment has resulted in the computation of a *floating point constant*. The experimenting mathematician wishes to understand how this constant may have come about, since an exact formula describing the floating-point number may contain useful information. In complete parallel to the case of integer sequences this task is not mathematically well defined, and is limited by the number of digits that may be computed for the constant. As we shall see, such computations are often prone to imprecisions and/or roundoff errors which introduce new challenges.

5.1.1 Transformations

As already touched upon, data given in a sequence $a_1, \ldots, a_n$ can often be understood by applying *transformations*, for example turning to successive differences

$$a_2 - a_1, a_3 - a_2, \ldots, a_n - a_{n-1}, \ldots$$

or successive quotients

$$a_2/a_1, a_3/a_2, \ldots, a_n/a_{n-1}, \ldots$$

If a descriptive formula for

$$a_{k+1} - a_k = b_k$$

Figure 5.2 All noncrossing spanning trees on 4 points ($c_4 = 12$).

may be obtained, we can reconstruct

$$a_n = a_1 + \sum_{k=1}^{n-1} b_k$$

(and similarly with products for successive quotients). Passing to differences is perhaps particularly promising when the given sequence is monotone. And as we shall see in numerous examples below, passing to quotients is very useful for understanding sequences of numbers that factorize systematically into products of relatively small primes, since small primes are often indicative of factorials or other basic combinatorial functions that may often be recognized this way.

Note, however, that this process comes at the price of reducing the number of data points by one, and may take us out of the realm of integers in the case of successive quotients.

Example 5.1.1: Noncrossing spanning trees. We seek a formula for the number c_n of trees that can span n points laid out evenly on a circle, so that no two edges cross, cf. Figure 5.2. Since no theoretical approach comes to mind, we will devise a procedure to compute the numbers by brute force as far as possible, and then attempt symbolic inversion.

Denoting the vertices $\{1, \ldots, n\}$ and the chosen edges by pairs (a, b) with $a < b$ allows an easy check for crossing edges: (a, b) will cross (a', b') precisely when $a < a' < b < b'$ or $a' < a < b' < b$. We know that a spanning tree must have $n - 1$ edges and be connected (or, equivalently, acyclic) but since programming this appears time-consuming we elect to generate all possible configurations with noncrossing edges by a simple recursive program based on the observation that the number we seek is $c(n, \emptyset)$ where c is defined recursively by

$$c(n, \mathcal{E}) = \begin{cases} 1 & |\mathcal{E}| = n - 1 \text{ and } \mathcal{E} \text{ is a tree} \\ 0 & |\mathcal{E}| = n - 1 \text{ and } \mathcal{E} \text{ is not a tree} \\ \sum_{e \in \text{succ } \mathcal{E}} c(n, \mathcal{E} \cup \{e\}) & \text{otherwise,} \end{cases}$$

where we have well ordered the set of all edges in some fashion and denote by succ $\mathcal{E}$ the set of edges that are larger than all elements in $\mathcal{E}$ and cross none of them.

```
[> with(GraphTheory):                                              1
  cycleTree := proc (n, edges)                                     2
    local a0, b0, a, b, found;                                     3
    if nops(edges) = n-1 then                                      4
      if IsTree(Graph(convert(edges, set))) then                  5
        return 1                                                   6
      else                                                         7
        return 0                                                   8
      end if;                                                      9
    end if;                                                        10
    if nops(edges) = 0 then                                        11
      a0 := 1; b0 := 1;                                            12
    else                                                           13
      a0 := edges[-1][1]; b0 := edges[-1][2];                      14
    end if;                                                        15
    found := 0;                                                    16
    for b from b0+1 to n do                                        17
      if noCrossing(edges, {a0, b}) then                          18
        found := found+                                            19
            cycleTree(n, [op(edges), {a0, b}])                     20
      end if;                                                      21
    end do;                                                        22
    for a from a0+1 to n-1 do                                      23
      for b from a+1 to n do                                       24
        if noCrossing(edges, {a, b}) then                         25
          found := found+                                          26
              cycleTree(n, [op(edges), {a, b}])                    27
        end if;                                                    28
      end do;                                                      29
    end do;                                                        30
    return found;                                                  31
  end proc;                                                        32
```

Figure 5.3 cycleTree.

To implement this, we use a built-in test from the GraphTheory package (discussed further in Section 8.1) to test whether a configuration is a tree. The program is written with a flagrant disregard for efficiency, and is certainly not fast, but nevertheless gives us $c_0, \ldots, c_{10}$ within 15 minutes. Since no pattern is immediate we decide to compute also c_{11} and after a couple of hours are rewarded with another term, so that in total we have

$$(c_0, \ldots, c_{11})$$
$$= (0, 0, 1, 3, 12, 55, 273, 1428, 7752, 43263, 246675, 1430715) \quad (5.2)$$

We notice by

```
[> ifactor(1430715);
```

$$3 \cdot 5 \cdot 11 \cdot 13 \cdot 23 \cdot 29$$

that c_{11} has a lot of small prime factors, and thus (cf. the discussion at the beginning of this section) decide to study the successive quotients c_{k+1}/c_k even though they are not integers. Since we have $c_0 = c_1 = 0$ we lose three terms this way, but applying ifactor to the remaining fractions certainly reveals some structure

$$3, 2^2, \frac{5 \cdot 11}{2^2 \cdot 3}, \frac{3 \cdot 7 \cdot 13}{5 \cdot 11}, \frac{2^2 \cdot 17}{13}, \frac{2 \cdot 19}{7}, \frac{3 \cdot 11 \cdot 23}{2^3 \cdot 17}, \frac{5^2 \cdot 13}{3 \cdot 19}, \frac{29}{5}$$

We notice first that the denominators contain the odd numbers in sequence, at least when these are primes, and considering $(2k+1)c_{k+1}/c_k$ instead we get

$$3 \cdot 5, 2^2 \cdot 7, \frac{3 \cdot 5 \cdot 11}{2^2}, \frac{3 \cdot 7 \cdot 13}{5}, 2^2 \cdot 17, \frac{2 \cdot 3 \cdot 5 \cdot 19}{7}, \frac{3 \cdot 11 \cdot 23}{2^3}, \frac{5^2 \cdot 13}{3}, \frac{3 \cdot 7 \cdot 29}{5}$$

which is a bit simpler. We note that similarly, the numerators contain $3k-1$ and $3k-2$ when these are primes, and hence attempt to compute

$$\frac{(2k+1)c_{k+1}}{(3k-1)(3k-2)c_k},$$

yielding

$$\frac{3}{2^2}, \frac{1}{2}, \frac{3}{2^3}, \frac{3}{2 \cdot 5}, \frac{1}{2^2}, \frac{3}{2 \cdot 7}, \frac{3}{2^4}, \frac{1}{2 \cdot 3}, \frac{3}{2^2 \cdot 5},$$

which is perhaps easier to process without applying ifactor:

$$\frac{3}{4}, \frac{1}{2}, \frac{3}{8}, \frac{3}{10}, \frac{1}{4}, \frac{3}{14}, \frac{3}{16}, \frac{1}{6}, \frac{3}{20},$$

which is simply $3/2k$. Thus we can backtrack to arrive at the hypothesis that

$$\frac{c_{k+1}}{c_k} = \frac{3(3k-1)(3k-2)}{2k(2k+1)}, k \geq 2, \tag{5.3}$$

which gives

$$c_n = \prod_{k=2}^{n-1} \frac{3(3k-1)(3k-2)}{2k(2k+1)}, n \geq 2.$$

EX. 5.1.4 ← Below we will see how this may be simplified further. ◁

We may try to reduce the task of recognizing floating point constants to the task of recognizing integer sequences. Indeed, we could certainly think of

$$3.1415926$$

as the sequence

$$3, 1, 4, 1, 5, 9, 2, 6$$

and try to recognize the number π this way. Such approaches may have merits, but unless the situation at hand is somehow connected to the number 10, it is generally much better to study the *continued fraction expansion*, rather than the decimal expansion, of a constant α.

For this, we let $\alpha_0 = \alpha$ and $a_0 = \lfloor \alpha \rfloor$, and then define a_n and α_n recursively as

$$a_{n+1} = \left\lfloor \frac{1}{\alpha_n} \right\rfloor \qquad \alpha_{n+1} = \frac{1}{\alpha_n} - a_{n+1}$$

as long as $\alpha_n \neq 0$. This is known as the *Euclidean algorithm*, and when it terminates, we can reconstruct α by

$$a_0 + \cfrac{1}{a_1 + \cfrac{1}{a_2 + \cfrac{1}{a_3 + \cfrac{1}{\ddots + \cfrac{1}{a_{n-1} + \cfrac{1}{a_n}}}}}} \tag{5.4}$$

When the algorithm does not terminate, that is, when α is irrational, we consider (5.4) as the $(n+1)$st so-called *convergent* which is usually denoted by p_n/q_n. As we shall see in detail in Section 5.3.1, the convergents indeed converge rapidly to α.

Maple has a `cfrac` command in the `numtheory` package which readily computes the integers a_n and the convergents p_n/q_n by commands such as

```
[> c:=cfrac(ln(2),10):                                                    1
    seq(nthconver(c,i),i=1..10);                                          2
```

$$1, \frac{2}{3}, \frac{7}{10}, \frac{9}{13}, \frac{61}{88}, \frac{192}{277}, \frac{253}{365}, \frac{445}{642}, \frac{1143}{1649}, \frac{1588}{2291}$$

Example 5.1.2: Fractions. To contrast decimal and continued fraction expansion, consider the fundamental question of symbolic inversion: given a floating point representation of a fraction p/q in lowest terms, how can we reconstruct p and q?

Theoretically, both the decimal expansion and the continued fraction contains all the information we need. The decimal expansion of a rational number is eventually periodic, that is, on the form

$$a.b_1 \cdots b_k (c_1 \cdots c_\ell)^\infty \tag{5.5}$$

from which we get that

$$\frac{p}{q} = a + \frac{b_1 \cdots b_k}{10^k} + 10^{-k-\ell} \sum_{i=0}^{\infty} \frac{c_1 \cdots c_\ell}{10^{i\ell}}$$

$$= a + \frac{b_1 \cdots b_k}{10^k} + \frac{(c_1 \cdots c_\ell) 10^{-k-\ell}}{1 - 10^{-\ell}}. \tag{5.6}$$

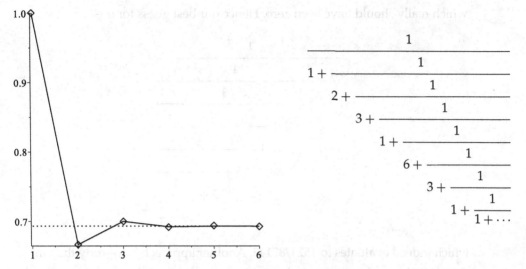

Figure 5.4 Left: The first 6 convergents to $\ln 2$. Right: The beginning of the continued fraction for $\ln 2$.

Given a continued fraction expansion, we may similarly reconstruct p/q as in (5.4).

However, when we only have a finite approximation of α with D digits, the two methods are far from equivalent. Consider the concrete example $\alpha = 1524/87143$ which to 15 digits of precision is

$$0.0174884959204985.$$

Running the Euclidean algorithm on this 15-digit number, we get

```
[> cfrac(evalf(1524/87143,15),10);
```

$$\cfrac{1}{57+\cfrac{1}{5+\cfrac{1}{1+\cfrac{1}{1+\cfrac{1}{5+\cfrac{1}{2+\cfrac{1}{10+\cfrac{1}{1+\cfrac{1}{14609026+\cfrac{1}{2+\cdots}}}}}}}}}}$$

which we interpret by asserting that the number 14609026 is the result of an imprecision in the computation as the reciprocal of a very small number, which really should have been zero. Hence our best guess for α is

$$\cfrac{1}{57+\cfrac{1}{5+\cfrac{1}{1+\cfrac{1}{1+\cfrac{1}{5+\cfrac{1}{2+\cfrac{1}{10+\cfrac{1}{1}}}}}}}}$$

which indeed evaluates to 1524/87143. Another approach is to study the *n*th convergents

```
[> seq(nthconver(cfrac(evalf(1524/87143,15),10),i),i=1..9);
```

$$\frac{1}{57}, \frac{5}{286}, \frac{6}{343}, \frac{11}{629}, \frac{61}{3488}, \frac{133}{7605}, \frac{1391}{79538}, \frac{1524}{87143}, \frac{22264157015}{1273074432256}$$

and trust the last approximation before the size of the numbers involved explode. To double check, we can relinquish one digit of precision and do

```
[> seq(nthconver(cfrac(evalf(1524/87143,14),10),i),i=1..8);
```

$$\frac{1}{57}, \frac{5}{286}, \frac{6}{343}, \frac{11}{629}, \frac{61}{3488}, \frac{133}{7605}, \frac{1391}{79538}, \frac{1524}{87143}, \frac{408743029}{23372108777}$$

We see that after the sought step the convergents differ at the two different precisions, supporting the hypothesis that what we are seeing after this step are results of irrelevant imprecisions.

By contrast, suppose we worked directly with the decimal expansion to extract the digits needed to compute α by Equation (5.6). Since the relevant period is 870 digits long—indeed $k = 139$ and $\ell = 870$ in (5.6)—we would need at least 1009 digits just to extract the $b_1 \cdots b_k$ and $c_1 \cdots c_\ell$, as well as a number of additional terms to convince ourselves that $c_1 \cdots c_\ell$ was repeating. Thus we would need around a thousand digits of α to reconstruct it directly using its decimal expansion, as opposed to the 15 or so needed by the Euclidean algorithm.   ◁

5.1.2 *Maple's Inversion Tools*

Maple contains a number of extremely useful procedures that help the experimenting mathematician with inversion. The most accessible of these methods addresses the question of recognizing floating point constants by the command `identify`. Using `identify` to analyze such constants as in

```
[> identify(3.1415926),identify(0.0174884959);
```

$$\pi, \frac{1524}{87143}$$

is completely straightforward when the floating point constants are given with sufficient precision, but as we will discuss in detail below, `identify` is quite sensitive to imprecisions and roundoff errors.

Example 5.1.3: Identify. We seek an expression for the infinite sum

$$\sum_{n=1}^{\infty} \frac{n}{2^n \binom{3n}{n}},$$

which Maple describes in closed form as a value of a hypergeometric function and estimates as

0.20502693452272468808609236770970673588038956164229

to 50 digits' precision. Applying `identify` gives the impressive formula

$$\frac{81}{625} + \frac{79}{3125}\pi - \frac{18}{3125}\ln 2. \qquad \triangleleft$$

In general, it is necessary with a rather high level of precision for `identity` to analyze constants this way. We will postpone the explanation of how `identify` works to Section 5.3.2.

The Maple package `gfun` contains a number of commands to help analyzing sequences of numbers, particularly helpful when trying to understand sequences of integers or fractions. For instance, when one searches for direct recursive relations between the terms of such a sequence, one may use a command such as

```
[> with(gfun):                                              1
   listtorec([0,1,1,2,3,5,8,13,21,34,55],u(n));             2
```

$$[-u(n+2) + u(n+1) + u(n), u(0) = 0, u(1) = 1, ogf]$$

which, as we see, manages to recognize the defining properties of the Fibonacci sequence (3.6) after just a few terms.

EX. 5.1.1 → **Example 5.1.4: Noncrossing trees by `listtorec`.** We store the observations found in a list

```
[> C:=[0,0,1,3,12,55,273,1428,7752,43263,246675,1430715]:
```

and run

```
[> listtorec(C,c(k));
```

$$[\{(21389k^2 + 5313k + 118)c(k+1) +$$
$$(5488k^2 + 11242k + 9114)c(k+2) +$$
$$(-7695k^2 - 30633k - 30318)c(k+3) +$$
$$(950k^2 + 5310k + 6820)c(k+4),$$
$$c(0) = 0, c(1) = 0, c(2) = 1, c(3) = 3\}, ogf] \tag{5.7}$$

Noting that this is not the same as what we found in (5.3), we realize that this may be because we are asking Maple to consider the two first terms which we had discarded in our first analysis, and instead try

```
[> listtorec(C[3..-1],c(k));
```

$$[\{(27k^2 - 135k + 168)c(k) + (-4k^2 - 26k - 42)c(k+1),$$
$$c(0) = 1, c(1) = 3\}, ogf]$$

Since we gave c_2 as our first term we have in fact found that

$$\frac{c_{k+1}}{c_k} = \frac{27(k-2)^2 - 135(k-2) + 168}{4(k-2)^2 + 26(k-2) + 42},$$

EX. 5.1.6 ← which reduces to (5.3). ◁

The `gfun` package is unfortunately not as straightforward to invoke as `identify`. To truly unleash its potential, and understand what is meant by ogf in (5.7), we need to understand the concept of *generating function*.

The *ordinary* generating function (ogf) for any sequence $(a_n)_{n=0}^\infty$ is the function defined by the power series

$$A(z) = \sum_{n=0}^{\infty} a_n z^n. \tag{5.8}$$

Although formally z is a complex number, it is often best thought of as a symbolic bookkeeping device, helping us keep track of indices (we elaborate on this in Section 5.2.2). The pivotal procedure of the `gfun` package is the command `guessgf` which attempts to recognize a pattern in a sequence of constants $a_0, a_1, \ldots, a_n$ and return a function $A(z)$ with the property that the power series expansion (5.8) matches the observations at index $0, \ldots, n$. When this can be done, subsequent terms can usually be computed easily, and very often the nature of $A(z)$ contains significant leads on the structure of the sequence (a_n).

Note that when A is given, the coefficients of the power series expansion can be computed by `series`. Very often, Maple even knows a formula for the terms in the power series expansion, available by `convert(...,FormalPowerSeries)`, which we then can consider as a conjectural formula for the entries of (a_n).

EX. 3.3.1 → **Example 5.1.5: Generating the Fibonacci numbers.** We can use `guessgf` to find the generating function $1/(1 - z - z^2)$ for the Fibonacci numbers by

```
[> guessgf([0,1,1,2,3,5,8,13,21,34,55],z);
```

$$\left[-\frac{z}{z^2 + z - 1}, ogf\right]$$

We see that the result matches the given data by

```
[> F:=unapply(%[1],z):
   series(F(z),z,10);
```

1

2

$$z + z^2 + 2z^3 + 3z^4 + 5z^5 + 8z^6 + 13z^7 + 21z^8 + 34z^9 + O(z^{10})$$

and by

```
[> convert(F(z),FormalPowerSeries);
```

$$\sum_{k=0}^{\infty} \left(\frac{\sqrt{5}}{5}(1/2 + (1/2)\sqrt{5})^k - \frac{\sqrt{5}}{5}(1/2 - (1/2)\sqrt{5})^k\right) z^k,$$

we obtain the important closed form formula for the Fibonacci numbers which may be known to the reader as *Binet's formula*:

$$f_k = \frac{1}{\sqrt{5}}\left(\left(\frac{1 + \sqrt{5}}{2}\right)^k - \left(\frac{1 - \sqrt{5}}{2}\right)^k\right). \tag{5.9}$$

Note that since $((1 - \sqrt{5})/2)^k \approx (-0.61)^k \to 0$ as $k \to \infty$, we get

$$f_k \approx \frac{\phi^k}{\sqrt{5}} \tag{5.10}$$

EX. 5.2.3 ← where $\phi = (1 + \sqrt{5})/2 \approx 1.68$ is the *golden mean*. ◁

EX. 5.1.4 → **Example 5.1.6: Noncrossing trees by** `guessgf`. Maple seems unable to process the full list C by `guessgf`, but after discarding one initial term we get

```
[> guessgf(C[2..-1],x);
```

$$\left[-1 - \frac{(-1)^{1/3}\sqrt{3}(-(12\sqrt{3}x + 4\sqrt{27x - 4})^{2/3} + 4(-1)^{1/3})}{6\sqrt{x}(12\sqrt{3}x + 4\sqrt{27x - 4})^{1/3}}, ogf\right] \tag{5.11}$$

Maple's suggestion for a generating function is hard to read—one needs to know that $(-1)^{1/3}$ is the root in the first quadrant of the complex plane—and `convert(...,FormalPowerSeries)` gives a complicated power series which is not so easy to understand. Using `simplify` as in

```
[> simplify(convert(guessgf(C[2..-1],x)[1],          1
                    FormalPowerSeries));               2
```

$$\sum_{k=0}^{\infty} \frac{3(3k+2)!}{k!(2k+3)!} x^{k+1}$$

gives a very promising hypothesis about the nature of c_k. Recalling that we have discarded one entry so that the coefficient of x^k is in fact c_{k+1} we get

$$c_{k+2} = \frac{3(3k+2)!}{k!(2k+3)!} = \frac{3}{3k+3}\frac{(3k+3)!}{k!(2k+3)!} = \frac{1}{k+1}\binom{3k+3}{k},$$

and hence,

$$c_k = \frac{1}{k-1}\binom{3k-3}{k-2} \tag{5.12}$$

for $k \geq 3$. We test with

```
[> seq(binomial(3*k-3,k-2)/(k-1),k=2..10);
```

$$1, 3, 12, 55, 273, 1428, 7752, 43263, 246675$$

that we have indeed found something that is consistent with our
EX. 5.1.7 ← observations.   ◁

5.1.3 Databases

The two key online resources for the experimental mathematician, the *Online Encyclopedia of Integer Sequences* and the *Inverse Symbolic Calculator* address the two different kinds of symbolic inversion we are considering in this chapter.

The *Online Encyclopedia of Integer Sequences*, universally referred to as the OEIS, has terms of roughly 200000 sequences along with explanations of how they are generated as well as relevant references to the mathematical literature. The database is continually updated and expanded by user submissions which are checked by a college of editors, and this makes it extremely useful for the purposes of an experimental mathematician.

Using the OEIS is rather self-explanatory; one simply enters the terms available in an online form on www.oeis.org and a list of "hits" is returned. One needs at least four terms, and having something like 8 is usually quite sufficient to ensure that hits are unique. As we will discuss in detail later, initial terms that may be considered irrelevant or—worse—subject to interpretation must be omitted.

Each sequence in the OEIS is given an index of the form **A**xxxxxx and this "**A** number" is the key reference to the sequence which can be used in references.

EX. 5.1.6 → **Example 5.1.7: Noncrossing configurations in OEIS.**   Submitting our observations from (5.2) to the OEIS gives no hits. Following the general principle of avoiding initial terms, we instead try

$$1, 3, 12, 55, 273, 1428, 7752, 43263, 246675.$$

This gives the entry A1764, revealing the formula (5.12) as well as a reference to the beautiful treatise [Fla97] from which this example was drawn. Studying
EX. 5.2.4 ← this reference leads to a proof of (5.12), which we will detail below.   ◁

EX. 3.2.3 → **Example 5.1.8: Bernoulli numbers.**   In Examples 1.6.3, 3.2.3 and Exercise 4.38 we were lead to understand quite a lot about how the coefficients of the polynomials q_m were developing downwards in the triangle of coefficients indicated in Example 1.6.3. But the initial term of each such column, that is, the coefficient $c_m^{(m)}$ of n in $q_m(n)$, remained mysterious apart from the obvious fact that it was alternately zero and nonzero after a few terms.

We easily compute these terms

```
[> seq(coeff(expand(sum(r^m,r=1..n)),n,1),m=0..20);
```

$$1, \frac{1}{2}, \frac{1}{6}, 0, -\frac{1}{30}, 0, \frac{1}{42}, 0, -\frac{1}{30}, 0, \frac{5}{66}, 0, -\frac{691}{2730}, 0, \frac{7}{6}, 0, -\frac{3617}{510}, 0, \frac{43867}{798}$$

but since they are not integers, we need to decide on a way to pass the observations to OEIS. Using ifactor we see that the denominators away from the zero entries are

$$2 \cdot 3, \quad 2 \cdot 3 \cdot 5, \quad 2 \cdot 3 \cdot 7, \quad 2 \cdot 3 \cdot 5, \quad 2 \cdot 3 \cdot 11, \quad 2 \cdot 3 \cdot 5 \cdot 7 \cdot 13, \quad 2 \cdot 3.$$

Although no obvious pattern emerges, it is certainly clear that we can cancel the denominators with $(n + 1)!$ to get an integer sequence

$$1, 1, 1, 0, -4, 0, 120, 0, -12096, 0, 3024000, 0, -1576143360, 0,$$
$$1525620096000, 0, -2522591034163200. \tag{5.13}$$

We can also separate numerators and denominators with numer and denom to get

$$1, 1, 1, 0, -1, 0, 1, 0, -1, 0, 5, 0, -691, 0, 7, 0, -3617, 0, 43867, 0, -174611$$

and

$$1, 2, 6, 1, 30, 1, 42, 1, 30, 1, 66, 1, 2730, 1, 6, 1, 510, 1, 798, 1, 330, 1, 138, 1, 2730.$$

In this particular case, each of these strategies works to get a hit in the OEIS: A129814, A27641, A27642, because we are considering one of the most important nontrivial sequences of rational numbers in existence: the *Bernoulli numbers* $B_0, B_1, B_2, \ldots$ defined by the implicit recurrence formula

$$\sum_{k=0}^{n} \binom{n+1}{k} B_k = \begin{cases} 1 & n = 0, \\ 0 & n > 0 \end{cases}, \tag{5.14}$$

which easily shows that we have found $c_n^{(n)} = B_n$ with the single exception that $c_1^{(1)} = 1/2 = -B_1$. Studying the OEIS entries leads to a multitude of ex-

EX. 7.3.1 ← amples where these numbers occur.   ◁

Whereas the OEIS is a unique database anchored at the same URL for decades, a variety of inverse symbolic calculators have appeared and disappeared over the years. At the time of writing, the best such resource is the ISC hosted by University of Newcastle, New South Wales at `isc.carma` `.newcastle.edu.au`. It is straightforward to use the ISC by simply entering a decimal approximant of the number one hopes to identify.

The key challenge of using the ISC is that it contains a staggering number of constants and thus the risk of encountering a false friend is high. Although the site tries to help by suggesting a "simple" hit among those in the vicinity of the number submitted, one will usually not be able to use the database meaningfully with less that 15 accurate digits of the number, and precision to this level is not always obtainable.

Example 5.1.9: A hard integral. We wish to study

$$b_n = \int_0^1 \left(\ln \frac{t}{1-t} \right)^n dt$$

for $n \in \mathbb{N}$, but find that Maple cannot evaluate the integral exactly. It fails even when n is odd, where $b_n = 0$ due to the obvious symmetry of the integrand around $t = \frac{1}{2}$. However, we may readily compute $b_2, b_4, \ldots, b_{20}$ with 50 digit precision, for instance

$$b_2 = 3.28986813369645287294483033329205037843789980241 36$$
$$b_4 = 45.45757581586780404367215525472905191653953998 0587$$
$$b_6 = 1419.19357146830654990175251205833413642303539 85958$$
$$b_8 = 80336.2292693975265936886059330772837453694528 59894.$$

With `identify`, we immediately get the hits

$$b_2 = \frac{\pi^2}{3} \qquad b_4 = \frac{7\pi^4}{15},$$

but this method does not lead to any identification of $b_6, \ldots, b_{20}$. The Inverse Symbolic Calculator also recognizes b_2 and b_4, and further finds that

$$b_6 = \frac{31\pi^6}{21}$$

but does not recognize any of $b_8, \ldots, b_{20}$. Formulating the hypothesis that b_n/π^n is rational, and using `identify` on b_n/π^n instead, readily gives subsequent hits of the form

$$\frac{127}{15}, \frac{2555}{33}, \frac{1414477}{1365}, \frac{57337}{3}, \frac{118518239}{255}, \frac{5749691557}{399}, \frac{91546277357}{165}.$$

The Bernoulli numbers

Diagram for the computation by the Engine of the Numbers of Bernoulli. See Note G. (page 722 et seq.)

The Swiss mathematician Jakob Bernoulli (1654–1705) was led to study the sequence of numbers that now bear his name while searching for efficient computations of sums of powers. He enthusiastically reported:

> With the help of this table, it took me less than half of a quarter of an hour to find that the tenth powers of the first 1000 numbers being added together will yield the sum 91409924241424243424241924242500

In fact, the numbers were discovered independently around the same time by the Japanese mathematician Seki Kōwa (1642–1708).

Because of the Bernoulli numbers' position at the cusp of computational and theoretical mathematics, they are ubiquitous in experimental mathematics, and for the same reason, they have the distinction of being the subject of the first published computer program. This was written by Ada Lovelace (1815–1852) for the "Analytical engine" invented by Charles Babbage (1791–1871). The engine was never realized due to lack of funding, but in a set of notes published by Lovelace in 1843, she showed as an example of the use and versatility of the machine how to compute the numbers with an iterative procedure based on (5.14).

The Bernoulli numbers have been determined to index 10^8 by computing $n!B_n$ modulo p for sufficiently many primes that the numbers can then be obtained by the Chinese remainder theorem, allowing for parallel computing. This of course has no practical applications in summing problems, but several open theoretical problems involve the Bernoulli numbers and may hence be studied this way.

Applying `ifactor` to the complete list of fractions we get

$$\frac{1}{3}, \frac{7}{3\cdot5}, \frac{31}{3\cdot7}, \frac{127}{3\cdot5}, \frac{5\cdot7\cdot73}{3\cdot11}, \frac{23\cdot89\cdot691}{3\cdot5\cdot7\cdot13}, \frac{7\cdot8191}{3},$$

$$\frac{7\cdot31\cdot151\cdot3617}{3\cdot5\cdot17}, \frac{43867\cdot131071}{3\cdot7\cdot19}, \frac{283\cdot617\cdot524287}{3\cdot5\cdot11}.$$

The systematic appearance of the numbers $n+1$ in the denominators whenever they are prime indicate that we can cancel the denominators by multiplying with $(n+1)!$, but the resulting sequence of integers

$$2, 56, 7440, 3072384, 3090528000, 6452730915840, 24992708412672000,$$

$$165315480832851148800, 1752936859075384958976000,$$

$$283465791665561231094251520000$$

is not known to the OEIS. However, we notice in the numerators each and every one of the first seven Mersenne primes, leading us to realize that in fact $2^{n-1}-1$ is a factor in every single case observed this far. Dividing out, we get a sequence of even numbers again unknown to the OEIS, but dividing by 2 we finally arrive at

$$1, 4, 120, 12096, 3024000, 1576143360, 1525620096000, 2522591034163200,$$

$$6686974460694528000, 27033456071346536448000,$$

which we, with the help of OEIS, recognize as closely related to (5.13): it is

$$(-1)^n B_{2m}(2m+1)!$$

where B_{2m} are the even Bernoulli numbers introduced in Example 5.1.8. Substituting back using that $B_{2m-1}=0$ when $m>1$ we get

$$\int_0^1 \left(\ln\frac{t}{1-t}\right)^n dt = \left|\pi^n B_n(2^n-2)\right|,$$

which actually holds for any n. The references given in A129814 lead to connections to the zeta function which could be studied to lead to a proof of the equality.   ◁

EX. 1.6.6 → **Example 5.1.10: Counting pyramids.**   Following the notation in Exercise 1.9, we wish to submit terms of the integer sequence p_n (defined as the number of pyramids which can be made with n LEGO bricks of width 2 in the same vertical plane) to OEIS in the hope of producing a formula for the number of such pyramids.

Introducing the concept of *width* for the levels in the obvious way, we already know from Example 1.6.5 that when every level has width 2, the number of such *towers* is 3^{n-1}, but of course there are many more pyramids. It is not obvious how to count them all, so let us use the fact (as indicated in Figure 5.5) that to obtain a level with a width of $2N$, at least $2N-1$ bricks are needed. Hence, to count all pyramids with 6 bricks or less, we only need to

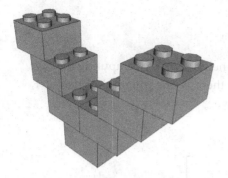

Figure 5.5 The smallest pyramid having a level of width 8.

concern ourselves with levels of width 6 or less. There is one possible level of width 2, 4 and 5, and two possible levels of width 6, and for each pair of these five types of levels we compute by hand the number of different ways one can be put on top of the other:

	3	1	0	0	0
	5	3	2	1	1
	6	4	3	2	2
	6	3	2	3	2
	7	5	4	3	3

This information is stored in a 5×5 Maple matrix A that will be used to count all pyramids with the property that every level is of width less than 6. To do so, we introduce a *formal variable* x to keep track of how many bricks are used by each level. Thus we set

```
[> B:=A.DiagonalMatrix([x,x^2,x^2,x^2,x^3]);
```

$$B := \begin{bmatrix} 3x & x^2 & 0 & 0, & 0 \\ 5x & 3x^2 & 2x^2 & x^2 & x^3 \\ 6x & 4x^2 & 3x^2 & 2x^2 & 2x^3 \\ 6x & 3x^2 & 2x^2 & 3x^2 & 2x^3 \\ 7x & 5x^2 & 4x^2 & 3x^2 & 3x^3 \end{bmatrix}$$

so that when we let

```
[> v:=<x|0|0|0|0>:
```

we may count the number of pyramids of height $i + 1$ by computing the row matrix vB^i. Indeed, v itself indicates that there is one pyramid of height 1, and that it is built of one brick, and we have

```
[> map(sort@expand,v.B);
```

$$\begin{bmatrix} 3x^2 & x^3 & 0 & 0 & 0 \end{bmatrix}$$

which tells us that there are four pyramids of height 2: three built of 2 bricks (the towers) and one pyramid which is not a tower. The Maple commands sort and expand make sure that entries are on the desired expanded form and have the monomials in descending order. Once more, we can compute

```
[> map(sort@expand,v.B^2);
```

$$\begin{bmatrix} 5x^4 + 9x^3 & 3x^5 + x^4 & 2x^5 & x^5 & x^6 \end{bmatrix}$$

to get all the different ways of making pyramids of height 3. They are organized from left to right according to what is on the top level, and the various powers of x indicate the "cost" of each pyramid in bricks. To organize the counting, we let

```
[> w:=<1|1|1|1|1>:
```

and compute

$$v(I + B + B^2 + B^3 + B^4 + B^5 + B^6)w$$

by

```
[> sort(expand(simplify(v.(sum(B^i,i=0..6)).w)));
```

$$81x^{18} + 1080x^{17} + 6259x^{16} + 20486x^{15} + 41311x^{14} + 53400x^{13}$$
$$+ 46892x^{12} + 32146x^{11} + 18491x^{10} + 9283x^9 + 4192x^8$$
$$+ 1711x^7 + 462x^6 + 126x^5 + 35x^4 + 10x^3 + 3x^2 + x$$

This computation gives us all pyramids of height 7 or less and width 6 or less, and as we have noted above, this must include all pyramids built of 6 or fewer bricks; the number of these are hence

$$1, 3, 10, 35, 126, 462$$

respectively. Taking these observations to the OEIS, we get several hits as described in Figure 5.6, where the rightmost column shows the next term in each sequence. Looking closer, we see that in fact A1700 equals A88218, and since neither of the descriptions in any of the other matches appear to be relevant for our situation, we decide to look closer at A1700. Shifting the

A1700	$\binom{2n+1}{n+1}$: number of ways to put $n+1$ indistinguishable balls into $n+1$ distinguishable boxes = number of $(n+1)$-st degree monomials in $n+1$ variables = number of monotone maps from $\{1, \ldots n+1\}$ to $\{1, \ldots, n+1\}$	1716
A88218	Total number of leaves in all rooted ordered trees with n edges.	1716
A167403	Number of decimal numbers having n or fewer digits and having the sum of their digits equal to n	1716
A72266	Number of words of length $2n$ generated by the two letters s and t that reduce to the identity 1 using the relations $ssssss = 1, tt = 1$ and $stst = 1$. The generators s and t along with the three relations generate the 14-element dihedral group D_7.	1717
A122068	Expansion of $x(1 - 3x)(1 - x)/(1 - 7x + 14x^2 - 7x^3)$	1715

Figure 5.6   Various hits for 1, 3, 10, 35, 126, 462.

entries to match our setup, we thus venture the hypothesis that the number of pyramids is indeed

$$\binom{2n - 1}{n - 1}$$

for $n \geq 1$ (one would probably, at $n = 0$, say that there is precisely one such empty pyramid, but then the formula does not make sense).

To test the hypothesis further, we see if it predicts the next number in the sequence correctly. We have already found 1711 pyramids with 7 bricks, characterized as the ones having every level of width 6 or less. The pyramids with 7 bricks and a level of width 7 or 8 are easily determined—they are depicted on Figures 1.6 and 5.5—and there are indeed 5 of these as predicted
EX. 5.2.5 ← by A1700.   ◁

5.1.4 False Friends

Just like conjectures can fail for the first time at very large indices, two sequences can be the same for a large number of indices or two mathematical constants can be so close that their decimal expansions agree for a large number of digits. We present a few instances of such cases below to alert the reader to this problem.

One must note, however, that these examples have in common that they are based on the lack of continuity of the floor function, and, admittedly, could be conceived as somewhat construed. In general, when two sets of data coincide for a long time it is advisable to assert that they are in fact the same, and attempt to understand why.

Example 5.1.11: Two sequences.   Consider the sequences

$$a_n = \left\lfloor \frac{2n}{\ln 2} \right\rfloor \qquad b_n = \left\lceil \frac{2}{\sqrt[n]{2} - 1} \right\rceil$$

The OEIS and Plouffe's inverter

SEQUENCES BEGINNING 1, 2, 11, 1, 2, 12, ...

787 1, 2, 11, 23, 24, 26, 33, 47, 49, 50, 59, 73, 74, 88, 96, 97, 107, 121, 122, 146, 169, 177, 184, 191, 193, 194, 218, 239, 241, 242, 249, 289, 297, 299, 311, 312, 313, 337, 338 **FORMING PERFECT SQUARES. REF MMAG 37 218 64.**

788 1, 2, 11, 32, 50, 132, 380, 368, 1135 **THE NO-THREE-IN-LINE PROBLEM. REF GU3. WE1 124.**

789 1, 2, 11, 35, 85, 175, 322, 546, 870, 1320, 1925, 2717, 3731, 5005, 6580, 8500, 10812, 13566, 16815, 20615, 25025, 30107, 35926, 42550, 50050, 58500, 67977, 78561 **STIRLING NUMBERS OF FIRST KIND. REF AS1 833. DKB 226.**

The OEIS dates back to 1965 when its creator, Neil Sloane (1939–), was a graduate student and encountered the sequence

$$0, 1, 8, 78, 944,$$

in an attempt to perform symbolic inversion. He not only managed to expand and explain the sequence, but also realized the need for a systematic way of allowing mathematicians to exchange information pertaining to integer sequences. The first sequences were digitized in 1967 and between 1973 and 1995 published in books, most recently in [SP95]. Since 1996 the sequences have been available electronically and the OEIS has grown into an active online community.

In a parallel effort, Simon Plouffe (1956–), who at one time also held the record for memorizing most digits of π, compiled a large database of floating point constants to create *Plouffe's inverter* which grew into The Inverse Symbolic Calculator at the Canadian Centre for Experimental and Constructive Mathematics in 1995.

Keeping the OEIS updated should be a key ambition for any experimental mathematician, in the sense that whenever a new interesting sequence of integers has been computed, the sequence should be submitted. Similarly, if additional information has been uncovered about a known sequence, a reference or similar should be submitted. This may not only help other mathematicians having similar problems, but could also provide the experimenter with future contacts to other mathematicians with interesting new perspectives on the given problem.

---

discussed in Exercise 2.30. These are easily seen to be identical for many n, both starting with

$$2, 5, 8, 11, 14, 17, 20, 23, 25, 28, 31, 34, 37, 40, 43, 46, 49, 51, 54, 57.$$

In fact, they agree until $n = 777451915729367$, but

$$a_{777451915729368} = 2243252046704766 \neq 2243252046704767 = b_{777451915729368}$$

In Example 7.4.5 we will explain how to find this discrepancy. For now note, using the elementary inequality

$$\alpha < e^\alpha - 1 < \frac{\alpha}{1 - \frac{\alpha}{2}}$$

which holds for all $0 < \alpha < 1$, that

$$\frac{\ln 2}{n} < 2^{1/n} - 1 < \frac{\frac{\ln 2}{n}}{1 - \frac{\ln 2}{2n}} = \frac{1}{\frac{n}{\ln 2} - \frac{1}{2}}$$

whence

$$\frac{2n}{\ln 2} - 1 < \frac{2}{\sqrt[n]{2} - 1} < \frac{2n}{\ln 2} \tag{5.15}$$

EX. 7.4.5 ← which explains why $a_n \le b_n \le a_n + 1$ for all n. ◁

Example 5.1.12: A fraudulous sum. Consider the sum

$$\sum_{n=0}^{\infty} \frac{\lfloor (e^\pi - \pi)n \rfloor}{3^n}$$

and note that it evaluates to

$$14.50000000$$

which we need neither identify nor the ISC to recognize as 29/2. We see by

```
[> seq(floor((exp(Pi)-Pi)*n),n=0..10);
```

$$0, 19, 39, 59, 79, 99, 119, 139, 159, 179, 199$$

that this unlikely phenomenon has something to do with the fact that

$$c_n = \lfloor (e^\pi - \pi)n \rfloor$$

seems to equal $20n - 1$ for all n. Indeed, it is easy to see that

$$\sum_{n=0}^{\infty} \frac{20n - 1}{3^n} = \frac{29}{2}.$$

But whereas $c_n = 20n - 1$ for all $n = 0, \ldots, 1111$, we get $c_{1112} = 22238 = 20 \cdot 1112 - 2$, showing that

$$\sum_{n=0}^{\infty} \frac{\lfloor (e^\pi - \pi)n \rfloor}{3^n} \le \frac{29}{2} - 3^{-1112}.$$

EX. 7.4.6 ← Since $3^{-1112} \approx 2.762 \cdot 10^{-531}$ there is a discrepancy at the 531st digit. ◁

5.2 Recognizing Integer Sequences

In this section we systematically discuss symbolic inversion of sequences of integers and fractions.

5.2.1 Transformations

We saw in Section 5.1.1 that looking at successive differences and quotients can often lead to a better understanding of sequences. Since it is easy to transform back with sums or products, a formula for such a derived sequence readily leads to a formula for the original. Other less immediate transformations that are sometimes useful are the *Möbius transform* given by

$$\sum_{k|n} a_k,$$

and the *Newton transform* given by

$$\sum_{k=0}^{n} \binom{n}{k} a_k.$$

Also, various *convolutions* such as

$$\sum_{k=0}^{n} a_k a_{n-k} \tag{5.16}$$

or

$$\sum_{m=1}^{\infty} \sum_{\substack{k_1+k_2+\cdots+k_m=n \\ k_i \geq 1}} a_{k_1} a_{k_2} \cdots a_{k_m} \tag{5.17}$$

may be relevant.

The Möbius transform should always be considered when the sequence found is *multiplicative* in the sense that

$$a_{mn} = a_m a_n$$

whenever $\gcd(m, n) = 1$. Indeed, then the transform will be multiplicative as well. The Newton transform is particularly natural to consider when the terms have alternating signs. As described below, the original sequence can in both cases be recovered by rather simple formulas if the corresponding transformed sequence can be understood.

Proposition 5.2.1. *When $(a_n)_{n=1}^{\infty}$ is a fixed sequence and*

$$b_n = \sum_{k|n} a_k$$

then

$$a_n = \sum_{k|n} \mu(n/k) b_k = \sum_{k|n} \mu(k) b_{n/k}$$

with the Möbius function μ defined as in (3.17). When

$$c_n = \sum_{k=0}^{n} \binom{n}{k} a_k$$

$$d_n = \sum_{k=0}^{n} (-1)^k \binom{n}{k} a_k$$

then

$$a_n = -\sum_{k=0}^{n} (-1)^k \binom{n}{k} c_k = \sum_{k=0}^{n} (-1)^k \binom{n}{k} d_k.$$

EX. 3.4.6 → **Example 5.2.2: Polya's conjecture revisited.** The functions L and Λ considered in Example 3.4.6 are, respectively, exactly the partial sums and the Möbius transform of the Liouville function λ. Note that λ is indeed multi-
EX. 7.1.5 ← plicative. ◁

Reconstructing from convolutions is more complicated, and is usually done via generating functions as described in the next section.

5.2.2 *Generating Functions*

As we have seen, the *ordinary* generating function for any sequence $(a_n)_{n=0}^{\infty}$ is the function defined by the power series

$$A(z) = \sum_{n=0}^{\infty} a_n z^n.$$

We usually define z to be a complex number, but it is often best thought of as a "place-holder," the powers of which keep track of indices signifying the number of used objects as in Example 5.1.10 or weights as in Example 5.2.7. One sometimes considers this as a formal sum, but of course $A(z)$ only makes sense whenever the series converges, which it will do for all $|z| < R$ and no $|z| > R$ with R the radius of convergence computable for instance as

$$R = \liminf \sqrt[n]{|a_n|}.$$

The key reason for working with generating functions is that many frequently occurring manipulations of sequences of numbers correspond directly to very basic operations on the corresponding generating functions. For instance, rules such as

$$cA(z) = \sum_{n=0}^{\infty} ca_n z^n, \quad c \in \mathbb{C} \tag{5.18}$$

$$z^m A(z) = \sum_{n=m}^{\infty} a_{n-m} z^n, \quad m \geq 0 \tag{5.19}$$

$$A(z^m) = \sum_{n=0}^{\infty} a_n z^{mn}, \quad m \geq 0 \tag{5.20}$$

$$A(cz) = \sum_{n=0}^{\infty} a_n c^n z^n, \qquad c \in \mathbb{C} \tag{5.21}$$

$$A(z)B(z) = \sum_{n=0}^{\infty} \left[\sum_{k=0}^{n} a_k b_{n-k} \right] z^n \tag{5.22}$$

$$\frac{A(z)}{1 - A(z)} = \sum_{\substack{k_1 + k_2 + \cdots + k_m = n \\ k_i \geq 1}} a_{k_1} a_{k_2} \cdots a_{k_m} z^n \tag{5.23}$$

$$A'(z) = \sum_{n=0}^{\infty} (n+1) a_{n+1} z^n$$

$$\int_0^z A(w)dw = \sum_{n=1}^{\infty} \frac{a_{n-1}}{n} z^n$$

can be combined with basic theory for power series to find that

$$1, 0, 0, 0, 0, 0, \ldots \sim 1 \tag{5.24}$$

$$1, 1, 1, 1, 1, 1, \ldots \sim \frac{1}{1-z}$$

$$1, 0, 1, 0, 1, 0, \ldots \sim \frac{1}{1-z^2} \tag{5.25}$$

$$1, 2, 3, 4, 5, 6, \ldots \sim \frac{1}{(1-z)^2} \tag{5.26}$$

$$0, 1, \frac{1}{2}, \frac{1}{3}, \frac{1}{4}, \frac{1}{5}, \ldots \sim \ln\left(\frac{1}{1-z}\right)$$

$$0, 1, \frac{1}{2}, \frac{1}{6}, \frac{1}{24}, \frac{1}{120}, \ldots \sim e^z \tag{5.27}$$

$$\binom{c}{0}, \binom{c}{1}, \binom{c}{2}, \binom{c}{3}, \binom{c}{4}, \binom{c}{5}, \ldots \sim (1+z)^c, \tag{5.28}$$

where $\sim$ indicates that the given function is the generating function for the given sequence of numbers, and the given sequence of numbers the coefficients in the power series for the given function. The last formula holds for any c by the definition

$$\binom{c}{n} = \frac{c(c-1) \cdots (c-n+1)}{n(n-1) \cdots 1}$$

(consistent with what we did in Exercise 3.11).

We see by comparison to (5.22) and (5.23) that the generating function for the sequences obtained by transforming by (5.16) and (5.17) become $A(z)^2$ and $A(z)/(1 - A(z))$, respectively. Thus, an explicit generating function of the transformed sequence can lead to an explicit generating function of the original sequence by solving a simple equation.

One often also considers the *exponential generating function* (egf):

$$\widehat{A}(z) = \sum_{n=0}^{\infty} a_n \frac{z^n}{n!}.$$

The basic relations here are

$$\widehat{A}(z)\widehat{B}(z) = \sum_{n=0}^{\infty}\left[\sum_{k=0}^{n} \binom{n}{k} a_k b_{n-k}\right]\frac{z^n}{n!} \tag{5.29}$$

$$\widehat{A}'(z) = \sum_{n=0}^{\infty} a_{n+1}\frac{z^n}{n!}$$

Using generating functions is a standard tool for investigating sequences of numbers, in particular when it comes to *solving recurrences*, that is, determining closed forms for sequences given by recursive definitions. It is beyond the scope of this book to cover the rich theory of generating functions, but we will record a few examples to illustrate the power and versatility of this tool.

EX. 5.1.5 → **Example 5.2.3: Fibonacci numbers.** We have already seen guessgf guess the generating function for the Fibonacci numbers f_n given by the recursive formula (3.6). Let us see how to extract a generating function $F(z)$ theoretically. We have by (5.19) that

$$F(z) = \sum_{n=0}^{\infty} f_n z^n$$

$$zF(z) = \sum_{n=1}^{\infty} f_{n-1} z^n$$

$$z^2 F(z) = \sum_{n=2}^{\infty} f_{n-2} z^n$$

so we see by inspecting the right hand sides that $F(z) - zF(z) - z^2F(z)$ has trivial coefficients at $n \geq 1$ because of (3.6). At the power z, we get $z - 0 - 0 = z$, so in total we have

$$F(z) - zF(z) - z^2F(z) = z,$$

which we may solve for $F(z)$ to get

$$F(z) = \frac{z}{1 - z - z^2}. \tag{5.31}$$

This description leads to a proof of (5.9) by expanding $F(z)$ in partial fractions. Indeed, we have

$$F(z) = \frac{\sqrt{5} - 1}{1 + 2z + \sqrt{5}} + \frac{1 - \sqrt{5}}{-1 - 2z + \sqrt{5}}$$

with two terms each of the form

$$\frac{a}{z - b} = \frac{-a/b}{1 - z/b},$$

which corresponds to the sequence

$$-a/b, -a/b^2, -a/b^3, -a/b^4, \ldots$$

by applying (5.18) and (5.21) to (5.24). Note that these computations form the
EX. 7.1.2 ← solid basis of a mathematical proof, in spite of their experimental origins. ◁

EX. 5.1.7 → **Example 5.2.4: Noncrossing trees.**   Revisiting the results found in Examples 5.1.1, 5.1.4, 5.1.6, and 5.1.7, we are led to consider whether perhaps our result that $c_1 = 0$ is problematic, wrong even. It would certainly seem reasonable to say that a cycle with a single vertex could be spanned according to our rules in one way rather than none. We trace this result back to the fact that IsTree does not accept a single vertex as a tree, and we decide to revise our observation to $c_1 = 1$ so that we can get the revised hypothesis

$$c_k = \frac{1}{3k-2}\binom{3k-2}{k-1}. \tag{5.32}$$

This is an extremely nice candidate for a formula for c_k, but we are still missing an argument to establish it as a mathematical fact. Very often, the best approach in such a situation is to study how Maple arrived at its suggestion for the generating function $C(x)$. The function found by guessgf in (5.11) may remind the reader of the solutions to cubic equations. Using our revised values for c_0 and c_1, we indeed get

```
[> guesseqn([0,1,1,3,12,55,273,1428,7752,43263,246675],    1
             C(x));                                          2
```

$$[-x + xC(x) - C(x)^3, ogf]$$

or equivalently

$$xC(x) = x^2 + C(x)^3.$$

By (5.19) and (5.22), this becomes

$$c_{n-1} = \sum_{\substack{k,\ell,m \geq 1 \\ k+\ell+m=n}} c_k c_\ell c_m + \begin{cases} 1 & n = 2 \\ 0 & \text{otherwise} \end{cases}$$

or better

$$c_n = \sum_{\substack{k,\ell,m \geq 1 \\ k+\ell+m=n+1}} c_k c_\ell c_m$$

for $n \geq 2$ with $c_0 = 0$ and $c_1 = 1$. Thus we are led to a proof by devising a method for uniquely producing a noncrossing spanning tree with n vertices out of three smaller such trees having a total of $n + 1$ vertices, cf. Exercise 5.43.

◁

EX. 5.1.10 → **Example 5.2.5: LEGO pyramids.** It is possible to prove the hypothesis from Example 5.1.10 using generating functions. Let the number of pyramids that can be built by n bricks be denoted by p_n, and define the generating function

$$P(z) = \sum_{n=1}^{\infty} p_n z^n.$$

We consider *half-pyramids* to be pyramids with the property that no block is placed to the left of the base block, denoting this number by h_n and the generating function by $H(z)$. We have $p_1 = h_1 = 1$, and it can be proved that

$$p_n = h_n + \sum_{k=1}^{n-1} p_k h_{n-k}, n \geq 0 \tag{5.33}$$

by noting that every pyramid which is not a half-pyramid can be divided uniquely into a smaller half-pyramid and a smaller pyramid. Similar reasoning gives the recursive formula

$$h_n = 1 + \sum_{k=1}^{n-1} h_k + \sum_{k=2}^{n-1} \sum_{\ell=1}^{k-1} h_\ell h_{k-\ell}. \tag{5.34}$$

The point of these recurrences is that (5.34) translates to

$$H(z) = \frac{1}{1-z} \left[1 + zH(z) + z^2 H^2(z) \right], \tag{5.35}$$

and (5.33) translates to

$$P(z) = H(z) + zH(z)P(z). \tag{5.36}$$

Solving (5.35) gives

$$H(z) = \frac{1 - 2z \pm \sqrt{1 - 4z}}{2z^2}.$$

Note that the relevant root is the one with a negative sign; indeed in the other case the fraction will diverge as $z \to 0$. We may then solve (5.36) using Maple to get

$$P(z) = -\frac{2z - 1 + \sqrt{1 - 4z}}{z(4z + \sqrt{1 - 4z} - 1)}$$

(this is not the most elegant form of P). With P defined this way in Maple, we can check that we are on the right track with

```
[> series(P(z),z,8);
```

$$1 + 3z + 10z^2 + 35z^3 + 126z^4 + 462z^5 + 1716z^6 + 6435z^7 + O(z^8).$$

Maple gives us

```
[> convert(P(z),FormalPowerSeries);
```

$$\sum_{k=0}^{\infty} \frac{(2k+1)! z^k}{k!^2 (k+1)},$$

showing that the power series of the function is

$$\sum_{k=0}^{\infty} \binom{2k-1}{k-1} z^k.$$

It is possible to derive this last step theoretically by simplifying the expression for P to

$$P(z) = \frac{1}{2z\sqrt{1-4z}}$$

and employing (5.27) along with the observation that

$$\binom{-1/2}{k} = \left(\frac{-1}{4}\right)^k \binom{2k}{k}$$

(see e.g. [GKP94, (5.37)]). Again, the experimental considerations lead di-
EX. 5.4.3 ← rectly to a solid proof.   ◁

5.2.3 *The* gfun *Package*

The key idea behind the gfun package (developed by Bruno Salvy and Paul Zimmermann) is to try to match a given segment of an infinite sequence with the power series associated to a "nice" function. More precisely, a generating function will be considered plausible if it is *hypergeometric*, which corresponds to the proposed infinite sequence being *holonomic*. We will not need to concern ourselves with the details of these classes of objects, but we note that the set of hypergeometric functions contains most of the functions which are holomorphic in a neighborhood of 0 and which the reader knows by name.

To use these tools, one supplies a list of numbers to the Maple command guessgf. For instance,

```
[> with(gfun):                                                            1
    guessgf([seq(n^2,n=0..10)],z);                                        2
```

$$\left[-\frac{-z^2 - z}{-z^3 + 3z^2 - 3z + 1}, ogf \right]$$

Here, the clause "*ogf*" informs us that this is an ordinary generating function. Some times, say with

```
[> guessgf([seq(n!,n=0..10)],z);
```

$$\left[\frac{1}{1-z}, egf \right]$$

an exponential generating function is found, as indicated with "*egf*."

EX. 3.2.1 → **Example 5.2.6:** guessgf.   In (3.2) of Example 3.2.1 we computed terms of the sequences (a_n) and (b_n) defined there. With these observations stored in SA and SB, respectively, we get

---

Sister Celine and the Wilf–Zeilberger algorithm

Examples such as the ones given above may make one wonder if it is possible to "cut out the middle man" and let the computer handle the entire process of establishing mathematical fact, from the realization that something may be true to the formal proof.

In the area of *hypergeometric identities*, this turns out to be possible, thanks to groundbreaking work by Mary Celine Fasenmyer (1906–1996), a nun from the Sisters of Mercy order who in her 1945 PhD thesis proved that all such identities in a special class had a certain recursive form which, in turn, could form the basis for a formal proof. But the result was overlooked until Doron Zeilberger (1950–) realized that Sister Celine's methods could be generalized to allow for identities such as

$$\sum_{k=0}^{n} \binom{n}{k}^2 = \binom{2n}{n}$$

to not only be automatically provable from certain rational functions, in this case by

$$R(n, k) = -\frac{k^2(3n + 3 - 2k)}{2(n + 1 - k)^2(2n + 1)},$$

serving as certificates for their correctness, but also to provide efficient algorithms to find such certificates or prove their nonexistence. The resulting so-called Wilf–Zeilberger algorithm is implemented in Maple's `SumTools` package.

Zeilberger is a tireless proponent for experimental mathematics, and often credits his computer Shalosh B. Ekhad on papers (both as a coauthor and as a single author which we may assume that Zeilberger helped type up the paper), to alert the mathematical community at large that new and powerful methods for doing mathematics are appearing. Zeilberger's *36th Opinion* containing claims such as "any theorem that a human can prove is, *ipso facto*, utterly trivial" and

> *since everything that we can prove today will soon be provable, faster and better, by computers, it is a waste of time to keep proving, in the same old-way, either by only pencil and paper, and even doing "computer-assisted" proofs, regarding the computer as a "pencil with power-stirring".*

instigated a large debate on the ends and means of 21st-century mathematics which is highly relevant for any experimental mathematician, irrespective of whether they agree or not.

```
[> guessgf(SA,z), guessgf(SB,z);
```

$$\left[\frac{\ln(z+1)+1}{(z+1)^2}, egf\right], \left[-\frac{1}{1+2z+z^2}, egf\right].$$

Starting with the function found to the right, note that by combining (5.20) and (5.25), it is seen that the ordinary generating function for $-1/(1+2z+z^2)$ is given by

$$\sum_{n=0}^{\infty}(-1)^{n+1}(n+1)z^n.$$

Hence, the coefficients of the exponential generating function at $n \in \mathbb{N}_0$ would seem to be

$$(-1)^{n+1}(n+1)n! = (-1)^{n+1}(n+1)!,$$

which is easy to guess from (3.2). However, the picture is muddled by the fact that we have used the entry corresponding to the nth derivative as the coefficient to z^{n-1}. Prepending 0 and redoing the computation yields

```
[> guessgf([0,op(SB)],z);
```

$$\left[-\frac{z}{z+1}, egf\right]$$

and we can conclude that $b_n = (-1)^n n!$ as before. Doing the same for the sequence (a_n), we get

$$\left[\frac{\ln(z+1)}{z+1}, egf\right].$$

The ordinary generating functions for $\ln(z+1)$ and $1/(z+1)$ are given by applying (5.20) with $c = -1$ to (5.26) and (5.24). They are, respectively, $(-1)^n\frac{1}{n}$ and $(-1)^n$, so by (5.22), and adjusting for the fact that the generating function is exponential, we get in particular

$$a_n = n!\sum_{k=0}^{n}(-1)^k\frac{1}{k}(-1)^{n-k} = (-1)^n n!\sum_{k=0}^{n}\frac{1}{k}.$$

These are known as the signed Stirling numbers of the first kind, cf. Exercise 5.20 and the box on p. 152.   ◁

5.2.4 *Using the OEIS*

As already mentioned, it is completely straightforward to use the OEIS: one simply enters the sequence of interest in a search form on www.oeis.org. However, to improve the chances for a hit, the sequences should be "cleaned up," by omitting obviously redundant factors. For instance, if every other term is zero, for example

$$1, 0, 2, 0, 4, 0, 8, 0, 16, 0, 32, 0, 64, 0,$$

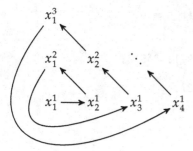

Figure 5.7 Organizing 2d observations.

it is suggested to omit these zeroes, and instead look up

$$1, 2, 4, 8, 16, 32, 64.$$

Sequences with several initial entries in $\{0, 1\}$ such as

$$0, 1, 1, 2, 5, 12, 32, 94, 289$$

should be submitted with only one initial "1." This will signal to the OEIS that such terms exist, while avoiding the problem that we have already encountered a number of times; that peculiarities at the start of a sequence make it impossible for the OEIS to recognize.

If the experimental data depends on two variables, it should be organized diagonally. For instance the observations in Figure 5.7 should be submitted as

$$x_1^1, x_2^1, x_1^2, x_3^1, x_2^2, x_1^3, x_4^1, x_3^2, x_2^3, x_1^4, \ldots$$

Alternatively, one can try row-by-row or column-by-column. A sequence of fractions can be submitted as sequences of nominators and denominators separately. We did this with success in Example 5.1.8, but note that often reductions to lowest terms will tend to confuse matters. Hence a systematic way of canceling denominators, when possible, should be preferred.

For each sequence in the OEIS, the entry will usually contain many more terms than what is needed to locate it, as well as an explanation of how it arises in various contexts. The OEIS also provides references to the literature, as well as snippets of code in Maple or other computer algebra software systems for their efficient generation.

The entries are rather self-explanatory, but let us note a few of them:

Offset: This line usually gives the subscript of the first term in the sequence. If two numbers are given, the second one indicates the first entry which is neither 0 nor 1. If the sequence gives the decimal expansion of a constant, the offset is the number of digits before the decimal point.

Formula: If a closed form for a sequence is known, it will be given here.

Crossrefs: This entry can often lead to interesting, related sequences.

```
A7576 Number of solutions to k_1 + 2*k_2 + ... + n*k_n = 0,
      where k_i are from {-1,0,1}, i=1..n.

1, 1, 1, 3, 7, 15, 35, 87, 217, 547, 1417, 3735, 9911, 26513,
71581, 194681, ·532481, 1464029, 4045117, 11225159,
31268577, 87404465, 245101771, 689323849, 1943817227,
5494808425, 15568077235, 44200775239, 125739619467
OFFSET
0,4
COMMENTS
Also, number of maximally stable towers of 2 X 2 LEGO blocks.
REFERENCES
N.J.A. Sloane and Simon Plouffe, The Encyclopedia of Integer
Sequences, Academic Press, 1995 (includes this sequence).
P.J.S. Watson, On "LEGO" towers, J. Rec. Math., 12
(No. 1, 1979-1980), 24-27.
LINKS T.D. Noe, Table of n, a(n) for n=0..100
       S.R. Finch, Signum equations and extremal coefficients.
FORMULA
Coefficient of x^(n*(n+1)/2) in
Product_{k=1..n}(1+x^k+x^(2*k)).
EXAMPLE
For n=4 there are 7 solutions: (-1,-1,1,0), (-1,0,-1,1),
(-1,1,1,-1), (0,0,0,0), (1,-1,-1,1), (1,0,1,-1), (1,1,-1,0).
MATHEMATICA
f[0] = 1; f[n_] := Coefficient[Expand@
Product[1 + x^k + x^(2k), {k, n}], x^(n(n + 1)/2)];
Table[f@n, {n, 0, 28}]] (from Robert G. Wilson v, Nov 10 2006)
PROG
(Maxima) a(n):=coeff(expand(product(1+x^k+x^(2*k),
k, 1, n)), x, binomial(n+1, 2));
makelist(a(n), n, 0, 24);
CROSSREFS
Cf. A007575, A063865, A039826.
```

Figure 5.8 The beginning of the OEIS entry A7576.

EX. 4.3.1 → **Example 5.2.7: LEGO towers in the OEIS.**   Consider again the maximally stable LEGO towers discussed in Example 1.6.5. Several years ago, the first named author looked up Watson's observations (3.8) in the OEIS, finding them submitted with reference to Watson's paper as A7576. But another match was found in A86821 which originated quite differently, namely as the number of solutions to

$$\sum_{i=1}^{n} i k_i = 0$$

with all $k_i \in \{-1, 0, 1\}$. It is easy to prove that these two sequences coincide, since the sum given precisely computes the center of gravity, and the two entries have now been merged into one in the OEIS. Most of the present entry can be found in Figure 5.8.

We note that the entry also contains an alternative method for computing the B_n, implemented in Mathematica and Maxima code (but not Maple). The fundamental idea in this method is that every choice of an entry in $\mathbf{x} \in \{-1, 0, 1\}^{N-1}$ corresponds to choosing one of the summands in each parenthesis in the expression

$$q_N(x) = (x^{-1} + 1 + x^1)(x^{-2} + 1 + x^2) \cdots (x^{-(N-1)} + 1 + x^{N-1}).$$

Expanding the expression, we get a monomial of the form x^ℓ for each of the 3^{N-1} different ways of choosing such $N - 1$ summands. Collecting the terms, we see that the coefficient of x^w is exactly $t_{w,N}$ as defined in Example 1.6.5.

To avoid negative coefficients, it is convenient to multiply by

$$x^1 x^2 \cdots x^{N-1} = x^{N(N-1)/2},$$

and instead extract the coefficient at $x^{w+N(N-1)/2}$ in

$$p_N(x) = x^{N(N-1)/2} q_N(x)$$
$$= (1 + x + x^2)(1 + x^2 + x^4) \cdots (1 + x^{N-1} + x^{2N-2}).$$

In Maple we obtain this by

```
[> q:=(N,x)->product((1+x^i+x^(2*i)),i=1..N-1);          1
   t:=(N,w)->coeff(q(N,x),x,w+N*(N-1)/2);                2
```

and we check by running

```
[> Q:=20;                                                1
   max([seq(seq(abs(dTower(N,w)-t(N,w)),w=-Q..Q),        2
     N=1..Q)]);                                          3
```

to obtain the value 0 that the old and new realizations of $t_{w,N}$ do coincide for small values of w and N. We obtain this way a completely new way of computing the numbers which, as we shall see, has merits over our previous

EX. 5.3.6 ← method.   ◁

5.3 Recognizing Floating-point Numbers

5.3.1 Continued Fractions

A complete discussion of continued fractions would take us too far, but in this section we collect a few key results to aid the reader's work with continued fractions. To conserve space we use the standard notation $[a_0; a_1, a_2, a_3, \dots]$ for the continued fraction

$$\alpha = a_0 + \cfrac{1}{a_1 + \cfrac{1}{a_2 + \cfrac{1}{a_3 + \cdots}}}$$

By assumption all $a_i \in \mathbb{N}$ for $i \geq 1$, but we must of course allow that $a_0 \in \mathbb{Z}$.

We have already noted:

Proposition 5.3.1.

(i) *The continued fraction expansion of a number α is finite if and only if α is rational.*
(ii) *The continued fraction expansion of an irrational number is unique.*
(iii) *Every rational number has exactly two continued fraction expansions:*

$$[a_0; a_1, a_2, a_3, \ldots, a_n + 1] = [a_0; a_1, a_2, a_3, \ldots, a_n, 1].$$

When α is irrational and given by an infinite continued fraction expansion

$$[a_0; a_1, a_2, a_3, \ldots]$$

we write

$$\frac{p_n}{q_n} = [a_0; a_1, a_2, a_3, \ldots, a_{n-1}],$$

and call p_n/q_n the nth convergent, with $\gcd(p_n, q_n) = 1$ and $q_n > 1$ assumed implicitly throughout. The behavior of the convergents to $\ln(2)$ illustrated in Figure 5.4 is generic: the convergents are alternately larger and smaller than the number being approximated, and each convergent is a better approximation that any of the preceding convergents. Further, the convergents are unique in the sense that they are the only rational approximations p/q closer to the approximant than $1/2q^2$. Precisely:

Proposition 5.3.2.

(i) $\dfrac{p_{2n}}{q_{2n}} \nearrow \alpha$ and $\dfrac{p_{2n-1}}{q_{2n-1}} \searrow \alpha$ as $n \to \infty$.
(ii) *For any integers p, q with $0 < q \le q_n$ we have*

$$\left| \alpha - \frac{p}{q} \right| \ge \left| \alpha - \frac{p_n}{q_n} \right|$$

with equality only at $p = p_n$ and $q = q_n$.
(iii) *When*

$$\left| \alpha - \frac{p}{q} \right| < \frac{1}{2q^2}$$

with $\gcd(p, q) = 1$, then $p/q = p_n/q_n$ for some n.

We also note:

Proposition 5.3.3. *Given an interval $I = [\alpha, \beta]$, a fraction $p/q \in I$ with q as small as possible is given by*

$$\frac{p}{q} = [a_0; a_1, \ldots, a_{k-1}, \min(a_k, b_k) + 1]$$

when the continued fraction expansions of α and β are given by

$$[a_0; a_1, a_2, \ldots] \qquad [b_0; b_1, b_2, \ldots]$$

with $a_0 = b_0, \ldots, a_k = b_k$ and $a_{k+1} \neq b_{k+1}$.

Proposition 5.3.3 can be used in situations where the constant one tries to recognize is given with so much imprecision that only a few digits can be trusted. As we shall see in Chapter 6, this approach is particularly useful in the context of pseudorandomness.

Example 5.3.4: Recognizing fractions. We wish to make sense out of five numbers arising from a computation so imprecise that we only know that they lie in the intervals

$$[[0.008314, 0.008365], [0.216699, 0.216941], [0.549744, 0.550021],$$
$$[0.216502, 0.216744], [0.008309, 0.008360]]'$$

A procedure such as

```
[> bestFraction:=proc(II)                                    1
       local L,a,b,alpha,beta;                               2
       L:=[];                                                 3
       a:=floor(II[1]); b:=floor(II[2]);                      4
       alpha:=II[1]-a; beta:=II[2]-b;                         5
       while(a=b) do                                          6
          L:=[op(L),a];                                       7
          a:=floor(1/alpha); b:=floor(1/beta);               8
          alpha:=1/alpha-a; beta:=1/beta-b;                  9
       end do;                                               10
       L:=[op(L),min(a,b)+1];                                11
       return cfrac(L);                                      12
    end proc;                                                13
```

works by running the Euclidean algorithm on the endpoints until the results differ, and then reconstructing the continued fraction using `cfrac`, to give

$$\left[\frac{1}{120}, \frac{18}{83}, \frac{11}{20}, \frac{13}{60}, \frac{1}{120} \right] \tag{5.38}$$

EX. 6.5.3 ←

◁

5.3.2 *identify and PSLQ*

Using `identify` on data arising from experiments, prone to imprecision or error, may be difficult. In Example 4.2.4, for instance, we encountered a floating point constant which was identified as ln(3) based on the given context, but even though we based our fit on the 51 observations $B_{250}, \ldots, B_{300}$, Fit gave the result

$$1.0968020,$$

which would have been impossible for `identify` to recognize, since in fact

$$\ln(3) \approx 1.0968123.$$

The command `identify(1.0968)` yields arcsinh $\frac{4}{3}$ which is correct (as can be seen with `convert(arcsinh(4/3),ln)`), even though it is hard to recognize. However, having one more correct digit, as in `identify(1.09681)`, would yield the false friend $\frac{78}{71}$. These kinds of volatility issues regularly arise when one uses `identify`, making it very important to know precisely how many digits to trust, and to have sufficiently many trustworthy digits.

In the very common situation where the constant one tries to `identify` is only computable to a low level of precision, it is instructive to apply `identify` to a variety of significant digits as in

```
[> multiIdentify:=c->                                                    1
    [seq(identify(evalf(c,i),all=true),i=1..15)];                        2
```

where we have added the option `all=true` to ask `identify` to try a full range of searches. This is usually worth doing unless one is traversing a lot of floating point constants.

This reveals that when we start with a given constant, `identify` will respond very differently depending on the number of digits given. We get, for instance,

$$\pi : 3, \frac{31}{10}, \frac{22}{7}, \frac{22}{7}, \pi, \pi, \pi, \frac{355}{113}, \pi, \ldots, \pi$$

$$e : 3, \frac{27}{10}, e, e, e, \pi - \operatorname{arccot}\frac{91}{41}, \pi - \operatorname{arccot}\frac{91}{41}, e, \ldots, e$$

$$\sqrt{\pi} : 2, \frac{9}{5}, \frac{23}{13}, \frac{39}{22}, \frac{39}{22}, \sqrt{\pi}, \ldots, \sqrt{\pi}$$

$$\ln 5 : 2, \frac{8}{5}, \frac{29}{18}, \frac{37}{23}, \ln 5, \operatorname{arcsinh}\frac{12}{5}, \ldots, \operatorname{arcsinh}\frac{12}{5}$$

$$e^{\pi/5} : 2, \frac{19}{10}, \frac{43}{23}, \frac{15}{8}, e^{-\frac{1}{2}+\frac{2}{\sqrt{\pi}}}, \frac{47}{26}\zeta(5), e^{\pi/5}, e^{\pi/5}, e^{\pi/5}, e^{\pi/5}, e^{\pi/5},$$

$$\pi - \operatorname{arccos}\frac{1153}{3856}, e^{\pi/5}, e^{\pi/5}, e^{\pi/5}.$$

Obviously, it is naive to try to recognize π from 3.1, but note how we quickly encounter some of the oldest approximations (cf. box on p. 249) this way. Note also how `multiIdentify` flip-flops between the correct value and less useful ones as precision increases, and that indeed

$$\operatorname{arcsinh}\frac{12}{5} = \ln 5$$

as above, so that this particular answer is in fact correct even though it is less immediately useful than $\ln(5)$. It is only in the last example that the option `all=true` plays a role.

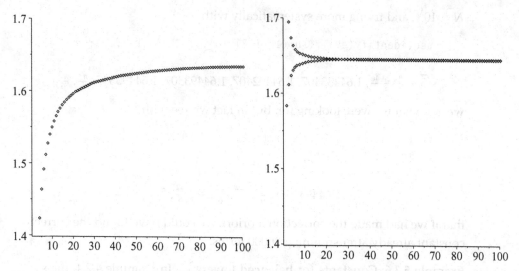

Figure 5.9   Left: Partial sums. Right: Sums adjusted by the lower and upper error estimates.

Example 5.3.5: Estimating errors.   Suppose we had forgotten Euler's beautiful formula

$$\sum_{n=1}^{\infty} \frac{1}{n^2} = \frac{\pi^2}{6}$$

and wanted to be reminded using identify. Trying

```
[> identify(evalf(sum(1/(i^2),i=1..1000000)));
```

gives nothing, so we are forced to think a little harder about the problem.

In general, in the situation where an increasing sequence converges to some theoretical value that we wish to identify, it is extremely difficult to decide how many digits to trust as indeed the limit is unknown to us. In this case, however, there is an easy estimate of the distance to the limit, since the error we are making when summing the first N terms is of course

$$\sum_{n=N+1}^{\infty} \frac{1}{n^2}$$

which we may approximate using integrals as

$$\frac{1}{N+1} = \int_{N+1}^{\infty} \frac{1}{x^2} dx \leq \sum_{n=N+1}^{\infty} \frac{1}{n^2} \leq \int_{N}^{\infty} \frac{1}{x^2} dx = \frac{1}{N}.$$

This tells us that the error is between $1/(N+1)$ and $1/N$, and when we adjust for this in the plot to the right in Figure 5.9, we no longer need to worry about how close we are to the goal; knowing that we have M correct digits when

$N \geq 10^M$, and trying more systematically with

```
[> seq(identify(evalf(sum(1/(i^2),i=1..10^k))),k=3..9);
```

$$\sqrt{3} - \tfrac{8\sqrt{2}+4e}{5}, \ 1.64483407, \ 1.64492407, \ 1.64493307, \ 1.64493397, \ \tfrac{\pi^2}{6}, \ \tfrac{\pi^2}{6}$$

we get what we were looking for. But in fact we see with

```
[> seq(identify(evalf(sum(1/(i^2),i=1..10^k))+                    1
      10^(-k)),k=3..9);                                           2
```

$$1.644934568, \ \tfrac{\pi^2}{6}, \ \tfrac{\pi^2}{6}, \ \tfrac{\pi^2}{6}, \ \tfrac{\pi^2}{6}, \ \tfrac{\pi^2}{6}, \ \tfrac{\pi^2}{6}$$

that if we had made the correction a priori, we could have found the correct constant already after summing 10000 terms.   ◁

EX. 5.2.7 → **Example 5.3.6: Constants for balanced towers.**   In Example 4.2.4, the sequences $\widehat{B}_n$ and $\widecheck{\beta}_n$ were shown to be decaying as $k_1 n^{-3/2}$ and $k_2 n^{-1/2}$, respectively. Let us try to identify k_1, using the rich supply of values of B_n computed for n up to 646 in Example 3.3.4. Assume that these values are stored in a list LL of the form

```
[> LL[1..10];
```

$$[[1, 1], [2, 1], [3, 1], [4, 3], [5, 7], [6, 15], [7, 35], [8, 87], [9, 217], [10, 547]]$$

so the approximations of k_1 can be computed by:

```
[> QL:=[seq(evalf(LL[i][2]*3^(-i+1)*(i)^(3/2)),            1
          i=1..nops(LL))]:                                 2
      QL[-5..-1];                                          3
```

$$[0.8468282408, 0.8468273949, 0.8468265513, 0.8468257106, 0.8468248723]$$

Here it is clear that no more than five digits can be expected to be correct, and this does not seem to be enough for identify, which ventures the guess $\tfrac{22}{45}\sqrt{3}$ that is clearly too low.

To get an idea of how far we are from the limit value, the approximants are plotted in Figure 5.10. The convergence seems clear, but it is also obvious that it is not very fast at the relevant scale. In fact, the behavior might remind us of what we saw in Figure 5.9, and a similar strategy can be employed. For the last 100 data points, the relative differences $\widehat{B}_n - \widehat{B}_{n-1}$ are plotted in a double logarithmic grid to the right in Figure 5.10, and they seem to decay as cn^{-2}. More precisely, setting

$$a = -1.997120 \quad \text{and} \quad b = -1.071713,$$

we get that $an + b$ is a fit to the doubly logarithmic transform of the observations. If the remaining terms developed according to the regime $-e^b n^a$, then

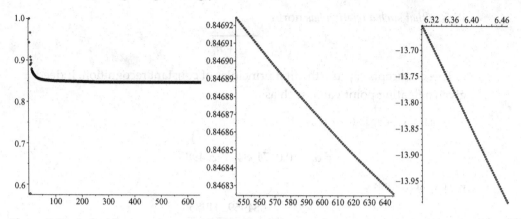

Figure 5.10   Left: All approximants. Middle: Last 100 approximants. Right: Relative difference for the last 100 observations.

the aggregated error would be roughly

$$\int_{647}^{\infty} -e^b x^a dx = 0.0005397883929.$$

Hence, the estimate is

$$0.8468248723 - 0.0005397883929 = 0.8462850839,$$

yielding

```
[> multiIdentify(0.8462850839);
```

$$\tfrac{4}{5}, \tfrac{17}{20}, \tfrac{11}{13}, \tfrac{1}{2} + \tfrac{1}{2}\ln 2, \arctan\left(\tfrac{4}{5} + \tfrac{e^{1/2}}{5}\right), \tfrac{3}{2\sqrt{\pi}}, \tfrac{3}{2\sqrt{\pi}}, \sin\left(\tfrac{3^{2/3}\pi^{7/5}}{10\ln(3)^{1/4}}\right),$$
$$.846285084, \arctan\left(\tfrac{3\sqrt{3}}{5} + \tfrac{e}{30}\right), \dots, \arctan\left(\tfrac{3\sqrt{3}}{5} + \tfrac{e}{30}\right)$$

Note that the appearance of a rational multiple of $1/\sqrt{\pi}$ reinforces our earlier idea (Example 4.3.1) that the problem studied is somehow related to the normal distribution. Note how using `multiIdentify` helps us avoid the unlikely conclusion that the constant should be interpreted as an angle given by arctan. In fact, $\tfrac{3}{2\sqrt{\pi}}$ is the correct constant as shown in [Fin], the notes already

EX. 7.1.4 ← identified as relevant in the OEIS entry in Figure 5.8.   ◁

5.3.3 *Integer Relations*

To understand how `identity` works, and prepare for more advanced discussions, let us formalize the notion of integer relations.

Definition 5.3.7. *Let a tuple* $(\alpha_1, \dots, \alpha_k) \in \mathbb{R}^k$ *be given. An* integer relation *of precision* ϵ *on this tuple is* $(n_1, \dots, n_k) \in \mathbb{Z}^k$ *with the property that*

$$|n_1\alpha_1 + \cdots + n_k\alpha_k| < \epsilon.$$

We say that such a relation has norm

$$\sqrt{n_1^2 + \cdots + n_k^2}.$$

These concepts capture the first principles of constant recognition. Indeed, given a floating point value such as

```
[> alpha:=evalf(1524/87143,15);
```

$$\alpha := 0.0174884959204985$$

we explicitly have

$$\alpha = \frac{174884959204985}{1000000000000000}$$

and hence of course there is an integer relation

$$1000000000000000\alpha - 174884959204985 \cdot 1 = 0,$$

but our aim is to find a relation which is *small in norm*, as that would lead to a better understanding of α. Indeed, we have already seen how to find

$$87143\alpha - 1524 \cdot 1 \approx 0$$

either using continued fractions or identify.

As we have seen, the problem of finding small integer relations is solved very satisfactorily by the Euclidean algorithm when $k = 2$. Indeed, Proposition 5.3.2(ii) can be interpreted as stating that such relations are optimal. Finding good integer relations for $k > 2$ is substantially harder, and was solved satisfactorily as late as the 1990s. Algorithms such as the PSLQ algorithm (named for "Partial Sums of Least sQuares") by Helaman Ferguson and David Bailey ([FBA99], [FF79]) were produced with the property of being able to find an integer relation of precision ϵ for any given tuple, or provide a large lower bound for the norm of any such relation. In Maple, the PSLQ implementation just returns a relation with a "small" norm in the sense that it is not guaranteed to be of minimal norm, but that the order of magnitude is correct. The experimenter must then decide whether such a relation is small enough to carry any explanatory weight. A general rule of thumb suggested in the implementation is that when the precision is 10^{-d}, the *sum* of the number of digits in the n_i should be well below d.

To work with PSLQ requires a high level of precision in the investigated floating point numbers, and it is generally advisable to increase precision substantially compared to the standard. We will discuss such issues further in Section 7.4, so here we will simply decide to use 50 digits in all remaining computations in this section. We first try

```
[> PSLQ([Pi,exp(1),1]);
```

$$[-11584053355521898, 7398898547413626, 16280085448453303]$$

In fact, it is not known if there is an exact integer relation between π, e, and 1, but certainly since the output looks like three random integers with roughly 50/3 digits each, our rule of thumb should lead us to discard the hypothesis that the relation found has any deeper meaning. In the other direction,

```
[> PSLQ([ln(9),ln(12),ln(8)]);
```

$$[3, -6, 4]$$

cannot be expected to be a coincidence since the sum of number of digits is much below 50, and of course it is not since

$$3\ln(9) - 6\ln(12) + 4\ln(8) = \ln\left(\frac{9^3 \cdot 8^4}{12^6}\right) = 0.$$

Example 5.3.8: PSLQ. Being a sum of two algebraic numbers,

$$\beta = \sqrt[3]{2} + \sqrt{3},$$

is certainly a root in a polynomial with integer coefficients. Let us use the PSLQ algorithm to try to determine such a polynomial with minimal degree. Asking PSLQ to search for integer relations between

$$1, \beta, \ldots, \beta^k$$

for increasing k with

```
[> for k from 1 to 8 do                                    1
    PSLQ([seq(beta^i,i=0..k)]);                            2
   end do;                                                 3
```

we get

$$[-6535101088729575120062481, 2184212084892162728882584]$$
$$[10178270372955303, 17788398546836608, -7082372390915209]$$
$$[191266011176, 1645990902651, 343755885064, -305904510887]$$
$$[4898801149, 3239552067, 8415546448, -3244163998, -37878393]$$
$$[11968627, 18142745, 51821131, 69862006, -47946790, 6009881]$$
$$[23, 36, -27, 4, 9, 0, -1]$$
$$[23, 36, -27, 4, 9, 0, -1, 0]$$
$$[0, 0, 23, 36, -27, 4, 9, 0, -1]$$

We see that as k reaches 6, the norm of the relation found decreases rapidly, and remains virtually unchanged as k increases. The conclusion suggested by the PSLQ algorithm is hence that we have found a polynomial

$$p(x) = x^6 - 9x^4 - 4x^3 + 27x^2 - 36x - 23$$

in which our constant is root, and that there are no such polynomials of lower degree. We can easily check that indeed $p(\beta) = 0$ and test using the `isirreduc` procedure that the p we have found is indeed irreducible, confirming this conclusion theoretically.   ◁

Example 5.3.9: Finding formulas for π. As investigated in Exercise 5.38, the classical formula

$$\ln(2) = \sum_{k=1}^{\infty} \frac{1}{k2^k} \tag{5.39}$$

can be used to compute individual binary digits of $\ln(2)$ without first calculating the preceding digits. An algorithm capable of producing individual digits in this manner is called an *arbitrary digit algorithm*. This is clearly a very desirable feature if one is interested in finding a large number of digits because it makes it possible to continue a previous calculation, to check other calculations without redoing them completely, and because it facilitates parallelization.

Inspired by this application of (5.39), Peter Borwein and Simon Plouffe began to search for an arbitrary digit algorithm for π in 1994. As discussed in Exercise 5.39, any constant α satisfying

$$\alpha = \sum_{k=1}^{\infty} \frac{p(k)}{b^n q(k)}, \tag{5.40}$$

where $b > 1$ is an integer, p and q are integer polynomials and q has no zeroes at positive integers can be computed with an arbitrary digit algorithm. More generally, it is possible to develop an arbitrary digit algorithm for any linear combination of constants obeying (5.40).

Unfortunately, no known formula for π had the required form, so Borwein and Plouffe began to search for one using an implementation of PSLQ written by David Bailey. Together, they identified a number of constants of the required type and used PSLQ to attempt to find an integer relation between π and these constants. After months of computations (and several restarts necessitated by the addition of new constants that had been identified in the literature), the program found the following integer relation:

$$\pi = {}_2F_1\left(\begin{matrix} \frac{1}{4}, \frac{5}{4} \\ 1 \end{matrix} \middle| \frac{-1}{4}\right) + 2\arctan\left(\frac{1}{2}\right) - \ln 5,$$

where the first term is a complicated hypergeometric function. Converting this equation to a series gives the Bailey–Borwein–Plouffe formula:

$$\pi = \sum_{k=0}^{\infty} \frac{1}{16^k}\left(\frac{4}{8k+1} - \frac{2}{8k+4} - \frac{1}{8k+5} - \frac{1}{8k+6}\right). \tag{5.41}$$

After discovering (5.41) through this carefully constructed experiment, Borwein, Bailey, and Plouffe were able to prove that the equation holds using traditional methods [BBP97]. In fact, this proof is not complicated, and the key to the result was clearly to establish *what* to prove. In this way, the

BOX P. 249 ← example showcases experimental mathematics at its best.   ◁

(i) Test if x rational.

(ii) Test if x is algebraic of degree 6 or less.

(iii) Test if $f(x)$ is a rational number for $f \in \mathcal{F}$

(iv) Test if $f(x)$ is algebraic of degree 6 or less for $f \in \mathcal{F}$

(v) Test if x is an integral combination of

$$1, t^{1/2}, t^{-1/2}, t, t^{-1}, t^2, t^{-2}, t^3, t^{-3}$$

with $t \in \{\pi, e, \ln 2\}$

(vi) Test if x is an integral combination of

$$1, \sqrt{2}, \sqrt{3}, \pi, \ln 2, \ln 3, \zeta(3), \zeta(5)$$

with no more than three nonzero terms.

(vii) Test if x is of the form

$$2^{a_1} \cdot 3^{a_2} \cdot 5^{a_3} \cdot 7^{a_4} \cdot \pi^{a_5} e^{a_6} (\ln 2)^{a_7} (\ln 3)^{a_8} \zeta(3)^{a_9} \zeta(5)^{a_{10}}$$

with $a_i \in \mathbb{Q}$.

Figure 5.11 Tests in `identify`.

In essence, the `identify` command is just a front-end to the PSLQ algorithm; Maple will search for various kinds of integer relations, and when a relation is deemed to be of sufficiently small norm to be of merit, this relation will be used for computing a closed form for an approximant of the given floating point number. For instance, when `identify` is passed an approximation of the golden mean ϕ

```
[> identify(.61803398874989484820);
```

Maple will locate the integer relation

$$\phi^2 + \phi - 1 = 0$$

among powers of ϕ, solve the equation symbolically, and return the root which is close to the given floating point number. If Maple is not able to solve the equation completely, partial information using Maple's standard syntax will be returned, as in

```
[> identify(evalf(2^(1/3)+3^(1/2),50));
```

$$Root\_Of\,(Z^6 - 9Z^4 - 4Z^3 + 27Z^2 - 36Z - 23, index = 1)$$

cf. Example 5.3.8.

In fact, `identify(x)` will by default do the tests in Figure 5.11 to look for an explanation of x. Here,

$$\mathcal{F} = \{\exp, \ln, \sin, \arcsin, \dots\}$$

is a family of household functions which is not obviously changeable. Most other parameters can be varied, for instance the degree in test 2 and 4, or the set of constants in test 5. Adding `all=true` will allow Maple to apply the latter three tests also to $f(x)$ with $f \in \mathcal{F}$ as in test 2 and 3, at a substantial cost in time.

5.4 The Mathematics of Inversion

We have seen that the way the experimenting mathematician infers using inversion must be coupled with nonmathematical notions of plausibility based on context. But tools for inversion such as `guessgf` or `identify` certainly operate in a well-defined mathematical setting and are based on very deep mathematical reasoning. It is beyond the scope of this book to explain in full detail how they work, but in the present section we will explain some of the key approaches and introduce a few more tools of use in inversion.

5.4.1 Padé Approximation

Just like `identify`, `guessgf` works by attempting a series of tests in order to locate a pattern in the provided sequences which may be used to either infer an expression of the generating function directly, or which leads to a formula describing the function that may then be solved by Maple's general symbolic methods. It would take us too far to describe all these methods, but let us detail one, arising from the notion of a *Padé approximant*:

Proposition 5.4.1. *Fix $M, N \in \mathbb{N}_0$ and an interval I with 0 an interior point. For any function $f : I \to \mathbb{R}$ which is differentiable up to order $M + N + 1$ there exists a unique rational function*

$$q(x) = \frac{a_M x^M + \ldots a_1 x + a_0}{b_N x^N + \ldots b_1 x + 1}$$

with the property that

$$q^{(i)}(0) = f^{(i)}(0) \qquad i \in \{0, \ldots, N + M\}.$$

When $N = 0$ we are of course just considering the Taylor polynomial.

Definition 5.4.2. *The function q thus determined is called the $[M/N]$ Padé approximant for f. We will say that it is degenerate if $a_M = 0$ or $b_N = 0$.*

Given a sequence of numbers $c_0, \ldots c_{2L}$, we can let

$$f(x) = \sum_{i=0}^{2L} c_i x^i$$

and compute the Padé approximant of order $[L/L]$. If both leading coefficients a_L and b_L are nonzero, such as

```
[> with(numapprox):                                               1
   sum(i!*z^i,i=0..8);                                            2
   pade(%,z,[4,4]);                                               3
```

$$40320z^8 + 5040z^7 + 720z^6 + 120z^5 + 24z^4 + 6z^3 + 2z^2 + z + 1$$

$$\frac{24z^4 - 154z^3 + 102z^2 - 19z + 1}{120z^4 - 240z^3 + 120z^2 - 20z + 1}$$

it does not appear particularly plausible that the given sequence of numbers has a generating function that is rational, nor that the found approximant could be used to predict more terms of the sequence. But if the Padé approximant degenerates, as for instance

```
[> sum(combinat[fibonacci](i)*z^i,i=0..8);                        1
   pade(%,z,[4,4]);                                               2
                                                                  3
```

$$21z^8 + 13z^7 + 8z^6 + 5z^5 + 3z^4 + 2z^3 + z^2 + z$$

$$\frac{z}{-z^2 - z + 1}$$

we have found something with explanatory power! Indeed, the [4/4] approximant is identical to the [1/2] approximant, and could thus have been determined by only the four first terms of the sequence. Since the remaining terms could have been inferred from the Taylor polynomial of the [1/2] approximant, it is a plausible conclusion that this holds even for (as yet) unknown elements in the sequence.

As we have seen, Padé approximation offers a way to recognize sequences that arise as the coefficients in the expansion of a rational function, but of course such sequences are not particularly common. However, just like in the case of identify, we can perform transformations of the sequences, search for rational descriptions of those, and transform back. For instance, when

$$A(z) = \sum_{k=0}^{\infty} a_k z^k$$

is given with $a_0 \neq 0$ so that $A(z) \neq 0$ in a neighborhood of 0, there is an efficient algorithm for computing the power series of the *logarithmic derivative*

$$\frac{A'(z)}{A(z)} = \sum_{k=0}^{\infty} b_k z^k,$$

starting

$$b_0 = \frac{a_1}{a_0}, b_1 = \frac{2a_0a_2 - a_1^2}{a_0^2}, b_2 = \frac{3a_0^2a_3 - 3a_0a_1a_2 + a_1^3}{a_0^3}, \dots$$

The pattern emerging that b_k may be determined from $a_0, \dots, a_{k+1}$ holds true in general, so the transformation can be done at the cost of a single term by applying `listtolist(L,ldgogf)`. If we can determine a closed form for A'/A, a closed form for A can be found by solving a simple differential equation.

Similarly, when $a_0 = 0$ and $a_1 \neq 0$, we can determine by `listtolist(L,revogf)` the coefficients of

$$A^{-1}(z) = \sum_{k=1}^{\infty} c_k z^k$$

starting

$$c_1 = \frac{1}{a_1}, c_2 = -\frac{a_2}{a_1^3}, c_3 = -\frac{a_1 a_3 - 2a_2^2}{a_1^5}, \cdots$$

where we only need $a_1, \ldots, a_k$ to compute c_k. Hence this transformation can be made at no cost of terms.

EX. 5.2.5 → **Example 5.4.3: Pyramids with `guessgf`.** Consider again the sequence

$$1, 3, 10, 35, 126, 462, 1716, 6435, 24310, 92378,$$

which we managed to identify by the use of OEIS in Example 5.1.10. We could also have found the generating function using `guessgf` as

```
[> guessgf(L,z);
```

$$\left[\frac{2}{\sqrt{1 - 4z}(1 + \sqrt{1 - 4z})}, ogf \right]$$

To try to understand how Maple could have obtained this, we attempt an [8/8] Padé approximation

$$\frac{-8z^8 + 84z^7 - 252z^6 + 330z^5 - 220z^4 + 78z^3 - 14z^2 + z}{17z^8 - 204z^7 + 714z^6 - 1122z^5 + 935z^4 - 442z^3 + 119z^2 - 17z + 1}$$

but find no good description of the generating function $A(z)$ this way. Trying instead to analyze $A^{-1}(z)$ with `listtolist(L,revogf)` we get an error arising from the convention that only lists starting with a zero may be inverted this way, so we try instead

```
[> RL:=listtolist([0,op(L)],revogf);
```

$$RL := [0, 1, -3, 8, -20, 48, -112, 256, -576, 1280, -2816, 6144,$$
$$-13312, 28672, -61440, 131072, -278528, 589824, -1245184,$$
$$2621440, -5505024]$$

Removing the initial 0 again and searching for a Padé approximant we get

```
[> pade(sum(RL[i+1]*w^i,i=1..20),w,[8,8]);
```

$$\frac{w^2 + w}{4w^2 + 4w + 1}$$

which does seem to carry explanatory power, degenerating all the way to a [2/2] approximant.

Thus we have a good description of $A^{-1}(w)$, which we may turn into a good description of $A(z)$ by solving

$$z = A^{-1}(w) = \frac{w^2 + w}{4w^2 + 4w + 1}$$

for z. Maple helps us find

$$w = \frac{\pm 1 - \sqrt{-4z + 1}}{\sqrt{-4z + 1}}$$

and we easily check that the solution with minus gives the desired answer. $\triangleleft$

5.4.2 *The PSLQ Algorithm*

When originally formulated by Ferguson, the PSLQ algorithm was somewhat complicated, but subsequent refinements simplified the algorithm enough for us to essentially present it here. Our starting point is a vector $\mathbf{x} = (x_1, \ldots, x_n)$ with n entries from $\mathbb{R}$.

We set

$$s_k = ||(0, \ldots, 0, x_k, \ldots, x_n)|| = \sqrt{\sum_{j=k}^{n} x_j^2}$$

and normalize $\mathbf{x}$ to

$$\mathbf{y} = \frac{1}{s_1}\mathbf{x}.$$

We also set

$$H_\mathbf{x} = \begin{bmatrix} \frac{s_2}{s_1} & 0 & & \cdots & & 0 \\ -\frac{x_1 x_2}{s_1 s_2} & \frac{s_3}{s_2} & 0 & & & 0 \\ -\frac{x_1 x_3}{s_1 s_2} & -\frac{s_2 x_3}{s_2} & \frac{s_4}{s_3} & 0 & & 0 \\ \vdots & \vdots & & \ddots & \ddots & \vdots \\ & & & & & 0 \\ & & & & & \frac{s_n}{s_{n-1}} \\ -\frac{x_1 x_n}{s_1 s_2} & -\frac{x_2 x_n}{s_2 s_3} & & \cdots & & \frac{x_{n-1} x_n}{s_{n-1} s_n} \end{bmatrix}, \tag{5.42}$$

noting that every column in $H_\mathbf{x}$ is orthogonal to $\mathbf{x}$ and $\mathbf{y}$, so that $H_\mathbf{x}$ represents a basis for the subspace of relations in which we are hoping to find an integer vector $\mathbf{n}$.

Formulating the PSLQ algorithm requires the concepts of *Hermite reduction* and a procedure we here call the *Ferguson swap*.

When an $n \times (n-1)$-matrix H is given on upper triangular form

$$
H = \begin{bmatrix}
d_1 & 0 & & \cdots & & 0 \\
* & d_2 & 0 & & & 0 \\
* & * & \ddots & \ddots & & \vdots \\
* & * & \cdots & d_{n-2} & 0 & \\
* & * & \cdots & * & d_{n-1} \\
* & * & \cdots & * & *
\end{bmatrix}
$$

with all diagonal entries $d_1, \ldots d_n$ nonzero, it is easy to obtain a diagonal matrix using row operations. Organizing these operations into a matrix E_0, we obtain that $E_0 H$ is diagonal and E_0 is lower triangular with ones in the diagonal, and one may prove, defining E by replacing each entry of E_0 by the closest integer, that E remains invertible and that the matrix EH is lower triangular with relatively small entries below the diagonal. We call EH the *Hermite reduction* of H and E the *Hermite reduction matrix*.

When an $n \times (n-1)$-matrix H is given on the form

$$
H = \begin{bmatrix}
d_1 & 0 & & & & & \cdots & & 0 \\
* & d_2 & 0 & & & & & & \vdots \\
* & * & \ddots & \ddots & & & & & \\
* & * & \cdots & d_m & c & & & & \\
* & * & \cdots & * & d_{m+1} & & & & \\
* & * & \cdots & * & & \ddots & \ddots & & \\
* & * & \cdots & * & & \cdots & d_{n-2} & 0 & \\
* & * & \cdots & * & & \cdots & * & d_{n-1} \\
* & * & \cdots & * & & \cdots & * & *
\end{bmatrix},
$$

we compute

$$
t_0 = \sqrt{d_m^2 + c^2}
$$
$$
t_1 = d_m / t_0
$$
$$
t_2 = c / t_0
$$

and define the matrix $\widehat{H}$ by replacing column number m and $m+1$ of H as

$$
\widehat{H}_m = t_1 H_m + t_2 H_{m+1} \qquad \widehat{H}_{m+1} = -t_2 H_m + t_1 H_{m+1}.
$$

Note that $\widehat{H}$ is lower triangular. Fixing $\gamma > 1$, the PSLQ can now be described by the pseudocode given in Algorithm 5.1.

Ferguson and Bailey prove that when the algorithm terminates without finding a relation, there can exist no relation of norm less than $\min 1/d_j$ with $d_1, \ldots, d_{n-1}$ the diagonal of the last occurrence of H_x. Thus, even when the search for small integer relations is not successful, at least one is provided a guarantee that no relation has been overlooked by the search. It is further

---

Algorithm 5.1 PSLQ

1: **procedure** PSLQ($\mathbf{x}, M, \delta$)

2:      Compute $\mathbf{y}$ and $H_{\mathbf{x}}$

3:      Set $A = B = I$

4:      Compute the Hermite reducing matrix E for $H_{\mathbf{x}}$

5:      Set $H_{\mathbf{x}} := EH_{\mathbf{x}}$, $\mathbf{y} := E^{-1}\mathbf{y}$, $A := EA$, $B := BE^{-1}$

6:      **while** $\max\{|a_{ij}|\} < M$ and $\min|y_i| > \delta$ **do**

7:           Extract the diagonal $d_1, \ldots, d_{n-1}$ from $H_{\mathbf{x}}$

8:           Select $1 \leq m \leq n - 1$ so that $\gamma^m|d_m|$ is maximal

9:           Let P be the permutation matrix of the transposition $(m, m+1)$

10:           Set $H_{\mathbf{x}} := PH_{\mathbf{x}}$, $\mathbf{y} := P^{-1}\mathbf{y}$, $A := PA$, $B := BP^{-1}$

11:           **if** $m < n - 1$ **then**

12:                Set $H_{\mathbf{x}} := \widehat{H_{\mathbf{x}}}$

13:                Compute the Hermite reducing matrix E for $H_{\mathbf{x}}$

14:                Set $H_{\mathbf{x}} := EH_{\mathbf{x}}$, $\mathbf{y} := E^{-1}\mathbf{y}$, $A := EA$, $B := BE^{-1}$

15:           **end if**

16:      **end while**

17:      **if** $\min|y_i| \leq \delta$ **then**

18:           A good integer relation is found in the ith column of B

19:      **else**

20:           No good integer relation exists at the given precision

21:      **end if**

22: **end procedure**

---

proved that any $\gamma > 1$ makes the procedure work, and heuristics are provided to show that $\gamma = \sqrt{4/3}$ makes the algorithm terminate faster.

Example 5.4.4: Hit and miss with PSLQ. It is instructive to study how the PSLQ works for the two triples $\mathbf{x} = (\pi, e, 1)$ and $\mathbf{x}' = (\ln(9), \ln(12), \ln(8))$ that we considered in Section 5.3.3. In the first case, the column of B corresponding to the smallest y_i will be

$$\begin{bmatrix} 0 \\ 0 \\ 1 \end{bmatrix}, \begin{bmatrix} 0 \\ 1 \\ -3 \end{bmatrix}, \begin{bmatrix} 0 \\ 1 \\ -3 \end{bmatrix}, \begin{bmatrix} 1 \\ 0 \\ -3 \end{bmatrix}, \begin{bmatrix} 1 \\ 0 \\ -3 \end{bmatrix}, \begin{bmatrix} -2 \\ -1 \\ 9 \end{bmatrix}, \begin{bmatrix} -3 \\ 2 \\ 4 \end{bmatrix}, \begin{bmatrix} 37 \\ -24 \\ -51 \end{bmatrix}, \begin{bmatrix} -2 \\ -1 \\ 9 \end{bmatrix}, \begin{bmatrix} -19 \\ -6 \\ 76 \end{bmatrix}, \begin{bmatrix} -37 \\ 24 \\ 51 \end{bmatrix}, \begin{bmatrix} 124 \\ -211 \\ 184 \end{bmatrix},$$

$$\begin{bmatrix} -19 \\ -6 \\ 76 \end{bmatrix}, \begin{bmatrix} 94 \\ -6 \\ -279 \end{bmatrix}, \begin{bmatrix} 124 \\ -211 \\ 184 \end{bmatrix}, \begin{bmatrix} -267 \\ 416 \\ -292 \end{bmatrix}, \begin{bmatrix} -30 \\ 205 \\ -463 \end{bmatrix}, \begin{bmatrix} -267 \\ 416 \\ -292 \end{bmatrix}, \begin{bmatrix} -267 \\ 416 \\ -292 \end{bmatrix}, \begin{bmatrix} 538 \\ -223 \\ -1084 \end{bmatrix}, \begin{bmatrix} 538 \\ -223 \\ -1084 \end{bmatrix},$$

$$\begin{bmatrix} 9955 \\ -3821 \\ -20888 \end{bmatrix}, \begin{bmatrix} -1985 \\ 4341 \\ -5564 \end{bmatrix}, \begin{bmatrix} 5970 \\ -4081 \\ -7662 \end{bmatrix}, \begin{bmatrix} 731 \\ 2412 \\ -8853 \end{bmatrix}, \begin{bmatrix} -523 \\ 9165 \\ -23270 \end{bmatrix}$$

and in the second we get

$$\begin{bmatrix} 0 \\ 0 \\ 1 \end{bmatrix}, \begin{bmatrix} 1 \\ -1 \\ 0 \end{bmatrix}, \begin{bmatrix} 1 \\ 0 \\ -1 \end{bmatrix}, \begin{bmatrix} 7 \\ -7 \\ 1 \end{bmatrix}, \begin{bmatrix} 1 \\ 0 \\ -1 \end{bmatrix}, \begin{bmatrix} 3 \\ -6 \\ 4 \end{bmatrix}.$$

We note that the algorithm may return to previously found good relations and thus that the norm is not strictly decreasing as the algorithm progresses, as seen in Figure 5.12. The rapid drop in the size of the error as a true relation

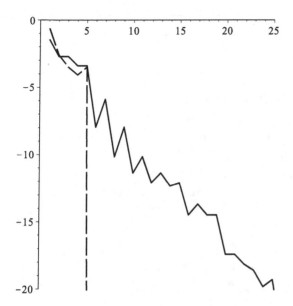

Figure 5.12   Smallest value of $|y_i|$ as PSLQ runs, semilogarithmic scale. $--$: $\mathbf{x}'$. Solid: $\mathbf{x}$.

is encountered is typical and indeed some implementations terminate and return a result when such a drop is seen.   ◁

5.5 Case Studies

When using databases such as the OEIS or ISC, we are depending on other mathematicians' judgment about the importance of sequences or numbers that they deem, or do not deem, sufficiently interesting to become a part of the body of information stored in such databases. But there are of course many more interesting sequences and constants than the ones mathematicians have previously come across and taken the effort to submit. For such sequences and constants, algorithmic tools and human ingenuity must be applied to understand the data.

In the worked examples below we will hence refrain from using the databases until absolutely necessary, to furnish the reader with examples of a more general approach.

Example 5.5.1: A class of determinants.   Suppose we are lead to study the determinant of the matrices A_n of the form

$$\begin{bmatrix} 1 & 2^{-1} & 3^{-1} & \ldots & n^{-1} \\ 2^{-1} & 3^{-1} & 4^{-1} & \ldots & (n+1)^{-1} \\ 3^{-1} & 4^{-1} & 5^{-1} & \ldots & (n+2)^{-1} \\ \vdots & \vdots & \vdots & & \vdots \\ n^{-1} & (n+1)^{-1} & (n+2)^{-1} & \ldots & (2n-1)^{-1} \end{bmatrix}.$$

Inspecting the first 10 such determinants, it seems safe to assert that these numbers are reciprocals of large integers, so we let $a_n = (\det A_n)^{-1}$ and consider

1

$2^2 \cdot 3$ $2^2 \cdot 3$

$2^4 \cdot 3^3 \cdot 5$ $2^2 \cdot 3^2 \cdot 5$

$2^8 \cdot 3^3 \cdot 5^3 \cdot 7$ $2^4 \cdot 5^2 \cdot 7$

$2^{10} \cdot 3^5 \cdot 5^5 \cdot 7^3$ $2^2 \cdot 3^2 \cdot 5^2 \cdot 7^2$

$2^{14} \cdot 3^9 \cdot 5^5 \cdot 7^5 \cdot 11$ $2^4 \cdot 3^4 \cdot 7^2 \cdot 11$

$2^{18} \cdot 3^{11} \cdot 5^5 \cdot 7^7 \cdot 11^3 \cdot 13$ $2^4 \cdot 3^2 \cdot 7^2 \cdot 11^2 \cdot 13$

$2^{24} \cdot 3^{14} \cdot 5^6 \cdot 7^7 \cdot 11^5 \cdot 13^3$ $2^6 \cdot 3^3 \cdot 5 \cdot 11^2 \cdot 13^2$

$2^{26} \cdot 3^{18} \cdot 5^8 \cdot 7^7 \cdot 11^7 \cdot 13^5 \cdot 17$ $2^2 \cdot 3^4 \cdot 5^2 \cdot 11^2 \cdot 13^2 \cdot 17$

$2^{30} \cdot 3^{18} \cdot 5^{10} \cdot 7^7 \cdot 11^9 \cdot 13^7 \cdot 17^3 \cdot 19$ $2^4 \cdot 5^2 \cdot 11^2 \cdot 13^2 \cdot 17^2 \cdot 19$

Figure 5.13 Prime factors of a_n (left) and a_n/a_{n-1} (right).

```
[> seq(1/Determinant(Matrix(n,n,(i,j)->1/(i+j-1))),          1
        n=1..10);                                             2
```

1, 12, 2160, 6048000, 266716800000, 186313420339200000,

206790904792577064960000, 36535684712573448587811225600000,

10287817843785696978870529629093888000000000,

46206893947914691316295628839036278726983680000000000

Using `guessgf` on even 30 terms of this sequence does not give any leads. Instead we let the observation that 10 divides these numbers an increasing number of times lead us to study the prime factorization of these numbers. It appears obvious from the observations to the left in Figure 5.13 that the numbers are composed of a lot of powers of small prime numbers, but the multiplicity with which the various primes appear is a bit mysterious. We do see that each multiplicity increases, so a_n must divide a_{n+1} and we can instead study the successive quotients a_{n+1}/a_n without having to leave the integers. Again, `guessgf` fails to recognize the sequence, but factoring the quotients yields the numbers to the right in Figure 5.13. The pattern remains a bit elusive, but we note a prevalence of even powers, suggesting that these numbers are close to being squares. We can use the `ifactors` variant of Maple's factorization command along with `select` as in

```
[> for n from 1 to N-1 do                                    1
      [n,select(x->is(x[2] mod 2=1),                         2
              ifactors(a[n+1]/a[n])[2])];                    3
   end do;                                                   4
```

to extract what is required to complete the square in each case

$$3, 5, 7, 1, 11, 13, 15, 17, 19, 21, 23, 1, 3, 29, 31.$$

The systematic appearance of numbers of the form $2n + 1$ whenever they are squarefree suggests that $b_n = (2n + 1)a_{n+1}/a_n$ is a square, and this we may confirm by

```
[> for n from 1 to N-1 do                                              1
      b[n]:=(2*n+1)*a[n+1]/a[n];                                       2
   end do:                                                             3
   seq(sqrt(b[n]),n=1..10);                                           4
```

$$6, 30, 140, 630, 2772, 12012, 51480, 218790, 923780, 3879876$$

Here, at last, we get a hit with `guessgf`

```
[> guessgf([0,seq(sqrt(b[n]),n=1..N-1)],x);                           1
   convert(%[1],FormalPowerSeries);                                    2
```

$$\left[\frac{4x\sqrt{1-4x} - \sqrt{1-4x} + 1}{(1-4x)^{3/2}}, ogf \right]$$

$$\sum_{k=0}^{\infty} \frac{2(2k+1)!(2k+3)}{(k+1)(k!)^2} x^{k+1}$$

and we conclude by backtracking that

$$\sqrt{b_n} = (4n+2)\binom{2n-1}{n}$$

$$\frac{a_{n+1}}{a_n} = \frac{(4n+2)^2}{2n+1}\binom{2n-1}{n}^2 = (8n+4)\binom{2n-1}{n}^2$$

$$a_n = \prod_{k=1}^{n}(8k+4)\binom{2k-1}{k}^2.$$

Consulting the OEIS would have given us this formula right away (A5778), telling us that the matrices are named after Hilbert and even providing a reference to a proof using the Cauchy formula for determinants of matrices on this general form.   ◁

Example 5.5.2: Triangles with sides of integer length.   We wish to study the number of triangles with perimeter n, identified up to rotations and translations, which can be obtained with all sides of integer length. Denoting the lengths a, b, c with the assumption

$$a \le b \le c$$

we observe that such triangles exists if and only if $c < a + b$. When $a = b$ or $b = c$ the triangle will of course be isosceles and thus uniquely defined, but when $a < b < c$ the choice of side lengths define two different such triangles as indicated on Figure 5.14 (cf. Exercise 4.15).

Thus, a viable strategy for counting all these triangles is to use our procedure `nextList` defined in Example 3.4.2 to iterate through all triples $[a, b, c]$ and record in an array when this gives rise to one or two triangles of perimeter $s = a + b + c$. We obtain this straightforwardly by

```
[> count:=Array(1..N):                                       1
   for i from 1 to N do                                      2
      count[i]:=0;                                           3
   end do:                                                   4
   L:=[1,1,1];                                               5
   while(L[1]<N) do                                          6
      if(L[1]<L[2]+L[3]) then                                7
         i:=L[1]+L[2]+L[3];                                  8
         if(i<=N) then                                       9
            if(L[1]>L[2] and L[2]>L[3]) then                 10
               count[i]:=count[i]+2;                         11
            else                                             12
               count[i]:=count[i]+1;                         13
            end if;                                          14
         end if;                                             15
      end if;                                                16
      L:=nextList(L);                                        17
   end do:                                                   18
```

We use Array for a reason we will explain in Section 7.3.3. We can afford not to worry about the unfortunate fact that when c (represented by L[1]) gets close to N, only very few choices of a and b give rise to a perimeter of length N or less, and easily compute all the way to $N = 50$. Denoting the number of triangles t_n, we find that $t_1, \ldots, t_{50}$ is

$$0, 0, 1, 0, 1, 1, 2, 1, 4, 2, 5, 4, 7, 5, 10, 7, 12, 10, 15, 12, 19, 15,$$
$$22, 19, 26, 22, 31, 26, 35, 31, 40, 35, 46, 40, 51, 46, 57, 51, 64,$$
$$57, 70, 64, 77, 70, 85, 77, 92, 85, 100, 92.$$

Plotting the sequence (see Figure 5.14) reveals that the numbers grow in a very systematic way which may roughly be described as given by a parabola overlaid with a small alternating motion which is a little harder to describe. We pass the observations to gfun using

```
[> guessgf([seq(count[i],i=1..N)],x);                        1
   convert(%[1],FormalPowerSeries);                          2
```

$$\left[-\frac{x^6 - x^4 + x^2}{x^7 - 2x^5 - x^4 + x^3 + 2x^2 - 1}, ogf \right]$$

$$\sum_{k=0}^{\infty} \left(\frac{41}{144} - \frac{1}{16}(-1)^k + \frac{1}{8}(-1)^k k - \frac{1}{24}k + \frac{1}{24}k^2 - \right.$$
$$\left. \frac{2(\sqrt{3} - i)\sqrt{3}(-\frac{1}{2} + \frac{i}{2}\sqrt{3})^k}{9i\sqrt{3} + 27} + \frac{i}{27}\sqrt{3}(i\sqrt{3} - 3)\left(-\frac{1}{2} - \frac{i}{2}\sqrt{3} \right)^k \right) x^k$$

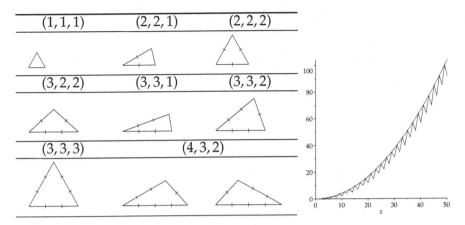

Figure 5.14 Left: Integer side triangles with perimeter ≤ 9. Right: $t_1, \ldots, t_{50}$ plotted with $x^2/24$.

Thus Maple provides a closed form for t_k which may appear a bit daunting at first. We note that there is indeed a dominating quadratic term $k^2/24$ explaining the parabolic behavior of t_n, as well as alternating terms $(2k-1)(-1)^k/16$ explaining the oscillations, but the appearance of complex constants in the last two terms of the large parenthesis provided by `convert` muddles the picture somewhat. Evaluating only these two terms, we get

$$-.222, .444 - 1.470 \cdot 10^{-11}i, -.222 - 10^{-10}i, -.222, .444 - 3.440 \cdot 10^{-11}i,$$
$$-.222, -.222, .444 + 3.965 \cdot 10^{-12}i, -.222,$$

which seems to indicate that they are cyclically of the form $-2/9, 4/9, -2/9$. Proceeding this way (cf. Exercise 5.5.2) we could arrive at a very convincing conjectural form for t_n. However, we still have not been served any facts that could lead to a proof that such a conjecture is true. Since rational generating functions are closely related to recurrence relations with constant coefficients, we try

```
[> listtorec([seq(count[i],i=1..N)],u(n));
```
1

but get no hit until allowing for recurrence relation of higher order by

```
[> Parameters('maxordereqn'=10);
```

after which we get

$$[\{u(n+7) - 2u(n+5) - u(n+4) + u(n+3) + 2u(n+2) - u(n),$$
$$u(0) = 0, u(1) = 0, u(2) = 1, u(3) = 0, u(4) = 1, u(5) = 1, u(6) = 2\}, ogf],$$

which can easily be transformed into the nice formula

$$t_n = 2t_{n-2} + t_{n-3} - t_{n-4} - 2t_{n-5} + t_{n-7},$$

but it is not easy to base a proof on this observation. Trying the OEIS we find sequence **A8742** which is clearly a match, but the description discusses a concept (Molien series) not immediately relevant for the problem at hand. However, a cross-reference establishes contact to *Alcuin's sequence* (**A5044**)

$$0, 0, 1, 0, 1, 1, 2, 1, 3, 2, 4, 3, 5, 4, 7, 5, 8, 7, 10, 8, 12, 10, 14, 12, 16, 14, 19, 16,$$
$$21, 19, 24, 21, 27, 24, 30, 27, 33, 30, 37, 33, 40, 37, 44, 40, 48, 44, 52, 48, 56, 52.$$

Among many other things, this sequence is stated to be the solution to a small variation of the counting problem we are studying where one identifies two triangles which have the same sides, such as the two matrices associated to $(4, 3, 2)$ in Figure 5.14.

The OEIS entry gives the reference [And79] which suggests a connection to the number of partitions (see Example 4.1.4) of n into 2, 3 and 4 parts. Even better, a paper ([Ekh12]) by Shalosh B. Ekhad (see box on p. 161) explains how to prove the corresponding identity in a way that may easily be translated to our original setting (see Exercise 5.44). But frankly, the easiest way of finding this material would have been to execute a Google search after "triangles with integer sides." ◁

In the final example of this section we will allow ourselves to use the OEIS freely.

Example 5.5.3: Balancing pyramids. Combining the notions introduced in Examples 1.6.5 and 1.6.6 we set out to study the number of pyramids that are stable or maximally stable, denoting these numbers by γ_n and Γ_n, respectively. As an initial approach, we decide to simply construct all pyramids and compute how many of them that are stable and maximally so. We know from Examples 5.1.10 and 5.2.5 that the number of pyramids is $\binom{2n-1}{n-1}$, but since this result was obtained by the advanced use of generating functions, it is not a priori obvious how to efficiently iterate through them all even though we know how many there are. Note that $\binom{2n-1}{n-1}$ is precisely the same as the number of ways we can select strings with $2n$ letters chosen in $\{0, 1\}$ in such a way that

- the first letter is 1
- there is an equal number of 0's and 1's.

Hence, it is natural to look for a map from the set S_n of such strings, to the set of pyramids $\mathcal{P}_n$.

Though not immediately providing a map

$$\Phi : S_n \to \mathcal{P}_n,$$

the proof in Example 5.2.5 does furnish the hint to first study the half-pyramids defined there, and use them to understand the full range. Since we have found the generating function $H(z)$, it is very easy to generate enough terms of (h_n) to locate the number of such pyramids in the OEIS. The entry at **A108** states "This is probably the longest entry in the OEIS, and rightly

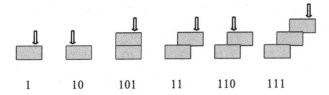

1   10   101   11   110   111

Figure 5.15 Reading off a positive string.

so," and indeed these *Catalan numbers* (named after the Belgian mathematician Eugéne Catalan) may be interpreted as the solution of a multitude of combinatorial problems. Browsing through the various descriptions, this one catches the eye:

```
Consider all the binomial(2n,n) paths on squared paper
that
  (i) start at (0, 0),
 (ii) end at (2n, 0) and
(iii) at each step, either make a (+1,+1) step or
       a (+1,-1) step.
Then the number of such paths that never go below the
x-axis (Dyck paths) is C(n). [Chung-Feller]
```

This suggests that the half-pyramids should be represented precisely by those strings that have the property that

$$\sum_{k=1}^{m}(1 - 2s_k) \geq 0 \qquad \text{all } m \geq 0.$$

When we interpret a 1 as a $(+1, +1)$ step and a 0 as a $(+1, -1)$ step, this corresponds exactly to the condition of never going below the x-axis. We know from the OEIS entry that the number of such strings, which we will call *positive*, is identical to the number of half-pyramids, and indeed one may produce a very natural map from the set of positive strings to the set of half-pyramids by reading the string as a building instruction where "1" means "place a brick and move the position to the right" and "0" means "move the position to the left." The y-coordinate placement of each brick is determined by letting it "fall from the sky" as in the computer game Tetris, letting the bottom align with the top of the highest brick at the relevant x-coordinates already placed. Figure 5.15 explains how the shortest positive strings are interpreted, with the current position indicated by an arrow.

Using the methods developed in Example 3.2.5 to generate all the $\binom{7}{3} = 35$ combinations producing strings of length 8 which satisfy our conditions, we may check after writing a visualization device (see Exercise 4.35) that we indeed get the set of half-pyramids this way, thus defining a map Φ sending positive strings to half-pyramids in a one-to-one fashion.

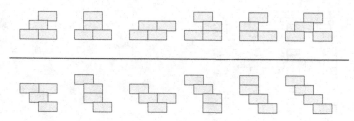

Figure 5.16 Top: Problematic constructions with nonpositive strings. Bottom: Constructions missed by the nonproblematic constructions.

But although Φ makes sense for all strings with an equal number of zeroes and ones, it does not always produce a pyramid away from the positive case. For a nonpositive string such as 10010011 the construction seems to work fine, allowing x-coordinates to the left of the base block as desired, but for the strings

$$10001110,\ 10001101,\ 11000011,\ 10100011,\ 10001011,\ 10000111,$$

we get problematic constructions as illustrated at the top of Figure 5.16.

To solve this problem, we again turn to Example 5.2.5 and note that the observation

$$P(z) = \frac{H(z)}{1 - H(z)} = H(z) + H^2(z) + H^3(z) + \cdots$$

translates to the fact that

$$p_n = s_n = \sum_{k=1}^{\infty} \sum_{m_1 + \cdots + m_k = n} h_{m_1} \cdots h_{m_k}$$

because of the observation just after (5.28). Hence, in a parallel fashion,

- every pyramid in $\mathcal{P}_n$ is obtained by combining a number of half-pyramids;
- every string in $\mathcal{S}_n$ is obtained by combining a number of positive strings.

Thus, to extend Φ to the not necessarily positive strings, we are led to the idea that general strings may be analyzed as a sequence of strings of even length that are alternately positive and *negative* in the sense that

$$\sum_{k=1}^{m} (1 - 2s_k) \leq 0 \qquad \text{all } m \geq 0.$$

For the problematic strings mentioned above we get

$$10|0011|10,\ 10|001101,\ 1100|0011,\ 1010|0011,\ 10|001011,\ 10|000111,$$

and by comparing this to the problematic buildings as well as the list of the pyramids that we missed by our naive construction, it becomes very natural to venture the idea that the negative strings should result in half-pyramids that are mirrored in the x-axis before assembly.

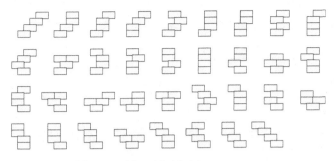

Figure 5.17 All pyramids with 4 bricks.

Thus, it becomes clear that a map $\Phi : \mathcal{S}_n \to \mathcal{P}_n$ may be usefully defined by analyzing the strings into alternately positive and negative substrings, composing half-pyramids accordingly, and assembling everything with the half-pyramids coming from negative strings reflected vertically and placed one unit to the left of the base block.

In fact, with the right candidate for such a map it is not hard to prove that this is a bijection (since we know the sets have the same size, it suffices to prove injectivity), and we may write Maple code that produces complete lists of pyramids as in Figure 5.17.

Implementing τ computing the x-coordinate of the center of gravity as given in (1.1) is trivial, so eventually we get data such as

$$\left[\tfrac{3}{2}, \tfrac{5}{4}, 1, \tfrac{3}{4}, 1, \tfrac{3}{4}, \tfrac{1}{2}, \tfrac{1}{2}, \tfrac{1}{4}, 0, \tfrac{3}{4}, \tfrac{1}{2}, \tfrac{1}{4}, \tfrac{1}{4}, 0, -\tfrac{1}{4}, 0, -\tfrac{1}{4}, -\tfrac{1}{2}, \right.$$
$$\left. -\tfrac{3}{4}, \tfrac{1}{2}, \tfrac{1}{4}, 0, 0, -\tfrac{1}{4}, -\tfrac{1}{2}, -\tfrac{1}{4}, -\tfrac{1}{2}, -\tfrac{3}{4}, -1, -\tfrac{1}{2}, -\tfrac{3}{4}, -1, -\tfrac{5}{4}, -\tfrac{3}{2}\right],$$

which is a complete list of all x-coordinates of centers of gravity for the pyramids of Figure 5.17. This establishes that $\Gamma_4 = 5$ and $\gamma_4 = 27$ and doing so for n up to 9 is straightforward.

For Γ_n, we obtain the observations

$$1, 2, 5, 12, 32, 94, 289, 910.$$

These numbers cannot be recognized by guessgf, but they match up with an OEIS entry A2838 taken directly from a 1969 paper by Odeh and Cockayne ([OC69]) with the abstract

The problem is to determine the function $f(n, r)$ which is the total number of balance positions when r equal weights are placed on a centrally pivoted uniform rod at r distinct point whose coordinates with respect to the center as origin are a subset of the $2n + 1$ integers $\{0, \pm1, \pm2, \ldots, \pm n\}$. The function is evaluated precisely for small n and estimated accurately for all n using asymptotic statistical theory.

Since this work also deals with questions of equilibrium, there is little doubt that we have in fact found a useful hit, so we study the paper to learn that the numbers $f(n, r)$ are defined algebraically as the number of solutions to

$$\sum_{i=-n}^{n} i x_i = 0$$

with $x_i \in \{0, 1\}$ and precisely r of the x_i nonzero. With this definition, OEIS is indicating that $\Gamma_N = f(N, N)$, and the paper contains a wealth of information allowing conclusions like

$$f(N, N) \approx \frac{\sqrt{12}}{\pi} \frac{4^N}{N^2}$$

to be drawn from the law of large numbers. But of course, we would have to prove that $\Gamma_N = f(N, N)$ to be able to appeal to these results. A key is found in

$$\tau(\Phi(s)) = \sum_{i=2}^{2n} (n - i + 1)s_i, \qquad (5.43)$$

which holds true for any $s \in S_n$. As surprising as this result may seem compared to the rather complicated way that we had to define Φ, as easy it is to test experimentally and indeed to prove by induction. The explanation is that when we reflect a half-pyramid vertically to read off a negative string, the x-coordinate of the center of gravity remains the same. Hence, the full range of results obtained in [OC69] can be used to explain the growth of the number of maximally balanced pyramids.

This mathematical experiment was particularly successful in two independent senses. First, Φ which was developed for the sake of the experiment, turned out to be useful for establishing a fundamental identity theoretically. And second, the experiment led to a complete analysis of the numbers in question which could then be applied directly. Of course one is not usually so lucky.

It is worth noting that the paper [OC69] has never been cited in the mathematical literature (according to the standard database MathSciNet), so it is not easy to imagine how a link could be established without the help of the OEIS.   ◁

5.6 Exercises

Warmup

EX. 5.1.2 → **Exercise 5.1**   Compute the period $C = c_1 \cdots c_{870}$ and the preperiod $B = b_1 \cdots b_{139}$ of 1524/87143 as described in Example 5.1.2, and check that indeed

$$B \cdot 10^{-139} + \frac{C \cdot 10^{-139-870}}{1 - 10^{-870}} = \frac{1524}{87143}.$$

[Hint: To extract the periods, print out 2000 decimals on the screen, and resize the window until you see the period. Then cut and paste.]

EX. 5.2.3 → **Exercise 5.2**   Use Maple to expand the expression found for $F(z)$ in (5.31) into partial fractions. Consult the help page for `convert(...,parfrac)` if you have problems doing so, and explain what happens.

EX. 5.2.5 → **Exercise 5.3**   Write recursive procedures H and P from (5.33) and (5.34) and test that they produce the desired output. *[Hint: You probably need to use* `add` *in stead of* `sum`.*]*

EX. 5.1.1 → **Exercise 5.4**   Implement `noCrossing` and run `cycleTree` to obtain the observations $c_0, \ldots, c_9$.

EX. 5.2.6 → **Exercise 5.5**   Note that the generating function found for a_n is closely related to the function we originally studied in Example 1.6.1. Explain why.

Exercise 5.6   Prove Proposition 5.3.3.

Exercise 5.7   Try to use the OEIS to find several plausible extensions of the sequence

$$1, 1, 2, 2, 3, .$$

Exercise 5.8   Determine ordinary generating functions for

$$1, 1, 2, 2, 3, 3, 4, 4, 5, 5, 6, 6, \ldots$$
$$1, 0, -1, 0, 1, 0, -1, 0, 1, 0, -1, 0, \ldots$$
$$1, 10, 100, 1000, 10000, 100000, \ldots$$

by appealing to the basic observations noted at the beginning of Section 5.2.2. Check your answers with `series`.

Exercise 5.9   Use `guessgf` to solve Exercise 5.8.

Exercise 5.10   Use the two procedures

```
[> get0coeffs:=proc(f::procedure,n)                            1
       return([seq((D@@i)(f)(0)/i!,i=0..n)]);                  2
    end proc;                                                  3
    getEcoeffs:=proc(f::procedure,n)                           4
       return([seq((D@@i)(f)(0),i=0..n)]);                     5
    end proc;                                                  6
```

to experiment with `guessgf`. Can Maple recognize the power series of $\exp(z)$, $1/(1+z^5-z^8)$, $1/\sqrt{1-4z}$, $\cos(z^2)$, $\sqrt{\exp(z^3)}$? How many terms are needed?

Exercise 5.11   Prove that every column in the matrix H_x defined in (5.42) is orthogonal to **x**.

Exercise 5.12 Which of the following constants can `identify` recognize from a floating point representation? And how many digits are needed?

$$260697/202, 2/\sqrt{\pi}, e^e, \pi/\sqrt{7}, \ln(173), 8e^7, \pi^2/6.$$

Exercise 5.13 Use the ISC to find an impressive mathematical formula for your phone number.

Exercise 5.14 Look up the sequences

$$1, 0, 1, 0, 1, 0, 1, 0, 1, 0$$
$$1, 1, 2, 4, 8, 16, 32, 64, 128, 256$$
$$1, 2, 5, 14, 41, 122, 365, 1094, 3281, 9842$$
$$1, 3, 10, 36, 136, 528, 2080, 8256, 32896, 131328$$
$$1, 4, 17, 76, 353, 1684, 8177, 40156, 198593, 986404$$
$$1, 5, 26, 140, 776, 4400, 25376, 148160, 872576, 5169920$$
$$1, 6, 37, 234, 1513, 9966, 66637, 450834, 3077713, 21153366$$
$$1, 7, 50, 364, 2696, 20272, 154400, 1188544, 9228416, 72147712$$

in the OEIS, noting down the **A** numbers. These are the results from Exercise 3.12; would the OEIS have helped you solve that exercise?

Exercise 5.15 It may be known to the reader that $\pi/4 = \arctan(1/2) + \arctan(1/3)$. Use PSLQ to find other integer relations between π, $\arctan(1/n)$ and $\arctan(1/m)$ for appropriately chosen m and n.

Exercise 5.16 Consider the procedure `IQtest` given by

```
[> with(gfun):                                              1
  IQtest:=proc(L) local p;                                  2
    p:=guessgf(L,x);                                        3
    if p=FAIL then                                          4
      return "?"                                            5
    else                                                    6
      if(p[2]=ogf) then                                     7
        return coeff(series(p[1],x=0,nops(L)+1),            8
                     x,nops(L));                            9
      else                                                  10
        return coeff(series(p[1],x=0,nops(L)+1),            11
                     x,nops(L))*(nops(L))!                  12
      end if;                                               13
    end if;                                                 14
  end proc;                                                 15
```

Analyze what `IQtest` does, and how it works. Give examples of its usage.

Exercise 5.17 Apply `identify` to the constant

$$0.123456789101112131415161718192021\cdots$$

Discuss the result.

Exercise 5.18 What is $\sum_{n=1}^{\infty} \frac{1+1/2+\cdots+1/n}{(n+1)^2}$?

Exercise 5.19 Write a Maple procedure to check the results in A93653 and extend the list of observations all the way to $n = 200$.

EX. 3.2.1 → **Exercise 5.20** Use the OEIS to look up the sequences (a_n), (b_n) in Example 3.2.1. Was the result consistent with your solution to Exercise 1.6.1?

Homework

Exercise 5.21 Attempt to determine exact formulas for the following integrals using each of the methods:

- exact evaluation in Maple
- approximate evaluation in Maple followed by `identify`
- approximate evaluation in Maple followed by an ISC look-up

For each integral, there is a closed form involving only π, e and the Euler constant γ combined with standard operations. Categorize the integrals according to their difficulty.

(a) $\displaystyle\int_0^1 \frac{x^2 dx}{(1+x^4)\sqrt{1-x^4}}$ (e) $\displaystyle\int_0^{\pi/2} \frac{x^2 dx}{\sin^2 x}$

(b) $\displaystyle\int_0^{\infty} xe^{-x}\sqrt{1-e^{-2x}}dx$ (f) $\displaystyle\int_0^{\pi/2} \ln(\cos x)^2 dx$

(c) $\displaystyle\int_0^{\infty} \frac{x^2 dx}{\sqrt{e^x - 1}}$ (g) $\displaystyle\int_0^1 \frac{\ln(x)^2 dx}{x^2 + x + 1}$

(d) $\displaystyle\int_0^{\pi/4} (\pi/4 - x\tan x)\tan(x)dx$ (h) $\displaystyle\int_0^{\infty} \frac{\ln x}{\cosh^2 x}dx.$

EX. 5.5.3 → **Exercise 5.22**

(a) Formalize the definition of Φ and implement it in Maple. Use visualization as in Exercise 4.35 to test the implementation.

(b) Prove (5.43).

EX. 2.5.7 → **Exercise 5.23** Implement a Maple procedure `runlength` which replaces a sequence (a_n) taking only two values $\{x, y\}$ by a sequence (b_n) given by counting the "run lengths" of x and y in (a_n):

$$\underbrace{x, \ldots, x}_{b_1} \underbrace{y, \ldots, y}_{b_2} \underbrace{x, \ldots, x}_{b_3} \underbrace{y, \ldots, y}_{b_4} \cdots\cdots$$

Apply `runlength` to sequences s[α] as in Example 2.5.7 and analyze the results by the methods introduced in Chapter 5.

Exercise 5.24 Prove that the Hermite reduction matrix is always invertible.

EX. 5.1.10 → **Exercise 5.25** Among the pyramids counted in Example 5.1.10, consider those that are *symmetric* around a vertical axis. When the number of bricks ranges from 1 to 4, there are, respectively,

$$1, 1, 2, 3 \tag{5.44}$$

of those. Use the approach of Example 5.1.10 to compute enough terms of the sequence in (5.44) to find the sequence in the OEIS. [*Hint: a 7 × 7-matrix will do the trick.*]

Exercise 5.26 We say that a permutation $\sigma : \{1, \dots, n\} \to \{1, \dots, n\}$ is *fixed-point free* if for all i we have

$$\sigma(i) \neq i.$$

The number of such permutations is denoted f_n for each n.

(*a*) Write a procedure to compute f_n for small n.

(*b*) Use symbolic inversion to guess an (exponential) generating function $\widehat{F}(z)$ with

$$\widehat{F}(z) = \frac{f_1}{1!}z + \frac{f_2}{2!}z^2 + \frac{f_3}{3!}z^3 + \frac{f_4}{4!}z^4 + \cdots$$

(*c*) Taking for granted that the result found in (b) is correct, convince yourself that

$$\lim_{n \to \infty} \frac{f_n}{n!}$$

exists. Use symbolic inversion to guess what this constant is.

Exercise 5.27 We say that a permutation $\sigma : \{1, \dots, n\} \to \{1, \dots, n\}$ is *up-down* if we have

$$\sigma(1) > \sigma(2) < \sigma(3) > \sigma(4) < \cdots$$

The number of such permutations is denoted u_n for each n.

Perform an analysis as in Exercise 5.26(a)-(c) to find an (exponential) generating function $\widehat{U}(z)$.

Exercise 5.28 Use inversion to come up with simple expressions for a_n, b_n given by

$$a_n = \sum_{k=1}^{n} \left\lfloor \frac{k}{2} \right\rfloor \left\lceil \frac{k}{2} \right\rceil \qquad b_n = \sum_{k=0}^{n} \left\lceil \frac{k}{2} \right\rceil \left\lceil \frac{n-k}{2} \right\rceil.$$

Exercise 5.29 Consider words with letters from $\{0, 1\}$ starting throughout by "1." Such a word is denoted *even* if there is always an even number of zeroes between two consecutive ones, and *odd* if there is always an odd number of zeroes between two consecutive ones. Thus, up to length 5, the even words are

$$1, 10, 11, 100, 110, 111, 1000, 1001, 1100, 1110, 1111,$$
$$10000, 10010, 10011, 11000, 11001, 11100, 11110, 11111$$

and the odd words are

$$1, 10, 100, 101, 1000, 1010, 10000, 10100, 10101, 10001.$$

Write procedures to count all even and odd words of a given length, and perform symbolic inversion on the numbers obtained.

Exercise 5.30 Program a search for $a_1, \ldots a_{10}$ of test 7 in Figure 5.11 directly using PSLQ.

Exercise 5.31 Compare, step by step, PSLQ to the Euclidean algorithm when the given vector **x** has precisely two entries.

EX. 5.3.8 → **Exercise 5.32** Use PSLQ to find polynomials $p_{a,b}$ of least possible order so that

$$p_{a,b}(\sqrt[a]{b} + \sqrt[b]{a}) = 0,$$

and search for patterns in the order and coefficients of $p_{a,b}$.

Exercise 5.33 Write a procedure which will compute the continued fraction expansion of a constant and pass it to guessgf. Then try to explain the patterns, if any, in the continued fraction expansions of

$$e, e^2, \sqrt{2}, \sqrt{3}, \sqrt[3]{2}, \sqrt{51}, \text{ and } \pi.$$

EX. 5.1.2 → **Exercise 5.34** Write a program to compute the values k and ℓ in the decimal expansion of a fraction p/q (*cf.* (5.5)). Make sure that the program returns $\ell = 0$ when the decimal expansion is finite. Compute ℓ for fractions on the form $1/n$ with $n = 1, \ldots, 50$ and use inversion to explain how ℓ varies with n.

Exercise 5.35 Writing Δa_n for $a_{n+1} - a_n$ we may iterate the idea of passing to successive differences and arrive at a diagram

$$
\begin{array}{cccccccc}
a_1 & a_2 & a_3 & a_4 & a_5 & a_6 & a_7 & a_8 \\
\Delta a_1 & \Delta a_2 & \Delta a_3 & \Delta a_4 & \Delta a_5 & \Delta a_6 & \Delta a_7 \\
\Delta^2 a_1 & \Delta^2 a_2 & \Delta^2 a_3 & \Delta^2 a_4 & \Delta^2 a_5 & \Delta^2 a_6 & \Delta^2 a_7 \\
\Delta^3 a_1 & \Delta^3 a_2 & \Delta^3 a_3 & \Delta^3 a_4 & \Delta^3 a_5 & \Delta^3 a_6 \\
\Delta^4 a_1 & \Delta^4 a_2 & \Delta^4 a_3 & \Delta^4 a_4 & \Delta^4 a_5 & \Delta^4 a_6 \\
& \ddots & & \ddots
\end{array}
$$

(*a*) Write Maple procedures to create such tables and apply them to the three sequences

$$1, 5, 12, 22, 35, 51, 70, 92, 117, 145, 176, 210, 247, 287, 330$$

$$0, 2, 5, 10, 19, 36, 69, 134, 263, 520, 1033, 2058, 4107, 8204$$

$$0, 2, 9, 31, 97, 291, 857, 2507, 7329, 21475, 63145, 186363, 551921.$$

(*b*) Suppose a closed form $\Delta^k a_n = b_n$ has been found for some $k \geq 1$. Express a_n in terms of the b_n.

(*c*) Suppose a closed form $\Delta^n a_1 = c_n$ has been found. Express a_n in terms of the c_n.

(*d*) Identify the three sequences in (a) this way without the use of the OEIS.

Exercise 5.36 Let $N(r)$ denote the number of integer lattice points inside a circle of radius r. Find an exact formula for $N(r)$.

Exercise 5.37 For which k can you find $n_1, \ldots, n_k$ for which there is an integer relation among π, $\arctan(1/n_1), \ldots, \arctan(1/n_k)$. Which of these found relations is best suited for determining digits of π using the Taylor expansion of arctan around 0?

EX. 5.3.9 → **Exercise 5.38** Show how Equation (5.39) can be used to compute individual digits of $\ln(2)$. Write a procedure which, given $m < n$, computes digits number m through n.

EX. 5.3.9 → **Exercise 5.39** Prove that there is an arbitrary digit algorithm for any constant α satisfying Equation (5.40). Prove that there is also an arbitrary digit algorithm for any linear combination of such constants.

EX. 5.3.9 → **Exercise 5.40** Write a procedure that, given $m < n$, uses the Bailey–Borwein–Plouffe formula (5.41) to compute digits number m through n of π.

Exercise 5.41 Prove that Equation (5.41) holds.

EX. 3.2.3 → **Exercise 5.42** Find a closed form for the exponential generating function for the Bernoulli numbers using the methods

- combining (5.14) and (5.29),
- using `guessgf`,
- looking in the OEIS.

EX. 5.2.4 → **Exercise 5.43** Prove the formula (5.32).

EX. 5.5.2 → **Exercise 5.44** Find a closed formula for the number of triangles of integer sides (not identifying a triangle with its mirror image, just like in our original approach in Example 5.5.2). Prove the formula, seeking inspiration in the references to A5044.

Projects and Group Work

Exercise 5.45 We consider finite words written with the symbols 0 and 1. When such a word w of length ℓ is given, we consider the sequence $\mathbf{m}^w = (m_n^w)_{n=0}^{\infty}$ counting the number of words with n letters containing the string w. It is straightforward to count such strings when n is not too large, using for instance the StringTools package as

```
[> with(StringTools):                                          1
   wMatch:=(s,x)->min(Search(s,x),1);                          2
   countAll:=proc(s, n) local L;                               3
     L:=Generate(n,"01");                                      4
     return add(i,i=map(x->wMatch(s,x),L));                    5
   end proc;                                                   6
```

(a) Experiment with countAll to extract as many relations as possible between $\mathbf{m}^w$ and $\mathbf{m}^{w'}$ for different w and w'.

(b) Combine countAll with guessgf to compute generating functions $M_w(z)$ for a suitably chosen class of words w.

(c) Analyze the class of generating functions, noting as many properties as possible. Compare the findings to what was found in (a).

Exercise 5.46 This exercise involves at least two teams consisting of one or more persons. Using five different Maple seq commands, each team produces five sequences of 10 positive integers starting with a number less than 100 and ending with a number less than 10^{30}. Keeping the last entry of each output a secret, data are exchanged with another team, which then tries to guess the seq command and the entry kept secret. Check your results with the other team and discuss. *[Hint: You may want to avoid sequences in the OEIS.]*

Exercise 5.47 This exercise involves at least two teams consisting of one or more persons. Using five different Maple evalf(...,30) commands, each team produces five floating point numbers with 30 significant digits. Keeping the last digit of each number a secret (remember to round off appropriately), data is exchanged with another team, which then tries to guess the evalf command and the digit kept secret. Check your results with the other team and discuss.

Exercise 5.48 We see with

```
[> identify(evalf(sin(100),30));                               1
   identify(evalf(sin(100),30),all=true);                      2
```

$$-.50636564110975879365655761046 0$$

$$\sin(100)$$

that the all=true option is important for Maple to recognize constants such as $\sin(100)$. Explain why and make a procedure to identify constants

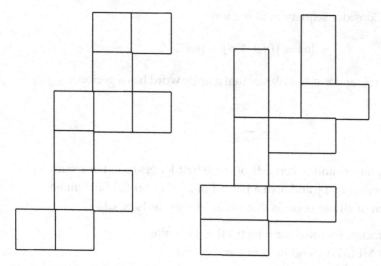

Figure 5.18   Left: A 1×1-animal. Right: A 1×2-animal.

of the form

$$\sin(p/q)$$

without `identify`, by appealing directly to PSLQ.

Exercise 5.49   Implement the PSLQ algorithm from Algorithm 5.1 and compare to the built-in Maple procedure PSLQ.

Exercise 5.50   By an $a \times b$-*animal*, cf. Figure 5.18, we understand a configurations of translates of the *tiles*

$$[0, a] \times [0, b] \text{ and } [0, b] \times [0, a]$$

so that

- every translated tile has its corners in $\mathbb{Z} \times \mathbb{Z}$,
- the translated tiles intersect only at their boundaries,
- the configuration generates a connected set even after $\mathbb{Z} \times \mathbb{Z}$ is removed.

Two examples of animals are shown in Figure 5.18. We wish to study the numbers $t_{a,b}(n)$ counting the number of different animals, identified up to translation. The case of 1×1-animals, also referred to as *polyominoes*, is very well studied, and quite a lot—although certainly not as much as one would want—is known about $t_{1,1}(n)$. In this exercise we emphasize the study of what happens when n is fixed while a and b are varied.

(a) Are $t_{1,a}(n)$ and $t_{a,a}(n)$ polynomials in a for fixed n? Is $t_{a,b}(n)$? Of which degree?

(b) Is there a pattern in the coefficients found?

(c) Do such patterns lead to insight into the rate of growth of $t_{a,b}(n)$?

EX. 2.5.7 → **Exercise 5.51** Consider sequences of the form

$$\mathbf{s}_n[\alpha] = \lfloor (n+1)\alpha \rfloor - \lfloor n\alpha \rfloor.$$

with $\alpha \in [0,1] \backslash \mathbb{Q}$ and $n \in \mathbb{N}_0$. We say that a finite word has a period $n + p/q$ if it has the form

$$\overbrace{v \cdots v}^{n} w,$$

where v has q letters and w consists of the p first letters of v. For example, 10101 has a period of $1\frac{1}{4}$ and also a period of $2\frac{1}{2}$. Let $MP(\alpha)$ be defined as the supremum of all the periods that occur in subwords of $\mathbf{s}_n[\alpha]$.

(*a*) What characterizes the α for which $MP(\alpha)$ is finite?

(*b*) How does $MP(\alpha)$ depend on α in these cases?

5.7 Notes and Further Reading

The last printed version of the OEIS [SP95] contains a chapter "How to deal with a strange sequence," which has inspired a lot of the material presented in this chapter and contains a wealth of additional information for what to do when a sequence cannot be found via the OEIS. It is available electronically via the OEIS.

The reader is referred to the excellent sources [Wil05] and [GKP94] for more information on generating functions. The latter is a standard textbook of advanced mathematics for students of computer science, and contains a wealth of other information that is useful for the experimental mathematician. The Wilf–Zeilberger algorithm is also described there, but for a more complete description, [PWZ96] is the obvious reference.

Apart from the opinions mentioned on p. 161, Zeilberger's homepage http://www.math.rutgers.edu/~zeilberg contains links to homepages of courses in experimental mathematics taught for about a decade. Several of the examples and exercises of this chapter were inspired by problems set by Zeilberger for his students.

The gfun package is described in [SZ94]. Many foundational ideas appear in [BP92].

A good general source on continued fractions is [RS92]. The PSLQ algorithm was analyzed in [FBA99]. We have followed the simplified exposition of [Str], which has also inspired several examples and exercises. Exercise 5.21 was extracted from [BB08]. For a collection of formulas discovered using the PSLQ algorithm, see [Bai].

Exercise 5.18 was inspired by [BD09, Exercise 4.2]. The description of the development of the Bailey–Borwein–Plouffe formula considered in Example 5.3.9 is based on the presentation given in [BD09, Chapter 2].

The false friend in Example 5.1.11 was identified as such in [GH02] during an analysis of higher-dimensional tic-tac-toe. However, as we shall discuss in Example 7.4.5, it is not correct when it is stated there that $a_{6847196937} \neq b_{6847196937}$.

The sequence of examples concerning noncrossing trees were taken from [Fla97]. The hard integral in Example 5.1.9 came to our attention when it was determined theoretically in [HM13].

The proof in Example 5.2.5 follows an idea developed in [BMR02]. The concrete map Φ defined in Example 5.5.3 is described in [DE10].

The discussion of IQ testing benefited from informal discussions with our colleagues Bruce Blackadar, Uffe Haagerup and Morten Risager. The "max power" idea in Exercise 5.51 was introduced to us by Jacob Thamsborg.

The Euler–Maclaurin summation formula can be used to compute sums or integrals more precisely, to allow for `identify` to recognize them, by relating $\int_a^b f(x)dx$ to $\sum_{n=a}^{b-1} f(n)$, but using the formula requires great care. A good source is [GKP94, 9.5].

6 *Pseudorandomness*

This chapter concerns the use of randomness, or rather pseudorandomness, in mathematical experiments. It may seem counterintuitive that randomness has a role to play in the investigation of mathematical problems, but we will see that randomness can be essential for generating samples and for simulating values that cannot be computed directly. Randomness can also be used to keep experiments honest by eliminating bias and forcing the experimenter to consider a representative set of data points.

6.1 Why Use Randomness?

In the previous chapters, we have seen numerous examples where an exhaustive search was used to find all instances of some mathematical structure, up to some predefined threshold of complexity. For instance, this was the approach used in the investigation of the LEGO buildings considered in Examples 1.6.5 and 1.6.6. Here, the number of possible buildings of various kinds were calculated using exhaustive searches of all the possibilities up to some maximum number of bricks. These searches were an essential part of the generation of examples and the foundation on which the developed hypotheses were based. In many cases, however, it is not possible to investigate a significant part of the considered examples exhaustively.

In particular, this happens in problems involving *uncountable* sets of possibilities, that is, an infinite set X where there is no way to construct a bijection from X to $\mathbb{N}$. In such cases, there is no way to enumerate the options, and hence, no reasonable way of trying them one at a time. The canonical example of this type is the problem of investigating a property defined for all $x \in I$ for some interval $I \subseteq \mathbb{R}$. Each nontrivial interval is uncountable, so there is no way to enumerate the elements and test them sequentially. Such an example has already been encountered in the case of the sequences considered in Example 2.5.7 which are defined for every $x \in (0, 1) \setminus \mathbb{Q}$. While this set is clearly not an interval, it is still uncountable.

However, countability is not sufficient to guarantee that it is practical to investigate the possibilities sequentially. Even if it is possible to enumerate the possible configurations, the number of possibilities may increase so quickly that they are only practically computable to a very low level, beyond which interesting examples may be hidden.

Example 6.1.1: Enumerating matrices. Given $n \in \mathbb{N}$, consider the set $M_n(0, 1)$ of $n \times n$ matrices with entries in $\{0, 1\}$. For each n, there are 2^{n^2} different matrices and this number grows very quickly with n. Suppose one is interested in investigating a property defined for each element of $M(0, 1) = \bigcup_n M_n(0, 1)$. This is a countable set, and it is straightforward to enumerate the elements based on enumerations of the individual $M_n(0, 1)$. However, the number of elements grows very quickly with n, so it is not practically possible to compute all elements of $M_n(0, 1)$ beyond a certain level. This is investigated further in Exercise 6.6. ◁

In cases like the ones described above, the best way to make a finite unbiased collection of data, is often to use randomness to choose which elements to consider. For the matrices, randomness could be used to generate a collection of matrices of dimension n beyond the level where it is practical to compute all the matrices. In short, randomness is the tool to use when there is no way to investigate (a sufficiently large part of) the considered structures using iteration or recursion. This will be investigated further at the end of the chapter.

EX. 3.3.3 → **Example 6.1.2: To simulate or not to simulate.** Example 3.2.4 investigated the case of a gambler with N dollars intending to play M fair games with 1 dollar at stake in each game. There, pseudorandomness was used to run a simulation of the process to arrive at an estimation of the frequency of bankruptcy. As seen in Example 3.3.3, this problem can also be solved using a recursive algorithm to make an exhaustive search of all the possibilities. Recall that the number of possible games grows exponentially with M, so that one might a priori think that it would be impossible to investigate all the outcomes for large values, like $M = 100$. However, through a recursive algorithm using `remember` and utilizing inherent symmetries in the problem, it was in fact possible to construct a precise and very fast solution to the problem. The lesson is that even though a problem seems to involve an impossibly big collection of objects, there may still be a way to investigate it through an exhaustive

EX. 6.5.2 ← search yielding far more accurate results than possible through a simulation.

◁

6.2 True Randomness vs. Pseudorandomness

It is an interesting philosophical question whether quantities exist that are unpredictable no matter the level of knowledge possessed, but that kind of discussion is not particularly important to the experimenting mathematician. At least there is no doubt that quantities exist which are unpredictable for all practical purposes. For instance, www.random.org uses meteorological data to construct random numbers, while certain operating systems will use fluctuations in precise measurements of the voltages in the computer to do the same. In the following, such procedures will be referred to as *true random number generators*, without worrying about the extent to which they produce true randomness in the strictest sense.

A *pseudorandom number generator*, on the other hand, is a *deterministic* procedure which is designed to produce output that shares many of the features of a sequence of truly random numbers. Pseudorandom number generators are usually designed to take an integer—known as the *seed*—as input and to return a sequence of pseudorandom numbers depending on the seed.

Several different statistical tools have been developed to test sequences of pseudorandom numbers to check whether they give a good simulation of true randomness. Clearly, such testing is a complex problem: a good sequence of pseudorandom numbers should not exhibit any structure whatsoever, but such structures can be hard to detect. In the past, new tests have invalidated previously used pseudorandom number generators, and it is certainly possible that future tests will invalidate some of the ones being used today. The testing of pseudorandom number generators will be discussed briefly in Section 6.3.5.

Having access to true random number generators like the ones described above, one might wonder why it could be desirable to use a pseudorandom number generator instead. While the degree of randomness in pseudorandom generator is presumably smaller than that of a true random generator, the pseudorandom generator does have one significant advantage: repeatability. As discussed in Chapter 1, it is extremely important for the experimenting mathematician to be able to re-investigate examples and counterexamples in particular. This would be theoretically impossible in an application depending on truly random events which, by the very nature of randomness, cannot be reproduced. The deterministic nature of pseudorandomness, on the other hand, makes it possible to repeat experiments and reexamine the output, and the high quality of the pseudorandom number generators used today means that they are able to produce approximations of true randomness that are more than sufficient for most practical purposes.

6.3 Pseudorandom Number Generators

The following sections will give three concrete examples of pseudorandom number generators to illustrate the fundamental ideas of pseudorandomness and to show what can go wrong in a poorly designed generator.

Having a generator that produces randomized bits (0s and 1s), it is straightforward to construct a generator of random integers by concatenating a number of random bits and considering them as the binary expansion of an integer. Similarly, a generator returning pseudorandom integers can easily be adapted to produce fractions by dividing by a suitably large integer. Hence, having a generator of one kind of pseudorandom output, it is generally straightforward to turn it into a generator producing another kind of output.

6.3.1 States and Periods

Most pseudorandom number generators are initialized using a *seed*, often an integer. This sets the initial *state* of the generator. Each subsequent call of the generator will return a pseudorandom number, and change the state to a new value. At each step, the generated pseudorandom number will only depend on the current state. The state could be a number or a more complex object such as a vector. For particularly simple generators, the state can be identical to the returned pseudorandom number.

Most pseudorandom number generators are periodic: After a fixed number of calls, P, the state of the generator will be returned to the initial state, and hence, the sequence of generated pseudorandom numbers will also repeat itself with period P. Clearly, it is desirable for a generator to have a long period, to avoid reusing numbers and thereby introducing unwanted dependencies. However, a long period is obviously not sufficient to guarantee a good simulation of true randomness.

6.3.2 RANDU

> One of us recalls producing a "random" plot with only 11 planes, and being told by his computer center's programming consultant that he had misused the random number generator: "We guarantee that each number is random individually, but we don't guarantee that more than one of them is random." Figure that out.
>
> W. H. Press et al.

RANDU is a simple pseudorandom number generator given by the recurrence relation

$$x_{j+1} \equiv (2^{16} + 3)x_j \pmod{2^{31}}.$$

This gives a formula for computing a sequence of pseudorandom numbers x_i in $\{0, \ldots, 2^{31} - 1\}$ recursively. Often, one would transform such an integer into a rational number in $[0, 1)$ by dividing with 2^{31}. RANDU was developed by IBM in the 1960s, and it was in widespread use on computer systems at the time.

In this generator, the state is simply the last generated pseudorandom number: to find the next number, it is sufficient to know the previous one. Starting from a seed $x_0 = 1$, these states are easy to generate, and they can be found in OEIS as the sequence A96555.

However, RANDU is no longer used as a serious pseudorandom number generator due to a very serious flaw that results in dependencies between consecutive numbers giving a very poor simulation of true randomness. To see this, consider an arbitrary $k \in \mathbb{N}$ and note that

$$x_{k+2} = (2^{16} + 3)^2 x_k = (2^{32} + 6 \cdot 2^{16} + 9)x_k \equiv (6(2^{16} + 3) - 9)x_k \pmod{2^{31}}.$$

Hence, $x_{k+2} \equiv 6x_{k+1} - 9x_k \pmod{2^{31}}$, and this relation between adjacent numbers in the sequence results in a poor quality of randomness as illustrated in Exercise 6.8. This problem has been demonstrated to be inherent in any use of a simple linear recurrence relation in the construction of pseudorandom numbers.

6.3.3 Blum Blum Shub

Blum Blum Shub is a pseudorandom number generator developed in 1986 by Lenore Blum, Manuel Blum, and Michael Shub [BBS86]. Each pair of (large) primes p and q defines a recurrence relation

$$x_{n+1} \equiv x_n^2 \pmod{pq},$$

and together with a seed x_0, this relation defines the states x_n of the Blum Blum Shub generator. Note that this is based on a nonlinear recurrence relation which allows the generator to avoid the problems inherent in RANDU. The seed x_0 should be an integer different from 1 where neither p nor q is a factor. For each state x_n, one can extract a pseudorandom number in $\{0, 1\}$ either as the parity of the binary expansion of x_n or as the last digit of this expansion. Note that unlike RANDU, this gives a distinction between the state x_n and the corresponding pseudorandom output. To make the period of the generator long, p and q should be congruent to 3 modulo 4.

Unlike RANDU, this procedure is still used to produce pseudorandom numbers in certain computer systems, and the Maple package `RandomTools` contains an implementation. The main drawback of this generator is that it is slow compared to other alternatives. The dependence on two large primes, on the other hand, means that the output could be used for cryptography.

6.3.4 Mersenne Twister

In Maple, the primary pseudorandom number generator is the *Mersenne Twister*. It is essentially given by a linear recurrence relation like the one defining RANDU, but the states involved in the recurrence are vectors rather than single numbers, and this solves the problems inherent in simple linear recurrence generators like RANDU.

The fundamental algorithm of the Mersenne twister depends on a number of variables which determine the precise behavior of the generator:

w: The *word length*. The returned pseudorandom numbers will be w-bit integers.

n: The *degree of recurrence* which—together with w—determines the size of the states of the generator.

m: An integer with $1 \leq m \leq n$ that determines the part of the current state used to compute the output.

r: An integer.

$\mathbf{a}$: A w-dimensional row vector with entries in the finite field with two elements $\mathbb{F}_2 = \{0, 1\}$, $\mathbf{a} = (a_0, \ldots, a_{w-1})$.

A *word vector* of the Mersenne twister is a binary integer between 0 and $2^w - 1$ interpreted as a w-dimensional row vector with entries in $\mathbb{F}_2 = \{0, 1\}$. Note that each word vector can be considered as a w-bit machine word.

The initial state of the generator consists of n word vectors $\mathbf{x}^0, \ldots, \mathbf{x}^{n-1}$ which must be initialized (seeded) manually. For $0 \leq i \leq j \leq w - 1$ and a word vector $\mathbf{x} = (x_0, \ldots, x_{w-1})$, let $\mathbf{x}_{[i,j]} = (x_i, \ldots, x_j)$. The evolution of the generator is given by the following linear recurrence relation:

$$\mathbf{x}^{k+n} = \mathbf{x}^{k+m} \text{ xor } (\mathbf{x}^k_{[0,w-r-1]}|\mathbf{x}^{k+1}_{[w-r,w-1]})A$$

where xor denotes bitwise addition modulo 2, $(\mathbf{y}|\mathbf{z})$ denotes concatenation of vectors, and A is the following $w \times w$-matrix:

$$A = \begin{bmatrix} 0 & 1 & 0 & \cdots & 0 \\ 0 & 0 & 1 & & 0 \\ & & & \ddots & \vdots \\ 0 & 0 & 0 & \cdots & 1 \\ a_0 & a_1 & a_2 & \cdots & a_{w-1} \end{bmatrix}.$$

After k iterations, the output of the Mersenne Twister is simply the word vector $\mathbf{x}^{n+k}$ interpreted as a w-bit integer while the state of the generator is the list $\mathbf{x}^k, \ldots, \mathbf{x}^{k+n-1}$. The recurrence relation has been constructed so that it can be implemented by relying on only a few basic operations (such as bitwise addition modulo 2 and binary logic operations), and this allows it to run very quickly even for large values of n and w.

To improve the quality of the pseudorandomness, actual implementations of the generator additionally multiply the matrix A on the right by a fixed invertible $w \times w$-matrix T (called the *tempering matrix*). This matrix is given by another set of parameters, but it goes beyond the scope of this book to discuss the precise construction.

With the right choice of parameters, it is possible to obtain a generator that passes a very wide range of tests for pseudorandomness and has an extremely long period. The maximal period of the generator is $2^{nw-r} - 1$, and the name of the generator stems from the fact that this upper bound can be achieved when $2^{nw-r} - 1$ is a Mersenne prime (see Example 1.5.1). The following definition allows a more precise description of the quality of the pseudorandomness generated by the Mersenne Twister.

Definition 6.3.1. *A sequence of pseudorandom w-dimensional word vectors (or, equivalently, w-bit integers)* $\mathbf{x}^i$ *of period P is said to be k-distributed to v-bit accuracy if each of the* 2^{kv} *possible vectors*

$$(x^i_{[0,v-1]}, x^{i+1}_{[0,v-1]}, \ldots, x^{i+k-1}_{[0,v-1]})$$

occurs the same number of times in a period (except for the all-zero combination which occurs once less often). For each $1 \leq v \leq w$, *let* $k(v)$ *denote the maximum number such that the sequence is* $k(v)$-*distributed.*

Note that $2^{k(v)v} - 1 \leq P$ since at most P patterns can occur in one period.

This definition has a nice geometric interpretation that makes it easy to see why it is desirable to have high $k(v)$-values in a pseudorandom sequence. Consider each $\mathbf{x}^i$ as a w-bit integer and normalize by dividing by 2^w to obtain a number $x_i \in [0, 1]$. For each $0 \leq i < P$, interpret $(x_i, \ldots, x_{i+k-1})$ as a point in the k-dimensional unit cube. Divide the interval $[0, 1]$ into 2^v equally big intervals, and consider the corresponding division of the k-dimensional unit cube into 2^{kv} nonoverlapping cubes. The sequence is k-distributed to v bit accuracy if and only if these cubes all contain equally many points (except for the cube at the origin which contains one less). Consequently, a high $k(v)$-value ensures high-dimensional equidistribution of the numbers. In particular, this prevents the kind of behavior exhibited by RANDU.

The fact that the Mersenne Twister relies on a linear recurrence relation means that in principle the state of the generator can be determined if one knows a sufficiently long sequence of successively generated pseudorandom numbers. Hence, the generator should not be used directly for cryptography.

Maple uses a variant of the Mersenne Twister known as MT19937 where the parameters are

$$w = 32, \qquad n = 624, \qquad m = 397, \qquad r = 31.$$

Hence, the word vectors can be considered as 32-bit integers, the output is a 32-bit integer, and the state of the generator consists of 624 such numbers. The vector $\mathbf{a}$ defining the recurrence matrix A corresponds to the binary number for which the hexadecimal expansion is 9908B0DF. The period of this generator is the Mersenne prime $2^{32 \cdot 624 - 31} - 1 = 2^{19937} - 1$. With the right choice of tempering matrix, this generator has very good k-distribution properties. In particular, $k(1) = 19937$ and $k(32) = 623$ and both these numbers achieve the theoretical maximum given by the period of the sequence. The word length is 32, so the latter implies that regarding the pseudorandom numbers returned by the generator as points in $[0, 1]$ and passing to the 623-dimensional unit cube as described above, each of the $2^{32 \cdot 623} = 2^{19936}$ sub-cubes will contain equally many points. This guarantees a very good distribution of the numbers.

6.3.5 Testing Pseudorandom Number Generators

Much of this book is dedicated to the art of recognizing and describing structure in collections of data, and Chapter 5 introduced an extensive collection of tools for this purpose. Recognizing structure may be hard, but recognizing the complete lack of structure is probably harder still, and it is a highly nontrivial problem to design a test that will determine whether any given sequence of pseudorandom numbers gives a good simulation of true randomness. After all, *any* kind of systematic structure in the pseudorandom sequence will in principle make it distinguishable from a truly random sequence, and such structure can take infinitely many different forms.

Let $x = (x_0, x_1, \ldots, x_N)$ be a finite binary sequence. To examine whether x gives a good simulation of true randomness, one can use it to generate a number of different data sets and check whether these behave as one would expect for a truly random sequence. At the most basic level, one could ask whether the sequences has the average that one would expect or look at the expected length of the longest block of adjacent ones. For a more complicated test, one could look at the distribution of subwords: For each $n \in \mathbb{N}$, let $B_n(x) \subseteq \{0, 1\}^n$ be the set of distinct subsequences of length n occurring in x, if x is a truly random sequence, then the elements of $B_n(x)$ should be uniformly distributed. But as N and n grow, the exponential growth in the number of subwords means that it quickly becomes impossible to carry out this test. Another basic idea is to interpret the data as 2d or 3d points and inspect them visually (as done in Exercise 6.8). For a more stringent analysis, one can apply a wide range of statistical tests that are beyond the scope of this book.

None of the tests mentioned above are capable of detecting all kinds of structure, indeed, given a single such test, it will most often be straightforward to construct an example of a highly structured sequence that passes the test. For professional testing of randomness, a wide range of tests are applied at once to increase the probability of detecting hidden structure.

6.4 Pseudorandomness in Maple

Maple has a wide range of commands for generating pseudorandom numbers and other data structures which all rely on the Mersenne Twister discussed above.

6.4.1 Generating numbers

In Maple, the procedures related to the generation of pseudorandom numbers are kept in the package `RandomTools`. The main tool for generating pseudorandom objects is the command `Generate`, which can be used for many different purposes. To generate an integer, the syntax is

```
[> Generate(integer);                                        1
    Generate(integer(range=2..7));                           2
```

If no additional parameters are given, the integer will be a number between -499999999994 and 499999999994.

The command Generate can also be used to construct pseudorandom rational numbers. It does so by generating a pseudorandom integer and dividing by a suitably large fixed integer. The basic syntax is:

```
[> Generate(rational);                                                    1
    Generate(rational(range=-3..3, denominator=1000));                   2
```

Specifying a denominator d will result in fractions with this denominator (before cancellation). The default denominator is 499999999994. Without additional options, the fraction will be an element of $[0, 1)$, but this can be changed as in the second command given above. It is also possible to specify that the interval should be closed in one or both ends. This can be important if working with small denominators where it will give a significant nonzero chance of choosing one of the endpoints.

The following commands demonstrate how to generate random floating point numbers

```
[> Generate(float);                                                       1
    Generate(float(range=1.234..1.567, digits=4));                       2
```

The basic form of the command gives a random floating point number in the interval $[0 + 10^{-d}, 1 - 10^{-d}]$, where d is the current value of the environment variable Digits, that is, 10^{-d} is the smallest floating point number that Maple can currently distinguish from 0. Setting a range from a to b will similarly give numbers between $[a + 10^{-d}, b - 10^{-d}]$. By default, the floating point number will be given with a number of digits equal to the current value of Digits, but this can be changed by adding a parameter as in the second command given above.

By default, the generated floating point numbers are *logarithmically* distributed in the sense that long sequences drawn from $[0 + 10^{-d}, 1 - 10^{-d}]$ will contain approximately equally many numbers between 10^{-n} and 10^{-n+1} for each value of $n \in \{1, \ldots, d\}$. This is obtained by drawing a random integer *significand* s and a random integer *exponent* e, and forming the floating point number $b \cdot 10^e$. In many cases, however, it is more relevant to have a *uniform* distribution of the numbers, and this can be achieved by the following command

```
[> Generate(float(method=uniform));
```

Figure 6.1 illustrates the difference between the two distributions by showing two plots of points $(x, y) \in (0, 1)$ drawn randomly using uniform and logarithmic distributions, respectively.

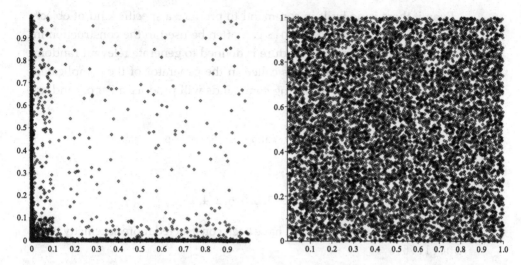

Figure 6.1 10000 points in $(0, 1)^2$ generated by `Generate(float)` with logarithmic distribution (left) and uniform distribution (right).

All of the commands considered above also come in complex versions with analogous syntax:

```
[> Generate(complex(integer));                                    1
   Generate(complex(rational));                                   2
   Generate(complex(float));                                      3
```

As for real numbers, parameters can be used to specify the required ranges, digits, and distributions.

Another option when generating floating point numbers is to use a specific statistical distribution. The package `Statistics` contains the commands necessary to produce random samples drawn from a wide range of distributions. For instance, the following commands will produce 10 values sampled from the normal distribution with mean 0 and variance 0.5:

```
[> with(Statistics);                                              1
   Sample(Normal(0,0.5),10);                                      2
```

Maple also has a more simple command, `rand`, that can be used to generate pseudorandom integers without loading the package `RandomTools`. Just like `Generate`, it relies on an implementation of the Mersenne twister. The command `rand(1..6)` will produce a procedure that generates random integers between 1 and 6. To actually produce such a number, use `rand(1..6)()`.

6.4.2 Other Data Structures

In addition to the commands considered above, `RandomTools` also contains various procedures for constructing more complicated objects such as polynomials and lists, as well as less complicated data structures such as boolean variables.

Even if there is no built-in command to produce a specific kind of object, the procedures from `RandomTools` can often be used in the construction in a two-step process: first a procedure is defined to generate relevant random numbers, then this procedure is called in the generator of the complicated object. For instance, the following commands will produce a list of random integers in $\{1, \ldots, 6\}$.

```
[> die := Generate(integer(range=1..6),makeproc=true):    1
    [seq(die(),i=1..10)];                                  2
```

$$[2, 1, 5, 3, 6, 6, 6, 2, 4, 1]$$

In this case, the procedure could have been constructed more succinctly with `rand(1..6)`.

6.4.3 Random Irrationals?

For the generation of the sequences introduced in Example 2.5.7, it was desirable to consider random irrational numbers in $I = (0, 1)$. However, this poses a problem: there is no fair way to draw a random element from such a set. As seen above, Maple contains good tools for generating random fractions or floating point numbers, and both these approaches can clearly be used to approximate elements of I. But what if one really needs an *exact* random irrational number?

To get an exact random irrational, one could define a procedure, such as the following, which takes three numbers (meant to be irrational) as input and returns a random linear combination with coefficients in $\mathbb{Q}$.

```
[> randomIrrational := proc(a,b,c)                 1
       local r;                                    2
       r := Generate(rational, range=0..1)*a+      3
           Generate(rational, range=0..1)*b+       4
           Generate(rational, range=0..1)*c;       5
       return r-floor(r);                          6
   end proc;                                       7
   randomIrrational(sqrt(2),Pi,exp(1));            8
```

While both e and π are transcendental numbers, it is (as mentioned in passing in Section 5.3.3) unknown whether $e + \pi$ is transcendental. Indeed, it is even unknown whether $e + \pi$ is irrational. Hence, the generator given above is not actually guaranteed to produce irrational numbers. However, if it turns out to produce a rational number, then this result is almost certainly a bigger mathematical discovery than whatever problem the random numbers were supposed to help investigate.

This also illustrates the inherent problem of a generator like this: the only reason to use exact irrational numbers rather than floating point approximations is the desire to use these numbers in exact computations. However, the numbers that this procedure generates are so complicated that Maple is unable to do meaningful symbolic computations with them. For instance, checking that such a number is a root of a given function will be impossible unless the function has been tailored to this specific number.

6.4.4 Repeatability

As already mentioned, the great benefit of using pseudorandomness rather than true randomness is that a sequence of pseudorandom numbers can be re-generated from the seed, or from an intermediate state of the generator. The ability to repeat calculations involving pseudorandom numbers can be essential in experimental mathematics in order to re-investigate examples and counterexamples. Hence, we need a way to manually change the state of the generator either by restarting it from the same initial seed or by specifically setting the state.

As described in Section 6.3.4, the state of the Mersenne Twister used by Maple is a 624-dimensional vector of 32-bit integers. The state vector of a newly initialized Mersenne Twister will contain many entries equal to zero, and this prevents it from producing high quality pseudorandom numbers. Hence, one would usually discard some of the initial numbers returned by the generator, and this is automatically done by Maple at start up. This explains why repeatability is obtained by saving and loading the state of the generator rather than by saving a seed and reseeding the generator: As an integer, the seed is a much simpler object than the 624 dimensional state vector, but a newly reseeded generator is not ready to produce pseudorandom numbers.

The internal state of the Mersenne Twister algorithm can be read and set by using GetState and SetState, respectively. These commands allow sequences of pseudorandom numbers to be regenerated. For instance, the following code will print two identical sequences of numbers.

```
[> s := GetState():                                          1
   seq(Generate(integer),i=1..10);                           2
   SetState(state=s):                                        3
   seq(Generate(integer),i=1..10);                           4
```

Note that all commands that produce pseudorandom output rely on the same underlying generator, so each execution of such a command will change the state of the generator. For instance, calling rand between SetState and seq above will result in a translation of the generated numbers.

As a less sophisticated alternative to SetState, one can use randomize to reseed the generator. This command is available without loading RandomTools, and it is primarily meant for applications relying on rand instead of Generate.

6.5 Using Pseudorandomness in Experiments

In this section, we will consider three applications of pseudorandomness in experimental mathematics: simulation, generation of samples, and testing of hypotheses. This is not an exhaustive list of the uses of pseudorandomness, and there is certainly some overlap between the three categories, but they will serve to give an idea about the possibilities and limitations of using pseudorandomness. Pseudorandomness may additionally find use in the construction of probabilistic algorithms, and this application will be examined in Section 6.6.

6.5.1 *Monte Carlo Methods*

The basic idea of Monte Carlo methods is to use repeated random sampling to obtain numerical results. Such methods are often useful in situations where there is no closed form description of the investigated quantity. We have already seen an example of a Monte Carlo simulation in the discussion of ruin probabilities in Example 3.2.4. Here, we will consider a much simpler, but illustrative, example.

Modern Monte Carlo methods were first used by Stanislaw Ulam and John von Neumann during their work on the Manhattan project (see the box on p. 215). Today, such methods are important tools in a wide range of scientific and commercial disciplines, and we will not attempt to give a detailed account of the subject here. It is worth noting, however, that one benefit of Monte Carlo methods is that they are very easy to parallelize, making it possible to run them quickly on supercomputers.

Example 6.5.1: Simulating π. As a basic example of a Monte Carlo method, consider the following procedure for finding the digits of π: Generate n uniformly distributed points (x, y) with $|x|, |y| \leq 1$ and let k be the number of points inside the unit circle. As n grows, k/n will converge to the relative area of the two geometric shapes, that is, for large n, k/n gives an approximation of $\pi/4$. Hence, this gives a method for computing π. Note, however, that this is not an efficient method (see Exercise 6.19).   ◁

When we undertake simulation for the purpose of mathematical experimentation, we usually have only very limited information about the situation at hand. In particular, the distribution of the random variable under consideration is rarely known. Hence, the experimental mathematician often cannot draw on deep results from probability theory or statistics to analyze results obtained by pseudorandom methods.

However, just as in other experimentation, fundamental concepts like *variance* and *confidence interval* can be useful for evaluating the usefulness of a simulated value, and to make decisions on how much computing power to expend on further simulation. We briefly recall the basic concepts and give a few examples in this section.

Manhattan and Monte Carlo

The first thoughts and attempts I made to practice were suggested by a question which occurred to me in 1946 as I was convalescing from an illness and playing solitaires. The question was: what are the chances that a Canfield solitaire laid out with 52 cards will come out successfully? After spending a lot of time trying to estimate them by pure combinatorial calculations, I wondered whether a more practical method than "abstract thinking" might not be to lay it out say one hundred times and simply observe and count the number of successful plays. [···] I immediately thought of problems of neutron diffusion and other questions of mathematical physics, and more generally how to change processes described by certain differential equations into an equivalent form interpretable as a succession of random operations. Later, I described the idea to John von Neumann, and we began to plan actual calculations.

– Stanislaw Ulam

As the quote above describes, the use of Monte Carlo methods was conceived and developed by Stanislaw Ulam (1909–1984) and John von Neumann (1903–1957) during their work on the Manhattan project. The term Monte Carlo Method refers to the casino in Monaco, where Ulam's uncle used to gamble. Using lists of truly random numbers was much too slow for this work, so von Neumann developed a pseudorandom number generator instead. This generator is called the *middle-squared method*, and he first described it to the scientific public in a talk in 1949. At that occasion, he made the following comment:

Any one who considers arithmetical methods of producing random digits is, of course, in a state of sin.

In other words, there is no way to use such methods to generate truly random numbers. Clearly, von Neumann was very well aware of the limitations of pseudorandomness in general (and his own generator in particular), but in spite of the lack of true randomness the approach proved very useful for the Monte Carlo simulations carried out at the Manhattan project.

We focus on the situation where we are aiming to estimate the *mean* $\mu = E(X)$ of a random variable X by drawing, by simulation, N values $X_1, \ldots, X_N$ and computing

$$\overline{\mu} = \frac{1}{N} \sum_{i=1}^{N} X_i.$$

The *variance* $V = E((X - \mu)^2)$ is then estimated by

$$V = \frac{1}{N} \sum_{i=1}^{N} (X_i - \overline{\mu})^2$$

or, equivalently, by

$$V = \frac{1}{N} \sum_{i=1}^{N} X_i^2 - \left(\frac{1}{N} \sum_{i=1}^{N} X_i \right)^2.$$

The *standard deviation* $\sigma = \sqrt{V}$ estimates how close the simulated values fall to the observed mean and can be used to compute indicators such as the 95% *confidence interval*

$$\left[\overline{\mu} - 1.96\sigma/\sqrt{N}, \overline{\mu} + 1.96\sigma/\sqrt{N} \right]$$

defined by the property that 95% of the time, the true value of $E(X)$ will lie in the interval found.

EX. 6.1.2 → **Example 6.5.2: Ruin probabilities.**   In Example 3.2.4, we estimated ruin probabilities for a gambler playing 100 games with $c = 10, 11, \ldots, 20$ dollars as initial capital by a simulation with $N = 100000$ samples. We can think of these probabilities as averages of a random variable taking values in $\{0, 1\}$, and hence, since $X_i^2 = X_i$ throughout, the variance can be reconstructed by the means found by

$$V = \frac{1}{N} \sum_{i=1}^{N} X_i^2 - \left(\frac{1}{N} \sum_{i=1}^{N} X_i \right)^2 = \mu - \mu^2$$

and the confidence interval becomes simply

$$\left[\mu - 1.96\sqrt{\mu - \mu^2}/\sqrt{N}, \mu + 1.96\sqrt{\mu - \mu^2}/\sqrt{N} \right]$$

giving the intervals (first row gives the capital c while the second and third rows give rounded values of respectively the lower and upper bound of the confidence interval)

10	11	12	13	14	15	16	17	18	19	20
0.313	0.270	0.225	0.192	0.155	0.132	0.105	0.085	0.069	0.056	0.043
0.319	0.276	0.230	0.197	0.160	0.136	0.109	0.088	0.072	0.059	0.045

In Example 3.3.3, we found that Maple was able to compute the exact probabilities in very little time, and we can easily check that the correct value falls in the confidence interval for each of the considered capitals except $c = 17$. Here the true value is

$$\frac{702168147827955751862174225}{792281625142643375935439503336} \simeq 0.08862.$$

This is completely consistent with the concept of confidence interval.   ◁

EX. 5.3.4 → **Example 6.5.3: Carries.**   When we add numbers one digit at a time, carries are generated as in

	1	0	0	2	1	0	0	0
	5	3	4	9	3	4	2	0
	3	3	0	3	7	1	0	0
	4	1	1	7	8	0	3	4
1	2	7	7	0	8	5	5	4

We are interested in the distribution of carries when k large numbers are added. It is easy to check that the possible carries are $\{0, 1, 2, \ldots, k-1\}$, but it is not obvious how frequently each of these occur. It is this we will address in the following.

Assume that we have constructed a procedure `ComputeCarry` that given a list L of numbers returns a list enumerating the carries that occur in the addition of all numbers from L. For instance, the command

```
[> computeCarry([53493420,33037100,41178034]);
```

should yield the result [5, 2, 1], representing that the carries 0, 1 and 2 occur respectively 5, 2, and 1 times in the addition of the three numbers as found by hand in the beginning of the example. Such a procedure is constructed in Exercise 6.21.

Given this procedure, we may now generate random numbers and feed them to `ComputeCarry` in order to estimate the frequencies of the carries.

Now, one might think that the distribution of carries occurring in the addition of k integers can be estimated from a single such addition of integers with an larger number of digits. After all, this is an easy way to generate a large number of carries. However, this approach is flawed: Observations of two successive carries in an addition are obviously not independent, so it is highly problematic to estimate the frequencies from such an experiment. Instead, we repeat the experiment M times, each time adding integers with a fixed moderate number N of digits, exploiting that the carries generated in two such additions must be independent of each other.

It is straightforward to use this approach to estimate the variance and compute confidence intervals. However, there is one more problem to overcome. In a concrete simulation $k = 2$, $N = 200$, and $M = 500000$, gave [0.5002, 0.5004] as the 95% confidence interval for the frequency of the carry 0 while the corresponding interval for the carry 1 is [0.4996, 0.4998]. On the one hand, this indicates that the true probability is 1/2 for both 0 and 1. On

Table 6.1 *For each k, the remaining columns list observed frequencies of carries occurring in the addition of k large integers. The frequencies are obtained by applying* BestFraction *to the confidence intervals of each sample as described in Example 6.5.3. Fractions that are theoretically correct are emphasized in bold.*

k	0	1	2	3	4	5	6	7
2	$\mathbf{\frac{1}{2}}$	$\mathbf{\frac{1}{2}}$						
3	$\mathbf{\frac{1}{6}}$	$\mathbf{\frac{2}{3}}$	$\frac{122}{733}$					
4	$\mathbf{\frac{1}{24}}$	$\mathbf{\frac{11}{24}}$	$\mathbf{\frac{11}{24}}$	$\mathbf{\frac{1}{24}}$				
5	$\mathbf{\frac{1}{120}}$	$\frac{18}{83}$	$\mathbf{\frac{11}{20}}$	$\mathbf{\frac{13}{60}}$	$\mathbf{\frac{1}{120}}$			
6	$\mathbf{\frac{1}{716}}$	$\frac{8}{101}$	$\frac{13}{31}$	$\frac{13}{31}$	$\frac{8}{101}$	$\frac{1}{717}$		
7	$\frac{1}{4938}$	$\mathbf{\frac{1}{42}}$	$\frac{13}{55}$	$\frac{23}{48}$	$\frac{13}{55}$	$\mathbf{\frac{1}{42}}$	$\frac{1}{4892}$	

the other, the two confidence intervals are disjoint, indicating that the two probabilities are different. Clearly, we must take this as an indication that there is something wrong with our simulation. Indeed, since the first carry is always 0, there is a systematic, although small, bias towards that value which could shift the probabilities at least by $1/200$ in this case.

We respond to this issue by the dual strategy of increasing N at the expense of M and adding 20 digits to the beginning of each number to generate carries that are not counted. With this adjustment we arrived for $k = 5$ at the confidence intervals given in Example 5.3.4 and identified as fractions in (5.38). Applying bestFraction to all observations in this way yields the data shown in Table 6.1. Note that except at $k = 2$ and $k = 4$, the fractions identified do not add up to 1, and hence cannot all be correct. Choosing to believe only in the fractions in bold leads us to the assumption that each of the probabilities at k is an integral multiple of $1/k!$.

Multiplying the midpoint of each confidence interval by $k!$ and passing to the nearest integer we get

$$1, 1$$
$$1, 4, 1$$
$$1, 11, 11, 1$$
$$1, 26, 66, 26, 1$$
$$1, 57, 302, 302, 57, 1$$
$$1, 120, 1191, 2416, 1191, 120, 1.$$

We can pass this to the OEIS row-by-row as
$$1, 4, 1, 1, 11, 11, 1, 1, \dots$$
to recognize the Eulerian numbers in **A8292**.   ◁

6.5.2 *Generating Random Collections*

Considering a randomly generated collection of samples allows an unbiased investigation of collections that are too extensive to be investigated exhaustively. In particular, pseudorandomness may be useful in the initial investigation of a new problem if the structures involved are largely unknown.

Example 6.5.4: Latin squares. An $n \times n$ *Latin square* is an $n \times n$ matrix where every row and every column contains each number $1, \ldots, n$ precisely once. For instance, the following are Latin squares:

$$A_2 = \begin{bmatrix} 1 & 2 \\ 2 & 1 \end{bmatrix} \qquad A_3 = \begin{bmatrix} 1 & 2 & 3 \\ 3 & 1 & 2 \\ 2 & 3 & 1 \end{bmatrix}.$$

In this example, we will investigate the determinants of Latin squares. For each $n \in \mathbb{N}$, let $\mathcal{D}_n \subseteq \mathbb{Z}$ denote the set consisting of every number that is the determinant of an $n \times n$ Latin square.

Recall that row and column additions do not change the value of the determinant of a matrix. For odd n, such operations can be used to prove that $\frac{n^2+n}{2}$ divides every element of $\mathcal{D}_n$ (see Exercise 6.22). But which possible multiples actually occur?

For now, we will restrict ourselves to the following questions: For which odd n is $0 \in \mathcal{D}_n$? And for which is $n(1 + 2 + \cdots + n) \in \mathcal{D}_n$? To answer this, we need a procedure that generates Latin squares. To avoid the resource use and bookkeeping involved in generating an exhaustive collection, we will use the following probabilistic generator:

```
[> firstZero := proc(A)                                          1
      local r,c;                                                 2
      for r from 1 to RowDimension(A) do                        3
          for c from 1 to ColumnDimension(A) do                 4
              if A[r,c] = 0 then return [r,c]; end if;           5
          end do;                                                6
      end do;                                                    7
      return [0,0];                                              8
   end proc:                                                     9
                                                                 10
   fill := proc(A)                                               11
      local allowed,nextEntry,newA,result,a,r,c;                 12
      nextEntry := firstZero(A);                                 13
      if nextEntry = [0,0] then return A; end if;                14
      r := nextEntry[1];                                         15
      c := nextEntry[2];                                         16
      allowed := {seq(i,i=1..RowDimension(A))} minus            17
                 (convert(Row(A,r),set) union                    18
                     convert(Column(A,c),set));                  19
```

```
        while allowed <> {} do                                          20
            a := allowed[                                               21
                Generate(integer(range=1..nops(allowed)))];            22
            newA := Copy(A);                                            23
            newA[r,c] := a;                                            24
            newA := fill(newA);                                         25
            if newA = FAIL then                                        26
                allowed := allowed minus {a};                          27
            else                                                       28
                return newA;                                           29
            end if;                                                    30
        end do;                                                        31
    return FAIL;                                                       32
    end proc;                                                          33
```

With these definitions, the command fill(Matrix(n)) will generate an $n \times n$ Latin square. Note that the recursive structure of the program guarantees that this will always produce a Latin square, but even for moderately sized values of n, it may need to run a long time to do so (see Exercise 6.23).

Using this tool, it is straightforward to check that 0 is an element of $\mathcal{D}_n$ for $n \in \{7, 9\}$, but not for $n \in \{3, 5\}$. Similarly, $n(1 + 2 + \cdots + n)$ is an element of $\mathcal{D}_n$ for each $n \in \{3, 5, 7, 9\}$ (see Exercise 6.24). In order to solve the problem in general, one would need to analyze the structure of Latin squares achieving these minimal values and use that information to construct explicit formulas for such Latin squares. With luck, such a formula can be generalized to larger values of n and used to construct Latin squares with minimal determinants

EX. 8.5.2 ← there.   ◁

There are several possible problems that one should be aware of when considering randomly generated collections. First and foremost, the objects constructed by the method may not be uniformly distributed among the possibilities. In particular, a random generator may be biased toward returning objects from a certain subclass. To take an extreme case, one could imagine a generator that practically always outputs the same object or one that is never able to produce certain elements of the class of objects under consideration. Naturally, this will lead to a poor representation of the investigated structure and ultimately to misguided hypotheses. Unfortunately, this problem is likely to go unnoticed unless one explicitly investigates the distribution of the generated objects. The distribution of the Latin squares constructed in Example 6.5.4 is investigated in Exercise 6.25.

The fundamental benefit of randomness is that it can be used to exclude the possibility of human bias, but the downside of this is that it can be very hard to detect patterns in a randomly constructed collection of objects. Depending on the problem, it may be better to first consider structured collections of objects to make it easier to detect patterns. Once the possibilities of systematic searches have been exhausted, one can then turn to randomness to investigate a collection of examples that lies beyond the class that could be investigated systematically. In such cases, randomness can be considered a last resort, when it is not possible to do an exhaustive—or at least systematic—search.

Even when using randomness, it may be beneficial to consider random collections with some kind of common internal structure. For real numbers, this could mean considering random simple fractions, integer/rational combinations of simple square roots, roots in small polynomials with integer/rational coefficients, sines of rational multiples of π, simple continued fractions and so on. Depending on the problem at hand, some of these might be more appropriate than others.

As mentioned above, randomness is the tool to use when lack of structure or an overwhelming number of cases makes it impossible to use iteration or recursion to investigate a sufficiently large systematically constructed subset of the possibilities. This means that randomness will often be employed in situations where there are very many different options to choose from. In such cases, it is important to understand what fraction of the possible configurations have actually been examined. Examining millions of examples might sound impressive, but in a situation where there are 10^{20} possibilities, this will actually only have been a vanishing fraction of the total. Naturally, this problem is exacerbated if the generated collection contains many repetitions or the interesting examples are few and far between.

This does not mean that one should refrain from using randomness in cases with many possibilities, but it is always important to be aware of the scale of the problem at hand. Rather than keeping track of the absolute number of cases tested, one should consider this number relative to the total number of cases. This helps the investigator from being mislead to believe that a hypothesis is more well supported than actually the case.

6.5.3 *Testing Hypotheses on Random Samples*

An important application of pseudorandomness is in the search for counterexamples to hypotheses. It is often straightforward to test a well formulated hypothesis on a collection of randomly generated examples, and this allows an unbiased search for counterexamples.

Often, one will be in a situation where iteration or recursion has been used to investigate a subset of the considered structures, but due to restraints of time and memory, it is impossible to continue in this manner. If this investigation has resulted in a hypothesis, then one might be able to test it on random elements outside the subset already considered, and this is a very powerful tool, because it allows the test of a generalized hypothesis beyond the data material on the basis of which is was formulated.

EX. 2.6.2 → **Example 6.5.5: Counting games.** Consider the game introduced in Example 2.6.2. As seen in Exercise 2.43, it is easy to devise a winning strategy for Player B in the case $n = 3$. Specifically, Player B can win by using the following strategy:

Always play the opposite of the last digit played by Player A   (6.1)

Having constructed winning strategies for $n = 2$ (see Example 2.6.2) and $n = 3$, it is natural to check whether these also work for other values of n.

As described in Exercise 3.15, it is possible to make a recursive procedure which for each n decides whether Player A or Player B has a winning strategy, and to extract this winning strategy as a list of instructions. However, such a list is potentially complicated, and it would be much more satisfactory to have compact descriptions of the winning strategies like the ones available for $n = 2$ and $n = 3$.

It is difficult to compute the exact number of games by hand, but the following recursive procedure can do so for small values of n. Given a binary string s and an N, this program returns the possible strings that a game starting with s can result in.

```
[> allGames := proc(s,N)                                          1
       local 1;                                                    2
       1:=length(s);                                              3
       if 1 <= N then                                              4
         return [op(allGames(cat(s,"0"),N)),                      5
                 op(allGames(cat(s,"1"),N))];                      6
       end if;                                                     7
       if is(Search(SubString(s,1-N+1..1),s)<1-N+1) then          8
         return [s];                                               9
       else                                                       10
         return [op(allGames(cat(s,"0"),N)),                      11
                 op(allGames(cat(s,"1"),N))];                     12
       end if;                                                    13
   end proc:                                                      14
```

The following output shows that the number of games grows drastically:

```
[> for N from 2 to 5 do                                           1
       print(N,2*nops(allGames("0",N)));                          2
   end do:                                                         3
```

$$2, 26$$

$$3, 236$$

$$4, 7882$$

$$5, 4445804$$

The complexity of the problem means that this approach fails at $n = 6$ or $n = 7$ unless you have access to very powerful computers. However, using the approach suggested in Exercise 3.15 it is straightforward to determine which player has a winning strategy for $n = 6$, at least.

Clearly, using a specific strategy for one of the players significantly reduces the number of possible different games, so one could test such a strategy exhaustively for $n \leq 7$, but beyond that, one is forced to use randomness. Specifically, we can test a strategy by letting one player take moves according to the strategy while the other plays at random. Such tests can easily be carried out for much larger values of n.

Using this approach, it is straightforward to check that the strategy shown in (6.1) works, not only for $n = 3$, but for every odd n as well (see Exercise 6.27). In fact, this is not hard to prove (see Exercise 6.28). This is a very satisfactory approach because it uses ideas based on knowledge from the analysis of the game for small values of n to formulate a hypothesis which can then be tested for large values of n using randomness. ◁

6.6 Randomness in Algorithms

By an *algorithm*, we usually mean a *deterministic* procedure for solving a specific problem that is guaranteed to finish in finite time and to produce the correct answer. By contrast, a *probabilistic* or *randomized* algorithm employs randomness as part of the procedure, sacrificing determinism for some other benefit, usually increased speed. For a computationally hard problem, a probabilistic algorithm may be the only practical way to find a solution.

6.6.1 *Primality Tests*

The command isprime has been used several times in the preceding chapters to test whether various numbers were primes. However, the description of isprime from the Maple help system reveals that it is not *guaranteed* to give the correct answer:

- The isprime command is a probabilistic primality testing routine [...].
- It returns false if n is shown to be composite within one strong pseudo-primality test and one Lucas test. It returns true otherwise.
- If isprime returns true, n is very probably prime [...]. No counterexample is known and it has been conjectured that such a counterexample must be hundreds of digits long.

In other words, any number identified as composite by isprime is guaranteed to be composite, while a number identified as a prime could conceivably be composite. But why would one want to use a procedure that is not guaranteed to produce the right result? After all, there exists a simple deterministic procedure for testing whether n is a prime: simply check whether $k | n$ for all $k \leq \sqrt{n}$. Naturally, the answer is speed: the latter method is much too slow for many practical applications.

Example 6.6.1: Pseudoprimes. In the following,

$$(\mathbb{Z}/n\mathbb{Z})^* = \{b \in \mathbb{Z}/n\mathbb{Z} \mid \gcd(n, b) = 1\}$$

will denote the multiplicative group of integers modulo n. By Fermat's Little Theorem

$$b^{n-1} \equiv 1 \pmod{n} \tag{6.2}$$

for any prime n and b with $\gcd(b, n) = 1$. Note that (6.2) may also hold in cases where n is not prime, but most often, it does not. This observation is the motivation behind the following definition.

Definition 6.6.2. *Let n an odd, composite number and let b be an integer with $\gcd(n, b) = 1$. If $b^{n-1} \equiv 1 \pmod{n}$ then n is said to be a* pseudoprime *to the base b.*

In other words n is a pseudoprime to the base b if it behaves like a prime with respect to the congruence in (6.2).

Proposition 6.6.3. *Let n be an odd integer. Let b, b_1, b_2 be relatively prime to n.*

(i) *n is a pseudoprime to base b if and only if the order of b in $(\mathbb{Z}/n\mathbb{Z})^*$ divides $n - 1$.*
(ii) *If n is a pseudoprime to the bases b_1 and b_2, then it is also a pseudoprime to the bases $b_1 b_2$ and $b_1 b_2^{-1}$.*
(iii) *If there exists $b \in (\mathbb{Z}/n\mathbb{Z})^*$ such that n is not a pseudoprime to the base b, then*

$$|\{b \in (\mathbb{Z}/n\mathbb{Z})^* \mid n \text{ not pseudoprime to base } b\}|$$
$$\geq |\{b \in (\mathbb{Z}/n\mathbb{Z})^* \mid n \text{ pseudoprime to base } b\}|.$$

The first two statements are straightforward to prove, while the last requires a little more work (see Exercise 6.31). Note that this result guarantees that if there exists a base b where the test fails, then it will fail for at least half of the possible bases. This leads to the nondeterministic primality test described in Algorithm 6.1. This test is implemented in Exercise 6.33.

Algorithm 6.1 A probabilistic primality test

1: **procedure** PSEUDOPRIMETEST(n, k)
2:　　**for** i from 1 to k **do**
3:　　　　generate a random b in $\{1, \ldots, n - 1\}$
4:　　　　**if** $\gcd(n, b) \neq 1$ **then**
5:　　　　　　**return** n is composite
6:　　　　**else if** $b^{n-1} \not\equiv 1 \pmod{n}$ **then**
7:　　　　　　**return** n is composite
8:　　　　**end if**
9:　　**end for**
10:　　**return** n is probably prime
11: **end procedure**

Assume that n is a composite number for which there exists a base b to which n is a not a pseudoprime. Then n is not a pseudoprime to at least half of the possible bases, so each iteration of the algorithm has at least 50% chance of revealing that n is composite. Repeating the test k times reduces the probability to 2^{-k}. Clearly, the rapid decrease of this probability gives an extremely efficient way to test whether n is composite, but only if the assumptions are satisfied. Now, the question is naturally whether there exist composite n which satisfy (6.2) for *every* b with $\gcd(n, b) = 1$. Unfortunately, the answer is yes:

Definition 6.6.4. *A* Carmichael number *is a composite integer n such that (6.2) holds for every $b \in (\mathbb{Z}/n\mathbb{Z})^*$.*

The smallest Carmichael number is $561 = 3 \cdot 11 \cdot 17$, and it has been proved that there are in fact infinitely many Carmichael numbers. A number of small Carmichael numbers are identified in Exercise 6.33. Naturally, tests based on pseudoprimes are of limited practical use since they necessarily fail for these composite numbers. That problem will be remedied in the following example. ◁

Example 6.6.5: The Solovay–Strassen test. As discussed in Exercise 6.34, any prime n satisfies the following congruence for every $1 < b < n$:

$$b^{(n-1)/2} \equiv \left(\frac{b}{n}\right) \pmod{n}, \tag{6.3}$$

where $\left(\frac{b}{n}\right)$ is the generalized Legendre symbol introduced in Example 4.1.5.

Definition 6.6.6. *Let n be an odd composite integer and let b be an integer with $\gcd(n, b) = 1$, then n is said to be an* Euler pseudoprime to the base b *if n and b satisfy (6.3).*

It is straightforward to check that every Euler pseudoprime is a pseudoprime to the same base. Every odd composite number is an Euler pseudoprime to the base ± 1, and these trivial bases will be excluded from the following discussion.

Note that there is no analogue of Carmichael numbers for Euler pseudoprimes: any composite number n fails to satisfy this congruence for at least half of the possible bases (see Exercise 6.34 and 6.35). This makes (6.3) much more attractive than (6.2) as the foundation of a primality test. Algorithm 6.2 gives pseudocode for the Solovay–Strassen test where (6.3) is checked for randomly chosen bases in order to test primality of the input.

Since each odd composite n fails the test for at least half the possible bases, the probability that the algorithm reports a composite number as a probable prime is at most 2^{-k}. The fast decay of this function allows primality to be established with a very high degree of certainty. Using fast algorithms for modular exponentiation, the Solovay–Strassen test runs in $O(k \log^3 n)$, where k is the number of bases considered. ◁

Example 6.6.7: isprime. As mentioned in the beginning of this section, Maple's isprime carries out two tests to check whether a given number

---

Algorithm 6.2 The Solovay–Strassen test

1: **procedure** SOLOVAYSTRASSENTEST(n, k)
2:     **for** i from 1 to k **do**
3:         generate a random b in $\{1, \dots, n-1\}$
4:         **if** $b^{(n-1)/2} \not\equiv \left(\frac{b}{n}\right) \pmod{n}$ **then**
5:             **return** n is composite
6:         **end if**
7:     **end for**
8:     **return** n is probably prime
9: **end procedure**

---

is a prime: A strong pseudoprime test and a Lucas test. It goes beyond the scope of this presentation to give a detailed description of these tests, but it is worth mentioning that they are both probabilistic. Like the two tests considered above, they use conditions that are satisfied by all primes, but few composite numbers to check for primality. As in the test considered in Example 6.6.1, there are known examples of composite numbers that cannot be detected by either of the two tests individually. The strength of the combined test comes from the fact that there are very few such pseudoprimes of each kind and no known overlaps between the two lists. In fact, it has been tested that no $n < 2^{64}$ is misclassified by both tests.   ◁

It is worth noting that there exist deterministic primality tests that are much faster than the primitive approach of checking every possible divisor. In fact, the so called AKS test can check primality for any number in polynomial time, but it is outperformed by probabilistic alternatives in practical applications. Often, the speed of a (probabilistic) primality test is improved by explicitly checking whether any element of a predefined set of small prime numbers divides the integer under investigation. This strategy is also employed by isprime.

EX. 3.4.4 → **Example 6.6.8: The weak Goldbach conjecture.**   As we discussed in Example 3.4.4 and Exercise 3.20, Helfgott reduced the proof of the weak Goldbach conjecture to establishing the existence of a collection of primes

$$p_1 < p_2 < \cdots < p_n$$

with $p_k - p_{k-1} < 10^{18}$ and $p_n > 10^{30}$. Since Helfgott's goal was to provide a computer-assisted proof rather than performing a mathematical experiment, a probabilistic method such as the one employed by isprime was clearly insufficient, but on the other hand, the numbers studied were of a magnitude where general deterministic algorithms are too slow, taking into account that at least 10^{12} such numbers would have to be found. The solution to this problem found in [HP13] was to look only for p_k being a *Proth number*, that is, of the form $k2^n + 1$ with odd $k < 2^n$. Indeed, a theorem of Proth establishes that whenever p is a Proth number, and we for some a have

$$\left(\frac{a}{p}\right) = -1$$

(i.e. a is a quadratic nonresidue modulo p as discussed in Example 4.1.5) then p is a prime exactly when

$$a^{(p-1)/2} \equiv -1 \pmod{p}.$$

In other words, the Solovay–Strassen test becomes deterministic for Proth numbers in the presence of such a number a, which, as we have already seen, may be found with probability $1 - 2^{-\ell}$ by trying ℓ different small primes.

Thus, although the a_k and the strategically positioned Proth numbers p_k passing the primality test must still be found by trial and error, the pair (p_k, a_k) provides an explicit certificate for the existence of the desired primes which in turn leads to the complete proof.

In fact, this approach failed partially since not enough Proth primes could be found to establish the result, but since only about 130000 additional primes had to be found (a very small number compared to the lower bound of 10^{12}), Ex. 7.1.3 ← this could be obtained by deterministic primality checks.   ◁

6.7 Exercises

Warmup

Exercise 6.1 Construct a procedure which, given N, returns the first N pseudorandom numbers generated by RANDU with seed $x_0 = 1$. Check with the OEIS.

Exercise 6.2 Construct a procedure that, given $n \in \mathbb{N}$, returns an $n \times n$ matrix with random 4 digit floating point entries.

Exercise 6.3 Construct a procedure that returns $\sin(p\pi/q)$ for a random rational p/q.

Exercise 6.4 Check `GetState` and `SetState` by generating the same vector consisting of 10000 pseudorandom integers twice. Check that the two vectors are in fact identical.

Exercise 6.5 Use `Generate(float(range=1..10))` with logarithmic distribution and `pointplot` to plot random elements of $(1, 10)^2$. Compare with Figure 6.1. Judging from this, how does Maple construct the random elements of an interval (a, b)?

Homework

Exercise 6.6 Given $n \in \mathbb{N}$ and $i \in \{0, \dots, 2^{n^2} - 1\}$, the binary expansion of i can be used as an encoding of an element of $M_n(0, 1)$. For instance, for $n = 2$

and $i = 7$, the binary expansion of i is 111, and padding this with an extra 0 at the start to produce a sequence of length n^2, gives 0111, corresponding to the matrix

$$\begin{bmatrix} 0 & 1 \\ 1 & 1 \end{bmatrix} \in M_n(0, 1).$$

Construct a procedure that, given n and i, returns the matrix defined by this encoding [*Hint: use* `convert(i,base,2)`]. Construct all elements of $M_2(0, 1)$ in this way. For how large values of n is it practically possible to construct all elements of $M_n(0, 1)$?

Exercise 6.7 Construct a procedure that, given $n \in \mathbb{N}$, uses the procedure constructed in Exercise 6.6 to return a randomly chosen element of $M_n(0, 1)$.

Exercise 6.8 Use the procedure constructed in Exercise 6.1 to generate a plot of random points in $[0, 1)^2$. Does the output look random? Use the procedure to make a plot of random points of the form $(x_i, x_{i+1}, x_{i+2}) \in [0, 1)^3$. Rotate the resulting figure and look at it from various angles. Does the output look random? Comment. Compare with the quote given at the start of Section 6.3.2.

EX. 4.1.6 → **Exercise 6.9** The plots constructed in Example 4.1.6 and Exercise 4.43 use a fixed grid of points to create plots of the Mandelbrot set. Modify the plots to make them use randomly generated points instead. What are the benefits and drawbacks to using randomness in this context?

Exercise 6.10 As discussed in Chapter 5, the PSLQ algorithm can be used to find integer relations among numbers. The aim of this exercise is to express $\sin(nx)$ in terms of $\sin(x)^i$ for $i = 1, \ldots n$. Execute the following commands in Maple a number of times:

```
[> x := Generate(float(method=uniform));          1
   n:=3:                                           2
   PSLQ([sin(n*x),seq(sin(x)^i,i=1..n)]);          3
```

Use the results to formulate a hypothesis about the relation between $\sin(3x)$ and $\sin(x)$, $\sin(x)^2$, and $\sin(x)^3$. Attempt to do the same for higher values of n [*Hint: The value of* `Digits` *must be increased to make this work.*] Test your hypothesis, and explain what any counterexamples have in common. Look up the identified sequences of coefficients in OEIS.

EX. 3.1.1 → **Exercise 6.11** Construct a procedure that given $N, n \in \mathbb{N}$ with $n \leq N$ returns n distinct random elements of $\{1, \ldots, N\}$. Use this to construct a procedure that can select a random subset when passed a set.

Exercise 6.12 Write a procedure that given d and N returns a random root from a random polynomial of degree d with integer coefficients between $-N$ and N. How are these roots distributed on the real line?

Exercise 6.13 Write a procedure in Maple which, given a finite sequence of bits, identifies the biggest n for which there is a subsequence consisting of n ones. Compute the expected value of this number for a sequence of N truly random bits. Does Generate produce sequences that look random with respect to this?

Exercise 6.14 What is the entropy of a sequence of random bits? Does Generate produce sequences with the correct entropy?

BOX P. 215 → **Exercise 6.15** For the Manhattan project, von Neumann used a pseudorandom number generator known as the *middle squared method*: Let x be a 4 digit seed and consider the digits of x^2 as a sequence. If needed, add leading zeroes to produce a sequence with 8 elements $a_1 \cdots a_8$. Let $x_1 = a_3 \cdots a_6$. Reiterating this procedure results in a sequence of pseudorandom numbers. Implement the middle square method and investigate its properties. Is it a good pseudorandom number generator?

Exercise 6.16 Invent an algorithm for the generation of pseudorandom bits and implement it. Can you demonstrate a flaw in your own generator?

Exercise 6.17 Use the test developed in Exercises 6.14 and 6.13 on RANDU and Blum Blum Shub as well as the pseudorandom number generators developed in Exercises 6.16 and 6.15.

Exercise 6.18 For each $n \in \mathbb{N}$, let D_n denote the fraction of the elements of $M_n(\{0, 1\})$ for which the determinant is 0. Use the procedure constructed in Exercise 6.6 to compute D_2. For how large values of n can D_n be computed exactly in this way? Let N be the largest number for which it is practically possible to compute the fraction. Use the procedure constructed in Exercise 6.7 to find an approximated value of D_{N+1} by computing the determinants of a collection of randomly chosen elements. Is it possible to make a reasonable hypothesis about how D_n depends on n?

EX. 6.5.1 → **Exercise 6.19** Implement the procedure for computing π considered in Example 6.5.1. How many random points are needed to get n correct digits?

EX. 6.5.1 → **Exercise 6.20** The following is a version of *Buffon's needle problem*: Let $t > 1$ be given and draw parallel line in the plane such that the distance between neighboring lines is t. What is the probability that a needle of length 1 dropped on the plane will cross one of the lines? Compute the answer theoretically. Set up a Monte Carlo simulation of the problem to estimate the probability. Use this to give an estimate of π. How does this method compare to the one considered in Example 6.5.1 and Exercise 6.19?

EX. 6.5.3 → **Exercise 6.21** Write a procedure that given a list L of numbers returns an enumeration of the carries occurring in the addition of the elements of L. Use this procedure to replicate the experiments carried out in Example 6.5.3.

EX. 6.5.4 → **Exercise 6.22** Use row and column additions to prove that $\frac{n^2+n}{2}$ divides the determinant of every $n \times n$ Latin square when n is odd. Is it possible to derive an analogous formula for even n?

EX. 6.5.4 → **Exercise 6.23** In principle, the algorithm constructed in Example 6.5.4 will always produce a Latin square, but the average running time increases with the size of the square. Investigate this growth.

EX. 6.5.4 → **Exercise 6.24** Do 0 and $\frac{n^2+n}{2}$ occur as determinants of $n \times n$ Latin squares for $n \in \{3, 5, 7\}$? Is it also possible to answer the question for $n = 9$?

EX. 6.5.4 → **Exercise 6.25** Investigate the distribution of the results produced by the generator constructed in Example 6.5.4.

EX. 6.5.4 → **Exercise 6.26** Modify the algorithm constructed in Example 6.5.4 to achieve a deterministic procedure which produces all $n \times n$ Latin squares. For which n is it feasible to use this procedure? Compare with the probabilistic method.

EX. 6.5.5 → **Exercise 6.27** Carry out the investigation discussed in Example 6.5.5 to test the hypothesis that the strategy given in (6.1) is a winning strategy for Player B when n is odd.

EX. 6.5.5 → **Exercise 6.28** Prove that the strategy given in (6.1) is a winning strategy for Player B when n is odd.

EX. 6.5.5 → **Exercise 6.29** Examine the distribution of the games generated by letting both players play at random. Similarly, examine the distribution of games generated by letting Player A play at random while Player B uses a winning strategy.

Exercise 6.30 Implement the naive primality test which tests whether k divides n for every $k \leq \sqrt{n}$.

EX. 6.6.1 → **Exercise 6.31** Prove Proposition 6.6.3.

Exercise 6.32 *Wilson's theorem* states that p is prime if and only if $(p-1)! \equiv -1 \pmod{p}$. Use this to implement a deterministic primality test in Maple.

EX. 6.6.1 → **Exercise 6.33** Implement the primality test discussed in Example 6.6.1. Use it to identify the first 10 Carmichael numbers. Let $C(x)$ denote the number of Carmichael numbers less than x. Visualize the growth of $C(x)$ and give an estimate of a nontrivial lower bound for $C(x)$.

EX. 6.6.5 → **Exercise 6.34** Let p be an odd prime and let b be an integer. Prove that

$$\left(\frac{b}{p}\right) \equiv b^{(p-1)/2} \pmod{p}.$$

EX. 6.6.5 → **Exercise 6.35** Let n be an odd composite number. Prove that

$$\left(\frac{a}{n}\right) \not\equiv a^{(p-1)/2} \pmod{n}.$$

for at least half of all $1 < b < n$ with $\gcd(n, b) = 1$.

EX. 6.6.5 → **Exercise 6.36** Implement the Solovay–Strassen test.

Exercise 6.37 Look up pseudocode for the algorithm *quick sort* online. Explain how and why one should use randomness in this algorithm.

Exercise 6.38 Develop a probabilistic algorithm which given matrices A, B, and C with appropriate dimensions determines whether $C = AB$ by comparing the value of Cx_i and $A(Bx_i)$ for k suitable randomly generated vectors $x_1, \ldots, x_k$ with entries in $\{0, 1\}$. Implement and test the algorithm. Determine the running time and the probability of error. Compare with the naive approach of comparing each entry.

Projects and Group Work

Exercise 6.39 This is an exercise for two teams. Each team must produce 5 sequences of 50 zeroes and ones by hand (no randomness tools allowed) and generate 5 such sequences using pseudorandomness in Maple. The lists are permuted and swapped. The opposing team must attempt to guess which are which.

Exercise 6.40 Let x be a complex random variable with mean 0 and variance 1. Consider a sequence $(X_n)_{n=1}^{\infty}$ of $n \times n$ matrices whose entries are independent and identically distributed copies of x. Let $\lambda_1, \ldots, \lambda_n$, $1 \leq j \leq n$ denote the eigenvalues of $\frac{1}{\sqrt{n}}X_n$. Define the empirical spectral measure of $\frac{1}{\sqrt{n}}X_n$ as

$$\mu_{\frac{1}{\sqrt{n}}X_n}(A) = n^{-1}\#\{j \leq n : \lambda_j \in A\}, \quad A \in \mathcal{B}(\mathbb{C}).$$

The sequence of measures $\mu_{\frac{1}{\sqrt{n}}X_n}$ converges in probability to a measure on the unit disk. Which measure is this?

Exercise 6.41 The plots constructed in Exercise 4.47 were hampered by the rapid growth of the number of points in the pre-images considered. Modify the procedure to make it choose a random pre-image at each step rather than considering all of them. Does this improve the plots? Answer the questions posed in Exercise 4.47 based on this.

6.8 Notes and Further Reading

RANDU is documented in [IBM67] and the quote at the beginning of Section 6.3.2 is from [PTVF92]. For a discussion of the problem inherent in linear recurrence relations like RANDU, see [Mar68]. The Blum Blum Shub generator and the Mersenne twister are documented in respectively [BBS86, SS05] and [MN98b], [Mat]. The current standard for the testing of randomness is the NIST test suite for random numbers (`csrc.nist.gov/rng/`). For a basic introduction to the testing of randomness and a useful bibliography, see `www.random.org/analysis/`.

The fact that the probabilities identified in Example 6.5.3 are correct is proved in [Hol97]. For more information about the investigation of carries, see [DF09]. The problem of finding a winning strategy in the game considered in Example 6.5.5 will be revisited in Exercise 8.42. Similarly, the investigation of determinants of Latin squares started in Example 6.5.4 is continued in Exercise 8.42.

The proof that there are infinitely many Carmichael numbers can be found in [AGP94]. Interestingly, the authors of that paper were inspired the experimental study of Carmichael numbers reported in [Zha92]. The Solovay–Strassen test was introduced in [SS77], [SS78]. For a detailed discussion of the primality tests discussed in this chapter, see [Kob94] which also contains an accessible introduction to the required number theory and covers the computational complexity of the tests.

It is worth noting that there is no theoretical obstruction to the existence of a composite number that is a pseudoprime with respect to both the tests employed by `isprime` as discussed in Example 6.6.7. Indeed, a heuristic argument has been made for the case that there should be infinitely many composite numbers that are pseudoprime with respect to both tests, and hence theoretically undetectable by `isprime` [Pom]. Maple has had such problems in the past, specifically [Pin93] documented cases where Maple V mistakingly reported certain composite pseudoprimes as primes.

The middle squared method discussed in Exercise 6.15 was first described by a Franciscan friar known as Brother Edvin sometime around 1250, but it was reinvented by von Neumann for his work on the Manhattan project [Eke93]. Exercise 6.10 was suggested in [Str].

7 Time, Memory and Precision

Mathematical experiments often exert high demands on the experimenter's computing resources. There are many different reasons for this, but three themes seem to reoccur:

- The problems studied are often infinite in nature and hence one wishes to obtain as large finite datasets as possible to describe them.
- Often, it is hard to say a priori how much data are needed for further analysis.
- The structures studied are often poorly understood—this is why they are subject to experimentation—and hence computations tend to be algorithmically inefficient.

In this chapter, we will look at problems of this nature and describe some tools to address them. The reader is warned that we are now moving into the territory of computer science rather than mathematics. Of course, we will not be able to provide deep insight into all aspects of this discipline which could be relevant for the experimental mathematician.

We reiterate that it is almost always a good idea to design experiments with little emphasis on efficiency at the outset and then turn to matters of improving efficiency later. First of all, it may be that the experiment has sufficient merits in its nonoptimized form to lead to the sought insights, and hence, one is spared the trouble altogether. But even if optimization turns out to be necessary, it is useful to have a simpler version of the algorithm, in particular when checking the correctness of the more advanced algorithm by comparing their outputs.

7.1 Order of Consumption

7.1.1 O-notation

The most common way of addressing the demands of a certain algorithm, drawing on O-notation, will be well known to the mathematician. Usually,

233

we will consider a function $f : \mathbb{N} \to \mathbb{R}$ which is to be interpreted so that $f(n)$ is the "cost" of running the algorithm (usually in terms of time or memory requirements) where n somehow describes the size of the problem that the algorithm is solving. The following definitions are standard and probably known to the reader:

Definition 7.1.1. *We say that $f = O(g)$ when there exists $N \in \mathbb{N}$ and $C > 0$ so that*

$$|f(n)| \le C|g(n)| \quad \text{for all } n \ge N.$$

When $f = O(g)$ and $g = O(f)$ we say the two functions are of the same order *and write $f = \Theta(g)$.*

We remind the reader that for any $\alpha \ge \alpha' > 0$ and $\beta > 1$ we have

$$n^{\alpha'} = O(n^{\alpha})$$
$$n^{\alpha} = O(\beta^{n})$$
$$(\alpha')^{n} = O(\alpha^{n})$$
$$\ln n = O(n^{\beta}).$$

Algorithms whose cost are of the same order as n, c^{n}, $\ln n$ will casually be said to have *linear*, *exponential*, and *logarithmic complexity* and so on.

EX. 5.2.3 → **Example 7.1.2: Computing Fibonacci numbers.** We saw in Example 3.3.1 that the use of a remember table leads to a substantial increase of speed in the computation of the Fibonacci numbers f_{n}. In fact, the naive approach would cost

$$\sum_{i=0}^{n-2} f_i + f_{n-3} \tag{7.1}$$

recursive calls, whereas the remember table would cost only n. Since we know by (5.9) that $f_n = O(\phi^n)$, with ϕ the golden mean, we immediately see that the remember table takes us from a complexity of $O(n\phi^n)$ to one of $O(n)$. In fact, being slightly more careful (cf. Exercise 7.13), we can prove that the complexity of the naive approach is $\Theta(\phi^n)$, which is of course is still terrible compared
EX. 7.1.8 ← to the linear time. ◁

EX. 6.6.8 → **Example 7.1.3: Testing the Goldbach conjecture.** The memory complexity of the sieve devised in Example 3.4.4 to check for counterexamples to the Goldbach conjecture up to N is linear in N. The time complexity is clearly $O(N^2)$, and since we note that the inner `for` loop of Algorithm 3.2 is only reached at the primes encountered, we can use the prime number theorem (cf. the box on p. 10) to see that it is in fact $O(N^2/\ln(N))$. ◁

EX. 5.3.6 → **Example 7.1.4: Counting balanced towers.** The procedure `towers` in Example 1.6.5 counts balanced towers with N bricks by three recursive calls at level $N - 1$. Hence the complexity is a priori $O(3^N)$, but using a remember table, we could reduce the number of calls dramatically. This speedup relied

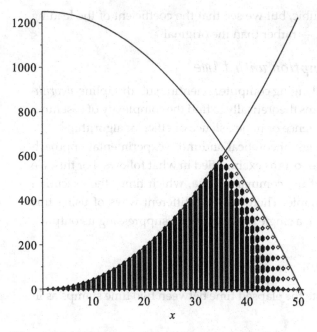

Figure 7.1 Necessary values of (n, w) in a call of dTower.

on the fact that to compute towers(N,0), we only needed to know the values of towers(n,w) for $0 \leq n \leq N$ and $-(n^2 - n)/2 \leq w \leq (n^2 - n)/2$. Thus, the number of values to be computed was capped at

$$\sum_{n=0}^{N} (n^2 - n) = \frac{1}{3} \left((N+1)^3 - 3(N+1)^2 + 2N + 2\right) = O(N^3).$$

We managed to further improve the efficiency of the procedure by using symmetry and the fact that certain values could be seen to vanish. Effectively, this means that the values (n, w) we need to consider are bounded by two parabolas and the x-axis as indicated in Figure 7.1. For instance, a call with $N = 50$ would result in 75810 entries being computed in the remember table of the original program, whereas 10027 values would suffice in the improved version.

A good estimate of the number of calls needed is provided by the area delimited by the two parabolas. We compute that they intersect at

$$x_N = \frac{1}{2}(1 + \sqrt{2N^2 - 2N + 1}),$$

and then get the area

$$A_N = \int_0^{x_N} \frac{1}{2} x(x-1) dx + \int_{x_N}^{N} \frac{1}{2} \left(N(N-1) - x(x-1)\right) dx$$

$$= \frac{1}{3} N^3 - \frac{1}{2} N^2 + \frac{1}{4} N - \frac{1}{12} \left(2N^2 - 2N + 1\right) \sqrt{2N^2 - 2N + 1} - \frac{1}{2}.$$

The complexity remains cubic, but we see that the coefficient of the leading

EX. 7.2.1 ← term is now $1/3 - \sqrt{2}/6 < \frac{1}{10}$ rather than the original $\frac{1}{3}$.   ◁

7.1.2 Gauging Time Consumption with *time*

In the mathematically challenging computer scientific sub-discipline *algorithmics*, one analyzes algorithms theoretically to find the complexity of cost functions and establish the existence or nonexistence of efficient algorithms.

We will mostly adopt a less theoretical and more experimental approach and use Maple to gauge the costs as exemplified in what follows. For this, we will make extensive use of the command `time`, which times the execution of a given procedure in Maple. There are two different ways of using this command: It can either time a single procedure call, suppressing its outputs, as in

```
[> time(evalf(log(sum(n^n,n=1..2000))));
```

or it can be used to compute the elapsed time between two time stamps as in

```
[> timestamp:=time();                                           1
     evalf(log(sum(n^n,n=1..2000)));                            2
     time()-timestamp;                                          3
```

To measure real time rather than only the time expended by the CPU, use the option `real`. Timing using `time[real]` will often give the most accurate estimate of the time-usage, but in general it is rarely important which method is used, as long as one does not try to compare observations made using one method with observations made with the other.

It is generally advisable to use `time` to produce ballpark estimates of time consumption before running a long computation, to avoid a situation where the long computation is not ready in any reasonable amount of time.

EX. 5.2.2 → **Example 7.1.5: Falsifying Pólya's conjecture.** Using Lehman's methods, we developed the procedure `LL` with the aim of computing `LL(905704815)`. Before embarking on this computation, we ran

```
[> seq(time(LL(10^i)),i=1..7);
```

$$0.001, 0.003, 0.021, 0.213, 1.963, 19.350, 195.645$$

which indicated that the time needed was growing linearly, roughly as $2 \cdot 10^{-5}n$ and that the estimated time consumption would thus be around 18000 seconds, exactly 5 hours. Finding this acceptable, we let the computer run

EX. 7.3.2 ← overnight to find that the time needed was slightly less, 17535 seconds.   ◁

EX. 3.1.1 → **Example 7.1.6: Power set algorithms.** In Example 3.1.1, four different algorithms for computing the power sets of $\{1, \ldots, n\}$ were studied. It is straightforward to use `time` do get an idea of their respective time-efficiency and produce a semilogarithmic plot of the time-consumption as in

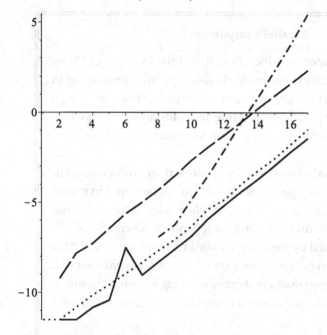

Figure 7.2 Time usage (semilogarithmic) for the four versions of powerset. [— powerset, —·— powerset1, ·· powerset2, — — powerset3.]

Figure 7.2. The figure shows that the three algorithms powerset, powerset2 and powerset3 appear to grow roughly as $C_i 2^n$, whereas powerset1 grows as something close to $C_1 4^n$. We infer of course that powerset1 should be avoided even though, at small n, it is working as efficiently as the built-in procedure.

For the remaining three versions, we quite obviously have that $C_0 < C_2 < C_3$. Hence, the built-in procedure is most efficient, but the one we designed using recursion keeps up pretty well.   ◁

EX. 3.4.3 → **Example 7.1.7: Finding sums of biquadrates.**   We wish to re-enact Frye's complete search for a solution to

$$a^4 + b^4 + c^4 = d^4$$

by testing all d up to $N = 500000$ in a two-pass approach:

- Go through all pairs (c, d), discarding pairs that can theoretically be seen to never lead to a solution, and collecting the rest in a file.
- Go through all pairs (a, b) to test for a solution for each entry in the file.

The only part of the procedure precheck (cf. Figure 3.8) that varies in time with (c, d) is the call of ifactor and the subsequent analysis of the divisors. After consulting the documentation for ifactor we make the qualified guess that the time expended for this call is $O(\ln N)$ so that the search in total is of order $O(N^2 \ln N)$. We time an analysis with $N = 10000$ and find that it

---

Parallel computing

The 1980s supercomputer on which Frye found the example (3.13) allowed only "Single instruction, multiple data" parallel processing in the sense that it could perform the same set of instructions on a large vector of data. Modern parallel computing generally allows the N CPUs (often denoted as cores) to compute completely independently, as N individual computers.

Writing programs that allow the cores to interactively work on a common dataset is very challenging, but algorithms encountered in experimental mathematics tend to be *embarrassingly parallel* in the sense that the computation may be divided into N independent subcomputations which may be performed by the cores without further interaction. This strategy applies even to personal computers, which often have several cores, and to experimental mathematicians working in teams, the members of which may each contribute a computer to such a distributed computation.

---

locates $v_0 = 428$ possible pairs of (c, d) in roughly $t_0 = 51$ seconds. It seems reasonable to expect that the time to compute to $N = 500000$ is

$$\frac{500000^2 \ln(500000)}{10000^2 \ln(10000)} \approx 3561.86$$

times longer, that is, around 50.5 hours.

The number of observations is more likely to grow as

$$\frac{500000^2}{10000^2} = 2500,$$

and hence we should expect to have 1070000 sets of possible pairs to check in the second pass. It seems fair to assert that each check in the second pass runs in linear time compared to N, and hence that the difference between checking the numbers found to $N = 10000$ and to $N = 500000$ also scales by 2500. Checking the 428 concrete values found to $N = 10000$ is timed to 35 seconds, so our total time expenditure is estimated to roughly 75 hours.

An analysis of this sort allows systematic optimization of precheck by changing the number, order, and types of checks to perform and then testing the altered procedure to extract the time usage t at $N = 10000$ and the number v of pairs left for the second pass. Our formula

$$0.989 \cdot t + 0.0563 \cdot v$$

will then predict the total computation time at $N = 500000$ and help us decide if it is worth saving time in the precheck phase at the expense of having more pairs to check in the second pass. We will discuss this further in the exercises. ◁

EX. 7.1.2 → **Example 7.1.8: Computing Fibonacci numbers.** In Section 3.3, the computation of the Fibonacci numbers was discussed, and it was shown that the straightforward definition

```
[> fibonacci0:=proc(n)                                    1
     if(n<=1) then                                        2
        return n;                                         3
     else                                                 4
        return fibonacci0(n-1)+fibonacci0(n-2);           5
     end if;                                              6
   end proc;                                              7
```

was not really useful, and had to be replaced by an identically defined version fibonacci1 using remember. We also found, in (5.9), a way of expressing the Fibonacci numbers using the roots of $z^2 - z - 1$, leading to alternatives

```
[> fibonacci2:=n->simplify((((sqrt(5)+1)/2)^n-            1
                ((-sqrt(5)+1)/2)^n)/sqrt(5));             2
   fibonacci3:=n->floor(1/2+((sqrt(5)+1)/2)^n/sqrt(5));   3
```

where in fibonacci2 we ask Maple to simplify the expression to get the integer, and in fibonacci3 we use the a priori information that the result is an integer to find it by computing the nearest integer to the approximation in (5.10), since the error can be seen to always be less than a half.

To compare the time-efficiency of the four procedures, and compare them in turn to the time-efficiency of the fibonacci procedure in the numtheory package, we decide to look at the time it takes to compute f_{2^k}. But since the procedures have dramatically different time-efficiency, it is a process which is hard to automate since the time it takes one of the procedures to compute a number is measured in hours whereas for another it is measured in seconds.

To help with this, we write the program Ftiming in Figure 7.3 which uses the Maple command timelimit to halt the computation if it takes too long. The construct with try and catch in lines 4 and 9 then allows the program to stop a kamikaze process as soon as the computation of f_{2^k} took longer than, say, a minute, and return a list of times for further inspection. The program also records the last 6 digits of each number computed for testing purposes.

The program works fine for gauging the time-consumption of all the procedures except fibonacci1, which gives an error mentioning "too many levels of recursion" when a computation at 2^{14} is attempted. Thus we time that separately, using forget between each call to not give the program an unfair advantage over the others.

The results in Table 7.1 show that our homemade attempts are not as efficient as the built-in procedure from the numtheory package, but that

```
[> Ftiming:=proc(f::procedure,T)                              1
     local N,L,p,t; N:=1; L:=[];                              2
     do                                                       3
        try                                                   4
           t:=time();                                         5
           p:=timelimit(T,f(2^N) mod 10^6);                   6
           L:=[op(L),[N,time()-t,p]];                         7
           N:=N+1;                                            8
        catch:                                                9
           break;                                            10
        end try;                                             11
     end do;                                                 12
     return L;                                               13
  end proc;                                                  14
```

Figure 7.3 The procedure Ftiming considered in Example 7.1.8.

fibonacci3 is clearly the fastest version so far. The time consumption of
EX. 7.4.2 ← the various versions is illustrated in Figure 7.5.   ◁

7.2 Balancing Time and Memory

Sometimes, memory is a greater concern for the efficiency of a program than
time. Frequently, but certainly not always, we are even able to choose between
an algorithm that takes a long time to run and one that is costly in memory
consumption. However, the limitations on time and memory resources are
not the same: there will be a hard limit on memory but not on time. Usually,
one will aim for a balance that uses as much memory as is available on the
system, while expending as little time as possible.

7.2.1 *Gauging Memory Consumption*

Measuring memory consumption in Maple is not straightforward since
Maple uses dynamic memory allocation to request memory from the operating system in larger chunks. The command

```
[> kernelopts(bytesalloc);
```

may be used to get the size, in bytes, of the memory currently requested by
Maple, and this can give an indication of the requirements of the previously

Table 7.1 *Largest number f_{2^k} computable in a minute*

fibonacci	fibonacci0	fibonacci1	fibonacci2	fibonacci3
31	5	13	16	23

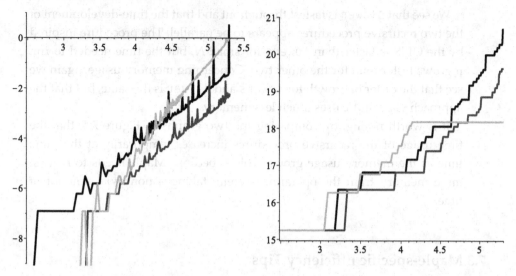

Figure 7.4 Memory and time consumption, doubly logarithmic scales. Black: `towers`, dark: `dTower`, light: `q/t`. Left: Time. Right: Memory.

executed commands. If the memory usage is essentially located in a single variable, like a list L, we may use

```
[> length(L);
```

to get the size of that list at any given time. This is measured in *storage words* which is a machine-dependent unit. To measure the size of a remember table of a recursive procedure f, we may use

```
[> length(op(eval(f)));
```

EX. 7.1.4 → **Example 7.2.1: Efficiency of tower counts.**   When trying to count with our recursive procedure `towers` in Example 1.6.5, we found that a remember table was essential, but also experienced problems with the table growing out of bounds. Thus we devised a more complicated recursive version `dTower` which reduced the number of remember table entries by employing symmetry and the a priori knowledge that certain entries would vanish. We also found in Example 5.2.7, by the help of the OEIS, an alternative way of computing the numbers by two Maple functions q and t each only one line long.

   To compare the usage of time and memory in these three approaches we can use commands of the form

```
[> [n,time(towers(n,0)),kernelopts(bytesalloc)];
```

to gauge the time and memory usage of the procedures. Such calls will return tuples of the form

$$[200, .251, 953950208]$$

which we may then study in plots such as the ones given in Figure 7.4.

We see that dTower is fastest throughout and that the time-development of the two recursive procedures appears to be parallel. The procedure inspired by the OEIS is faster than towers for small N, but the time needed to run it grows faster than for the other two. Concerning memory-usage, again we see that the order of growth for towers and dTower is the same, but that the approach via q and t uses much less memory.

It is worth noting, by comparing the two graphs in Figure 7.4, that the time usage of the recursive procedures increases temporarily at the same time as the memory usage grows. This is because Maple needs to request more memory from the operating system, taking a nontrivial amount of time.   ◁

7.3 Maple-specific Efficiency Tips

In this section, we discuss a few selected efficiency tips specific to Maple.

7.3.1 *add versus sum*

Maple has two independent commands for summing terms. So far, we have mainly used sum, which is a command for *symbolic* summation, handling both infinite sums and sums with variable limits, such as

```
[> sum(i^2,i=1..N);                                                       1
   sum(1/i^2,i=1..infinity);                                              2
```

$$\frac{1}{3}(N+1)^3 - \frac{1}{2}(N+1)^2 + \frac{1}{6}N + \frac{1}{6}$$
$$\frac{\pi^2}{6}.$$

Even if the limits of the summation are explicitly given, sum will attack the computation symbolically: rather than just adding up the given terms, it will look for a closed form for the sum and evaluate that. By contrast, add simply computes all the summands and adds them up.

When one is not concerned about efficiency, it is advisable to use sum whenever it works. There are, however, situations when sum will give a wrong answer, and add is the only option. For an example of this, consider

```
[> sum(rand(0..1)(),i=1..10^5),                                          1
   add(rand(0..1)(),i=1..10^5);                                          2
```

$$0, 50144$$

Both commands would seem to request the summation of 100000 random numbers from $\{0, 1\}$, but clearly sum does something else. To understand the problem, consider

```
[> sum(f(i),i=1..10);                                               1
    sum(g(),i=1..10);                                                2
```

$$f(1) + f(2) + f(3) + f(4) + f(5) + f(6) + f(7) + f(8) + f(9) + f(10)$$
$$10g()$$

Since `rand(0..1)()` does not depend on the summation variable, `sum` interprets the command as equivalent to `10^5*rand(0..1)()`, which it then evaluates to 0 or 100000 with equal probability.

In most situations, however, both `sum` and `add` will give the desired result, and when efficiency is of the essence, we need to choose between them. In general, `sum` is more efficient when Maple can exploit the power of mathematics to reduce the expression, such as

```
[> time(add(i,i=1..10^7)),                                         1
    time(sum(i,i=1..10^7));                                         2
```

$$0.649, 0.002$$

where `sum` will insert 10^7 in the formula $n(n + 1)/2$ rather than actually summing all terms. On the other hand, `add` is faster than `sum` if Maple does not have access to a closed formula, as in

```
[> time(add(floor(n*Pi),n=0..10^3)),                               1
    time(sum(floor(n*Pi),n=0..10^3));                               2
```

$$0.148, 0.162$$

Presumably, the slight overhead in `sum` stems from an unsuccessful attempt at finding an efficient formula to apply to the sum, before giving up and calling `add` instead.

EX. 5.1.8 → **Example 7.3.1: Using Bernoulli numbers.**   When we were experimenting with `sum` to understand the coefficients of the polynomial

$$q_m(n) = \sum_{k=1}^{n} k^m,$$

we were in some sense putting the carriage before the horse. Indeed, Maple knows full well how $q_m(n)$ may be computed using the Bernoulli numbers, and thus whenever `sum` is applied to a sum on this form, Maple will employ the formula rather than adding n numbers.   ◁

7.3.2 *Avoid (Re)calculation*

Maple has inert functions `Sum` and `Int` that may be used to define a sum or an integral without asking Maple to try to evaluate it. In situations where such an object is being passed to `evalf` quite a lot of time may be saved by using the inert versions:

```
[> time(evalf(int(log(t/(1-t))^2,t=0..1))),          1
   time(evalf(Int(log(t/(1-t))^2,t=0..1)));           2
```

$$0.139, 0.001$$

We have already noted in Example 5.1.9 that this particular integral is beyond the capacity of Maple, and substantial time will be spent before Maple knows that it cannot solve the problem exactly.

Problems of this nature are made worse when expressions that take a long time to evaluate are passed to procedures that may cause them to be evaluated multiple times. For instance, even though we remember to pass the inert version of this complicated integral to multiIdentify (defined in Section 5.3.2) as

```
[> time(multiIdentify(Int(log(t/(1-t))^2,t=0..1)));
```

we get a substantial time consumption of almost 9 seconds. The same computation only takes 0.2 seconds when the constant we are trying to identify is evaluated once before running multiIdentify, as in:

```
[> timestamp:=time():                                 1
   x:=evalf(int(log(t/(1-t))^2,t=0..1),30);           2
   multiIdentify(x);                                   3
   time()-timestamp;                                   4
```

EX. 3.4.6 → **Example 7.3.2: Saving time to falsify Pólya's conjecture.** We sped up our procedure LL substantially by avoiding recalculation of values of λ by encapsulating the calls in a procedure with a remember table, and by doing the computation of $\lfloor\sqrt{x}\rfloor$ once and for all before the loop in the middle of the procedure.   ◁

7.3.3 *Array versus* list

We have mainly been using Maple's list data structure to collect and manipulate sequential data, employing constructs like L:=[op(L),x] to append data to the end or beginning of given lists. This allows us the freedom to not decide a priori how long the lists should be, but it only works satisfactorily when we are only changing the lists at the beginning or end. In cases where it is necessary to alter the individual entries of a sequence of data, the Maple Array should be used instead.

To access the entries of an Array, say A, is straightforward using the standard index notation A[i], but as opposed to lists, an Array must be declared from the start. In particular, its size must be known a priori and cannot be changed.

The minimal array declaration has the form

```
[> A1:=Array(1..10000);
```

but it is generally advisable to provide information to Maple about the content of the array, such as in

```
[> A2:=Array(1..10000,datatype=integer[1]);
```

Declarations of this type allow Maple to conserve memory by adjusting the array to the size of the desired content, and to ensure that data of other types is not accidentally stored. For instance, using `integer[1]` tells Maple that we intend to store only numbers in $\{-128, \ldots, 127\}$ in A2, and hence (as we can check with `length`), Maple saves memory by only reserving one byte for each entry. Thus, in situations where memory constraints are of the essence, we may declare the `Array` to fit our needs exactly.

EX. 3.4.5 → **Example 7.3.3: More counterexamples to the other Goldbach conjecture.**
It is not hard to search for additional counterexamples to the lesser-known Goldbach conjecture by a variation of the sieve of Eratosthenes (see Algorithm 2.1). The most obvious approach would be to create two arrays each taking values `true` or `false` and use one to mark composite numbers and another to mark those on the form $p + 2m^2$ with p a prime.

However, if we were aspiring to test the conjecture very far, we should think about storing the two arrays efficiently in order to exploit the given capacity. It is clear that we only need to record the odd numbers, but beyond that we run into the problem that an `Array` cannot store less than a byte in each entry. Because of this, we might as well work with just one array, and use the least significant bit to flag for whether the number is composite or not, and the second smallest bit to flag for numbers of the form $p + 2m^2$.

```
[> othergoldbach:=proc(M)                                          1
      local sieve,i,j;                                             2
      sieve:=Array(1..M,datatype=integer[1]);                     3
      for i from 1 to M do                                         4
        if(sieve[i] mod 2=0) then                                  5
          for j from 1 to iquo(M-i,2*i+1) do                       6
            sieve[i+j*(2*i+1)]:=                                    7
              2*iquo(sieve[i+j*(2*i+1)],2)+1;                      8
          end do;                                                  9
          for j from 1 to floor(sqrt(M-i)) do                     10
            sieve[i+j*j]:=(sieve[i+j*j] mod 2)+2;                 11
          end do;                                                 12
        else                                                      13
          if(sieve[i]<2) then                                     14
            printf("%d is a counterexample\n",2*i+1);             15
          end if;                                                 16
        end if;                                                   17
      end do;                                                     18
    end proc;                                                     19
```

EX. 7.3.4 ←   ◁

7.3.4 *Use the Maple Compiler*

Maple is by default an *interpreted* programming language, in the sense that the high-level commands issued are continually translated to low-level code, which the computer's CPU can understand. This process takes time, and in situations where time is of the essence and the task to be completed is sufficiently simple, one can instead *compile* the program, once and for all, into machine-readable code. This is done by invoking a command `Compiler:-Compile` which works as

```
[> compiledOG:=Compiler:-Compile(othergoldbach);
```

When successful, this gives a version `compiledOG` of the procedure `othergoldbach` that produces the same results faster.

Regrettably, using Maple's compiler is often difficult and time-consuming, since many of the constructs in the original procedure are not recognized by the compiler. But in cases where such an approach is successful, speedups of up to a factor 50 are not uncommon.

EX. 7.3.3 → **Example 7.3.4: More counterexamples to the other Goldbach conjecture.** Most systems would allow us to define an array of 10^9 bytes, but since looking for counterexamples up to 10^6 takes 8 seconds and the algorithm is most likely $\Theta(N^2/\ln N)$, we would expect such a search to take several months. Thus, since the algorithm is rather straightforward, we attempt to compile it.

This does not immediately work, and by consulting the help system we learn that this is because Maple does not allow a compiled procedure to declare an `Array`. Instead, the array must be declared globally and passed to the procedure as an input variable. Further, we learn that the compiler only allows arrays of 32-bit integers, but when we take this into account and start the procedure

```
[> proc(sieve::Array(1..100000,datatype=integer[4]))
```

we actually get something that the compiler agrees to process. Note how we are forced to state a "magic number" explicitly in this case.

The speedup is substantial: what took 8 seconds before can now be done in 0.18 seconds, and the estimated time to test the whole array similarly reduced to one and a half day. But now the memory requirements have been quadrupled, and if our system does not allow an array of $4 \cdot 10^9$ bytes to be defined, we need to consider further programming constructs to use more than 2 out of the 32 bits in each array entry.   ◁

7.4 Floating-point Precision

By default, Maple does floating point arithmetic with ten digits' precision, and we have already seen various instances where it was necessary to increase the number of digits by assigning a value to `Digits` to perform the desired experiments. It is essential to realize that there is no guarantee that Maple will always compute a given floating point result with `Digits` correct digits; the constant defines the number of digits with which Maple will work, but accumulated rounding errors may propagate trough the computations and lead to further imprecision. For instance, by comparing

```
[> Digits:=10:                                                    1
   evalf(Pi^50);                                                  2
```

$$7.202671992 \ 10^{24} \tag{7.2}$$

and

```
[> Digits:=20;                                                    1
   evalf(Pi^50);                                                  2
```

$$7.2026719447158033106 \ 10^{24} \tag{7.3}$$

we see that the two last digits found at precision 10 were in fact wrong. The same is true of the last three digits at precision 20. It is tempting to work at higher precision throughout to avoid problems of this nature, but this leads to a large overhead in both time and memory consumption, so it is not generally advisable. Instead, resource limits may force us to strike a balance and find the correct level of precision for the task at hand.

7.4.1 Interval Arithmetic

Maple has very useful tools for the analysis of precision issues, most notably through the *interval arithmetic* available via the command `shake`. The idea of this command is to let Maple deal explicitly with rounding errors, computing bounds of the largest conceivable error and returning an interval guaranteed to contain the correct value. The command `shake` can be applied to a constant to determine how precisely Maple can evaluate it at a given number of digits, d. The command works by replacing each constant, say π, by an interval $[\pi - 10^{-d}, \pi + 10^{-d}]$ and letting the imprecisions propagate trough the computation using rules such as

$$[a_1, b_1] + [a_2, b_2] = [a_1 + a_2, b_1 + b_2]$$
$$-[a_1, b_1] = [-b_1, -a_1]$$

and

$$f([a, b]) = \left[\min_{t \in [a,b]} f(t), \max_{t \in [a,b]} f(t) \right].$$

For instance, we get

```
[> shake(Pi^50,10);                                               1
   shake(Pi^50,20);                                               2
```

$$[7.20267158479 \ 10^{24}, 7.20267230469 \ 10^{24}]$$
$$[7.202671944715803270410 \ 10^{24}, 7.202671944715803342401 \ 10^{24}]$$

which is consistent with our observations above.

EX. 7.3.2 → **Example 7.4.1: Precision issues in Haselgrove's proof.**   In Example 3.4.6, we computed a number $A_{1000}(831.847)$ by the use of approximants of the imaginary parts of 1000 zeroes of the zeta function which we found in [Odl]. These values are guaranteed to be correct to at least to 9 digits, so with

```
[> shake(AA(831.847),9)
```

$$[0.00494515562, 0.00494518780]$$

we may satisfy ourselves that the approximation 0.00495 provided by Haselgrove was correct to the precision given. In particular, the number is certifiably positive, and we have verified that Haselgrove did indeed have the precision to conclude that Pólya's conjecture was false.   ◁

EX. 7.1.8 → **Example 7.4.2: Error estimation.**   Continuing our efforts to compute large Fibonacci numbers in reasonable time, we try to employ floating point arithmetic to speed things up. A naive approach to avoid the symbolic manipulations necessary for applying (5.10) is to apply evalf before floor, as in

```
[> fibonacci4:=n->floor(evalf                              1
      (((sqrt(5)+1)/2)^n/sqrt(5)+1/2));                     2
```

However, this does not work:

```
[> fibonacci3(100),fibonacci4(100);
```

$$573147844013817084101, 573147816800000000000$$

The problem is that evalf works with the precision given by Digits, here set to 10. To solve this, we note that we have, by (5.10), a good upper bound on how many digits the nth Fibonacci number has, given by

$$\log_{10}\left(\frac{\phi^n}{\sqrt{5}}\right) + 1 \le 0.21n + 1,$$

where we use that $\log_{10}(\phi) \le 0.21$. Implementing this as

```
[> fibonacci5:=n->floor(evalf                              1
      (((sqrt(5)+1)/2)^n/sqrt(5)+1/2,floor(n*.21+1)));      2
   fibonacci5(100);                                         3
```

$$573147844013817084080$$

gets us closer to a functioning procedure, but again the result is not correct. This time, the problem is the result of rounding errors. Indeed, one easily sees by shake that a precision of 25 digits is needed to get the rounding error so small that floor finds the right 21-digit integer.

To more systematically study how many extra digits of precision are needed, we develop procedures that look for the smallest number of digits

The quest for π

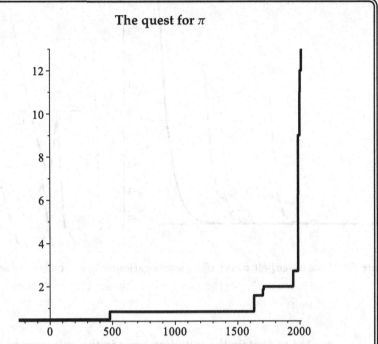

Around 250 BC, Archimedes (287–212 BC) used the circumferences of inscribed and circumscribed polygons of the unit circle to estimate π. Considering 96-sided polygons, he was able to prove that $\frac{223}{71} < \pi < \frac{22}{7}$. Variations of this polygonal algorithm were developed and used by many different mathematicians for hundreds of years. Around AD 480 the Chinese mathematician Zu Chongzhi (429–500) applied an algorithm based on the areas of inscribed and circumscribed polygons to a 12288-sided polygon, finding that $\pi \approx \frac{355}{113}$, correct to 7 decimal digits.

The calculation of π was revolutionized when mathematicians began to study infinite series, as algorithms based on the power series of trigonometric functions allow much faster convergence than the geometric methods previously employed.

While it was still unresolved whether π was rational, the search for more digits was clearly a case of experimental mathematics: After all, finding a period in the decimal expansion would have settled this fundamental question. Ten correct digits are sufficient for most numerical applications, and it is hard to imagine any such application requiring more than a hundred digits. And yet, the quest for more digits continued even after the irrationality of π was proved by Johann Heinrich Lambert (1728–1777) in 1761.

Naturally, digital computers have completely revolutionized the search for digits of π, and now trillions of digits are known. The continuing search for more digits has little practical or theoretical purpose, but experimental mathematics and integer relation tools were crucial in the development of some of the formulas on which modern algorithms are built, as explained in Example 5.3.9.

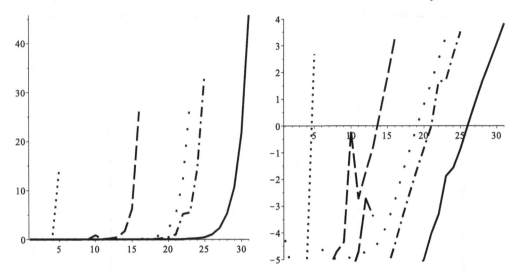

Figure 7.5   Time usage [left: direct, right: semilogarithmic] for `fibonacciX` at 2^n. [`··` `fibonacci0`, `−−` `fibonacci1`, `−−` `fibonacci2`, `··` `fibonacci3`, `·−·` `fibonacci6`, `—` Built-in procedure].

needed to contain the rounding error in the unit interval, so that `floor` returns the correct value:

```
[> inUnitInterval:=INT->is(op(1,op(1,INT))>0 and          1
                  op(2,op(1,INT))<1);                      2
   howManyExtraDigits:=proc(n)                             3
      local d0,d1;                                         4
      d0:=floor(n*.21+1);                                  5
      d1:=0;                                               6
      while(not inUnitInterval(shake(((sqrt(5)+1)/2)^n     7
           /sqrt(5)+1/2-fibonacci3(n),d0+d1) do            8
         d1:=d1+1;                                         9
      end do;                                             10
      return d1;                                          11
   end proc;                                              12
```

Running `howManyExtraDigits` on a large set of integers convinces us that adding 5 digits' precision is always sufficient, so we are led to

```
[> fibonacci6:=n->floor(evalf(((sqrt(5)+1)/2)n/sqrt(5)     1
               +1/2,floor((n+1)*.21+6)));                  2
   fibonacci6(100);                                        3
```

This version can run to 2^{16} in less than a minute, and is the fastest functioning procedure we have found. It is still not as efficient as the built-in procedure, though. Figure 7.5 illustrates the time development of our various

EX. 8.2.1 ← `fibonacciX`.   ◁

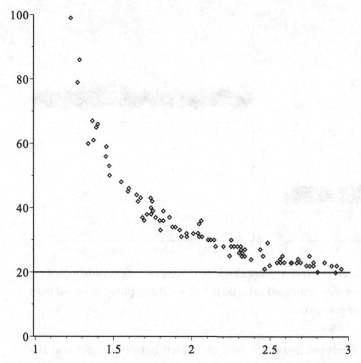

Figure 7.6 First mismatch between the exact sequence and the corresponding approximated sequence obtained by using 10 digits of precision for 100 randomly generated rational $\beta \in [1, 3)$.

EX. 2.8.2 → **Example 7.4.3: Approximated beta-sequences.** The computation of the first 1000 entries of $\mathbf{b}[\beta, 1]$ for a randomly generated rational $\beta \in [1, 3)$ takes about two seconds. This may not sound like much, but the time consumption grows rapidly with the number of entries and the situation is even worse for irrational numbers (see Exercise 7.17). For instance, the first 62 entries of $\mathbf{b}[\sqrt{2}, 1]$ can be computed almost instantaneously while entry number 63 takes about a minute to compute. Clearly, the growth of this computation time severely hampers any experimental investigation of these sequences (see Exercises 2.23, 2.24, 2.44 and 4.39).

However, the same computation of the first 63 entries of $\mathbf{b}[\sqrt{2}, 1]$ can be done with a hundred digits precision in 0.005 seconds. Clearly, this makes it very desirable to work with floating point approximations rather than exact rational and irrational numbers, but the speed comes at a price: When using a nonexact input, rounding errors are going to accumulate, so the calculated sequence is bound to deviate from the correct sequence from some point onwards. Hence, in order to be able to extract information from experiments with these sequences, it is first necessary to gauge how many digits that are needed to compute the first N entries of $\mathbf{b}[\beta, x]$ without errors.

For short sequences, it is easy to find the needed number of digits by comparing with the sequence obtained with exact input. For instance,

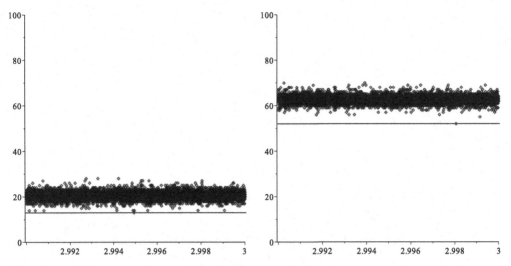

Figure 7.7 First mismatch between the exact sequence and the corresponding approximated sequence for 10000 randomly generated rational $\beta \in [2.99, 3]$ computed using 10 (left) and 30 (right) digits of precision.

when using the default precision the first mismatch between exact and the approximated sequence for **b**[17/6, 1] occurs at entry number 21. Figure 7.6 shows a plot of the first mismatch between the exact sequence and the approximated sequence computed with 10 digits precision for 100 randomly chosen rational $\beta \in [1, 3)$. Note that the best approximations are achieved for small values of β and that the mismatch values tend to decrease as β increases towards 3.

Among all the values considered in Figure 7.6, the minimal first mismatch was 20. However, there seem to be some fluctuations, so these numbers should be considered more closely. Figure 7.7 shows the first mismatches for 10000 randomly generated rational $\beta \in [2.99, 3)$ with a precision of respectively 10 and 30 digits. As expected, the minimal mismatch values grow when the number of digits is increased. Note that based on the data in Figure 7.6, it would seem that the first 20 terms are always calculated correctly when using 10 digits of precision, but the closer investigation in Figure 7.7 reveals that the actual number is at most 11. There is clearly a spread in the first mismatch values such that only a very few values of β achieve the minimal value in each case. Indeed, one might start to wonder if the minimal mismatch can actually become arbitrarily small (cf. Exercise 7.39). Certainly, there can be no doubt that to accurately gauge the number of digits needed in order to trust the first N entries, it is really necessary to consider this amount of different values of β, and more values would naturally be even better. However, such calculations require a lot of time because each exact calculation of a sequence is time consuming. In this way, the ability to estimate the error caused by using an approximation instead of an exact value is hampered by the exact same time constraints that made it appealing

EX. 7.4.4 ← to consider approximations in the first place.   ◁

7.4.2 *Heuristic Estimates of Error*

The previous section demonstrated how the precise estimation of error in a floating point calculation may be a serious computational problem in itself. This is not an uncommon occurrence in experimental mathematics, and it is often necessary to accept a level of uncertainty in order to be able to proceed with the actual experiments. Nevertheless, it is important to have an idea of the precision of the obtained data in order to be able to formulate and test hypotheses.

A *heuristic* estimate of error, is an estimate of the error of an approximate calculation based on experience gained through an experimental investigation. Note the difference from the error estimation of interval arithmetic, where an exact upper bound for the error is obtained.

Consider a mathematical object x (e.g. a number or a sequence) that can be computed approximately with various degrees of precision p (e.g. number of digits or sample size). An often used approach to heuristic error estimation is to compute the value of x for a given precision, p_1, and then recompute it with a significantly increased precision, p_2. Let x_1 and x_2 be the two objects computed in this manner, then x_1 and x_2 will likely agree about some—but not all—of the structure (e.g. digits or terms) of x. After such an analysis, one would heuristically believe that the precision p_1 is sufficient to correctly compute the part of the structure that x_1 and x_2 agree on, just like we were led to estimate that the first 8 digits of π^{50} were computed correctly when using 10 digits of precision by comparing (7.2) to (7.3).

EX. 7.4.3 → **Example 7.4.4: Frequencies.** Consider again the sequences introduced in Example 2.8.2. The goal of this example is to do a detailed heuristic analysis of the errors induced by using floating point rather than exact input in order to find out, given N, how many digits are required to compute the first N terms of the sequences correctly.

In Example 7.4.3, it was difficult to gauge the necessary number of digits precisely: it takes a significant amount of time to compute a long sequence exactly and the spread in the values of the first mismatch makes it necessary to consider many such sequences to estimate the minimal value of the first mismatch. The basic idea of the heuristic analysis is the same as before, but here, each approximated sequence will be compared to a better approximation rather than to the exact sequence. This will speed up the process significantly. More precisely, given a number of digits D, and a $\beta \in [1, 3)$, the terms of $\mathbf{b}[\beta, 1]$ are computed using, respectively, D and $D + 10$ digits of precision until the first mismatch between the two sequences is encountered. In Example 7.4.3, it became clear that the number of digits required varies significantly even among close values of β, hence, it makes sense to find first mismatch values for a large collection of values of β.

Figure 7.8 shows the result of such an investigation as a series of box plots of data sets which each consists of first mismatch values calculated for 1000

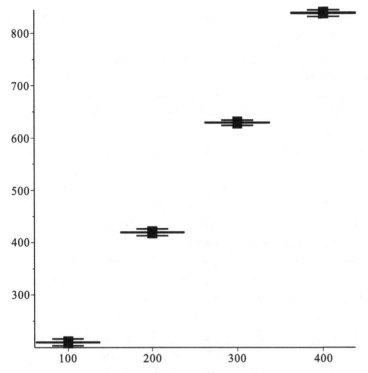

Figure 7.8 Box plots of first mismatch values between the approximated sequence constructed using N digits of precision and the approximated sequence constructed using $N + 10$ digits. Each sample consists of 1000 randomly generated $\beta \in [1, 3)$.

randomly generated $\beta \in [1, 3)$ as a function of the number of digits used in the construction of the sequences. Note that this figure supports the results of Example 7.4.3: The required number of digits grows linearly with the number of terms in the sequence. As before, there is a significant spread in the values, and there is no way to accurately measure the actual minimal values. However, including a wide margin of safety, to account for the possible spread in the values, this analysis makes it reasonable to believe that using N digits is more than sufficient to compute the N first terms of the sequences correctly in almost all cases.

The goal of Exercise 4.39 was to plot the frequency of, respectively, 0s, 1s and 2s in the first N elements of $\mathbf{b}[\beta, 1]$ as functions of $\beta \in [1, 3)$, and to look for interesting structure in the results. This is a tricky problem, and in fact it is impossible to draw reliable conclusions from the plots unless one finds a way to handle the trade-off between rounding errors and time consumption considered above. Indeed, it is very easy to come to the wrong conclusion if one is not aware that fluctuations in the data points are due to genuine differences rather than random noise. Now that we have a reliable estimate of the number of terms to trust, we are much better prepared to solve Exercise 4.39.

Figure 7.9 shows the frequencies of zeroes, ones and twos in the first 5000 terms of $\mathbf{b}[\beta, 1]$ for 1000 randomly generated floating point values of

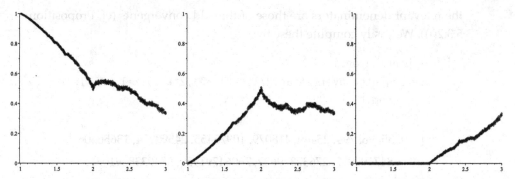

Figure 7.9   Frequencies of zeroes (left), ones (middle), and twos (right) in the first 5000 terms of $b[\beta, 1]$ for 1000 randomly generated $\beta \in [1, 3)$. Calculations were carried out using 5000 digits to ensure that all terms were calculated correctly.

$\beta \in [1, 3)$. Using the heuristic error analysis above, the computations were carried out with a precision of 5000 digits. Note that without a precise estimate of the error, there would have been no way to know how many digits to use in the computations, and in that case, it would be tempting to ascribe the many bumps and apparent changes in slope in the graphs in Figure 7.9 to rounding errors. Indeed, such a lack of precision could easily mislead the experimenter to believe that there is a simple functional dependency between β and the frequencies when in fact there is none.   ◁

7.4.3 Continued Fractions and Precision

In this section, we show how continued fractions can be a useful tool for analyzing computations leading to conjectures that are perhaps too good to be true.

Ex. 5.1.11 → **Example 7.4.5: Proving that two sequences differ.**   We found in (5.15) an explanation of why $a_n \le b_n \le a_n + 1$ with a_n and b_n as defined in Example 5.1.11, but it also became clear that if for some integer m we could arrange that

$$x_n = \frac{2n}{\ln 2} < m < \frac{2}{\sqrt[n]{2} - 1} + 1 = y_n,$$

then $a_n < b_n$. Since one can prove that

$$\frac{2}{\sqrt[n]{2} - 1} - \frac{2n}{\ln 2} \to 1 \text{ as } n \to \infty,$$

with the difference decaying as $O(n^{-2})$, we should look for n where $2n/\ln 2$ is close to being an integer.

Such an n can be found by considering the continued fraction expansion of $\ln 2$ and focusing on the denominators of the nth convergents. In fact, since we are looking for an n where $x_n = 2n/\ln 2$ undershoots an integer just slightly, the relevant denominators are those of the odd convergents (cf. Proposition 5.3.2(i)). We easily compute these by

```
[> with(numtheory):                                                      1
   L:=[seq(nthconver(cfrac(2/log(2),50),2*k-1),k=1..25)]:                2
   map(denom,L);                                                         3
```

$$[1, 9, 35, 96, 794, 25469, 418079, 10975455, 24590254, 136566069,$$
$$6847196937, 27637329632, 76064791959, 574033809103,$$
$$2669611999270, 25423560120208, 200718868962394, 777451915729368,$$
$$23611923995264527, 140894092055857794]$$

so we attempt to compare $a_n = \lfloor x_n \rfloor$ and $b_n = \lfloor y_n \rfloor$ at these values of n. However, when we reach $n = 6847196937$ Maple is no longer able to compute the rounded values with standard precision. But increasing precision to 50 digits is not a problem, and we get that $a_n \neq b_n$ at the values

$$777451915729368, \quad 140894092055857794.$$

However, since Golomb and Hales claimed in [GH02] that $a_n \neq b_n$ already at $n = 6847196937$, we decide to use interval arithmetic to satisfy ourselves that the choice of working with a precision 50 digits is sufficient to reach these conclusions. Using shake we see that x_n at $n = 6847196937$ gives

$$19756834129.9999999999599190646137158691842264789$$

with all digits certifiably correct, so we have certainly succeeded in undershooting an integer this way. But y_n in this case is certifiably

$$19756834129.9999999999976790863563891766$$

so this n is not a counterexample. At $n = 777451915729368$, however, we are sure to have x_n equal to

$$2243252046704766.99999999999999995741119755426714$$

and y_n equal to

$$2243252046704767.0000000000000010,$$

so here there is certifiably a counterexample.   ◁

EX. 5.1.12 → **Example 7.4.6: Disproving an identity.** We were led to challenge the hypothesis that $\lfloor (e^\pi - \pi)n \rfloor = 20n - 1$ at $n = 1112$ by noting that the second convergent of $e^\pi - \pi$ was $\frac{22219}{1111}$. Since the second convergent undershoots slightly, the floors at $n = 1111$ are as expected, but at $1111 + 1$ they differ. But Maple seems unwilling to confirm our claim that the sum

$$\sum_{n=0}^{\infty} \frac{\lfloor (e^\pi - \pi)n \rfloor}{3^n}$$

differs from 29/2 at the 531st digit. Indeed, Maple 2015 will compute thousands of decimals and claim they are all zero.

We cannot use `shake` directly on the infinite sum, but Maple can compute

$$\sum_{n=0}^{1112} \frac{\lfloor (e^{\pi} - \pi)n \rfloor}{3^n} + \sum_{n=1113}^{\infty} \frac{20n - 1}{3^n}$$

exactly. Since $e^{\pi} - \pi < 20$ and is known to be irrational, this is no larger than the original sum, and may easily checked (exactly or with `shake`) to be less than $29/2 - 10^{-531}$.

◁

7.5 Exercises

Warmup

EX. 7.1.6 → **Exercise 7.1**   In Figure 7.2, computing times down to 10^{-9} seconds was presented, yet `time` gauges times only to thousands of a second. How is that possible?

EX. 2.6.1 → **Exercise 7.2**   Write a procedure implementing the sieve of Eratosthenes using an `Array`. Write another procedure to systematically check the result against Maple's built-in procedures.

EX. 2.5.7 → **Exercise 7.3**   Make a heuristic estimate of the number of digits needed to correctly compute the first N terms of the sequences $s[\alpha]$ considered in Example 2.5.7.

EX. 5.3.5 → **Exercise 7.4**   Gauge how much time Maple needs to compute

$$\sum_{n=1}^{N} \frac{1}{n^2}.$$

Is it conceivable that all N summands are computed?

EX. 7.4.2 → **Exercise 7.5**   Make a systematic test with `howManyExtraDigits` of how many extra digits are needed to compute f_n exactly. Do the n which require many extra digits have anything in common?

Exercise 7.6   Find three algorithms described in this book which are embarrassingly parallel, and three algorithms that would be difficult to parallelize.

Exercise 7.7   There is a relation similar to the one between `sum` and `add` between `product` and `mul`. Try to guess which of these is more efficient for computing

$$\prod_{i=1}^{10^6}(i^2 + i) \quad \text{and} \quad \prod_{i=-10^6}^{10^6}(i^2 + i).$$

Test with `time`.

Exercise 7.8 Compute the computational complexity of the test constructed in Exercise 6.30.

Exercise 7.9 Compute the computational complexity of the test constructed in Exercise 6.32.

Exercise 7.10 Compute the computational complexity of the test constructed in Exercise 6.33.

Exercise 7.11 Compute the computational complexity of the test constructed in Exercise 6.36.

Exercise 7.12 Use inversion to solve Exercise 3.14 by guessing formulas for the number of calls needed.

EX. 7.1.2 → **Exercise 7.13** Prove that (7.1) implies that the run time is $O(\phi^n)$.

Exercise 7.14 Experiment with the time complexity of matrix multiplication and computation of determinants by generating random $n \times n$-matrices and gauging how the time consumption grows with n. Is it conceivable that Maple uses the formula

$$\det A = \sum_{\sigma} \text{sgn}(\sigma) a_{1\sigma(1)} \cdots a_{n\sigma(n)}?$$

Exercise 7.15 Produce formulas for $[a_1, b_1] \cdot [a_2, b_2]$ and $[a_1, b_1]^{-1}$ where in the latter case, $0 \notin [a_1, b_1]$.

Exercise 7.16 Why was it necessary to use `add` in place of `sum` in the solution of Exercise 5.3?

Homework

EX. 7.4.3 → **Exercise 7.17** Investigate and plot the growth in the time consumption of the computation of $\mathbf{b}[\beta, 1]$ when β is rational and the sequence is generated exactly. What happens if β is irrational?

EX. 7.4.4 → **Exercise 7.18** Construct versions of the plots shown in Figure 7.9 where interval arithmetic is used to represent each frequency as an interval. Compare with Figure 7.9.

Exercise 7.19 Devise a way to estimate how the time consumption of `ifactor(n)` grows with the number of digits in n. [*Hint: Use pseudorandomness.*]

EX. 6.5.5 → **Exercise 7.20** Analyze how the time consumption of the call `win("",n)` of the procedure defined in Exercise 3.15 varies with n (warning: small n only!). What seems to be the order of growth?

BOX P. 249 → **Exercise 7.21** The following list gives a few historic π records achieved by hand calculation. In each case, determine the number of terms/iterations needed to achieve the listed precision.

- **c. 250 BC**: 2 digits (Archimedes). Formula:

$$a_0 = 2\sqrt{3} \quad b_0 = 3 \quad a_{n+1} = \frac{2a_n b_n}{a_n + b_n} \quad b_{n+1} = \sqrt{a_{n+1} b_n} \qquad (7.4)$$

$b_n < \pi < a_n$ and both sequences converge to π.

- **c. AD 480**: 7 digits (Zu Chongzhi). Formula: Areas of inscribed and circumscribed polygons.
- **c. AD 1400**: 11 digits (Madhava of Sangamagrama). Formula:

$$\frac{\pi}{4} = 1 - \frac{1}{3} + \frac{1}{5} - \frac{1}{7} + \frac{1}{9} - \frac{1}{11} + \cdots \qquad (7.5)$$

- **AD 1630**: 38 digits (Christoph Grienberger). Formula: (7.4)
- **AD 1699**: 71 digits (Abraham Sharp). Formula: (7.5).
- **AD 1706**: 100 digits (John Machin). Formula: Power series of

$$\frac{\pi}{4} = 4 \arctan \frac{1}{5} - \arctan \frac{1}{239}. \qquad (7.6)$$

BOX P. 249 → **Exercise 7.22** Prove that Archimedes' sequences given in Equation (7.4) converge to π.

Exercise 7.23 Prove the Machin formula (7.6).

Exercise 7.24 Let $N(r) = \pi r^2 + E(r)$ be the number of integer lattice points inside a circle of radius r. Estimate the error term $E(r)$.

Exercise 7.25 The efficiency of the probabilistic primality tests discussed in Section 6.6.1 rely on fast modular exponentiation. Design and implement a fast procedure for computing $a^k \pmod{b}$ in Maple. Compute its complexity and compare with actual run times. Compare your procedure to the built-in command. Which is better?

EX. 4.1.7 → **Exercise 7.26** Several different series are known to converge to the Riemann zeta function in an area containing the critical line $\Re(z) = \frac{1}{2}$. In particular:

$$\zeta(s) = \frac{1}{-1 - 2^{1-s}} \sum_{n=1}^{\infty} (-1)^{n-1} n^{-s}, \qquad \Re(s) > 0$$

$$\zeta(s) = \frac{1}{1 - 2^{1-s}} \sum_{n=0}^{\infty} \frac{1}{2^{n+1}} \sum_{k=0}^{n} (-1)^k \binom{n}{k} (k+1)^{-s}, \qquad s \neq 1$$

$$\zeta(s) = \frac{1}{s-1} \sum_{n=0}^{\infty} \frac{1}{n+1} \sum_{k=0}^{n} (-1)^k \binom{n}{k} (k+1)^{1-s}, \qquad s \neq 1$$

For each of these, implement a procedure that uses the series to compute an approximation of ζ. Compare their usefulness. Use the best one to improve the computation of zeroes considered in Example 4.1.7. Compare with Figure 3.9.

EX. 7.4.6 → **Exercise 7.27**   Create your own "high-precision fraud" by using the ISC to locate a constant α close to an integer and then find a rational number q so that

$$\sum_{k=0}^{\infty} \frac{\lfloor n\alpha \rfloor}{10^k} \approx q$$

to many digits of precision. Find the first digit where the equality fails and compare to the continued fraction expansion of α.

EX. 3.4.6 → **Exercise 7.28**   In the procedure LL from Example 3.4.6 we chose w close to the square root of x. Is this optimal? Combine theory and time experiments to answer the question.

Exercise 7.29   How did you choose w and v in your solution of Exercise 3.18? Was this optimal? Combine theory and time experiments to answer the question.

EX. 5.1.1 → **Exercise 7.30**   Analyze the procedure cycleTree both theoretically and with time to estimate how long it would take the original program to compute c_{12}.

Exercise 7.31   Compute at least 6 terms of the continued fraction of the constant defined in Exercise 5.17. Compare with your solution of Exercise 5.17.

Exercise 7.32   Let $e, o : \mathbb{N} \to \mathbb{N}$ be the functions defined by counting the number of even, respectively, odd digits of the decimal expansion of a given integer (for instance, $e(12243) = 3$, $o(12243) = 2$). Confirm that

$$\sum_{n=1}^{\infty} \frac{o(2^n)}{2^n} \approx \frac{1}{9} \quad \text{and} \quad \sum_{n=1}^{\infty} \frac{e(2^n)}{2^n} \approx \frac{3166}{3096}.$$

Decide whether these approximate identities are in fact exact identities.

EX. 3.4.1 → **Exercise 7.33**

(a) Note that just storing the number F_{16} requires $2^{16} + 1$ bits of memory. Can you theoretically devise an algorithm for checking if $D \mid F_{16}$ using less that $2N + 100$ bits of memory when $D < 2^N$? [*Hint: First try on paper a direct long division in binary when the number to be divided is of the form* $10 \cdots 01$.]

(b) Implement the procedure using the same memory specifications as Selfridge (see the description of the SWAC on p. 75). [*Hint: Use only one bit of each entry in an array* Array(1..256*37-m*16, integer[1]) *and* m *variables of type* integer[2].]

(c) Selfridge described his experiment.

> *The writer's SWAC routine has tested all numbers of the form* $(2k + 1)2^r + 1$ *with* $D < 2^{36}$ *and* $k < 2^{15}$ *which are possible divisors of Fermat numbers. This took* $3\frac{1}{4}$ *hours running time.*

How many "hours of running time" did you need? Compile the results into a list of factors.

EX. 3.4.6 → **Exercise 7.34** Design a time-efficient procedure to compute $L(n)$ from Example 3.4.6 using a sieve to compute $\lambda(i)$ for all $i \in \{1, \ldots, n\}$. Can you confirm that $L(906180359) = 1$ this way? Would (3.16) help?

EX. 7.3.4 → **Exercise 7.35** Write a version of `othergoldbach` which uses all 32 bits of an entry in an `Array` with entries from `integer[4]`. Compile it and compute the number N up to which your computer can look for counterexamples in 24 hours.

Exercise 7.36 Attempt to compile your solution to Exercise 3.13.

EX. 7.4.5 → **Exercise 7.37** Use the estimate

$$\frac{e^x + 1}{e^x - 1} - \frac{2}{x} \leq \frac{x}{6}$$

to prove that $a_n \neq b_n$ is only possible when n is the denominator of a convergent of $2 \ln 2$.

Projects and Group Work

EX. 7.4.4 → **Exercise 7.38** Construct new versions of the graphs shown in Figure 7.9 where the βs used are *nice* irrational algebraic numbers (e.g. roots in small polynomials). Compare with Figure 7.9.

EX. 7.4.3 → **Exercise 7.39** Which values of β have small values of minimal first mismatch? Do they have anything in common? How small can the minimal first mismatch become?

EX. 7.1.7 → **Exercise 7.40** We list a number of ways that a re-enactment of Frye's experiment could be sped up. The entire group should discuss the merits of these strategies, decide on a strategy, and then execute it.

(a) Divide the search space into N equally sized chunks and let each of the N group members perform that. What must N be to allow an overnight computation?

(b) Compile the test in pass two.

(c) Replace the slow test by factorization by specific tests of the property (3.15) at the M smallest primes.

(d) Compile the test in pass one.

(e) Replace the test at residues $9, 13, 19$ by a test at residues $169, 81, 128, 29, 49, 121$.

BOX P. 249 → **Exercise 7.41** The following gives a few historic π records achieved using computer calculations. If possible, carry out the computation and determine the number of terms/iterations needed to achieve the listed precision. If not,

- identify the limiting resource(s)
- estimate the number of terms/iterations needed

Compare the efficiency of the methods.

- **1945**: 530 digits (Ferguson). Formula: Power series of:

$$\frac{\pi}{4} = 3\arctan(1/4) + \arctan(1/20) + \arctan(1/1985).$$

- **1985**: $1.7 \cdot 10^6$ digits (Gosper). Formula: A series discovered by Ramanujan:

$$\frac{1}{\pi} = \frac{2\sqrt{2}}{9801} \sum_{k=0}^{\infty} \frac{(4k)!(1103 + 26390k)}{k!^4 (396^{4k})}.$$

- **1987**: 10^9 digits (Chudnovsky brothers). Formula:

$$\frac{1}{\pi} = \frac{12}{640320^{3/2}} \sum_{k=0}^{\infty} \frac{(6k)!(13591409 + 545140134k)}{(3k)!(k!)^3(-640320)^{3k}}.$$

- **2002**: 10^{12} digits (Kanada). Formula:

$$\pi = 48\arctan(1/49) + 128\arctan(1/57)$$
$$- 20\arctan(1/239) + 48\arctan(1/110443) \quad (7.7)$$

and

$$\pi = 176\arctan(1/57) + 28\arctan(1/239)$$
$$- 48\arctan(1/682) + 96\arctan(1/12943)$$

Exercise 7.42 Investigate the complexity of the search carried out in Exercise 5.37. How much time would your program need to discover the relation in Equation (7.7)?

EX. 3.4.2 → **Exercise 7.43** Consider the three fundamentally different ways of searching for solutions to

$$\sum_{i=1}^{k} x_i^n = y^n,$$

where all $x_i, y \in \mathbb{N}$ and $y \leq M$:

- Search iteratively through all $x_1 \leq x_2 \leq \cdots \leq x_i \leq M$ as in Example 3.4.2,
- Search recursively for all $y \leq M$ by isPower as in Exercise 3.13
- Construct sieves marking sums of nth powers

(a) Perform a theoretical analysis of the time and memory consumption needed as a function of k, n, and M.

(b) Implement all three approaches and gauge their usage to test the theoretical results and determine concrete cost estimation functions.

(c) Launch a systematic search for the smallest possible solutions for $k = n$, using your most efficient method (cf. Exercise 3.19).

7.6 Notes and Further Reading

A thorough and mathematician-friendly introduction to algorithmics is [CLRS09]. More Maple efficiency tips are available in the `efficiency` section of the Maple online help system. For an introduction to the history of the computation of π, see [BBBP97]. The paper [BB92] contains many interesting examples of "high-precision fraud" as well as how to expose it. The number considered in Exercise 7.31 is called the Champernowne number.

8 *Applications of Linear Algebra and Graph Theory*

When doing experimental mathematics, the objects considered are often not completely understood theoretically. Otherwise, there would be little need for the knowledge that an experimental investigation might produce. This means that the experimental investigation will often encounter problems where novel programming techniques are needed to solve the tasks at hand. However, sometimes, it is possible to reformulate a problem to make it accessible to techniques from more developed areas of mathematics and computer science. This chapter is dedicated to showcasing two areas of mathematics where efficient algorithms exist that can be applied to a wide range of problems: linear algebra and graph theory.

8.1 Graphs

Graph theory is an example of a mathematical discipline that is often useful to experimenting mathematicians working in other fields. In many cases it is possible to rephrase questions in a graph theoretical language to take advantage of the efficient algorithms available there.

  Graph theory is a large and active area of mathematical research, and it is beyond the scope of this book to give a thorough introduction to the subject. In the following, a brief introduction to the basic properties of graphs will be given, followed by descriptions of three concepts that can be useful for facilitating the study of a variety of mathematical structures: graph colorings, spanning trees, and Hamiltonian paths.

8.1.1 Basic Definitions and Properties

A *graph* G consists of an ordered pair (G^0, G^1) of sets, known respectively as the *vertices* and *edges* of G. Each element of G^1 is a set $\{u, v\} \subseteq G^0$ of two vertices called the *ends*. Two vertices are *adjacent* if they are connected by an edge in this way. A *loop* is an edge with identical ends. The *degree* of a vertex is the number of edges incident with v (counting each loop twice). Graphs

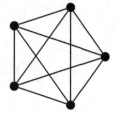

Figure 8.1 A planar graph with 4 vertices and 6 edges (one of which is a loop) and a nonplanar graph with 5 vertices and 10 edges.

show up in a number of different mathematical disciplines where it makes sense to describe certain structures as adjacent, for example in the study of polyhedra, lattices, and groups.

Graphs can be visualized by drawing the vertices as points and drawing each edge as a curve connecting its ends. Figure 8.1 shows an example. This graphical representation is very useful when working with graphs and gives a powerful tool for understanding their behavior. A graph is said to be *planar* if it can be visualized on a plane surface in such a way that edges only meet at vertices. The graph shown to the left in Figure 8.1 is planar while the graph to the right is not (the latter requires a proof).

A graph is *simple* if it has no loops. A *path* is a simple graph whose vertices can be arranged in sequence such that two vertices are adjacent if and only if one follows consecutively after the other in the sequence. A *cycle* on three or more vertices is a simple graph whose vertices can be arranged in a cyclic sequence. A graph G is *connected* if, for every partition of $V(G)$ into two non-empty disjoint subsets, there is an edge connecting an element of one set to an element of the other.

The *adjacency matrix* of a graph G is the $|V(G)| \times |V(G)|$-matrix with entries in $\{0, 1\}$ for which entry (i, j) is 1 if and only if an edge connects the ith and the jth vertex. By construction, the adjacency matrix of a graph is symmetric. The adjacency matrix gives a complete description of the graph, and several graph theoretical computations can be carried out by applying techniques of linear algebra to the adjacency matrix.

8.1.2 Graph Theory in Maple

In Maple, the tools for working with graphs are contained in the package GraphTheory. A graph can be defined using a set of two-element sets specifying the adjacent vertices:

```
[> G := Graph({{1,2},{2,3},{3,1},{3,4}}):      1
   Vertices(G);                                2
   Edges(G);                                   3
```

$$[1, 2, 3, 4]$$
$$\{\{1, 2\}, \{1, 3\}, \{2, 3\}, \{3, 4\}\}$$

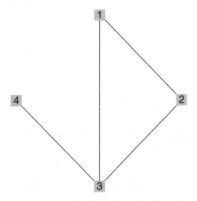

Figure 8.2   A graph drawn in Maple.

To draw the graph, use `DrawGraph(G)` which will produce the output shown in Figure 8.2. Maple will attempt to display the graph nicely, but this can be difficult for large graphs. The package `SpecialGraphs` contains definitions of a number of important graphs. Note that Maple does not allow graphs to have loops.

8.1.3 Graph Coloring

A *k-coloring* of a graph G is an assignment of k colors to its vertices. The coloring is said to be *proper* if no two adjacent vertices have the same color. The abundant theory of graph colorings has, to a great extent, been developed in attempts to prove the celebrated 4-color theorem:

Theorem 8.1.1. *Every loop-less planar graph is 4-colorable.*

The proof of this theorem is very complicated (and computer assisted), but there is a much easier proof of the corresponding result for 5 colors, and a simple proof of the 6-color version.

The minimal number of colors needed for a proper coloring of a given graph, G, is known as the *chromatic number* of G and denoted $\chi(G)$. Chromatic numbers are useful in a wide range of applications where a set of objects must be grouped according to some given criterion, and Maple can compute them efficiently:

```
[> G := Graph({{1,2},{2,3},{3,1},{3,4}}):                          1
   ChromaticNumber(G);                                             2
   ChromaticNumber(G,'myColors'):                                  3
   myColors;                                                       4
```

$$3$$

$$[[1, 4], [2], [3]]$$

The second form stores the coloring in the supplied variable as a list of lists of vertices with the same color. Computing the chromatic number can be

The Four Color Theorem

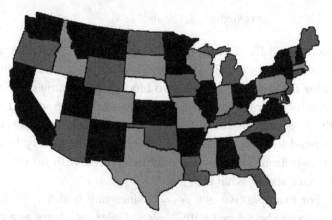

Any subdivision of the plane into contiguous regions can be colored with four colors in such a way that no two adjacent regions have the same color. This is the statement of the *Four Color Theorem*. Using the language of graph theory, it can be translated into: Every planar graph has chromatic number at most 4.

The result was first conjectured in 1852, and the tantalizing combination of a question that is easy to pose and extremely hard to answer has made the Four Color Problem well known even outside the mathematics community. Indeed, among mathematical problems its fame is perhaps second only to Fermat's Last Theorem.

The Four Color Theorem was finally proved in 1976 by Kenneth Appel (1932–2013) and Wolfgang Haken (1928–). The proof relied heavily on computer calculations and it was the first major theorem to be proved this way.

The idea of the proof is the following: If the conjecture is false, then there must exist a minimal map requiring five colors, that is, no other map requiring five colors has fewer countries. Appel and Haken proved that such a *minimal map* cannot exist.

An *unavoidable set* is a set of configurations of countries such that every minimal map requiring five colors must contain at least one configuration from the set. A *reducible configuration* is a configuration that can be reduced to a smaller configuration without altering the number of colors required, and hence such a configuration cannot occur in a minimal map requiring five colors. The computer assisted proof resulted in an unavoidable set of reducible configurations, proving that there is no minimal map requiring five colors.

The work by Appel and Haken is primarily known as a spectacular example of a computer assisted proof. However, their result also deserves to be mentioned here because the process that led to the proof involved a great deal of experimental work in order to find the right set of configurations to study.

time-consuming, so Maple also has a command for computing an estimate of the number rather than the exact value:

```
[> ChromaticNumber(G,'bound');
```

Example 8.1.2: Coloring LEGO buildings. Consider a structure made entirely of $b \times w$ LEGO-bricks. How many different colors are needed to color the structure so that two blocks of the same color never meet in the sense of having two sides adjacent over a positive area? This number is called the *chromatic number* of the structure. The $b \times w$ LEGO *chromatic number* is defined to be the smallest number $\chi_{b,w}$ so that every building constructed entirely from $b \times w$-blocks may be colored with no more than $\chi_{b,w}$ colors. Given b and w, what is $\chi_{b,w}$?

For example, we get $\chi_{1,1} = 2$ since any building built entirely of 1×1 blocks can be colored with 2 colors: Color each layer as a chessboard and alternate between black and white in the even and odd layers. For 2×4-blocks, it is easy to construct a building which requires 5 colors, and one requiring 6 is known. Because of the 4-color theorem, every layer can be colored with 4 colors, so by using different colors for even and odd layers, it can be seen that 8 colors always suffice; hence $1 < \chi_{b,w} \leq 8$ for every $b, w \in \mathbb{N}$.

To investigate the problem experimentally, it is very useful to first translate it into a problem concerning graph colorings: Construct a graph with a vertex for each block in the building and an edge between two vertices if and only if the corresponding blocks are adjacent to each other. Then the chromatic number of the building is simply the chromatic number of the graph, so the powerful algorithms for computing the chromatic number of a graph can be applied.

This makes it straightforward to use Maple to compute the chromatic number of a given building, but there is no complete description of the graphs that may be induced by LEGO buildings in this way, and the general problem remains open. Exercise 8.43 concerns the experimental investigation of this problem.   ◁

It is probably not surprising that the theory of graph colorings can be applied to the problem of coloring LEGO buildings. The following example demonstrates that the theory of graph colorings can also be applied to problems that may not be immediately recognizable as coloring problems.

Example 8.1.3: Guarding a museum. The following problem was first considered by Victor Klee: Consider an art museum in the shape of a polygon with n sides guarded by a number of guards stationed at fixed points within the museum. Each guard can turn around, but their view is obstructed by the walls of the museum. How many guards are needed to make sure that every point inside the museum is within the field of vision of at least one guard?

If the polygon is convex, one guard (stationed at an arbitrary point in the museum) is clearly sufficient, and experiments by paper and pencil

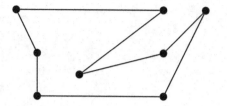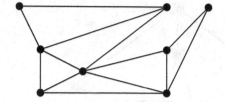

Figure 8.3 Left: A museum in the shape of a polygon as considered in Example 8.1.3. Right: A triangulation of the polygon.

(cf. Exercise 8.10) show that at least $\lfloor n/3 \rfloor$ guards are needed. The aim is to prove that this number is always sufficient.

First, draw $n - 3$ noncrossing diagonal edges between nonadjacent vertices of the polygon to form a triangulation, that is, a plane graph where every face is bounded by precisely three edges. The triangulation is not generally unique, but it is always possible to construct one (see Exercise 8.9). An example is shown in Figure 8.3.

The next goal is to use induction to prove that such a triangulation is always 3-colorable. This is trivial for $n = 3$. Let $n > 3$ and assume that every triangulation of a polygon with at most $n - 1$ edges is 3-colorable. Given a polygon with n vertices, construct a triangulation and pick any two vertices u, v connected by a diagonal (i.e. adjacent in the triangulation but not in the original polygon). This divides the triangulation into two triangulated polygons which each has at most $n - 1$ vertices. By assumption, these triangulations can be 3-colored with colors $\{1, 2, 3\}$. By rearranging the colors if needed, it can be assumed that u has color 1 and v has color 2 in both the colored triangulations. Hence, the two colorings can be pasted together to form a 3-coloring of the entire triangulation.

At least one of the color classes contains at most $\lfloor n/3 \rfloor$ vertices. Place a guard at each of these vertices and note that every triangle in the triangulation must contain precisely one vertex with a guard. This means that every triangle is guarded, and hence, so is the entire museum. In other words, $\lfloor n/3 \rfloor$ guards will always suffice.

The corresponding argument in three dimensions fails because it is not possible to triangulate an arbitrary polyhedron. ◁

8.1.4 Spanning Trees and Hamiltonian Paths

A graph is called *acyclic* if it contains no cycles, and a connected acyclic graph is called a *tree*. In a tree, any two distinct vertices are connected by exactly one path. Every tree contains a vertex of degree at most 1. A *subtree* of a graph G is a subgraph which is a tree. If every vertex of G is also a vertex of the subtree, then the subtree is said to be a *spanning tree* of G. It is not hard to prove that every connected graph has a spanning tree. In Maple, a spanning tree can be computed using the command `SpanningTree`:

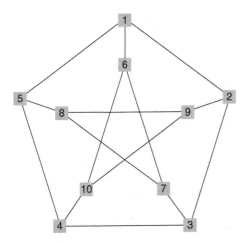

Figure 8.4 The Petersen graph.

```
[> with(SpecialGraphs):                                          1
    W := WheelGraph(5);                                          2
    SpanningTree(W);                                             3
```

In some graphs, it is possible to visit every vertex by sequentially traversing the edges of the graph. A *Hamiltonian path* in a graph *G* is a path that visits
every vertex precisely once. A graph admitting a Hamiltonian cycle is said to
be *Hamiltonian*. Let *P* be the graph shown in Figure 8.4. Then the command
IsHamiltonian(P) returns false, indicating that no Hamiltonian path exists. However, adding an extra edge results in a graph with a Hamiltonian
path:

```
[> AddEdge(P,{1,3});                                             1
    IsHamiltonian(P,'C');                                        2
```

The extra parameter 'C' is used to store the Hamiltonian cycle found in the
graph obtained by adding an edge between vertices 1 and 3 in *P*, that is, after
executing these commands C is [1, 2, 9, 8, 5, 4, 10, 6, 7, 3, 1],
indicating that this sequence of vertices constitutes a Hamiltonian cycle. A
number of other graph properties can be tested by similar procedures in
Maple.

8.2 Linear Algebra

Linear algebra is used in an extremely wide range of applications, and very
efficient algorithms have been developed to solve many of the standard problems in the field. Hence, being able to recognize that a given problem can be
translated into the setting of linear algebra allows the experimenting mathematician to draw on a vast body of knowledge. Often, this will give access to
efficient algorithms that it would be difficult and time consuming to develop
from scratch.

A fundamental example of the power of linear algebra is the techniques for solving systems of linear equations quickly. Solving a system of linear equations is easy using the standard tools of linear algebra, and obviously, no mathematician would attack such a problem in any other way. Indirectly, linear algebra has also been shown to play an important part in a wide range of mathematical experiments via the method for obtaining a linear fit to data discussed in Section 4.2. More fundamentally, simply framing a problem in the language of linear algebra will often provide insight and computational tools that far outclass other approaches. This is such an example:

EX. 7.4.2 → **Example 8.2.1: The builtin** `fibonacci` **command.** Although in Examples 7.1.2 and 7.4.2 we managed to improve our homemade procedures for computing Fibonacci numbers substantially, we did not get close to the efficiency of the built-in procedure from the `numtheory` package. To understand how this works, note that with

$$A = \begin{bmatrix} 1 & 1 \\ 1 & 0 \end{bmatrix}$$

we may easily prove by induction that

$$A^n = \begin{bmatrix} f_{n+1} & f_n \\ f_n & f_{n-1} \end{bmatrix}.$$

This observation in itself does not improve computational speeds, but since we may obtain A^{2^k} by only k matrix multiplications, computing first

$$A^2, A^4, A^8, \ldots, A^{2^{k-1}}$$

by successive squaring, we note that we have an efficient way of computing precisely the numbers f_{2^k} considered while benchmarking the different procedures. In fact, an experiment with `timelimit` shows that this is possible up to $k = 31$ if one is willing to allow 60 seconds' computing time, just like what we saw for `fibonacci` in Figure 7.1 (cf. Exercise 8.12). For general n, `fibonacci` computes f_n by expanding n in binary, computing the relevant A^{2^k}, and multiplying these together. ◁

As in the preceding example, matrix algebra was a crucial element of the calculations carried out in the Example 5.1.10, providing a simple framework for efficient computations. This is the strength of linear algebra: once a problem has been framed in the correct language, established theory provides the tools needed to proceed. In many cases, however, it requires an open mind to realize that the tools of linear algebra can be applied, and this is particularly true for linear algebra over other fields than $\mathbb{R}$ or $\mathbb{C}$.

8.2.1 *Linear Algebra over Fields*

The reader is probably mainly familiar with linear algebra over the number fields $\mathbb{R}$ and $\mathbb{C}$, but many problems can be treated with a powerful theoretical framework by considering them as problems in linear algebra over other fields or rings.

Let $(F, +, *)$ be a field, and let $M_{m,n}(F)$ be the set of all $m \times n$-matrices with entries in F. For each $\lambda \in F$ and $A \in M_{m,n}(F)$, the scalar multiple λA is defined to be the matrix obtained by multiplying each entry in A by λ. Similarly, given two matrices $A, B \in M_{n,m}(F)$, the sum $A + B$ is defined as the matrix where each entry is the sum of the corresponding entries from A and B:

$$(\lambda A)_{ij} = \lambda * A_{ij} \quad \text{and} \quad (A + B)_{ij} = A_{ij} + B_{ij}.$$

Note that multiplication and addition are carried out among elements of F and that this turns $M_{m,n}(F)$ into a vector space over F where the additive identity is the $m \times n$-matrix for which every entry is the additive identity of F.

A natural matrix product can be defined as follows: for $A \in M_{m,k}(F)$ and $A \in M_{k,n}(F)$, AB is defined to be the element of $M_{m,n}(F)$ for which

$$(AB)_{ij} = \sum_{k} A_{ik} * B_{kj}.$$

Note that the structure of this matrix product is completely analogous to the one known for $\mathbb{R}$ and $\mathbb{C}$ with the familiar addition and multiplication replaced by addition and multiplication in F. The matrix product is bilinear, and hence, $M_{n,n}(F)$ is an associative algebra over F.

Most of the important theorems used in linear algebra over $\mathbb{R}$ and $\mathbb{C}$ can be imported and applied directly to matrices over F, and anything that relies solely on the basic algebraic operations has an obvious counterpart in this more general setting. In particular, this is true for matrix addition, matrix multiplication, solutions to systems of linear equations, determinants, and Gaussian elimination. Note, however, that not everything taught in a standard linear algebra course can be imported. For instance, theorems that rely on inner products and norms are not available over a general field.

It may not be easy to recognize that a problem or structure can be described in terms of linear algebra, but when such a description is possible, it is almost always worthwhile to pursue it. Partly because a formulation in terms of linear algebra allows fast computations, but also because it gives a structure that makes it easier to formulate and test hypotheses. The following application gives a simple example of this kind.

Example 8.2.2: Oddtown. Consider the following problem: The n citizens of Oddtown like to form various *clubs*, but to limit the escalating number of clubs, the city council has introduced the following rules:

- Each club must have an odd number of members.
- Each pair of two distinct clubs must have an even number of members in common.

How many clubs can maximally be formed?

Clearly, n singleton clubs can always be formed, and experiments by hand reveal no allowed configurations with more than n clubs. The following will show that this is in fact the maximal number.

Enumerate the citizens $1, \ldots, n$ and assume that there are m distinct clubs $C_1, \ldots, C_m \subseteq \{1, \ldots, n\}$ obeying the rules given above. Define an $m \times n$-matrix A over the field with two elements, $\mathbb{F}_2$, by

$$A_{ij} = \begin{cases} 1 & , \quad j \in C_i \\ 0 & , \quad \text{otherwise} \end{cases}.$$

Consider the $m \times m$-matrix AA^T, and note that entry (i, k) is

$$(AA^T)_{i,k} = \sum_{j=1}^{n} A_{ij} A_{kj}.$$

Considered as a sum in $\mathbb{Z}$, this counts the number of elements in $C_i \cap C_k$, but working in $\mathbb{F}_2$, this number is 0 if $|C_i \cap C_k|$ is even and 1 if $|C_i \cap C_k|$ is odd. Hence, the rules dictate that $AA^T = \text{Id}_m$. In particular, $\text{rank}(AA^T) = m$. However, $\text{rank}(AA^T) \leq \min(\text{rank} A, \text{rank} A^T) = \text{rank} A \leq n$ (see Exercise 8.14), so at most n clubs can be formed. ◁

Finite fields are important in several branches of mathematics and—apart from the number fields $\mathbb{R}$ and $\mathbb{C}$—they are probably the most common underlying algebraic structures used for linear algebra. Section 8.4 examines how to define such finite fields as well as more complicated algebraic structures and use them for linear algebra computations in Maple.

8.2.2 Linear Algebra over Semirings

Let R be a semiring and let $M_{m,n}(R)$ be the set of $m \times n$-matrices with entries in R. Clearly, the structure of a semiring is sufficient to define matrix addition and matrix multiplication as above, but the lack of a multiplicative inverse means that it is not generally possible to carry out a Gaussian elimination, for instance. Nevertheless, even this restricted algebraic structure can be very useful for the design of clear and efficient algorithms. For instance, this was all that was used to enumerate the pyramids considered in Example 5.1.10.

Example 8.2.3: Boolean matrix. Consider $\{0, 1\}$ with the binary operations $\wedge$ and $\vee$ defined by the group tables

$\wedge$	0	1
0	0	0
1	0	1

and

$\vee$	0	1
0	0	1
1	1	1

.

Note that $\wedge$ acts as the logic operator *and*, while $\vee$ acts as the logic operator *or* when 0 and 1 are interpreted as the boolean values *true* and *false*, respectively. Alternatively, one can think of these operators as returning the minimal and the maximal value, respectively. As seen in Exercise 8.20, $(\{0, 1\}, \vee, \wedge)$ forms a semiring. Matrices over this semiring are called *boolean matrices*, and they are

useful in a variety of contexts. In particular, the adjacency matrix of a graph
is a boolean matrix.   ◁

8.3 Generalizations and Variations of Graphs

This section introduces a number of relevant generalizations and variations
of the basic definition of a graph which are useful in a variety of situations.

8.3.1 Directed Multigraphs

As discussed in Section 8.1, graphs model adjacency: For each pair of vertices, the graph contains information about whether the two are neighbors.
In some cases, however, it is relevant to consider vertices that can be connected in more than one way and to count the number of ways each pair of
vertices are connected. This could, for instance, be a count of the number of
airline routes connecting each pair of cities in a country. A *multigraph* is the
mathematical object used to describe such situations. One might also be interested in modeling a situation where it is possible to get from one vertex to
another while the reverse is not true. This could, for instance, be the case for
a graph modeling transportation in a city with (some) one-way streets. Such
a generalization is called a *directed graph*. The following definition captures
both these features at once.

Definition 8.3.1. *A* directed multigraph *is a four-tuple $E = (E^0, E^1, r, s)$ where
E^0 and E^1 are countable sets and $r, s \colon E^1 \to E^0$.*

Here, E^0 is a set of vertices, E^1 is a set of edges, and r, s determine, respectively,
the *range* and *source* of each edge. Note that there is nothing preventing two
edges from having the same range and source, and such edges are said to
be *parallel*. A *directed graph* is simply a directed multigraph without parallel
edges.

Analogously to graphs, a finite directed multigraph is conveniently represented by drawing each vertex as a circle and each edge as an arrow going
from the source to the range.

Example 8.3.2: Directed multigraph.   Figure 8.5 shows the directed multigraph defined by $E^0 = \{v_1, v_2\}$, $E^1 = \{e_1, e_2, e_3, e_4\}$ and

$$s(e_1) = v_1 \qquad\qquad\qquad r(e_1) = v_1$$
$$s(e_2) = v_1 \qquad\qquad\qquad r(e_2) = v_2$$
$$s(e_3) = v_2 \qquad\qquad\qquad r(e_3) = v_1$$
$$s(e_4) = v_2 \qquad\qquad\qquad r(e_4) = v_1.$$

◁

A *path* of length k in a directed multigraph E is a finite sequence of edges
$e_1, \ldots, e_k \in E^1$ for which $r(e_i) = s(e_{i+1})$. For each k, E^k denotes the set of paths

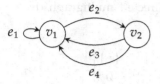

Figure 8.5 The directed multigraph considered in Example 8.3.2.

of length k. The notation is consistent if one considers the vertices to be paths of length 0. The set of all finite paths is $E^* = \cup_k E^k$. The range and source maps r and s are naturally extended to E^* by letting $s(e_1 \cdots e_k) = s(e_1)$ and $r(e_1 \cdots e_k) = r(e_k)$. A simple path $e_1 \cdots e_k$ is a path for which the vertices $r(e_1), \ldots, r(e_k)$ are all distinct. A *cycle* is a path $\lambda \in E^*$ with $r(\lambda) = s(\lambda)$.

Most of the commands from the package GraphTheory can also be applied to directed graphs. For instance, the following commands serve to define and draw a directed graph with four vertices:

```
[> G := Digraph({[1,2],[2,4],[3,1],[4,1]});          1
   DrawGraph(G);                                      2
```

Note that the edges are defined as (ordered) lists of vertices to specify the ranges and sources. Unfortunately, there is no built-in representation of multigraphs, and Maple does not allow directed graphs to have loops.

8.3.2 *Matrix Representations of Directed Multigraphs*

Let E be a finite directed multigraph with $E^0 = \{v_1, \ldots, v_n\}$. It is natural to associate three $n \times n$-matrices to E containing varying degrees of information about the graph:

- The *transition matrix* of E is the boolean (i.e. the entries are 0 and 1) $n \times n$-matrix T where $T_{ij} = 1$ if and only if there exists at least one edge $e \in E^1$ with $s(e) = v_i$ and $r(e) = v_j$. Note that this is analogous to the definition of the adjacency matrix of a graph with the notable difference that the transition matrix of a directed multigraph is not generally symmetric.
- The *path counting matrix* of E is the $n \times n$-matrix C with entries in $\mathbb{N}$ for which $C_{ij} = m$ if and only if there are precisely m edges with source v_i and range v_j. Note that $T_{ij} = 0$ if and only if $C_{ij} = 0$.
- The *path specifying matrix* of E is the $n \times n$-matrix P with entries in $\mathcal{P}(E^1)$ for which $P_{ij} = S$ if and only if $S \subseteq E^1$ is the set of edges with source v_i and range v_j. Note that $C_{ij} = |P_{ij}|$.

It is worth noting that the names and notation used for these matrices are not standard. In particular, both the transition matrix and the path counting matrix are sometimes known as the adjacency matrix.

Example 8.3.3: Matrix representations. For the directed multigraph defined in Example 8.3.2, the matrices are:

$$T = \begin{bmatrix} 1 & 1 \\ 1 & 0 \end{bmatrix}, \ C = \begin{bmatrix} 1 & 1 \\ 2 & 0 \end{bmatrix}, \text{ and } P = \begin{bmatrix} \{e_1\} & \{e_2\} \\ \{e_3, e_4\} & \emptyset \end{bmatrix}. \qquad \lhd$$

The great benefit of these matrix representations is that they allow us to use linear algebra to study paths in directed multigraphs, more specifically: Let E be a directed multigraph with $E^0 = \{v_i, \ldots, v_j\}$ and path counting matrix C. It is straightforward to prove that for each $k \in \mathbb{N}$, $(C^k)_{ij}$ is the number of paths of length k with source v_i and range v_j. Similarly, if the transition matrix T is considered as a boolean matrix, $(T^k)_{ij}$ is 1 if and only if there exists a path of length k from v_i to v_j (see Exercise 8.25).

The next goal is to construct an algebraic structure that defines a matrix product satisfying that $(P^k)_{ij}$ is the set of paths with source v_i and range v_j. Let $(E^1)^*$ be the set of strings (finite sequences) of edges from E. Note that there is a natural embedding of E^* into $(E^1)^*$, but in general the sequences in $(E^1)^*$ are not required to form paths in the graph. Define concatenation of strings as a binary operation on $(E^1)^*$:

$$u * w = u_1 \cdots u_k w_1 \cdots w_l \in (E^1)^{k+l}$$

for $u = u_1 \cdots u_k \in (E^1)^k$ and $w = w_1 \cdots w_l \in (E^1)^l$. Note that $((E^1)^*, *)$ is a semigroup where the identity is the empty path ϵ (see Exercise 8.22). Consider the power set $S_E = \mathcal{P}((E^1)^*)$, and extend the binary relation to this set by defining

$$U * W = \{u * w \mid u \in U \text{ and } w \in W\}$$

for $U, W \in S_E$. Considering set union as a binary operation on S_E, it is now possible to prove (see Exercise 8.23):

Lemma 8.3.4. $(S_E, \cup, *)$ *is a semiring with additive identity* $\emptyset$ *and multiplicative identity* $\{\epsilon\}$.

Hence, there is an associated matrix product for matrices with entries in S_E, and this matrix product has been constructed to have the desired properties when applied to matrices with entries in $\mathcal{P}(E^*)$.

It may seem strange that the definition of concatenation allows the construction of sequences of edges which do not form paths in the directed multigraph E, but as will be seen below, it is the structure of the matrix product that will guarantee that the entries of powers of the path specifying matrix P will always be sets consisting of well formed paths. In fact, this is a great strength of the construction: The structure of the algebraic operation guarantees that the only sequences formed are proper paths, and this means that there is no need to check the constructed paths explicitly.

Example 8.3.5. Considering the matrices given in Example 8.3.3 as, respectively, a boolean matrix, a regular matrix, and a matrix over S_E, one finds:

$$T^2 = \begin{bmatrix} 1 & 1 \\ 1 & 1 \end{bmatrix}, C^2 = \begin{bmatrix} 3 & 1 \\ 2 & 2 \end{bmatrix}, \text{ and } P^2 = \begin{bmatrix} \{e_1e_1, e_2e_3, e_2e_4\} & \{e_1e_2\} \\ \{e_3e_1, e_4e_1\} & \{e_3e_2, e_4e_2\} \end{bmatrix}.$$

Note that $(C^2)_{ij} = |(P^2)_{ij}|$, and $(C^2)_{ij} = 0$ if and only if $(T^2)_{ij} = 0$. ◁

The following result shows that considering a matrix with entries in $\mathcal{P}(E^*)$ (such as the path specifying matrix P) as a matrix over the semiring of sets of paths defined above yields a matrix product with the desired properties. In particular, the computations from Example 8.3.5 can be carried out for arbitrary directed multigraphs and arbitrary path lengths. The proof of this result is carried out in Exercises 8.25 and 8.26.

Theorem 8.3.6. *Let E be a directed multigraph with $E^0 = \{v_i, \ldots, v_n\}$, path counting matrix C, transition matrix T, and path specifying matrix P. For each $k \in \mathbb{N}$ and $1 \le i, j \le n$:*

(i) *$(C^k)_{ij}$ is the number of paths of length k from v_i to v_j.*

(ii) *$(T^k)_{ij}$ is 1 if and only if there exists a path of length k from v_i to v_j when T is considered as a boolean matrix.*

(iii) *$(P^k)_{ij}$ is the set of paths of length k with source v_i and range v_j when P is considered as a matrix over the semiring of sets of paths $(S_E, \cup, *)$.*

As an immediate consequence, this leads to the following corollary, generalizing the relations between T, C, and P mentioned in the definitions of the three matrices. Note that this result is consistent with Example 8.3.5.

Corollary 8.3.7. *For E, C, T, and P defined as in Theorem 8.3.6. For all $k \in \mathbb{N}$ and $1 \le i, j \le n$, $(C^k)_{ij} = |(P^k)_{ij}|$, and $(C^k)_{ij} = 0$ if and only if $(T^k)_{ij} = 0$.*

The great benefit of using matrix multiplication to study paths is that it allows an efficient and structured investigation. In the following sections, tools will be developed to carry out such computations by using linear algebra over user-defined fields, rings, and semirings in Maple.

8.4 Generic Linear Algebra in Maple

In Maple, it is possible to carry out several standard operations from linear algebra over custom-made algebraic structures. Some operations (such as Gaussian elimination) obviously require the underlying algebraic structure to be a field, while simpler operations (such as matrix products) can be defined for matrices over rings or semirings.

As the name implies, the sub-package `LinearAlgebra[Generic]` contains commands for making computations in linear algebra over generic fields, rings, and semirings. To use these commands, one must first define a suitable ring or field and then apply the commands from `LinearAlgebra[Generic]` with an explicit reference to this algebraic structure so that the right rules can be applied in the computation.

8.4.1 Defining and Using Fields in Maple

Consider a set F. In order to give F the structure of a field, one must define two maps $+, *: F \times F \to F$ as well as a multiplicative identity and an additive identity. Together these objects must satisfy the familiar relations in order to form a field. With the set F, this four-tuple is sufficient for a mathematical definition of the field, and in order to meaningfully define the field in Maple, it is clearly necessary to specify these four objects. From a computational viewpoint, however, it is practical to define the field with more of the structure given explicitly. For instance, Maple requires explicit procedures for the computation of additive and multiplicative inverses to allow meaningful computations with these objects. For that reason, a field is defined in Maple by specifying:

- An additive identity
- A multiplicative identity
- A procedure used to check whether two elements in the field are equal. (Maple may not always have a built-in procedure for the this purpose.)
- A procedure which, given $a, b, c, \ldots \in F$, returns $a + b + c + \cdots$.
- A procedure which returns $-a$ when given a single variable $a \in F$ as input, but returns $a - b - c - \cdots$ when given $a, b, c, \ldots \in F$ as input.
- A procedure which, given $a, b \in F$, computes the product $a * b$.
- A procedure which, given $a, b \in F$, computes $a * b^{-1}$.

Note, however, that Maple does not require a specification of the underlying *set*. This may be surprising to a mathematician, but it would be impractical if one was forced to specify (list?) all the elements of a field in order to work with it. Instead, Maple simply leaves it to the programmer/user to make sure that the operations of a field are only applied to elements of that field.

A field is defined as an abstract indexed parameter containing the objects mentioned above. For instance, to define a field as an algebraic object `myField` in Maple, one would assign appropriate values (constants and procedures) to `myField['0'], myField['1'], myField['='], myField['+']` and so on. In order to construct these objects, it will be necessary to use the technique from Example 2.5.5 to construct procedures that take an a priori undetermined number of variables as input.

The following examples show the process of defining a field as an algebraic object in Maple and using it to solve problems in linear algebra.

Assuming that a field has been defined in Maple as an algebraic object `myField` and that A, B are appropriate matrices, the commands from

`LinearAlgebra[Generic]` can be used to carry out various normal tasks from linear algebra such as:

```
[> with(LinearAlgebra[Generic]):                              1
   Determinant[myField](A);                                   2
   MatrixMatrixMultiply[myField](A,B);                        3
   MatrixInverse[myField](A);                                 4
   ReducedRowEchelonForm[myField](A);                         5
```

Note how the field is explicitly given as input to the commands to tell Maple how to carry out the additions and multiplications involved in the computations.

Example 8.4.1: The finite field $\mathbb{F}_2$. Consider the finite field with two elements $\mathbb{F}_2$. The following commands serve to define $\mathbb{F}_2$ as an algebraic object in Maple:

```
[> F2['0'] := 0:                                              1
   F2['1'] := 1:                                              2
   F2['='] := (x,y)->evalb( x=y ):                            3
   F2['+'] := ()->add(x,x in args) mod 2:                     4
   F2['-'] := proc()                                          5
                 if nargs = 1 then                            6
                   return -args[1] mod 2;                     7
                 else                                         8
                   return args[1]                             9
                     - add(x,x in args[2..-1]) mod 2;         10
                 end if;                                      11
              end proc:                                       12
   F2['*'] := (x,y)->x*y:                                     13
   F2['/'] := (x,y)->x/y:                                     14
```

Note that the definitions of addition and subtraction are simply modulo 2 versions of the standard operations in $\mathbb{R}$ or $\mathbb{C}$ while the multiplication and division operations can be used unmodified. Clearly, the operations only work as intended if they are never used on numbers different from 0 and 1, and one could build safeguards into the definitions to make sure that the user is alerted if one of the operations is used on an illegal element. ◁

Once an algebraic structure is defined as in the example above, the defined procedures and constants can be used to do computations. For instance, if x, y are elements of a field F defined in Maple then one could use the following commands to check whether the sum of x and y is equal to the multiplicative identity:

```
[> F['='](F['+'](x,y),F['1']);
```

Note, however, that Maple may not be able to put elements of a field on a standard form that allows easy comparison, and it falls on the programmer to define a sufficiently efficient procedure for F['='].

8.4.2 Defining and Using (Semi)rings in Maple

A very similar approach to the one presented in the previous section can be used to carry out computations over a ring (or a semiring) instead of a field simply by specifying an appropriate subset of the objects used to define fields.

Example 8.4.2: String semi-ring.   As seen previously, the semiring of sets of strings from Lemma 8.3.4 is useful for analyzing paths in directed multi-graphs. The following commands serve to define this semiring as an algebraic object in Maple:

```
[> S['0'] := {}:                                           1
   S['='] := (x,y)->evalb( x=y ):                          2
   S['+'] := proc()                                        3
                 return 'union'(args);                     4
             end proc:                                      5
   S['*'] := proc(L1,L2)                                   6
                 local newL,v,w;                           7
                 newL := {};                               8
                 for v in L1 do                            9
                    for w in L2 do                         10
                       newL := {cat(v,w),op(newL)}:        11
                    end do;                                12
                 end do;                                   13
             end proc:                                     14
```

In Exercise 8.29, this definition is used for concrete calculations involving the path specifying matrix of a directed multigraph.   ◁

8.5 Isomorphism and Equivalence

The concepts of *isomorphism* and *equivalence* play important roles in practically all branches of mathematics. They allow one to focus on the essential core of the problem at hand, disregarding superficial discrepancies between otherwise identical objects. In an experimental investigation, these terms often become important when one is interested in examining an collection of mathematical objects where internal symmetries mean that computing a quantity of interest for one object will immediately give the answer for other, related, objects as well. It is worth noting that problems involving isomorphism can be extremely difficult or impossible to solve.

$$A_0 = \begin{bmatrix} 0 & 0 \\ 0 & 0 \end{bmatrix} \quad A_1 = \begin{bmatrix} 0 & 0 \\ 0 & 1 \end{bmatrix} \quad A_2 = \begin{bmatrix} 0 & 0 \\ 1 & 0 \end{bmatrix} \quad A_3 = \begin{bmatrix} 0 & 0 \\ 1 & 1 \end{bmatrix}$$

$$A_4 = \begin{bmatrix} 0 & 1 \\ 0 & 0 \end{bmatrix} \quad A_5 = \begin{bmatrix} 0 & 1 \\ 0 & 1 \end{bmatrix} \quad A_6 = \begin{bmatrix} 0 & 1 \\ 1 & 0 \end{bmatrix} \quad A_7 = \begin{bmatrix} 0 & 1 \\ 1 & 1 \end{bmatrix}$$

$$A_8 = \begin{bmatrix} 1 & 0 \\ 0 & 0 \end{bmatrix} \quad A_9 = \begin{bmatrix} 1 & 0 \\ 0 & 1 \end{bmatrix} \quad A_{10} = \begin{bmatrix} 1 & 0 \\ 1 & 0 \end{bmatrix} \quad A_{11} = \begin{bmatrix} 1 & 0 \\ 1 & 1 \end{bmatrix}$$

$$A_{12} = \begin{bmatrix} 1 & 1 \\ 0 & 0 \end{bmatrix} \quad A_{13} = \begin{bmatrix} 1 & 1 \\ 0 & 1 \end{bmatrix} \quad A_{14} = \begin{bmatrix} 1 & 1 \\ 1 & 0 \end{bmatrix} \quad A_{15} = \begin{bmatrix} 1 & 1 \\ 1 & 1 \end{bmatrix}$$

Figure 8.6 All Boolean 2×2 matrices.

8.5.1 Graph Isomorphism

In this section, graphs and directed graphs will used as motivating examples for the discussion of isomorphism. Let G and H be graphs. In the following, $\phi: G \to H$ will represent a pair of maps $\phi^0: G^0 \to H^0$ and $\phi^1: G^1 \to H^1$. For notational convenience, define $\phi(v) = \phi^0(v)$ and $\phi(\{u, v\}) = \phi^1(\{u, v\})$ for $u, v \in G^0$.

A bijection $\phi: G \to H$ is a *graph isomorphism* if it satisfies $\phi(\{u, v\}) = \{\phi(u), \phi(v)\}$ for all $\{u, v\} \in G^1$. I other words, the graphs G and H must be identical up to a renaming of edges and vertices given by the map ϕ. When such a map exists, G and H are said to isomorphic. This defines an equivalence relation of the set of graphs, and the equivalence classes are called *isomorphism classes*. Similarly, for directed graphs G and H, a bijection $\phi: G \to H$ is a *directed graph isomorphism* if it satisfies that $s_H(\phi(e)) = \phi(s_G(e))$ and $r_H(\phi(e)) = \phi(r_G(e))$ for all $e \in G^1$.

Example 8.5.1: Isomorphism of directed graphs. Assume that we are interested in computing some value for all directed graphs on 2 vertices. Since each graph is given by a transition matrix, it is straightforward (but inefficient) to construct all graphs by first constructing all Boolean 2×2 matrices and considering the corresponding directed graph. Figure 8.6 shows all Boolean 2×2 matrices, and Figure 8.7 lists the corresponding graphs. Inspecting this list reveals six pairs of directed graphs that are essentially identical. In each case, the two graphs are isomorphic since one is obtained from the other by transposing the two vertices.

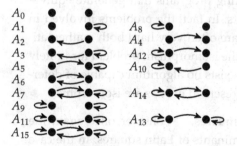

Figure 8.7 Isomorphism classes of directed graphs on 2 vertices as considered in Example 8.5.1. Graphs in the same row are isomorphic. The corresponding transition matrix is given to the left of each graph (see Figure 8.6).

Table 8.1 *Number of graph isomorphism classes (A595) for graphs on n vertices compared to the number of graphs obtained through the naive construction discussed in Example 8.5.1. The last column lists the approximate average size of the isomorphism classes*

n	2^{n^2}	Directed graph iso. classes	Average size
1	2	1	2
2	16	2	8
3	512	10	51
4	65536	104	630
5	33554432	3044	11023
6	68719476736	291968	235366

Note that the number of elements of each equivalence class grows rapidly as the number of vertices increases, so this naive construction becomes progressively less useful as n increases. This is illustrated in Table 8.1. The number of directed graph isomorphism classes are calculated in [Dav53] (cf. **A595**). The paper does not contain a constructive method for producing (representatives of) the isomorphism classes, relying instead on group theoretical and combinatorial arguments.   ◁

8.5.2 Invariants

Assume that an experimental investigation focuses on some class $\mathcal{A}$ of mathematical structures and that we are interested in a quantity $f(A)$ for all $A \in \mathcal{A}$. If $\sim$ is an equivalence relation on $\mathcal{A}$ and $f(A) = f(B)$ whenever $A \sim B$, then f is said to be an *invariant* of $\sim$. In that case, the investigation of f may as well be carried out for the equivalence classes in $\mathcal{A}/\sim$ rather than all the elements of $\mathcal{A}$. If there are many elements in each equivalence class, as in the case of graph isomorphism considered above, then this approach can drastically reduce the number of cases one needs to consider. However, this requires a procedure for generating representatives of equivalence classes (or equivalently, precisely one element from each class). Clearly, generating all elements of $\mathcal{A}$ and then subdividing based on $\sim$ is not a desirable solution.

There is no general approach to writing programs that generate equivalence classes rather than single elements. In fact, the problems involved in efficiently constructing such programs are often very hard both mathematically and algorithmically. For instance, the isomorphism problem for finitely presented groups is undecidable: there exists no algorithm capable of determining whether two arbitrary finitely presented groups are isomorphic.

EX. 6.5.4 → **Example 8.5.2: Equivalence of Latin squares.**   Consider once again the problem of determining possible determinants of Latin squares. In the case of D_7, it was relatively easy to construct a Latin square achieving the minimal positive determinant. However, continuing this investigation for larger values of n is difficult because it becomes progressively harder to construct Latin

Table 8.2 *Counts of Latin squares and reduced Latin squares*

n	Reduced Latin squares	All Latin squares
1	1	1
2	1	2
3	1	12
4	4	576
5	56	161280
6	9408	812851200
7	16942080	61479419904000
8	535281401856	108776032459082956800
9	377597570964258816	5524751496156892842531225600

squares as n grows. In fact, the total number of Latin squares is only known up to $n = 11$.

A Latin square is said to be *reduced* if the entries of the first and second rows are $1, 2, \ldots, n$ and $2, 3, \ldots, n, 1$, respectively. Any Latin square can be transformed into a unique reduced Latin square through a series of permutations of the rows and columns. Two Latin squares are said to be *equivalent* if they correspond to the same reduced Latin square in this way. Note that the absolute value of the determinant of a Latin square is an invariant for this equivalence relation since the involved operations only change the sign. Hence, we may as well restrict our investigation to reduced Latin squares.

It is straightforward to show hat each equivalence class of $n \times n$ Latin squares contains $n!(n-1)!$ elements. Hence, constructing reduced Latin squares rather than general Latin squares will allow a much more efficient investigation by avoiding repeated investigations of essentially identical squares. However, even the number of reduced Latin squares grows very quickly as illustrated in Table 8.2. Note that there is no known explicit formula for the number of reduced $n \times n$ Latin squares, so the numbers in the table are a result of direct constructions.

Depending on the application, there are further symmetries of Latin squares that it may be possible to exploit. For instance, two Latin squares are said to be *isotopic* if one can be obtained from the other through a permutation of rows, columns, and symbols. Unlike the first two operations, permuting symbols will generally change the absolute value of the determinant.

However, given a representative of an isotopy class, it would be straightforward to plug in all the possible permutations of the symbols and determine the corresponding determinants. Hence, an algorithm which constructs representatives of isotopy classes would also be useful for generating determinants, even though the determinant is not an isotopy invariant (cf. Exercise 8.34). Even without such an algorithm, it might be possible to take advantage of the isotopy classes in the construction of determinants and this is examined in Exercise 8.35. ◁

Example 8.5.3: House of Graphs.   It is nontrivial to write a program which generates all graphs on n vertices up to isomorphism, and it goes beyond the scope of this book to describe such an algorithm. Fortunately, this problem has already been investigated by others. As always in experimental mathematics, one should attempt to avoid unnecessary repetition of previous work, and in the case of graphs, it is easy to find online resources that give collections of graphs with various properties, for example exhaustive collections of representatives of graph isomorphism classes for small graphs. An example of such a resource is *The House of Graphs* [BCGM13]. At the time of writing, this database contains a large collection of interesting graphs as well as links to exhaustive collections of isomorphism classes of, for example, general graphs and planar graphs.

If one is interested in computing a quantity or testing a hypothesis for all graphs, then one can download a collection of representatives of isomorphism classes and carry out the test on that collection. Most often, this will save time in both the design and the execution of the test.   ◁

As illustrated by these examples, there is often an enormous potential for increased efficiency if one is able to find a way to consider equivalence classes rather than individual elements. However, finding a concrete way to do this may be highly nontrivial.

8.6 Exercises

Warmup

Exercise 8.1 Look up the following commands in the Maple help system and use each one in an example: `IsStronglyConnected`, `IsTree`, `AdjacencyMatrix`, `MinimumDegree`.

Exercise 8.2 Draw a map that has no proper 3-coloring and construct the corresponding graph.

Exercise 8.3 Construct a building from 2×4 LEGO bricks with chromatic number 5.

Exercise 8.4 Define the full graph on 5 vertices (shown in Figure 8.1) in Maple and plot it. Find a spanning tree and plot it.

Exercise 8.5 Use the command `Digraph` to attempt to define the directed multigraph from Example 8.3.2 in Maple. How does Maple handle the parallel edges?

Homework

Exercise 8.6 Prove the 6-color Theorem.

EX. 8.1.2 → **Exercise 8.7** Construct a graph with chromatic number 6 that does not contain the full 6-graph as a subgraph. Check whether it can be realized as the graph of a LEGO building constructed with 2 × 4-bricks.

EX. 8.1.2 → **Exercise 8.8** Construct a building from 2 × 4 LEGO bricks with chromatic number 6.

EX. 8.1.3 → **Exercise 8.9** Prove that every polygon can be triangulated. *[Hint: Identify a vertex where the internal angle is smaller than π, construct a diagonal, and use induction.]*

EX. 8.1.3 → **Exercise 8.10** Construct a polygonal art museum with n edges that achieves the maximum found in Example 8.1.3 by needing $\lfloor n/3 \rfloor$ guards.

EX. 8.2.1 → **Exercise 8.11** Prove that for any n, the number of matrix multiplications necessary in the procedure needed to compute A^n in Example 8.2.1 is $O(\ln(n))$. Does it follow that f_n can be computed exactly in $O(\ln(n))$ time?

EX. 8.2.1 → **Exercise 8.12** Implement the algorithm for the computation of Fibonacci numbers outlined in Example 8.2.1. Perform a time measurement and compare with Figure 7.1.

Exercise 8.13 An $n \times n$ boolean matrix M is said to be irreducible if there exists k such that every entry of M^k is 1. Let $k(n)$ be the largest value of k required to ensure that for every irreducible $n \times n$ matrix M, every entry in M^k is 1. For small n, use pseudorandomness to determine $k(n)$. How does $k(n)$ depend on n? *[Hint: matrices with fewer ones than zeroes are unlikely to be irreducible.]*

EX. 8.2.2 → **Exercise 8.14** Prove that $\operatorname{rank}(AB) \leq \min(\operatorname{rank} A, \operatorname{rank} B)$ whenever A and B are matrices for which the product is well defined.

Exercise 8.15 Define the finite field with 4 elements as an algebraic structure in Maple. Use it to find the 10 lowest powers of the matrix

$$\begin{bmatrix} 1 & 1 \\ 1 & 1 \end{bmatrix}.$$

Exercise 8.16 Let $\mathbb{F}_2$ be the finite field with two elements and consider the matrices $A, B \in M_{3,3}(\mathbb{F}_2)$ defined by

$$A = \begin{bmatrix} 1 & 0 & 1 \\ 0 & 1 & 1 \\ 1 & 1 & 1 \end{bmatrix} \quad \text{and} \quad B = \begin{bmatrix} 0 & 1 & 0 \\ 1 & 0 & 0 \\ 0 & 1 & 0 \end{bmatrix}.$$

Compute $A + B$, AB, and $\det A$. For each matrix, find the inverse if it exists.

Exercise 8.17 Define $\mathbb{F}_2$ as an algebraic object in Maple and use suitable commands from `LinearAlgebra[Generic]` to solve Exercise 8.16.

Exercise 8.18 Let F be a field. Prove that $M_{n,n}(F)$ is an associative algebra.

Exercise 8.19 Let $(R, +, *)$ be a semiring. Prove that $M_{n,n}(R)$ is a semiring and identify the additive and multiplicative identities.

EX. 8.2.3 → **Exercise 8.20** Prove that the structure constructed in Example 8.2.3 is a semiring.

EX. 8.2.3 → **Exercise 8.21** Define the semiring considered in Exercise 8.20 in Maple. Use it to calculate all distinct powers of the transition matrix of the Petersen graph shown in Figure 8.4.

Exercise 8.22 Let $\mathcal{A}$ be a finite set, let $\mathcal{A}^*$ be the set of finite sequences of elements from $\mathcal{A}$, and let $*$ denote concatenation of strings. Prove that $(\mathcal{A}^*, *)$ is a semigroup for which the identity is the empty string.

Exercise 8.23 Let $(S, *)$ be a semigroup. Prove that $(\mathcal{P}(S), \cup, *)$ is a semiring when $U \cup W$ denotes the usual union of the sets U and W, and

$$U * W = \{u * w \mid u \in U \text{ and } w \in W\}$$

for $U, W \subseteq S$.

EX. 8.3.3 → **Exercise 8.24** Consider the matrices given in Example 8.3.3. Compute T^3, C^3, and P^3 using, respectively, the boolean matrix product, the regular matrix product, and the matrix product over the semiring S_E. Compare the results.

Exercise 8.25 Let E be a directed multigraph with $E^0 = \{v_i, \dots, v_n\}$, path counting matrix C, and transition matrix T. Prove that for each $k \in \mathbb{N}$:

- $(C^k)_{ij}$ is the number of paths of length k from v_i to v_j.
- Considering T as a boolean matrix, $(T^k)_{ij}$ is 1 if and only if there exists a path of length k from v_i to v_j.

Exercise 8.26 Prove part (iii) of Theorem 8.3.6.

Exercise 8.27 Define the field $\mathbb{Q}\left[\sqrt{2}\right]$ as an algebraic object in Maple. Compute $A + B$, AB, and $\det A$ for the matrices $A, B \in M_{3,3}(\mathbb{Q}\left[\sqrt{2}\right])$ given by

$$A = \begin{bmatrix} \sqrt{2} & 0 & 1 \\ 0 & 3\sqrt{2} & 1 \\ 1 & 1 & 1 \end{bmatrix} \quad \text{and} \quad B = \begin{bmatrix} 0 & -2 & 0 \\ 1 & 0 & 0 \\ 0 & \sqrt{2} & 0 \end{bmatrix}.$$

For each matrix, find the inverse if it exists.

EX. 8.3.5 → **Exercise 8.28** Consider the directed multigraph from Example 8.3.5. Use boolean matrix multiplication in Maple to compute T^2 and compare with the result given in the example. Compute P^3 and C^3 and compare them.

EX. 8.3.5 → **Exercise 8.29** Use the semiring S_E from Lemma 8.3.4 to compute the matrix P^2 given in Example 8.3.5. Compute P^3, P^4, P^5 and compare with C^3, C^4, C^5.

Exercise 8.30 Construct 100 random boolean 100×100-matrices, and consider these as transition matrices for directed graphs [*Use smaller matrices if the problem becomes unmanageable.*] For each $k \in \{1, \ldots, 10\}$, compute the regular matrix power C^k of each of the matrices in the collection. Plot the time it takes to find these 100 matrix powers as function of k. Similarly, plot the time it takes find the 100 boolean matrix powers as a function of k. Compare the two results. Which matrix product is best to use if one is interested in knowing whether there is a path of some fixed length between two vertices in a directed multigraph?

EX. 8.5.2 → **Exercise 8.31** Prove that each Latin square can be transformed into a reduced Latin square through a series of permutations of the rows and columns. Prove that each equivalence class of $n \times n$ Latin squares contains $n!(n-1)!$ elements.

EX. 8.5.2 → **Exercise 8.32** Explain why choosing the right input for the procedure from Example 6.5.4 results in a method for producing reduced Latin squares.

EX. 8.5.2 → **Exercise 8.33** Use the observation from Exercise 8.32 to construct a procedure that counts the number of reduced $n \times n$ Latin squares. To what extent is it possible to verify the numbers in Table 8.1?

EX. 8.5.2 → **Exercise 8.34** Give a (simple) example to show that the determinant of a Latin square is not an isotopy invariant.

EX. 8.5.2 → **Exercise 8.35** Modify the method for constructing reduced Latin squares considered in Example 8.32 in the following way: After constructing a reduced Latin square A, construct all isotopic Latin squares obtained by permuting the symbols. Does this provide a more efficient way of generating determinants? Quantify and explain.

Exercise 8.36 A *labeled directed multigraph* is a pair consisting of a directed multigraph E and a map $\mathcal{L} \colon E^1 \to \mathcal{A}$. Note that a labeled directed multigraph can be represented visually by drawing the corresponding directed multigraph and annotating each edge e with the corresponding label $\mathcal{L}(e)$. Associate to each labeled directed multigraph, a L with entries in $\mathcal{P}(\mathcal{A})$ specifying the labels of edges between the individual vertices. Define a matrix multiplication such that L^n contains information about the labels of paths of length n.

EX. 5.1.1 → **Exercise 8.37** Use a procedure from the GraphTheory package (e.g. IsForest) to stop cycleTree from computing further on configurations that already have a cycle and hence will never contribute to the count. Analyze with time if the program executes faster with such an approach.

Exercise 8.38 Implement your own version of Padé approximation by generating a linear system of $N + M + 1$ equations in $N + M + 1$ indeterminates as in proposition 5.4.1 and solving it using `LinearAlgebra` tools. Compare its results and efficiency to the built-in procedure.

Projects and Group Work

Exercise 8.39 Investigate the *Lovász conjecture*: Every finite connected vertex-transitive graph contains a Hamiltonian path.

Exercise 8.40 For small values of n, calculate the number of labeled trees on $n \in \mathbb{N}$ vertices up to graph isomorphism. Do the same for unlabeled trees. If possible, formulate and test formulas for how these numbers grow with n.

EX. 6.5.4 → **Exercise 8.41** What is the structure of the set $\mathcal{D}_n$ of determinants of $n \times n$ Latin squares?

EX. 6.5.5 → **Exercise 8.42** Consider the game introduced in Example 2.6.2.

- Who has a winning strategy when n is even?
- Is it possible to give short descriptions of these winning strategies?

EX. 8.1.2 → **Exercise 8.43** Given b and w, what is the $b \times w$ LEGO chromatic number? Most buildings constructed from $b \times w$-blocks can be colored with fewer than $\chi_{b,w}$ colors so to investigate the problem, it is necessary to look actively for complex buildings, where every block has many adjacent blocks. A fruitful approach may be to combine experiments with physical LEGO-bricks with computer assisted calculations of chromatic numbers.

- What is $\chi_{b,w}$ for small values of $b, w \in \mathbb{N}$?
- Create a procedure that can construct LEGO-buildings and the corresponding graphs and compute the chromatic number.
- Is the problem easier to handle for, for example, square or very oblong bricks?
- Is $\chi_{b,w}$ an increasing function of b, w?

8.7 Notes and Further Reading

For a thorough introduction to graph theory, see for example [BM08]. Appel and Haken's proof of the 4-color theorem was published in[AH77] and [AHK77]. For a proof of the much simpler 5-color theorem, see [Hea49]. The description of the experimental aspects of the proof of the Four Color Theorem given in the box on p. 267 is based on [BD09]. For a more detailed account, see [Dev90].

The museum problem considered in Example 8.1.3 was first solved in [Chv75], but the solution given here is due to Fisk [Fis78], and the presentation is based on [AZ10]. Example 8.2.2 comes from the collection of beautiful and often unexpected applications of linear algebra found in [Mat10]. For a proof of the undecidability of the isomorphism problem for finitely presented groups see [MKS04].

As a nontrivial application of the ideas discussed in Section 8.5, consider the paper [AJS] which contains algorithms for the exhaustive generation of certain kinds of automorphisms of graph algebras. The great speed of these methods is partially achieved by constructing representations of equivalence classes rather than the individual elements.

Illustration notes

All illustrations in this book have been produced by the authors (either using Maple, lCad, Gimp, or TikZ) except:

- Figure 1.1 is reproduced from *Popular Science Monthly*, Volume 26, 1884–85.
- Figure 1.2 was produced by Peter Michael Reichstein Rasmussen.
- The letter from Gauss in the box on p. 10 appears by permission of the Niedersächsische Staats- und Universitätsbibliothek Göttingen. *[Reference: SUB Göttingen, Cod. Ms. Gauss Briefe B: Encke, No. 75.]*
- The picture in the box on p. 75 is a work of the United States Federal Government, specifically an employee of the National Institute of Standards and Technology, under the terms of Title 17, Chapter 1, Section 105 of the US Code.
- Figure 3.6 is a reproduction of [LP66] which is ©The American Matematical Society 1966. Reproduction rights acquired via RightsLink licence number 3836540829257.
- The model in the box on p. 96 appears by permission of the Department of Mathematical Sciences, University of Copenhagen. Photography by Rune Johansen.
- The figure in the box on p. 101 was produced by Peter Michael Reichstein Rasmussen.
- The program in the box on p. 147 is scanned from the original [Tay43] in the collection of Gösta Mittag-Leffler and is reproduced by permission of Institut Mittag-Leffler.
- The excerpt of [Slo73] in the box on p. 152 is ©Academic Press and Elsevier Books 1973. Reproduction rights acquired via RightsLink licence number 3841900034582.
- The picture of a Canfield solitaire in the box on p. 215 was photographed by Rune Johansen.

References

[AGP94] W. R. Alford, Andrew Granville, and Carl Pomerance. There are infinitely many Carmichael numbers. *Ann. of Math. (2)*, 139(3):703–722, 1994.

[AH77] K. Appel and W. Haken. Every planar map is four colorable. I. Discharging. *Illinois J. Math.*, 21(3):429–490, 1977.

[AHK77] K. Appel, W. Haken, and J. Koch. Every planar map is four colorable. II. Reducibility. *Illinois J. Math.*, 21(3):491–567, 1977.

[AJS] James Avery, Rune Johansen, and Wojciech Szymański. Visualizing automorphisms of graph algebras. In preparation.

[And79] George E. Andrews. A note on partitions and triangles with integer sides. *Amer. Math. Monthly*, 86:477–478, 1979.

[AZ10] Martin Aigner and Günter M. Ziegler. *Proofs from The Book*. Springer-Verlag, Berlin, 4th edn, 2010.

[Bai] David H. Bailey. A compendium of BBP-Type formulas for mathematical constants. http://crd-legacy.lbl.gov/~dhbailey/dhbpapers/bbp-formulas.pdf.

[BB92] J. M. Borwein and P. B. Borwein. Strange series and high precision fraud. *Amer. Math. Monthly*, 99(7):622–640, 1992.

[BB08] Jonathan Borwein and David Bailey. *Mathematics by Experiment: Plausible reasoning in the 21st century*. A. K. Peters Ltd., Wellesley, MA, 2nd edition, 2008.

[BBBG96] D. Borwein, J. M. Borwein, P. B. Borwein, and R. Girgensohn. Giuga's conjecture on primality. *Amer. Math. Monthly*, 103(1):40–50, 1996.

[BBBP97] D. H. Bailey, J. M. Borwein, P. B. Borwein, and S. Plouffe. The quest for pi. *Math. Intelligencer*, 19(1):50–57, 1997.

[BBP97] David Bailey, Peter Borwein, and Simon Plouffe. On the rapid computation of various polylogarithmic constants. *Math. Comp.*, 66(218):903–913, 1997.

[BBS86] L. Blum, M. Blum, and M. Shub. A simple unpredictable pseudorandom number generator. *SIAM J. Comput.*, 15(2):364–383, 1986.

[BCD+05] L. Bernardin, P. Chin, P. DeMarco, K. O. Geddes, D. E. G. Hare, K. M. Heal, G. Labahn, J. P. May, J. McCarron, M. B. Monagan, D. Ohashi, and S. M. Vorkoetter. Maple Introductory Programming Guide. www.maplesoft.com/documentation_center, 2005.

[BCD+16] L. Bernardin, P. Chin, P. DeMarco, K. O. Geddes, D. E. G. Hare, K. M. Heal, G. Labahn, J. P. May, J. McCarron, M. B. Monagan, D. Ohashi, and S. M. Vorkoetter. Maple Programming Guide. www.maplesoft.com/documentation_center, 2016.

[BCGM13] Gunnar Brinkmann, Kris Coolsaet, Jan Goedgebeur, and Hadrien Mélot. House of Graphs: a database of interesting graphs. *Discrete Appl. Math.*, 161(1–2):311–314, 2013.

[BD08] Christian Berg and Antonio J. Durán. The fixed point for a transformation of Hausdorff moment sequences and iteration of a rational function. *Math. Scand.*, 103(1): 11–39, 2008.

[BD09] Jonathan Borwein and Keith Devlin. *The Computer as Crucible: An introduction to experimental mathematics.* A. K. Peters, Ltd., Wellesley, MA, 2009.

[BFM08] Peter Borwein, Ron Ferguson, and Michael J. Mossinghoff. Sign changes in sums of the Liouville function. *Math. Comp.*, 77(263):1681–1694, 2008.

[BH78] Carter Bays and Richard H. Hudson. Details of the first region of integers x with $\pi_{3,2}(x) < \pi_{3,1}(x)$. *Math. Comp.*, 32(142):571–576, 1978.

[Bla89] François Blanchard. β-expansions and symbolic dynamics. *Theoret. Comput. Sci.*, 65(2): 131–141, 1989.

[BM08] J. A. Bondy and U. S. R. Murty. *Graph Theory*, volume 244 of *Graduate Texts in Mathematics*. Springer, New York, 2008.

[BMR02] Mireille Bousquet-Mélou and Andrew Rechnitzer. Lattice animals and heaps of dimers. *Discrete Math.*, 258:235–274, 2002.

[Bor15] Jonathan Borwein. The life of modern homo habilis mathematicus: Experimental computation and visual theorems. In John Monaghan, Luc Troche, and Jonathan Borwein, editors, *Tools and Mathematics: Instruments for Learning*. Springer-Verlag, 2015.

[BP92] F. Bergeron and S. Plouffe. Computing the generating function of a series given its first few terms. *Experiment. Math.*, 1(4):307–312, 1992.

[BS11] Jonathan M. Borwein and Matthew P. Skerritt. *An Introduction to Modern Mathematical Computing—With Maple*. Springer Undergraduate Texts in Mathematics and Technology. Springer, New York, 2011.

[BSD65] B. J. Birch and H. P. F. Swinnerton-Dyer. Notes on elliptic curves. II. *J. Reine Angew. Math.*, 218:79–108, 1965.

[Chv75] V. Chvátal. A combinatorial theorem in plane geometry. *J. Combinatorial Theory Ser. B*, 18:39–41, 1975.

[CLRS09] Thomas H. Cormen, Charles E. Leiserson, Ronald L. Rivest, and Clifford Stein. *Introduction to Algorithms*. MIT Press and McGraw-Hill, 3rd edition, 2009.

[Dav53] Robert L. Davis. The number of structures of finite relations. *Proc. Amer. Math. Soc.*, 4:486–495, 1953.

[DE10] B. Durhuus and S. Eilers. Combinatorial aspects of pyramids of one-dimensional pieces of fixed integer length. In *21st International Meeting on Probabilistic, Combinatorial, and Asymptotic Methods in the Analysis of Algorithms (AofA'10)*, pp. 143–158. Assoc. Discrete Math. Theor. Comput. Sci., Nancy, 2010.

[Dev90] Keith Devlin. *Mathematics: The New Golden Age*. Penguin Books, New York, 1990.

[DF09] Persi Diaconis and Jason Fulman. Carries, shuffling, and an amazing matrix. *Amer. Math. Monthly*, 116(9):788–803, 2009.

[Eke93] Ivar Ekeland. *The Broken Dice, and Other Mathematical Tales of Chance*. University of Chicago Press, Chicago, IL, 1993. Translated from the 1991 French original by Carol Volk.

[Ekh12] Shalosh B. Ekhad. A Maple one-line proof of George Andrews' formula that says that the number of triangles with integer sides whose perimeter is n equals $\{\frac{n^2}{12}\} - \lfloor \frac{n}{4} \rfloor \lfloor \frac{n+2}{4} \rfloor$. arXiv:1202.1156v1, 2012.

[Elk88] Noam D. Elkies. On $A^4 + B^4 + C^4 = D^4$. *Math. Comp.*, 51(184):825–835, 1988.

[FBA99] H. R. P. Ferguson, D. H. Bailey, and S. Arno. Analysis of PSLQ, an integer relation finding algorithm. *Math. Comp.*, 68(225):351–369, 1999.

[FF79] H. R. P. Ferguson and R. W. Forcade. Generalization of the Euclidean algorithm for real numbers to all dimensions higher than two. *Bull. Amer. Math. Soc. (N.S.)*, 1(6):912–914, 1979.

[FGM96] H. Ferguson, A. Gray, and St. Markvorsen. Costa's minimal surface via mathematica. *Mathematica in Educ. Res.*, 5:5–10, 1996.

[Fin] Steven R. Finch. Signum equations and extremal coefficients. Notes on mathematical constants. http://www.people.fas.harvard.edu/~sfinch/.

[Fis78] Steve Fisk. A short proof of Chvátal's watchman theorem. *J. Combin. Theory Ser. B*, 24(3):374, 1978.

[Fla97] Phillipe Flajolet. Enumeration of planar configurations in computational geometry. http://algo.inria.fr/libraries/autocomb/nc-configs-html/nc-configs1.html, 1997.

[Fog02] N. Pytheas Fogg. *Substitutions in Dynamics, Arithmetics and Combinatorics*, volume 1794 of *Lecture Notes in Mathematics*. Springer-Verlag, Heidelberg, 2002.

[Fry88] Roger E. Frye. Finding $95800^4 + 217519^4 + 414560^4 = 422481^4$ on the connection machine. In *Supercomputing 88. Vol.II: Science and Applications*, volume 2, pp. 106–116. IEEE, 1988.

[Gar16] Frank Garvan. *The Maple Book*. Chapman & Hall/CRC, 2nd edition, 2016.

[GH02] Solomon W. Golomb and Alfred W. Hales. Hypercube tic-tac-toe. In *More Games of No Chance (Berkeley, CA, 2000)*, volume 42 of *Math. Sci. Res. Inst. Publ.*, pp. 167–182. Cambridge University Press, Cambridge, 2002.

[GKP94] Ronald L. Graham, Donald E. Knuth, and Oren Patashnik. *Concrete Mathematics: A Foundation for Computer Science*. Addison-Wesley, 1994.

[Gol08] Catherine Goldstein. How to generate mathematical experimentation, and does it provide mathematical knowledge? In U. Feest, G. Hon, H.-J. Rheinberger, J. Schickore, and F. Steinle, eds, *Generating Experimental Knowledge*, number 340 in MPIWG Preprints, pp. 61–85. Max-Planck-Institut für Wissenschaftsgeschichte, Berlin, 2008.

[Gup40] Hansraj Gupta. On a table of values of $L(n)$. *Proc. Indian Acad. Sci., Sect. A.*, 12:407–409, 1940.

[Guy04] Richard K. Guy. *Unsolved Problems in Number Theory*. Problem Books in Mathematics. Springer-Verlag, New York, 3rd edition, 2004.

[Has58] C. B. Haselgrove. A disproof of a conjecture of Pólya. *Mathematika*, 5:141–145, 1958.

[Hea49] P. J. Heawood. Map-colour theorem. *Proc. London Math. Soc. (2)*, 51:161–175, 1949.

[Hel13] H. A. Helfgott. The ternary Goldbach conjecture is true. arXiv:1312.7748, 2013.

[HM90] David Hoffman and William H. Meeks, III. Embedded minimal surfaces of finite topology. *Ann. of Math. (2)*, 131(1):1–34, 1990.

[HM13] Uffe Haagerup and Sören Möller. The law of large numbers for the free multiplicative convolution. In *Operator algebra and dynamics*, volume 58 of *Springer Proc. Math. Stat.*, pp. 157–186. Springer, Heidelberg, 2013.

[Hol97] John M. Holte. Carries, combinatorics, and an amazing matrix. *Amer. Math. Monthly*, 104:138–149, 1997.

[HP13] H. A. Helfgott and David J. Platt. Numerical verification of the ternary Goldbach conjecture up to $8.875 \cdot 10^{30}$. arXiv:1305.3062, 2013.

[HW79] G. H. Hardy and E. M. Wright. *An Introduction to the Theory of Numbers*. The Clarendon Press, Oxford University Press, New York, 5th edition, 1979.

[IBM67] IBM. *System/360 Scientific Subroutine Package Version II Programmer's Manual*. IBM, 1967.

[Ing42] A. E. Ingham. On two conjectures in the theory of numbers. *Amer. J. Math.*, 64:313–319, 1942.

[KLS01] Michal Křížek, Florian Luca, and Lawrence Somer. *17 Lectures on Fermat Numbers: From number theory to geometry, With a foreword by Alena Šolcová*. CMS Books in Mathematics/Ouvrages de Mathématiques de la SMC, 9. Springer-Verlag, New York, 2001.

[Knu] Donald E. Knuth. *The Art of Computer Programming, Volume 4A: Combinatorial Algorithms, Part 1.* Addison-Wesley, Reading, MA, 2011.

[Kob94] Neal Koblitz. *A course in number theory and cryptography*, volume 114 of *Graduate Texts in Mathematics.* Springer-Verlag, New York, 2nd edition, 1994.

[Lag10] Jeffrey C. Lagarias, editor. *The Ultimate Challenge: The $3x + 1$ Problem.* American Mathematical Society, Providence, RI, 2010.

[Leh60] R. Sherman Lehman. On Liouville's function. *Math. Comp.*, 14:311–320, 1960.

[LP66] L. J. Lander and T. R. Parkin. Counterexample to Euler's conjecture on sums of like powers. *Bull. Amer. Math. Soc.*, 72:1079, 1966.

[Luc85] Edouard Lucas. Calculating-machines. *Popular Science Monthly*, 26:441–452, 1885.

[map16] Maple user manual. www.maplesoft.com/documentation_center, 2016.

[Mar68] George Marsaglia. Random numbers fall mainly in the planes. *Proc. Nat. Acad. Sci. U.S.A.*, 61:25–28, 1968.

[Mat] Makoto Matsumoto. http://www.math.sci.hiroshima-u.ac.jp/~m-mat/MT/emt.html.

[Mat10] Jiří Matoušek. *Thirty-three Miniatures: Mathematical and algorithmic applications of linear algebra*, volume 53 of *Student Mathematical Library.* American Mathematical Society, Providence, RI, 2010.

[Mau97] R. Daniel Mauldin. A generalization of Fermat's last theorem: the Beal conjecture and prize problem. *Notices Amer. Math. Soc.*, 44(11):1436–1437, 1997.

[MKS04] Wilhelm Magnus, Abraham Karrass, and Donald Solitar. *Combinatorial Group Theory.* Dover Publications, Inc., Mineola, NY, 2nd edition, 2004. Presentations of groups in terms of generators and relations.

[MN98a] Jiri Matousek and Jaroslav Nesetril. *Invitation to Discrete Mathematics.* Clarendon Press, Oxford, 1998.

[MN98b] Makoto Matsumoto and Takuji Nishimura. Mersenne twister: A 623-dimensionally equidistributed uniform pseudorandom number generator. *ACM Trans. on Modeling and Computer Simulation*, 8, No 1(1): 3–30, 1998.

[Mül04] E. Müller. Literaturberichte: Katalog mathematischer Modelle. *Monatsh. Math. Phys.*, 15(1):A4, 1904. für den höheren mathematischen Unterricht. Veröffentlicht durch die Verlagshandlung von Martin Schilling in Halle a. S. 6. Aufl. Halle a. S. 1903. XIII + 130 S.

[OC69] R. E. Odeh and E. J. Cockayne. Balancing equal weights on the integer line. *J. Combinatorial Theory*, 7:130–135, 1969.

[Odl] Andrew Odlyzko. Zeros of the zeta function. http://www.dtc.umn.edu/~Odlyzko/zeta_tables/.

[OeS] Tómas Oliveira e Silva. Goldbach conjecture verification. http://sweet.ua.pt/tos/goldbach.html.

[Pin93] R.G.E. Pinch. Some primality testing algorithms. *Notices Amer. Math. Soc.*, 40(9):1203–1210, 1993.

[Pom] Carl Pomerance. Are there counter-examples to the Baillie PSW primality test? http://www.pseudoprime.com/dopo.pdf.

[PTVF92] William H. Press, Saul A. Teukolsky, William T. Vetterling, and Brian P. Flannery. *Numerical Recipes in FORTRAN: The art of scientific computing.* With a separately available computer disk. Cambridge University Press, Cambridge, 2nd edition, 1992.

[PWZ96] Marko Petkovšek, Herbert S. Wilf, and Doron Zeilberger. $A = B$. A K Peters, Ltd., Wellesley, MA, 1996. With a foreword by Donald E. Knuth, With a separately available computer disk.

[Rob54] Raphael M. Robinson. Mersenne and Fermat numbers. *Proc. Amer. Math. Soc.*, 5:842–846, 1954.

[Rob58] Raphael M. Robinson. A report on primes of the form $k \cdot 2^n + 1$ and on factors of Fermat numbers. *Proc. Amer. Math. Soc.*, 9:673–681, 1958.

[Row13] David E. Rowe. Mathematical models as artefacts for research: Felix Klein and the case of Kummer surfaces. *Math. Semesterber.*, 60(1): 1–24, 2013.

[RS92] Andrew M. Rockett and Peter Szüsz. *Continued Fractions*. World Scientific, Singapore, 1992.

[RS02] Karl Rubin and Alice Silverberg. Ranks of elliptic curves. *Bull. Amer. Math. Soc. (N.S.)*, 39(4):455–474 (electronic), 2002.

[Sel53] J. L. Selfridge. Factors of Fermat numbers. *Math. Tables Aids Comput.*, 7:274–275, 1953.

[Ske33] S. Skewes. On the difference $\pi(x) - \mathrm{li}(x)$. I. *J. London Math. Soc.*, S1-8(4):277–283, 1933.

[Ske55] S. Skewes. On the difference $\pi(x) - \mathrm{li}(x)$. II. *Proc. London Math. Soc. (3)*, 5:48–70, 1955.

[Slo73] N. J. A. Sloane. *A Handbook of Integer Sequences*. Academic Press [A subsidiary of Harcourt Brace Jovanovich, Publishers], New York–London, 1973.

[SP95] N.J.A. Sloane and S. Plouffe. *The Encyclopedia of Integer Sequences*. Academic Press, 1995.

[SS77] R. Solovay and V. Strassen. A fast Monte-Carlo test for primality. *SIAM J. Comput.*, 6(1):84–85, 1977.

[SS78] R. Solovay and V. Strassen. Erratum: "A fast Monte-Carlo test for primality" (SIAM J. Comput. 6 (1977), no. 1, 84–85). *SIAM J. Comput.*, 7(1):118, 1978.

[SS05] Andrey Sidorenko and Berry Schoenmakers. Concrete security of the Blum-Blum-Shub pseudorandom generator. In *Cryptography and Coding*, volume 3796 of *Lecture Notes in Comput. Sci.*, pp. 355–375. Springer, Berlin, 2005.

[Str] Armin Straub. A gentle introduction to PSLQ. `http://arminstraub.com/downloads/math/pslq.pdf`.

[SZ94] Bruno Salvy and Paul Zimmerman. Gfun: a maple package for the manipulation of generating and holonomic functions in one variable. *ACM Trans. Math. Software*, 20(2):163–177, 1994.

[Tay43] Richard Taylor, editor. *Scientific Memoirs: Selected from the Transactions of Foreign Academies of Science and Learned Societies, and from Foreign Journals*, volume 3. 1843.

[Tsc06] Yuri Tschinkel. About the cover: On the distribution of primes—Gauss' tables. *Bull. Amer. Math. Soc. (N.S.)*, 43(1): 89–91 (electronic), 2006.

[Tuf01] Edward Tufte. *The Visual Display of Quantitative Information*. Graphics Pr, 2nd edition, 2001.

[Vin37] I. M. Vinogradov. The method of trigonometrical sums in the theory of numbers. *Trav. Inst. Math. Stekloff*, 10, 1937.

[Was04] Larry Wasserman. *All of Statistics: A concise course in statistical inference*. Springer Texts in Statistics. Springer-Verlag, New York, 2004.

[Wat80] P. J. S. Watson. On "LEGO" towers. *J. Recreational Math.*, 12:24–27, 1979-80.

[Wil05] Herbert S. Wilf. *generatingfunctionology: Third Edition*. A. K. Peters/CRC Press, 2005.

[Zha92] Ming Zhi Zhang. A method for finding large Carmichael numbers. *Sichuan Daxue Xuebao*, 29(4):472–479, 1992.

Index

he United States
aylor Publisher Services